Developing Enterprise Applications- An Impurist's View

Developing Enterprise Applications—
An Impurist's View

Paul Tindall

Copyright © 2000 by Que Corporation

International Standard Book Number: 0-7897-2269-0

Library of Congress Catalog Card Number: 00-100187

Printed in the United States of America

First Printing: April, 2000

02 01 00   3 2 1

Trademarks

Warning and Disclaimer

Associate Publisher
Tracy Dunkelberger

Acquisitions Editor
Michelle Newcomb

Development Editor
Bryan Morgan

Technical Editor
Jay Aguilar

Managing Editor
Matt Purcell

Project Editor
Tonya Simpson

Copy Editor
Christy Parrish

Indexer
Erika Millen

Proofreaders
Rachel Lopez Bell
Megan Wade

Team Coordinator
Cindy Teeters

Interior Designer
Gary Adair

Cover Designer
Jay Corpus

Copywriter
Eric Borgert

Editorial Assistant
Angela Boley

Layout Technicians
Ayanna Lacey
Heather Hiatt Miller
Stacey Richwine-DeRome

Contents

About the Author

Paul Tindall is a project manager at emerging.com, an e-business incubator and consulting company located in Houston, Texas. In this role, Paul is responsible for bringing emerging e-business ventures online in an expedient and robust fashion. Prior to joining emerging.com, Paul was an applications development manager and senior manufacturing engineer for Compaq Computer Corporation in Houston, Texas. At Compaq, Paul was responsible for developing applications to support their global manufacturing operations using Visual Basic, SQL Server, MTS, IIS, and Internet Explorer. He possesses more than 8 years of experience in enterprise application design and integration with more than 12 years of experience in software development in general. Paul has written articles that have appeared in *Enterprise Development* and *Visual Basic Programmer's Journal*, covering various aspects of enterprise application development.

Paul received his Bachelor of Science degree in electrical engineering from the University of Louisville, and he is currently an MBA candidate at the University of Texas at Austin.

Dedication

I dedicate this book to my wife, Kimberly. Her encouragement and support throughout this latest and most challenging endeavor in writing has allowed me to deliver what I hope to be a book of high value.

Acknowledgments

I wish to thank the staff at Macmillan USA for their support and assistance in putting this book together. Special thanks to Michelle Newcomb for helping me work around my other schedules, to Bryan Morgan, Jay Aguilar, Christy Parrish, and Tonya Simpson for applying their superb editing skills to my manuscripts, and to Tracy Dunkelberger for giving me the opportunity to write this book. I would also like to thank Fawcette Technical Publications for giving me my original avenues of writing, with special thanks to Lee Thé for bringing this sort of content into the forefront of technical media.

I also wish to thank the current and former management at Compaq Computer Corporation for allowing me to work on the applications that led to the formation of the techniques and architecture presented in this book. Thanks go to Marshall Bard for allowing me to build the applications that we could not buy and supporting these efforts every step of the way. Special thanks to George Bumgardner for constantly being a champion (to both management and our customer base) for the applications we were building. Finally, I would like to thank all the end users who validated the value of our efforts. Without their constant feedback and push for ongoing added value, these topics would not have come about.

I want to pay particular thanks to Bill Erzal of MSHOW in Austin, Texas. Bill has been my partner in development of applications at Compaq for the last several years and has been the original implementer of many of these techniques on a large scale. I thank him for being candid with me when I have presented a bad architectural decision, for biting his lip and pushing on when he was unsure of a design, and for saying "this looks good" when he knew one was right. In addition, many of the user interface design techniques covered in the book have been lifted directly from his work, which has been the result of an aggregation of experiences from his broad career in application development. I thank him for allowing me to include them with this book.

The Technical Validation Group for *Developing Enterprise Applications—An Impurist's View*

John E. Jackson (Eddie) is a senior software engineer with Computer Science Corporation (CSC) in Shalimar, Florida. At CSC Eddie spends his time designing, implementing, testing, debugging, and shipping applications designed for the Microsoft Windows family of operating systems.

Jay Aguilar (jaguilar@OpenTable.com, aguilarjay@usa.net) is a senior software developer/architect/B2B (Business to Business) consultant currently employed at OpenTable.com (http://www.OpenTable.com). He specializes in developing enterprise n-tier solutions for corporate intranets and Internet applications. Jay now focuses on developing and implementing the infrastructure for Internet B2B commerce. In the future, he hopes to write more technical publications and technical journals. His biggest passion is always trying to be on the cutting edge of technology and not losing his edge. He enjoys relaxing in the great outdoors and spending it still connected to the Internet.

Tell Us What You Think!

As the reader of this book, you are our most important critic and commentator. We value your opinion and want to know what we're doing right, what we could do better, what areas you'd like to see us publish in, and any other words of wisdom you're willing to pass our way.

As an associate publisher for Que, I welcome your comments. You can fax, email, or write me directly to let me know what you did or didn't like about this book—as well as what we can do to make our books stronger.

Please note that I cannot help you with technical problems related to the topic of this book, and that due to the high volume of mail I receive, I might not be able to reply to every message.

When you write, please be sure to include this book's title and author as well as your name and phone or fax number. I will carefully review your comments and share them with the author and editors who worked on the book.

Fax: 317-581-4666

Email: queprof@mcp.com

Mail: Associate Publisher
Que
201 West 103rd Street
Indianapolis, IN 46290 USA

Preface

This book is the culmination of many years of experience in using Visual Basic and SQL Server to build first client/server, and then, with the advent of MTS, distributed applications. Although many would say that this combination of tools is incapable of developing sophisticated enterprise applications, I offer up the techniques outlined in this book as a counter-argument. I offer up all the positive user feedback about how intuitive, user-friendly, and capable these applications are. These same users do not provide similar positive comments for the other commercial enterprise applications running on their desktops. A good enterprise application designer must always remember that the user is what drives the smarts under the hood. If you make your application difficult to use, users will perceive it to be a poorly designed application, no matter what value it is providing to the underlying business. Similarly, a great user interface design means nothing if the business value is not there. Thus, these applications require a sophisticated balance between both the user and business perspectives. This book provides the solutions to this problem.

With the advent of the Internet and the new user interface paradigm and application delivery model it provides, we must rethink the traditional development model. Many Internet models are patched onto existing applications, sometimes effectively, but many times not. The architecture in this book makes the Internet an integral part of the application. Counter to this, it does not force an unwarranted Internet basis when it is unnecessary.

The code samples in this book have been developed using Microsoft Visual Basic 6, Enterprise Edition, Service Pack 3. SQL Server schema were developed in version 6.5 but should also work on version 6.x ad 7.0.

The source code listings that appear in the book are also available at
http://www.mcp.com.

An Overview of Tools and Technologies

I

1

An Introduction to the Enterprise

YOU MIGHT BE WONDERING ABOUT THE REASON for the word *Impurist* in the title of this book. Before delving into an introductory definition, I would like to state that the application development industry is undergoing a significant transformation in how it develops applications. New tools and technologies are emerging at a rapid pace. With this emergence come experts that profess the techniques on how to employ these tools and technologies to their best use to solve the problems at hand. The tool vendors themselves provide guidance in how to use their products to solve a broad range of problems. It follows, then, that these techniques begin to coalesce within the industry and form the conventional wisdom on how we must use these tools and technologies. On the other end of the spectrum, we have the theoretical view on how to perform application development, and we chastise the tool vendors for not following a pure approach. Somewhere in between are the upper-level managers screaming the "on time, under budget" mantra, hoping to keep the development team focused on the tasks at hand. The effect of this mantra is that conventional wisdom typically takes on a "quick and dirty" component that runs counter to what we would otherwise do as we develop applications.

Thus, the approach of this book is not to necessarily utilize a technique because it is part of the accepted conventional wisdom or because it meets certain theoretical criteria. This is the root of the statement on impurity in the title. Although we all strive for the perfect solution to a given problem, we must remember that we cannot always do so in the corporate application landscape. We must perform a constant balancing act between the functionality we deliver, the resources required to do so, and the time we take to arrive at completion. These constraints invariably lead to conflicts in the decision-making process that we have to deal with as managers, architects, and developers. Thus, the intent of this book is to discuss how to look at the possible solutions within the realm of the constraints and make an appropriate decision. Although in many cases we will provide a specific solution, we will provide supporting reasons for why we have done something in a particular manner.

The underlying goal of corporate application development is not necessarily to remain pure to the industry or theoretical trends simply for the sake of doing so. We must realize that companies entrust us with their resources of money and time with the expectation that we will add value to their business processes. Good design decisions are an investment that we make as developers to meet these expectations. No value is added to a company when we constantly rework already delivered functionality due to poor design decisions we needlessly make because we follow a purist viewpoint. We add value not only when we deliver functionality in the first round, but also when we continue to deliver added functionality in following rounds. Our stretch goal is that we can do so at a diminishing cost structure with each round we successfully complete. Sound decision-making with these latter goals in mind is how we should proceed through our development efforts, even if it means being a little impure at times.

Enterprise Development

Although the term *enterprise development* is a common buzzword in the software industry these days, it is an ambiguous term. Enterprise application development is by no means a new concept to business because mainframes have existed for some 20 years or so, performing the daily chores to take care of corporate informational needs. It is, however, a new concept to some software developers, many of whom might have only had to implement simple departmental productivity applications up to this point. Corporate IS departments are becoming increasingly decentralized, with functionality leaving the glass house and its mainframes and moving toward organizations and their servers. At the same time, the development tools used to build applications are simultaneously becoming more powerful and easier to use. The same tools used to build productivity applications of yesterday can now deploy applications of today on a much grander scale. Indeed, it might be some of the smaller applications of today that will become the *de facto* enterprise applications of tomorrow. Because of this shift, the organizational-level IS leaders, designers, and implementers must pick up the reins and begin building the next generation of corporate solutions. This is logical because each organization understands its own business processes and informational needs best.

Coupled with this change in IS philosophy and the shift in application development responsibilities is the globalization of corporations in geography, business activities, and the underlying information driving the corporate business processes. It should be clear by now that planet Earth has become a much smaller space in which to do business because of the Internet revolution. As such, corporate competitive advantages are becoming more defined not only by their capability to tap into their vast knowledge bases, but also by their capability to transfer that knowledge into systems and information to enforce best practices. After it is tapped, the company can raise the level of capabilities across all geographical locations and business practices.

Still one other factor helps to define the enterprise application—that of flexibility in architecture. When a company fuels its growth through mergers and acquisitions, it must meld disparate business processes into a unified model. This invariably affects the applications running the enterprise, because part of the impetus for the combination of companies is to leverage greater economies of scale by eliminating overlapping functions.

Some would argue that high availability is an absolute requirement of the enterprise application as well. Although this is true in the ideal sense, it is not necessarily a rigid requirement in all cases. In many interpretations, "high availability" is synonymous with gargantuan servers. Many enterprise applications, though critical to the business, might need to support only several hundred users at any given time and might not need to follow a 99.999999% uptime model. The cost benefit justification of overly capable hardware might be difficult to make. In these cases, only robust application design techniques and appropriately matched hardware are needed to constitute high availability. It is important to understand that we can be less than perfect in an attempt to be economically prudent.

With these concepts in mind, we can start defining what the term *enterprise development* embodies. At its most succinct level, enterprise development means the capability to support multiple sites, geographies, organizations, and users with their informational needs. This support comes by way of focused applications embedded within the business processes needed to run core activities of an organization. The number of users supported by such an application can range into the hundreds or even thousands. If one then considers the capabilities afforded by the Internet and Dial-Up Networking, then it also means the capability to support the mobility of the user base. This would not only indicate a high level of application availability and accessibility to the users, but also ease of administration and maintenance for the developers and support teams over such diverse connection modes.

Taken to the next level, corporations realize that information from disparate systems becomes more valuable when taken in aggregate. Thus, the term *enterprise development* takes on an additional form of interfacibility—the capability to gather information from other applications, coupled with the capability to provide information to other applications. Some would also call this feature interoperability. Examples of such systems would be the corporate Enterprise Resource Planning (ERP) system, in-house applications supporting other organizations, or third-party applications implemented by the company.

Another feature of enterprise applications is that of extensibility. Although it can be easy to throw an application together that meets the needs of today, it is more difficult to anticipate the needs of tomorrow and design accordingly. If we follow an incremental develop-and-deploy approach, we must make sure that for every step forward we make, we will not have to take a few backward with the next release. Expanding our mode of thinking a bit more, we realize that after we implement a successful application within an individual organization, most likely other organizations will want to follow suit after we demonstrate the benefits. If we design accordingly, it should be trivial to replicate the majority of an application to meet new business needs. Expanding our thinking yet again, we realize that as a company goes through mergers and acquisitions, we might need to enhance the business processes within our application. Again, if we design accordingly, this should not be an issue. This leads us to define "application extensibility" within the realm of enterprise development.

At yet another level, the corporation begins hooking its enterprise applications together in modes beyond just simple information sharing. Whether they are internal or external to the company, few applications can drive a corporation's business processes in isolation. As such, they must begin working together within the context of some business workflow. Thus, the term *enterprise development* takes on a collaborative definition. As an example, one system, in the course of providing its functionality, can signal other systems into action; this in turn can signal still other systems. Although human interaction might be required somewhere in the process, it is not mandatory.

Because users with differing roles exist across the user base, no single user typically exercises the entire breadth of functionality provided by an enterprise application. The application is multifaceted, although that can mean different things to different people. There can be many human interfaces, both of the input and output variety. There are information generators as well as consumers. In most cases, the number of consumers far outweighs the number of generators because it is this dispersal of information and knowledge that drives such applications.

Thus, we have a series of attributes that help define what an enterprise application really entails. To summarize, an enterprise application has the following features:

- Support for many sites, geographies, organizations, and users
- Extensibility by design because it will need enhancement over its lifetime
- Two-way interoperability with other systems
- Collaboration capabilities with other systems, both internal and external to the company
- Multi-faceted from a user perspective—a single user rarely exercises the full breadth of functionality

Although these attributes are applicable to any application, they become mandatory when we face the rigors of the enterprise.

Patterns and Frameworks

Other ambiguous terms abound when speaking of enterprise development, most notably *patterns* and *frameworks*. Both are critical to successful enterprise development, but they have different meanings. A pattern represents the design of a core functional element in an abstract form, although it extends beyond pure theory because it typically evolves from ideas and techniques proven out in repeated, real-world situations. There are many industry-accepted patterns for implementing a variety of tasks across a diverse range of development tools and technologies. Because we typically implement patterns in an object-oriented language, patterns and object orientation share a common modeling methodology.

A framework is the tangible, reusable implementation of multiple patterns on a given platform using a specific set of development tools and technologies. A framework can also define the necessary communication and distribution mechanisms to make the pieces work together. Frameworks have existed for quite some time in commercial form. In the not-too-distant past, they came to us as Fourth Generation Languages (4GLs), used to develop client/server applications. Alternatively, they existed in the form of source-level GUI and I/O libraries meant to deliver applications in a consistent, cross-platform manner. Before that, they came in the form of mainframe development and control software, such as IBM's CICS and JCL tools. Now, they manifest themselves in several incarnations.

Commercial Frameworks

One incarnation of a modern framework is that of modeling tools with accompanying source-code generators. Here, an application or application component is first defined using a standard or proprietary modeling language. With a few mouse clicks after the model is complete, the tool generates source code. Some tools produce database schemas as well. The framework might fully realize itself simply as a set of runtime components referenced by the source code, as framework source code interspersed with the application code, or as a combination somewhere in between the two. Some of the more sophisticated tools can even generate code for multiple deployment languages (Visual Basic, C++, Java, and so on), database servers (SQL Server, Oracle, and so on), and distribution architectures (for example, COM/DCOM, CORBA, Java RMI, and so on).

Some commercial frameworks extend beyond the infrastructure side and actually begin to layer on some of the business process functionality. Examples include IBM's San Francisco Project, which attempts to define a core set of frameworks across several business domains. For some time, Oracle has provided business frameworks for accounting, manufacturing, and other popular problem domains.

Application Servers

Another incarnation of a framework is that of an application server. The term *application server* is itself a multi-aspect term because it attempts to implement some or all of the components that make up an enterprise application. In this form, the application server not only embodies the hardware and operating system, but also inherently defines a framework through its programming model. This model typically rests upon selected design patterns implemented by the application server vendor. This form of framework has similarities to the modeling approach in that support exists for multiple development languages, database servers, and distribution architectures. Some in the industry feel that a full-function application server is simply a reincarnation of the mainframe on updated hardware.

Custom Frameworks

With the emergence of enterprise development tools and components, it is not too difficult to develop a framework suited to a specific business process or organization. Microsoft has provided a suite of server products, development tools, and distribution technologies to enable the development of a custom framework for enterprise applications. The official moniker for this is the Microsoft Distributed interNet Applications (Microsoft DNA) architecture. Although DNA is Microsoft's attempt to fully define the tools, technologies, and implementation details needed to build such applications, it is not itself a framework.

Microsoft DNA

Whether you are a devout promoter, a casual user, or merely an observer, Microsoft is a major player in the enterprise development market. No other set of tools and technologies enable you to have a dynamic, database-driven Web site up and running in a short amount of time. No other set of tools and technologies enables you to build a robust, multi-tier application in a short amount of time. No other company provides the set of online support and technical information that Microsoft does. Although Microsoft has provided the tools, guidelines, and sample applications, this does not mean it is the definitive source on how to build our applications. It is merely a component of the conventional wisdom mix that we mentioned earlier.

Microsoft presents sample architecture implementation in the form of DNA. This is a bit of a misnomer in that it really does not use the Internet as much as one might surmise. True, we can set up a dynamic Web site that enables users to connect to it through the Internet, but we cannot create a DCOM link across the Internet unless we have a virtual private network in place. DCOM, a technology that we will discuss in further detail in Chapter 2, "Layers and Tiers," is what puts the "D" in DNA, but it does not work with the "N" portion of the acronym (it should really be *intraNet*). Although we use the same tools and technologies as DNA, the architectural concepts presented by this book vary from the Microsoft model in ways that should bode well for your enterprise application.

Although Microsoft can give us the tools and a basic model to follow through DNA, they have to do so in such a way that is applicable to their entire customer base, which means a lowest common denominator approach. In many cases, their efforts at simplification work adversely to your application's requirements, potentially reducing performance to a much lower level than the underlying technology is capable of delivering. Microsoft's prime directive is to provide the horizontal infrastructure for application development, whereas your job as an enterprise application developer is to use these tools to provide the vertical applications that your business needs. That they help you a bit by defining DNA is a bonus. We should not hold Microsoft to blame for this approach because they do provide a viable solution to cover a wide range of applications. It is only as we peel back the layers that we can see room for improvement.

The Decision Process

The framework decision process can be complex based on individual project situations. Unfortunately, it is probably the most important decision to make at the outset of an application development project. The project team spends considerable time and money for software licensing, developer training, and so on before the actual start of the software project. A bad decision at this early stage can wreak havoc after the team is further into the effort. The decision-making tree is not easy. The capabilities of the development staff are only one of the factors. For a given framework option, there are learning curves, costs of development, costs of deployment, and feature lists to consider. A common issue with commercial framework solutions is that the vendors spend a lot of effort trying to implement the lowest common denominator of functionality required across their potential customer base. In so doing, they can spend a significant amount of time perfecting some feature you find unnecessary at the expense of a feature that is of higher value to you.

The view of this book toward commercial frameworks is agnostic—it neither supports nor condones them. The industry rule of thumb is that a commercial framework provides between 40% and 60% of an application's functionality. Although this sounds appealing, it is hard to determine the level of difficulty encountered or success rate at implementing the remaining functionality required by the application. In addition, the 80/20 rule applied to application development says that 20% of the time is spent implementing 80% of the functionality, and 80% of the time is spent implementing 20% of the functionality. In most cases, the former 80% represents the template functionality of the application—for example, database interaction, network access, system services, client/user-interface design, and so on. The latter 20% represents the functionality that is more difficult to implement and also what gives the application its character and competitive advantage, along with the look and feel that matches the business process flow. Put another way, this 20% represents the value-added business logic embedded within the application. Looking back at the commercial framework and where the effort savings resides—in the 80% realm or the 20% realm—is what should drive the decision for using a particular commercial framework.

For example, if the effort savings reside completely in the 80% template functionality area, it probably does not offer significant value. If, on the other hand, it covers the 20% value-added functionality, it is probably worth a look. The former category is indicative of horizontal frameworks, whereas the latter is where vertical-based frameworks reside. We should note that good vertical frameworks typically implement up to 60% of an application's code, as part of the framework.

Our Framework Approach

We will take the approach of building our own framework for the purpose of this book. The framework topics presented in the rest of this book use several fundamental patterns that have emerged over the course of successful enterprise application development. These patterns are, in turn, implemented using a specific set of development tools and deployment technologies loosely based on Microsoft DNA. It is important to note that the framework topics presented in this book are not simply a rehash of DNA. There are many critical areas where we diverge from the Microsoft model for various reasons. Although the remainder of this book is devoted to presenting various framework design and implementation topics, it does not necessarily represent all the implementation options. Please be sure to use the topical information as a guideline to foster the appropriate design for your situation.

Aim of the Book—A Framework Cookbook

This book targets those readers interested in learning about the concepts of building a distributed enterprise framework using industry-standard tools and technologies. Specifically, this book covers the use of Visual Basic 6.0 Enterprise Edition, Transaction Server 2.0, Internet Information Server 4.0, and SQL Server 6.5 as the core components of an enterprise framework. It will also present pragmatic examples in the form of sample applications and accompanying source code, to further strengthen the topics of discussion.

Target Audience

This book targets the software architect, developer, and manager who wants to understand both the capabilities and limitations of the Microsoft tools and technologies available to them within the realm of enterprise applications. Readers of this book should also want to understand how such tools and technologies could be used to provide business-critical functionality in the form of world-class applications to their organizational customer base. Readers of this book need to have an intermediate to advanced understanding of the tools and technologies outlined in the following sections. These readers will learn how to take their existing skills in these areas and apply them to building enterprise applications.

Tools and Technologies

You can use a myriad of available development tools and implementation technologies to create enterprise applications. For the purposes of this book, a specific subset of these available tools and technologies will apply.

Windows NT Networking

Although it might seem strange to make an apparently obvious statement about Windows NT Networking as a core component of an enterprise framework, it is still worth mentioning because of several key features. Most importantly, Windows NT Networking represents an integrated security model. If properly configured, a user need only log in to the network once to gain access to areas beyond the network. Because the other server products that make up this framework run on top of Windows NT Server, they have access to this same security mechanism. This makes it easier on both the end user, who does not have to remember another set of passwords, and the developer, who does not have to implement a login and password management process. Windows NT Networking also has the capability to support various network configurations including Wide Area and Dial-Up Networking.

SQL Server

In any large-scale application, it is important to have a database server that can meet performance and load handling requirements. It is also important to have a database server that has sufficient online backup facilities, recovery features, transaction logging, two-phase commits, triggering, stored procedures, and so on. Small-scale database systems simply will not hold up to the extreme needs of managing enterprise-level data. Additionally, advanced features, such as integrated replication and an administrative API, are highly desirable.

Although there are several server options here, SQL Server 6.x or 7.0 will meet these requirements handily. In addition, SQL Server offers a graphical user interface in the form of the SQL Enterprise Manager, eliminating the need to use a query console window to perform administrative and developmental tasks. SQL Server also exposes the underpinnings of the Enterprise Manager in the form of an SQL-DMO (SQL-Data Management Objects). This programming module can be invaluable when it comes to automating complex administrative tasks on the server. This might include activities such as setting up a new server or simply running a weekly re-index and recompile of the views and stored procedures that need to follow a certain processing order.

Additionally, SQL Server has an SQL Executive component. This component is responsible for managing the replication tasks, backups, restores, and so on. The SQL Executive can also manage tasks that are external to SQL Server with its capability to call the NT command processor.

COM/DCOM

We will cover COM (Component Object Model) and DCOM (Distributed COM) in sufficient detail in Chapter 3. Still, we need some overview here before we can proceed with the remaining tools and technologies that build upon COM.

The COM architecture is the foundation for Microsoft's OLE (Object Linking and Embedding) and ActiveX technologies. COM is both a formal specification and a binary implementation. Technically, any platform can implement COM, not just Win32. The reason that it is so ubiquitous on the Win32 platform is that Microsoft has provided the reference (and hence the standard) implementation of the specification. On the Win32 platform specifically, COM relies on Microsoft's Dynamic Link Library (DLL) mechanism. The DLL architecture allows for a high level of runtime modularity (as opposed to source-code level), allowing binary modules to load in and out of a process address space at runtime. COM, and hence our framework, relies heavily on this dynamic nature of COM to support long-term flexibility over the life of the application.

Any programming language that can access the Win32 COM API and implement a virtual function table can generate a COM class. Visual Basic, which we will discuss shortly, is such a language, allowing a developer to build these types of classes while simultaneously hiding the gory implementation details.

DCOM takes COM across process boundaries. Although applications frequently implement DCOM boundaries on a single physical machine, it is really a technology meant for communicating between machines. DCOM adds the necessary functionality to make a client application think that it is simply invoking a local COM object, when it is really invoking a COM-style proxy locally that invokes the object remotely. There are some optimizations in the DCOM engine to minimize the effects of remote invocation because COM's original design did not account for network latency. DCOM also adds a modicum of a security infrastructure to ensure that only privileged clients can invoke a given object.

Visual Basic 6.0, Enterprise Edition

The development of the user interface is one of the critical areas of overall application development. It does not matter how elegant or robust your architecture is underneath if it is difficult for the user because of a poorly designed interface. After the development team clearly understands the business process flow for a particular area of the application, it must be able to easily transform that into the user interface. As such, the developer needs a capable development tool at his or her disposal.

Visual Basic 6.0 (VB6) is just such a tool, but its capabilities extend far beyond form design. One particularly nice feature of VB6 is that it enables the developer to build custom ActiveX controls that encapsulate core business process flows into a component that can run in a variety of locations. VB6 also enables the developer to create ActiveX Dynamic Link Libraries (DLLs) that are also usable in a variety of locations. Turning things around, VB6 is not only able to create these ActiveX components, but also able to host many of those created by other development tools.

VB development extends beyond simply the user interface and client machine, allowing us to develop modules that run on a server as part of a distributed application. We will discuss distribution in much more detail in Chapter 5.

Concerning the ease of development, VB6 has all sorts of goodies within the Integrated Development Environment (IDE). These features include IntelliSense, which can help the developer finish a variable reference with just the first few letters being typed, or show the calling convention for a native or user-defined function or method. VB6 also has a feature known as the Class Builder Utility, a simple class modeler and code generator that can save significant time in generating well-formed class modules. The IDE also performs an auto-correction of the code, color-coding key words and comment blocks, and block indenting. Although these features might seem minor, developers will spend the majority of their time during the coding phase within the IDE; therefore, every little improvement in productivity adds up over the life of the project.

Internet Explorer 4/5

The preferred browser in this architecture is the Internet Explorer 4/5 (IE4/5) based on its DHTML and ActiveX control hosting capabilities. In many corporate settings, IE4/5 has been adopted as the standard browser for a multitude of reasons.

The architecture we will present in Part II uses browser interfaces to support the basic reporting needs, or output side of the application. Using standard HTTP form processing techniques, the browser will work in conjunction with the IIS server, using ASP to support simple data management. VB-based client applications, or browser-hosted ActiveX controls, implement complex data management that is too difficult to implement using the HTTP form approach.

Microsoft Transaction Server

Microsoft Transaction Server (MTS) provides several functions that might not be apparent from its name. First, it is a DCOM surrogate, improving the management and administration of these components on a server. Second, it is a transaction coordinator, assisting in performing disparate database transactions as a group and rolling them back as a group if any part fails. Third, MTS is a resource-pooling manager, allowing multiple logical objects to run in the context of a pool of physical ones. It also provides database connection pooling for the DCOM libraries to minimize the performance issues associated with login and connection.

Internet Information Server 4.0/5.0

We choose Internet Information Server (IIS) as our Web server for several reasons. First, it is the foundation for Active Server Pages (ASP), a VBScript-based environment for the dynamic generation of browser-agnostic HTML pages. In addition, IIS and MTS integrate tightly when the two are running on the same physical machine, bypassing some of the normal activation processes to improve overall performance.

Visual InterDev 6.0

We use Visual InterDev as our primary ASP development tool. It has a powerful IDE much like Visual Basic, allowing us to develop our ASP pages more rapidly than we could in a conventional text editor (which up until release 6.0 was the primary path). In addition, Visual InterDev provides debug facilities that we can use to step through some server-side pages during generation or through the completed page on the client side, which might also have some embedded scripting code.

OLEDB/ADO

Database access is foundational to any enterprise application. Although many applications might still be using ODBC or other forms of legacy driver methods, OLEDB and ADO are the most appropriate choices for new application development or significant refreshes to existing applications. In addition to providing access to an RDBMS, OLEDB/ADO is the foundation upon which Microsoft plans to allow access to other structured data, such as network directory services. Additionally, ADO provides a mechanism to represent structured data created by your application and can serve as a temporary storage space or a transport mechanism, as we will see throughout the remainder of Part I.

XML and the MSMXL Parsing Engine

The Extensible Markup Language (XML) is currently one of the hottest topics in the enterprise application community. Similar to HTML, XML is a textual format for representing structured information. The difference between HTML and XML is that the former represents format and the latter represents data.

Although XML is a straightforward specification, its flexibility makes the development of a parser a nontrivial task. IBM has made a publicly available, Java-based parser for some time. It has only been with the release of IE5 that Microsoft has provided a standalone COM-based parser in the form of `MSXML.DLL`. Now that Microsoft has provided this invaluable tool, we can divert our attention from trying to build a complex parser and begin creating the value-added solutions from it. XML is a data-transfer mechanism with multiple roles, including providing a data conduit between processes within a system (P2P), processes across systems (S2S interfaces), and processes across businesses (B2B interfaces).

What is powerful about MSXML is its COM basis that gives it the capability to run within Visual Basic, ASP, and IE. Even more powerful is that data formatted as XML in a Windows-based COM environment is readable by a UNIX-based Java XML reader in another environment.

CDONTS

The final technology that we will use is that of CDONTS, or Collaborative Data Objects for NT Server. CDONTS provides many features, but the one of interest to us is its SMTP (Simple Mail Transport Protocol) capability that bypasses MAPI (Mail API). The reason that this is important is that MAPI requires the use of a mail service, such as Exchange, that adds additional overhead in administration and performance. Although there is a similar CDO (non-NT server) version, it lacks this SMTP-based messaging engine that we need. Fortunately, we can run CDONTS on our NT Workstation development machine. In production mode, we can use CDONTS with both IIS and MTS to provide server-side mail processing for collaboration and notification activities.

Organization of the Book

The remainder of Part I of this book first presents a quick overview of elements that will be used throughout the rest of the book. This overview is purposefully just that—an overview. The goal is to provide a quick familiarization of what we are using and why we are using it. Many books are available that go into in-depth coverage of these topics. This overview will then be followed by some fundamental design topics concerning object orientation, components, databases, distribution, and interface-based development.

Although the reader does not technically need to be a master of each of these areas to understand the framework topics in this book, he or she will need to be comfortable with each of the technologies. Along the way, hints and warnings provide helpful implementation techniques that have come about after many long hours and late nights of scouring through Microsoft documentation to find the solution to some particular quirk.

Part II discusses actual enterprise components built upon the concepts outlined in Part I. This book presents each framework component by first discussing the architectural reasoning behind the component and the types of trade-off decisions that were made during its development. The book then presents the component design in detail accompanied by the full source code required for its proper implementation.

Chapter Layout

Chapter 2, "Layers and Tiers, " presents an overview of the layered approach to application development. It then discusses 2-, 3-, and N-tier architectures. It concludes with a summary on how application layers map to tiers.

Chapter 3, "Objects, Components, and COM," provides an overview of object orientation. It then follows with a discussion on component-based development. It concludes with a discussion on how object-orientation and component-based development relate to Microsoft's Component Object Model.

Chapter 4, "The Relational Database Management System," discusses some basic features of an RDBMS. It follows with a discussion on the persistence of the state of an object. It concludes with the mapping of objects to databases.

Chapter 5, "Distribution Considerations," discusses the distribution of objects across multiple tiers. It provides several approaches to set up the necessary communication channels between objects across process boundaries. It concludes with a discussion of MTS best practices for distributed development.

Chapter 6, "Development Fundamentals and Design Goals of an Enterprise Application," discusses some best practices to follow for the programming languages involved with the framework. This includes Visual Basic, used for the application and its components, and Visual Basic Script, used by Active Server Pages. It also suggests entity design standards for the RDBMS part of the system. Finally, we will present the high-level design goals that we will use to drive the development of the framework in subsequent chapters.

Chapter 7, "The ClassManager Library," introduces the ClassManager component that is used to drive class definitions and the mapping of objects to databases.

Chapter 8, "The DataManager Library," introduces the DataManager component that is used to provide a non-invasive data layer for the business layer objects of the system.

Chapter 9, "A Two-Part, Distributed Business Object," discusses the splitting of the traditional business object into several parts that run on multiple tiers.

Chapter 10, "Adding an ActiveX Control to the Framework," discusses the development of the user interface using ActiveX control technology, allowing front-end deployment in a variety of hosts.

Chapter 11, "A Distributed Reporting Engine," discusses how to leverage ASP as your primary reporting engine. It is followed by a discussion on how to implement more complex reporting through an MTS-based reporting component.

Chapter 12, "Taking the Enterprise Application to the Net," discusses how to make your application functionality available to a larger client base through the corporate intranet.

Chapter 13, "Interoperability," discusses how to set up links to other systems, both internal and external to the corporation. It presents several models to deal with the most common needs that arise in the corporate setting.

Chapter 14, "A Task Management Component," presents the issues surrounding task automation, message queuing, and cross-system collaboration.

Chapter 15, "Concluding Remarks," presents several topics that have been left uncovered. These include security and scalability.

2
Layers and Tiers

I N AN EFFORT TO MOVE FROM A MONOLITHIC application model to a modular one, industry experience over the years has determined that there is a logical partitioning of functionality into distinct groups known as layers. Furthermore, experience has determined that there are certain physical locations where these layers reside—whether they are different machines—that are referred to as tiers. Although there is little debate in the industry on what these layers and tiers are, there are various viewpoints on how to best accomplish the implementation of these elements to arrive at a robust application.

Layers

Modern applications partition the system into at least three distinct logical layers of code known as user, business, and data. The Microsoft DNA architecture names these layers as presentation, application, and data, respectively. A fourth layer, named system, provides access to the services provided by the network and platform operating systems. This system layer should not be confused with Microsoft's workflow layer because the two are different in nature. For the purposes of the framework presented in this book, Microsoft's view of workflow logic is embedded in the user and business layers as part of the distribution mechanism.

This partitioning of functionality across layers not only allows the distribution of processing across multiple machines, but also creates a high level of modularity and maintainability in the code base. Figure 2.1 shows an overview of these layers and the interactions between them.

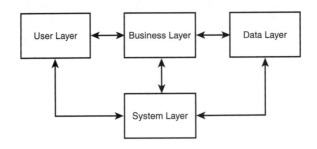

Figure 2.1   The layered development model.

The User/Presentation Layer

User services provide the presentational and navigational aspects of the application. The user services layer is the part of the system the user sees and interacts with regularly. In most cases, the user considers the user interface to be the application because they are unaware that any other parts of the system exist. We can define a user interface within the context of an application screen that contains complex interactive controls. These might include tables, drop-down lists, tree views, list views, button bars, tab strips, and so on. Similarly, we can define a page with simple form elements rendered in a Web browser as a simple user interface. In addition, we can also define a user interface in terms of a Web page that hosts an ActiveX control or Java applet.

To build a complex user interface, a language, such as Visual Basic, is required to host the interactive controls and provide the navigational logic for the user to move about the system. In a Web browser-based application, we can use a static HTML page to present the interface, or we can rely on Active Server Pages to build the interface for us based on dynamic requirements.

The Business/Application Layer

Although the user interface is what the end user sees, the business layer is what defines the application in terms of what it does from an information management perspective. It is logical to assume that all data input and output comes from the user layer; however, this is not the case. It is convenient to first define the business layer in these terms, but it will become clear in the development of the framework that inputs and outputs can be comprised of interfaces to other applications as well as to end users.

The modularity of the layered approach drives the ability to support both types of interfaces with a common business layer.

We often refer to the business layer as the heart of the system, and for good reason. Besides being the location where we implement all business logic, it is also the center point of a multilayer system. On one side of this layer stack, it interfaces with the user layer, providing the information needed to populate the interface and the validation logic needed to ensure proper data entry by the user. On the other side of the layer stack, it interfaces with the data layer that in turn interacts with the data storage and retrieval subsystems. The business layer can also communicate with other business layers either within or external to the application.

With respect to the user interface, the business layer provides both inputs and outputs. On the input side, the business layer handles the validation logic needed to ensure appropriate information entry by the user. If we take an example from an accounting application, a simple field-level validation might be necessary to ensure that the posting date on a ledger transaction constitutes a valid date. Complex logic, on the other hand, validates across an information set, but we still handle this on the business layer. An example taken from the same accounting application might be to make sure a check's posting date occurs before its clearing date. The business layer also defines the output aspects of the system. This might be in the form of the content that makes up human-readable reports or in data feeds to other systems. This could go beyond just a simple dump from a database system, where a standard query against a server provides the data, to a system that performs transformation of the data from one or more data storage systems.

When we start the definition process for a new application, we must focus on how to meet both the high-level business needs and the needs of the end user. Although common sense might seem to indicate a user-layer focus, we should really look to the business layer to drive our design efforts because the users understand the real world the best. As we will see in the next chapter, we can model the real world using object-oriented techniques, creating business-layer objects that drive the application. By using this approach, we can avoid an initial focus on the user and data layers that can side-track our efforts. Instead, we will implement a robust framework that will allow these outer layers to become a natural extension of our inner business layer.

The Data Services Layer

The data services layer performs all interactions with the data storage device, most often a Relational Database Management System (RDBMS) server. This layer is responsible for providing the rudimentary CRUD (Create, Retrieve, Update, and Delete) functionality on behalf of the system. It can also enforce business-entity relationship rules as part of its administrative duty. Typically, it not only involves the database server itself, but also the underlying data access methodology, such as Active Data

Objects (ADO), and the formal database language, such as Structured Query Language (SQL).

From an interaction standpoint, only the data layer should deal directly with the business layer. If we look around, we will see many systems deployed wherein the developer has directly coupled the user and data layers, effectively eliminating the business layer. Data-bound controls follow just this approach. Although this is a viable solution, it is inflexible in terms of extensions to the business processes because it does not implement them to begin with. If we do not implement a solid business process within our application, we have effectively created a dumb, fragile, and data-centric solution to a business problem.

Tip

Do not use controls while in data-bound mode in enterprise applications. They offer no flexibility for extensibility, minimal capability for business process implementation, and represent a poor design.

The System Layer

The system layer is somewhat of a catch-all category for functionality that is required but does not necessarily fit into one of the other layers. Each of the user, business, and data layers can have its own unique system layer to assist in providing its own requisite functionality. The system layer can include functionality to interact with the file system, network, or registry. It can include the login functionality, general-purpose functions, error handling, user messaging, and so on. It can also include security verification, mailing functionality, event-logging functions, and the like.

The Application Spread Across Tiers

Although often considered synonymous, tiers differ from layers in that they represent the physical hardware employed by the system. It is the number of such pieces of hardware that give a particular deployment strategy its tiering nomenclature. Common sense says that increasing the number of pieces of hardware has the effect of distributing the processing load, thereby increasing application performance. Although this is the design intent of a tiered architecture, simply adding hardware into the application does not necessarily improve the overall application. We must be careful to add hardware in an appropriate manner so that we achieve the desired effect.

Single-Tiered Architecture

In a single-tiered architecture, all the software layers that make up an application reside on the same physical computer. This is typically the case of an application running against a local database and a local database engine, such as Microsoft Access.

Single-tiered architectures usually represent a user base of one, because multiple users cannot simultaneously share the database. This architecture is also the worst-performing because the application and the database engine are running on the same machine, eliminating any chance for cooperative processing. Figure 2.2 shows the single-tiered architecture.

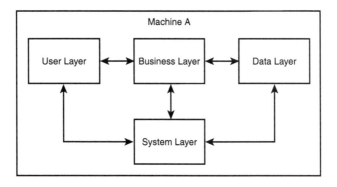

Figure 2.2   The generic single-tiered architecture.

2-Tiered Architecture

The 2-tiered architecture is synonymous with client/server technology. As the name suggests, we are using two pieces of hardware in this scenario: a client side that provides the user and business layers and a server side that provides the data layer. The server side is typically the database server itself. This architecture is much better at distributing the processing load between two machines—to be sure, client/server applications represent the largest installation base within the corporate world. One of the drawbacks to this approach is that it still places a significant burden on the client machine to provide both the user and business layers of the application. It also means that as we enhance (or fix) the business layer, we will have to re-deploy the necessary files across the user base as well. This can be a significant feat if the user base is large and extends across a vast geographic space. Figure 2.3 shows the 2-tiered architecture.

3-Tiered Architecture

A 3-tiered architecture fixes some of the problems of a 2-tiered model by introducing a third computer. In this mode, we insert a special business-layer tier between the client and server. This not only further improves performance (assuming it is done correctly), but it also puts the business layer at a single point, reducing the need to re-deploy the application as we make many of the enhancements and fixes to the application.

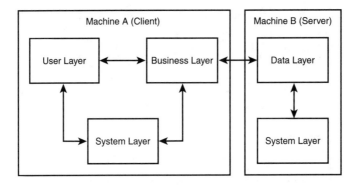

Figure 2.3   The generic 2-tiered architecture.

Many developers feel that a 3-tiered architecture is the same as the user/business/data layering approach. Although this is a technically valid assumption, it represents a pure layer to tier mapping that is difficult to implement in real-world situations for a variety of reasons that will be discussed later. Figure 2.4 shows a generic 3-tiered architecture.

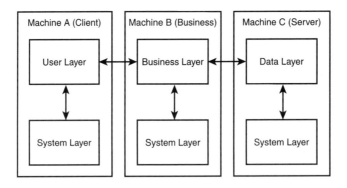

Figure 2.4   The generic 3-tiered architecture.

N-Tiered Architecture

An N-tiered architecture starts with a 3-tiered approach but allows the addition of new business or data layers running on additional hardware. This might be typical of applications that interface with other applications, but can simply be an application with multiple business, data, or user tiers. Figure 2.5 shows a realistic, albeit contrived, complex N-tiered architecture. Figure 2.6 shows a similar, complex N-tiered architecture specifically using our selected tools and technologies.

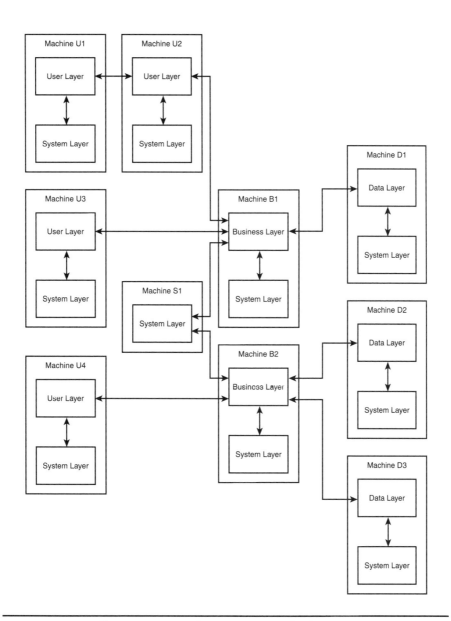

Figure 2.5   A complex, generic N-tiered architecture.

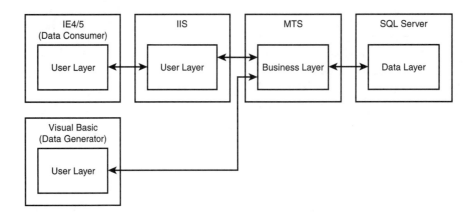

Figure 2.6   The N-tiered architecture using our chosen tools and technologies.

From Figure 2.5, we can see that for each tier, there can be a system layer to support the primary layer implemented by the tier. It is important to note that a middle tier might only be home to a system layer. This arises when we implement the functionality needed to drive administration tasks, workflow routing, and collaboration activities that take place as part of the application's daily chores.

N-tier distribution is critical to successful implementation of enterprise applications relative to the interfacibility and collaborative attributes discussed in Chapter 1, "An Introduction to the Enterprise." It is on these middle tiers that we can build the infrastructure for business layers from disparate systems to interface and work together. This other system can constitute either internally developed or third-party applications. We can see a good example of this in the form of a commercial ERP system that provides access to its business layer through a Business Application Programming Interface (BAPI). SAP is one such system that provides access to a limited portion of its functionality through a BAPI interface, also known as the SAP DCOM Connector, running on an MTS box. In implementing our business layers on a middle tier, we effectively create our own BAPI into our application as a secondary process.

Note

The cost and complexity of building either 3- or N-tier applications can be much higher than that for a standard 2-tier model. This is especially true when going through the first development project using such a model because the learning curve is steep and the number of decision-making points is high. With these issues in mind, you should plan to use such architectures only in applications with large user bases, such as those found in medium to large corporate environments. If you do decide to tackle a 3- or N-tier model in a smaller-scale application, start with some of the framework components presented in Part II of this book. This will help make the transition easier, whether the goal is a proof of concept or simply a plan for the future.

Mapping Layers to Tiers

As we have shown, layers and tiers are different; yet they relate to each other in that we have to decide where to physically put our functionality. Depending on how we perform this mapping, we can define the level of client-side functionality required by the application. This is important when it comes to the hardware cost goals of the application, which the development team often has little or no control over.

Thick Client

A thick client approach is indicative of the single- or 2-tiered models where a significant amount of functionality resides on the client-side computer. In the single-tier model, all three layers reside on the client. In the 2-tier model, only the user and business layers reside on the client. In either case, this usually requires client machines with higher performance than would otherwise be required.

Thin Client

When a thin client approach is used, only the user layer resides on the client machine. The business and data layers reside elsewhere, leading us to a 3- or N-tiered model. In this case, we need a machine with only minimal capabilities. In this approach, we are limited to a user interface with little complexity because a simple Web browser constitutes the application. Because of the lowered capabilities, we use thin clients primarily for data consumption or only light-duty data generation.

Typically in a thin client approach, we are providing a pure layer to tier mapping. The user layer maps completely to the client, the business layer maps to a middle tier (such as MTS), and the data layer maps to a back-end database server. Because of this mapping approach, all user input must cross from the client to the middle tier for simple activities, such as data validation, a process known as server round-tripping. In input-intensive applications, this can be frustrating for the end user because there is a performance penalty.

Plump Client

A plump client is somewhere in between the thin and thick varieties. Here we use a 3- or N-tiered model as well. In this mode, the user layer and a portion of the business layer reside on the client side. The remainder of the business layer resides on a middle tier. This solution represents a best-of-both-worlds scenario in which we can isolate the business process logic on a middle tier server, yet still enable a complex user interface. In this mode, we need a client machine that is somewhere in between the requirements of the thin and thick client modes as well. Although we can use a Web browser in this mode as well, it usually hosts a complex user layer object, such as an ActiveX control or a Java applet. Because of the balance afforded by a plump client, we use it primarily for heavy-duty data generation activities.

In a plump client mode, we modify the pure mapping described in the thin client approach by making the lines between the tiers a bit fuzzier. In this mode, the client tier has the user layer and a user-centric portion of the business layer. The middle tier has the business layer and a data-centric portion of the data layer. The data tier has the data layer and a business-centric portion of the business layer. While our tongue is untwisting after reading that series of sentences, we should look at Figure 2.7.

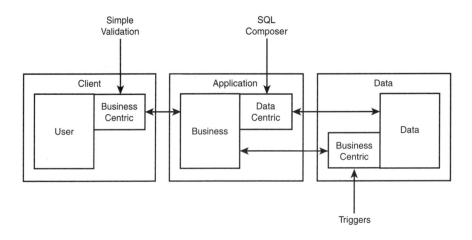

Figure 2.7   The split-layer distribution model.

Mapping Layers and Tiers to Your Development Team

Beyond mapping layers to tiers, we also need to consider how the two relate to the development team. Although it is important to have experts in each of the user, business, and data layer categories, it is also important to maintain a breadth of knowledge across the team. Any developer should be able to go into any layer of the application and perform work on the code base. The reason for this is that the layered approach means a certain level of cooperation is required between these functional areas. As such, it is important for one layer to provide the functionality needed by its attached layer, meaning, for example, that the user layer expert must understand the requirements of the business layer expert, and vice-versa. Such a full understanding of all layers by all developers will make the overall development and maintenance process more robust.

We will also see as we get into the component-based development discussions in Chapter 4, "The Relational Database Management System," that a one-to-one mapping between expert and layer bodes well for the development process in general.

Because we have a clearly defined separation of functional areas, each developer can work on a layer in isolation. In this mode, we can simulate the functionality of the attached layer through code stubs. During development, we can perform a high level of unit testing before hooking the application together for the integrated testing phase. This form of development, with clearly defined interfaces and stubs, also enables us to generate automated testing routines for regression testing after the application enters a release candidate or production mode.

Summary

In this chapter, we learned that enterprise application development consists of more than just code running on a single machine. With today's technologies, we can put the various pieces of functionality on multiple machines in ways that increase performance, decrease costs, and improve administration and maintenance. Such splitting of the functionality also simplifies the implementation of the interoperability and accessibility aspects of the application. In the next chapter, we will discuss object orientation as it relates to Visual Basic, MTS, and Microsoft's Component Object Model.

3

Objects, Components, and COM

WHETHER YOU ARE A SEASONED OBJECT-ORIENTED developer or someone who is just coming up to speed, it is important to understand some of the basic features that object-oriented programming imparts. Because we will be leveraging these features heavily in our framework in Part II of this book, we are providing a suitable overview in this chapter. To add depth, we will intersperse notes and tips relative to using object-orientation to your advantage in building enterprise applications throughout this chapter.

Object Orientation

Object orientation is not an entirely new concept, but it is becoming more prevalent in the underpinnings of modern applications. It has just been within the last ten years or so that object-orientation migrated from academia and experimentation to a true, commercial-grade development methodology. Since then, non–object-oriented development has moved into the minority position.

Note

One important thing to remember is that simply using an object-capable language does not constitute object-oriented development. In addition, simply defining classes within an object-capable language, without taking advantage of the power of object-orientation, does not necessarily make an enterprise application more robust.

To start a definition of object-orientation is to understand that it is rooted in the management of complexity. Modern applications, with their intrinsic business logic and interactions among data elements, can become burdensome to develop and maintain in a traditional procedural environment. Sometimes just the analysis of the business problem domain can become increasingly overwhelming as the system's scope grows from one of simple data management to one that embodies business process knowledge. Object-orientation helps throughout application development by allowing us to use a similar thought process across the analysis, design, and implementation phases. The basic pillars of object-orientation are abstraction, encapsulation, polymorphism, and inheritance. We will discuss these features of object-orientation and how they enable us to build modular, maintainable, and extensible applications.

Abstraction and Class Modeling

What is most striking about object-orientation is that it follows the true sense of the business world. In this world, anything that a business deals with, whether it is a widget that a company produces or a financial account that a bank maintains on behalf of a client, is definable in software terms through a class model. This class model defines the information pertinent to the business entity, along with the logic that operates on that information. Additionally, a class definition can contain references to one or more external classes through association or ownership relationships. In the case of a financial account, informational elements might include the account number, the names of the account owners, the current balance, the type of account, and so on. We call these items *properties* (also known as *attributes*) of the class. Similarly, the class can define a function to add a new transaction to the account or modify/delete an existing transaction. We call these items methods (also known as operations) of the class. What differentiates a class from an object is that a class is a definition, whereas an object is an instance of that definition.

We can also graphically represent our objects using a class diagram. There are many different views on how to represent these diagrams, but the most pervading forms are the Yourdon/Coad and the Rumbaugh methods, named after the individuals who developed them. Many drawing programs have templates predefined for these models, whereas many modeling tools can support some or all of the more popular styles. You can also create your own object modeling technique using simple lines and boxes. We have chosen to use the Rumbaugh model in this book because of the popularity of the Unified Modeling Language (UML), of which it is a component. It also happens to be the model used by the Microsoft Visual Modeler that is bundled with Visual Studio 6.0 Enterprise Edition. Figure 3.1 shows an example of a graphical depiction for a financial account class.

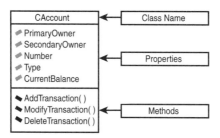

Figure 3.1   The CAccount class using the UML graphical model.

Tip

It is important to decide on a graphical object representation model early in the project. Make sure that everyone understands how to read it and feels comfortable with it. This model will be your roadmap as you work your way through all phases of the application development process and will be critical as the complexity starts to build.

As you can see, we modeled our real-world Account business entity in terms of properties and methods. We call this modeling process *abstraction*, which forms the basis for object orientation. With this in mind, we can further our discussion of other features of object-orientation.

Encapsulation

What should be apparent from Figure 3.1 is that we have bundled everything about the class into a nice, neat package. We formally define everything that the outside world needs to know about this class in terms of these properties and methods. We call the public properties and methods of a class its interface, which represents the concept of encapsulation. In the real-world account example, a customer does not necessarily need to know how the current balance is calculated based on transactions that are added, modified, or deleted. They just need to know their current balance. Similarly, users of the account class do not need to know how the class calculates the current balance either—just that the class properly handles it when the transaction processing methods are called. Thus, we can say that encapsulation has the effect of information hiding and the definition of narrow interfaces into the class. This concept is critical to the development of robust, maintainable applications.

A class might implement internal methods and properties but choose not to expose them to the outside world through its interface. Because of this, we are free to change the internal workings of these private items without affecting how the outside world uses our class through its public interface. Figure 3.2 shows how a public method calls a private method to perform a calculation that updates the value of a public property.

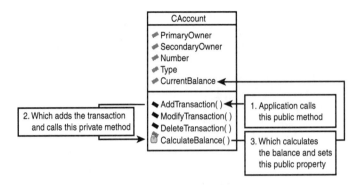

Figure 3.2   The interactions between public and private methods and properties.

Suppose, for the sake of argument, we were to expose the internal function (also known as a private method) that calculates current balances. We would do this by defining it to be public versus private. An application using this class, for whatever reason, might deem it acceptable to call this internal method directly and does so in a multitude of places. Now suppose that we must change the calling convention of this method by adding a new parameter to the parameter list, such that we have to modify every piece of software that references this internal method. Assume also that the public transaction methods would not have had to change, only the formerly private method. We have effectively forced ourselves into a potentially large code rewrite, debug, test, and deployment cycle that we could have otherwise handled simply within the object's private methods while leaving the public interface intact. We will see, in the COM model discussion to follow, that we can easily modify only the class and redeploy it across the user base with a minimum of effort. In the corporate world, this translates into time and money.

Because the term *interface* might be a difficult concept to grasp at first, it might be easier to think of as an electrical socket. In the 220-volt parts of the world, there are three-pronged sockets with one of the prongs oriented 90 degrees out from the other two. In the 110-volt parts of the world, there are two- and three-pronged plugs with a different geometry such that you cannot plug a 110-volt oriented plug into a 220-volt socket and vice-versa. Imagine if the 110-volt world suddenly began using 220-volt–style plugs and sockets (assuming voltage will not change). We would have to replace the plug on every electrical device along with all the wall sockets. It would be a huge mess. The same goes for properties and methods. After we define the interfaces of a class and write applications against them, making changes becomes difficult and costly.

Tip

When defining a class, assume every method is to be defined as private in scope (that is, hidden) unless there is good reason to make it public. When making a method public, take steps to ensure the stability of the calling convention (that is, the parameter list) over the life of the application. Use optional parameters as necessary to cover anticipated future needs.

Encapsulation also has the effect of protecting the integrity of objects, which are instantiated using the class definition. We have already touched on this when we stated that a class is responsible for its own inner workings. Outsiders cannot meddle in its internal affairs. Similarly, property definitions can be implemented such that the class rejects invalid property states during the setting process. For example, a date-based property could reject a date literal, such as "June 31, 1997," because it does not constitute a date on any calendar. Again, because the validation logic is contained within the class definition itself, modifying it to meet changing business needs occurs in a single place rather than throughout the application base. This aspect of encapsulation is important, especially for enterprise applications, when we discuss the implementation of validation logic in Chapter 9, "A Two-Part, Distributed Business Object." It further adds to our ability to develop robust, maintainable, and extensible applications.

Note

One of the common comments that newcomers to object-oriented development make is that it seems like unnecessary effort to package data and functionality together into a unit called a class. It also seems like extra work to define properties and methods, deciding what is to be public and what is to be private. It is much easier to just take a seat behind the keyboard and begin banging out some code. Although it is true that object-oriented development requires a different mindset and a somewhat formal approach to analysis and design, it is this formalization process that leads to less complex development over the long term. The old saying "penny-wise and dollar-foolish" applies here because some time saved up front will lead to potentially huge problems further into the development, and worse yet, the application launch process.

Let us switch gears by defining a class with some complexity—with a financial bond—so we can illustrate some other points and begin setting the stage for other features of object-orientation. Let us call it CBond (for Class Bond). We define several properties in tabular form in Table 3.1, methods in Table 3.2, and we provide a graphical depiction in Figure 3.3.

Table 3.1   **Properties of a *CBond* Class**

Property	Data Type	Description
Name	String	The descriptive name of the bond.
FaceValue	Single (Currency)	The final redemption value of the bond.
PurchasePrice	Single (Currency)	The price to purchase the bond.
CouponRate	Single (Percent)	The yearly bond coupon payment as a percentage of its face value.
BondTerm	Integer	The length of time to maturity for the bond, expressed in years, in the primary market.
BondType	Integer: (Enumeration [CouponBond, DiscountBond, ConsolBond])	The bond type used to drive calculation algorithms.

Table 3.2   **Methods of a *CBond* Class**

Method	Description
YieldToMaturity	Calculates the interest rate that equates the present value of the coupon payments over the life of the bond to its value today. Used in the secondary bond market.
BondPrice	Calculates the bond price as the sum of the present values of all the payments for the bond.
CurrentYield	Calculates the current yield as an approximation of the yield to maturity using a simplified formula. Note: Available only on CouponBond types.
DiscountYield	Calculates the discount yield based on the percentage gain on the face value of a bond and the remaining days to maturity.

Each method uses one or more of the public property values to perform the calculation. Some methods require additional information in the form of its parameter list, as can be seen in Figure 3.3. As you might guess, the BondType property helps each method determine how to perform the calculation. A sample Visual Basic implementation of the BondPrice method might be as follows in Listing 3.1.

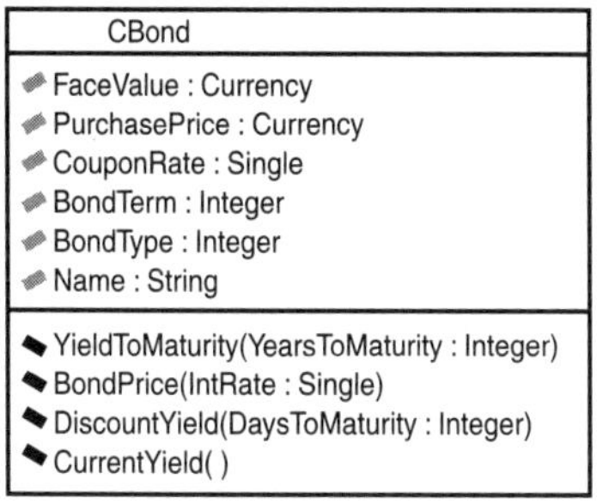

Figure 3.3　UML representation of a CBond class.

Listing 3.1　**The *BondPrice* Method**

```
Public Function BondPrice(IntRate as Single) as Single
 Dim CouponPayment as Single
 Dim j as integer
 Dim p as single
 CouponPayment = CouponRate * FaceValue
 Select Case BondType
  Case btCouponBond
   For j = 1 to BondTerm
    p = p + CouponPayment/(1 + IntRate)^j
   Next j
   p = p + FinalValue/(1 + IntRate)^BondTerm
   BondPrice = p
  Case btDiscountBond
   BondPrice = FaceValue/(1 + IntRate)
  Case btConsolBond
   BondPrice = CouponPayment/IntRate
 End Select
End Sub
```

As you can see, each value of the BondType property requires a different use of the properties to perform the correct calculation. The application using the class is not concerned with how the method performs the calculation, but only with the result. Now suppose that you need to modify the calculation algorithm for the BondPrice method. Because of encapsulation, you only need to modify the contents of the BondPrice method and nothing more. Better yet, because you have not changed the calling convention, the applications using the CBond class are none the wiser that a change occurred.

Polymorphism

Polymorphism is another standard feature of object-oriented programming. Fundamentally, polymorphism means the capability to define similar properties and methods on dissimilar classes. In essence, we define a common interface on a set of classes such that a calling application can use these classes with a standard set of conventions. Because this sounds complex, let us provide an example.

Suppose you are developing classes that must interact with a relational database. For each of these classes, there can be a standard set of methods to retrieve property values for an object instance from a database. We call this process of storing and retrieving property values *object persistence*, a topic we will discuss in detail in Chapter 5, "Distribution Considerations." We can illustrate an abstract definition of a couple of methods as follows:

```
Public Function RetrieveProperties(ObjectId As Long) As Variant
 ' code to retrieve the property values
End Function

Public Sub SetStateFromVariant(ObjectData As Variant)
 ' code to set the property values from ObjectData
End Sub
```

For each class that is to follow this behavior, it must not only define, but also provide the implementation for these two methods. Suppose you have three such classes—CClassOne, CClassTwo, and CClassThree. An application that creates and loads an object might implement polymorphic code in the following manner (see Listing 3.2).

Listing 3.2   **The *RetrieveObject* Method**

```
Public Function RetrieveObject(ClassType As Integer,
                               ObjectId As Long) As Object
 Dim OClassAny As Object
 Dim ObjectData as Variant
 Select Case ClassType
  Case CLASS_TYPE_ONE
   Set OClassAny = New CClassOne
  Case CLASS_TYPE_TWO
   Set OClassAny = New CClassTwo
  Case CLASS_TYPE_THREE
   Set OClassAny = New CClassThree
  End Select
 ObjectData = OClassAny.RetrieveProperties(ObjectId)
 Call OClassAny.SetStateFromVariant(ObjectData)
 SetRetrieveObject = OClassAny
End Function
```

In the preceding code example, we use a technique known as *late binding*, wherein Visual Basic performs type checking at runtime rather than at compile time. In this mode, we can declare a generic object (a variable type intrinsic to Visual Basic) to represent the instantiated object based on any of the three class definitions. We must assume that each of these classes defines and implements the `RetrieveProperties` and `SetStateFromVariant` methods as mandated by our polymorphic requirements. If the classes deviate from these conventions, a runtime error will occur. If the classes meet these requirements, we can simplify the coding of the object retrieval process into a single function call on the application. This not only leads to code that is easier to maintain over the life of the application, but also makes extending the application to support new class types much simpler.

The late binding technique of Visual Basic presents us with some concerns. Because late binding performs type checking at runtime, some errors might escape early testing or even propagate into the production application. Furthermore, late binding has a performance penalty because Visual Basic must go through a process known as *runtime discovery* with each object reference to determine the actual methods and properties available on the object. This said, we should scrutinize the use of late-binding approaches in the application wherever possible and choose alternative approaches. We will discuss several approaches to circumvent these issues when we discuss the framework components in Part II of the book.

Inheritance

The final pillar of object orientation is that of inheritance. Fundamental to this concept is the capability to define the common methods and properties of a related group of classes in a base class. Descendants of this base class can choose to retain the implementation provided by the base class or can override the implementation on its own. In some cases, the base class provides no implementation whatsoever, and it is focused solely on the definition of an interface. We consider these types of base classes abstract because each subclass must provide the complete implementation. Regardless of the mode, the descendent class must maintain the definition of all properties and methods of its base class. Said in another way, the descendent class must define the same interface as its base. This is similar in concept to polymorphism, except that inheritance forces the implementation in a formal manner, such that Visual Basic can perform type checking at compile time.

Looking again at our `CBond` class, we notice that there is a `BondType` property to force certain alternative behaviors by the calculation methods. We can modify our `CBond` class into a single `IBond` base class and three subclasses called `CCouponBond`, `CDiscountBond`, and `CConsolBond`. We use `IBond` here (for Interface Bond) instead of `CBond` to coincide with Microsoft's terminology for interface implementation. Graphically, we represent this as shown in Figure 3.4.

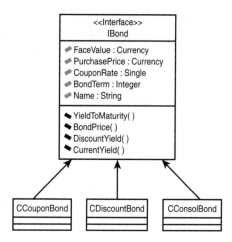

Figure 3.4   An inheritance diagram for the IBond base class.

If we revisit our bond calculation functions in the context of inheritance, they might look something like Listing 3.3. Disregard the IBond_ syntax for now because it is a concept that we gain a thorough understanding of in our work in Part II of this book.

Listing 3.3   **The *CalculateBondPrice* Method**

```
' From the application
Public Function CalculateBondPrice(BondType as Integer, _
                                   IntRate as Single) As Single
 Dim OBond As IBond
 Select Case BondType
  Case BOND_TYPE_COUPON
   Set OBond = New CCouponBond
  Case BOND_TYPE_DISCOUNT
   Set OBond = New CDiscountBond
  Case BOND_TYPE_CONSOL
   Set OBond = New CConsolBond
 End Select
 CalculateBondPrice = OBond.BondPrice(IntRate)
End Function

' From CCouponBond
Implements IBond
Public Function IBond_BondPrice(IntRate As Single) As Single
 Dim CouponPayment as Single
 Dim j as integer
 Dim p as single
 CouponPayment = IBond_CouponRate * IBond_FaceValue
 For j = 1 to IBond_BondTerm
  p = p + CouponPayment/(1 + IntRate)^j
```

```
 Next j
 p = p + IBond_FinalValue/(1 + IntRate)^IBond_BondTerm
 IBond_BondPrice = p
End Function

' From CDiscountBond
Implements IBond
Public Function IBond_BondPrice(IntRate As Single) As Single
 IBond_BondPrice = FaceValue/(1 + IntRate)
End Function

' From CConsolBond
Implements IBond
Public Function IBond_BondPrice(IntRate As Single) As Single
Dim CouponPayment as Single
 CouponPayment = IBond_CouponRate * IBond_FaceValue
 IBond_BondPrice = CouponPayment/IntRate
End Function
```

Although the application portion of this example might look somewhat similar to the polymorphic mechanism from before, there is an important distinction. Because we have defined these subclasses in the context of a base class IBond, we have forced the interface implementation of the base class. This, in turn, allows Visual Basic to perform early binding and therefore type checking at compile time. In contrast to late binding, this leads to better application performance, stability, and extensibility.

Tip

Any class definition that contains a Type property is a candidate for inheritance-based implementation.

Critics have chastised Microsoft for not implementing inheritance properly in Visual Basic in that it does not support a subclass descending from more than one base class, a concept known as multiple-inheritance. Although this lack of implementation technically is a true statement, in reality, multiple inheritance scenarios arise so infrequently that it is not worth the extra complexity that Microsoft would have had to add to Visual Basic to implement it.

Many critics would further argue that Visual Basic and COM, through their interface implementation technique, do not even support single inheritance properly and that the notion of the capability to subclass in this environment is ludicrous. Without taking a side in this debate, we can sufficiently state that interface implementation gives you some of the features afforded by single-inheritance, whether or not you want to formally define them in this manner. The particular side of the debate you might fall into is immaterial for the purposes of our framework development in Part II of this book.

Interface inheritance lends itself to maintainability and extensibility—essential attributes of enterprise applications as discussed in Chapter 1, "An Introduction to the Enterprise." If the implementation of a base method or property must change, we have to make the modifications only to the base class. Each descendent then inherits this new implementation as part of its interface implementation. If the base class physically resides in a different component than its descendants, something we will discuss later in this chapter, we only have to redeploy the component defining the base class.

Association Relationships

After we have defined the basics of classes with simple property types, we can expand our view to show that classes can have associative relationships with other classes. For example, a class might reference another class in a one-to-one manner, or a class might reference a group of other classes in a one-to-many fashion.

One-to-One Relationships

We might consider one-to-one relationships as strong or weak in nature. Weak relationships are just simple references to other classes that are shareable across multiple object instances. For example, a CPerson class can be referenced by many other classes, with a particular OPerson instance being referenced by multiple object instances of disparate classes. Strong relationships, on the other hand, are usually the result of containment relationships, where one object is the sole user of a subordinate object. In an automotive manufacturing application that tracks the serial numbers of finished units, an example might include the CSerializedEngine and CSerializedAutomobile classes, where each OSerializedEngine object can belong to only one OSerializedAutomobile object. Figure 3.5 shows a weak reference, whereas Figure 3.6 shows its strong counterpart.

In Figure 3.5, we show a graphical representation of a weak reference. In this example, the CPerson class (and thus, object instances based on the class) is referenced by both the CAccount and CLoan classes. In the real world that forms the basis for this mini-model, the relationship diagram indicates that it is possible for the same person to have both a checking account and a house or car loan at the bank. The same person could have multiple accounts or loans at the same bank.

In Figure 3.6, we show the graphical representation of a strong, or containment, reference. In this example, we show how a finished, serialized automobile has an engine and transmission, both of which the manufacturer serializes as well for tracking purposes. Each OSerializedEngine and OSerializedTransmission instance will reference only one instance of the CSerializedAutomobile class.

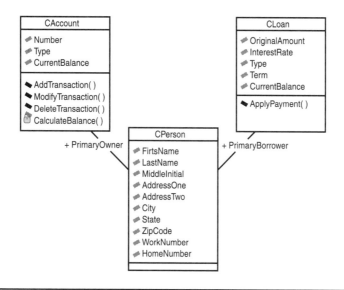

Figure 3.5 A weak association relationship.

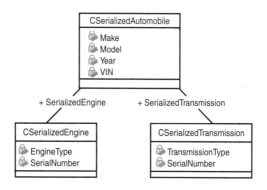

Figure 3.6 A strong association relationship.

One-To-Many Relationships

One-to-many references occur so often that we have developed a special class, known as a *collection*, to implement this type of relationship, as shown graphically in Figure 3.7. In this example, the CIBonds class indicates a collection of IBond interfaces, each of which can be subclassed as before. This CIBonds class has several methods associated with group management, such as Add, Remove, Item, and Count. If we defined a CPortfolio class, it might have a reference to a CIBonds class, as well as CIStocks and CIAssets classes, each of which are collections of IBond, IStock, and

`IAsset` classes, respectively. Again, each of these final interface classes can be subclassed to provide specific implementations, yet the collection can manage them in their base interface class.

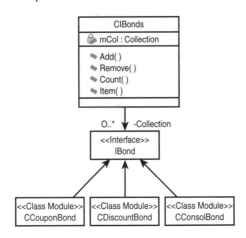

Figure 3.7 A one-to-many relationship and the collection class.

One-to-many relationships and the collection classes that implement them are synonymous with the master-detail relationships found across many applications. We will be using these collection classes frequently throughout our framework architecture. We will cover collections in detail in Chapter 7, "The ClassManager Library."

Class and Object Naming Conventions

Throughout our discussions in this chapter, we have been alluding to a naming convention for classes and objects without having given any formal definitions. Although the naming convention is arbitrary, it is important to decide on one and adhere to it throughout all phases of the project. This will not only provide a degree of standardization across multiple developers, but also make it easier for developers and maintainers to understand the code without the need for an abundant supply of comments. Standardization is important in classes and objects because the two are often confused. In our examples and throughout the remainder of this book, we will be using an uppercase `C` prefix to denote a class. Similarly, we will be using an uppercase `O` prefix for an object. Furthermore, we will be using the same suffix for both the class and its object instances, as in the case of the `CPerson` class and its `OPerson` instances. For example:

```
Set OPerson = New CPerson
```

Component-Based Development

With some object-orientation fundamentals behind us, we turn our discussion to component-based development (CBD). Many people feel that objects and components are synonymous, when in fact, they are more like siblings. Objects can exist without components, and vice-versa. A component is a reusable, self-contained body of functionality that we can use across a broad application base. Imagine an application suite that has a core piece of functionality contained in an includable source code module. Making a change to this functionality requires that we modify and recompile the source code, testing all applications that are using it. We must then distribute every application that references it. In large applications, this compile time can be extensive. In a component-based model, we can simply modify the component and do the same recompile, test, and distribute just on that component without affecting the applications.

As we alluded in our discussion on layers and tiers in Chapter 2, "Layers and Tiers," a CBD approach has some distinct advantages during the development process. Chief among these is the ability to develop and test components in isolation before integrated testing.

Component-Based Development and COM

Object-based CBD allows the packaging of class definitions into a deployable entity. Under the Microsoft Component Object Model (COM) architecture, these packages are special Dynamic Link Libraries (DLLs), a dynamic runtime technology that has been available since the earliest days of Microsoft Windows. Microsoft renamed these COM-style DLLs to ActiveX to indicate that there is a difference. An application gains access to classes in an ActiveX DLL by loading the library containing the class definitions into memory, followed by registration of the classes by the COM engine. Applications can then instantiate objects based on these classes using the COM engine.

The traditional DLL (non-ActiveX) meets the definition for CBD, but it is procedurally based (that is, non–object-based). ActiveX DLLs also meet this definition, being object-based in nature. Because an object-based approach is already rooted in the reusability of functionality, the ActiveX DLL implementation of CBD is widely considered the most powerful and flexible technology when working solely on the Win32 platform.

Although COM is both a component and object engine, it differs from other CBD technologies in that it represents binary reusability of components versus source-code level reusability. Because of its binary basis, we can write COM libraries in any language on the Win32 platform that adheres to the COM specification and its related API. The basic requirement to support the COM API is the capacity of a language to implement an array of function pointers that follow a C-style calling syntax.

The COM engine uses this array as a jumping point into the public methods and properties defined on the object. Visual Basic is one of many languages with this capability.

COM actually has two modes of operation: local and remote invocation. The distinction between these two will become important as we discuss distribution in Chapter 6, "Understanding Development Fundamentals and Design Goals of an Enterprise Application."

In local invocation, a component is loaded into the memory space of a single computer. This component can load directly into an application's process space, or it can be loaded in a separate process space with an interprocess communication mechanism. In this latter approach, we must establish a communication channel between the process spaces. In the case of distributed computing, these processes reside on physically different machines, and the communication channel must occur over a network connection. We call the local invocation method an *in-process* invocation, and we call the remote invocation method *out-of-process*. We can actually make a local, out-of-process reference as well, which effectively removes the network portion of the communication channel. Microsoft developed a local, out-of-process mode of invocation for application automation, for example, when a Microsoft Word document activates an embedded Microsoft Excel worksheet.

With in-process servers, an application can reference an object, its methods, and its properties using memory pointers as it shares a memory space with the component. Figure 3.8 depicts the local, in-process invocation.

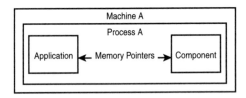

Figure 3.8   The local, in-process invocation mode of COM.

In the out-of-process server mode, all data must be serialized (that is, made suitable for transport), sent over the interprocess boundary, and then deserialized. We call this serialization process *marshalling*, a topic that we will cover in detail in Chapter 6. Additionally, the out-of-process mode must set up a "proxy" structure on the application (or client) side, and a "stub" structure on the component (or server) side. Figure 3.9 depicts the local, out-of-process mode.

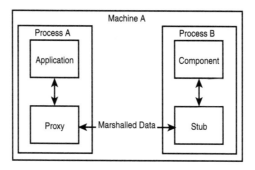

Figure 3.9   The local, out-of-process invocation mode of COM.

The reason for this proxy/stub setup is to allow the client and server sides of the boundary to maintain their generic COM programming view, without having to be concerned about the details of crossing a process boundary. In this mode, neither side is aware that a process boundary is in place. The client thinks that it is invoking a local, in-process server. The server thinks that we have called it in an in-process manner. The in-process mode of COM is fast and efficient, whereas the out-of-process mode adds extra steps and overhead to accomplish the same tasks.

Tip

We should not use an out-of-process approach in speed-critical areas of an application. Examples of where not to use an out-of-process approach would include graphic rendering or genetic algorithm processing.

If the processes reside on different machines, we must add a pair of network interface cards (NICs) to the diagram. Additionally, we must use the remote procedure call (RPC) mechanism to allow the proxy/stub pair to communicate. We refer to the remote, out-of-process mode of COM as Distributed COM (DCOM). Figure 3.10 depicts DCOM. As we might imagine, DCOM is expensive from an overall performance standpoint relative to standard COM.

COM-Definable Entities

A COM library not only enables us to define classes in terms of properties and methods, but also to define enumerations, events, and interfaces used in inheritance relationships. We already have talked about properties, methods, and interfaces, so let us complete the definition by talking about enumerations and events.

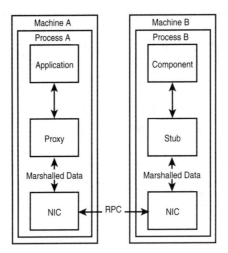

Figure 3.10   The remote, out-of-process invocation mode of COM.

Enumerations are nothing more than a list of named integral values, no different from global constants. What differentiates them is that they become a part of the COM component. In essence, the COM component predefines the constants needed by the application in the form of these enumerations. By bundling them with the classes that rely on them and giving them human-readable names, we can ensure a certain level of robustness and ease of code development throughout the overall application.

Tip
Use public enumerations in place of constants when they tie intrinsically to the operation of a class. This will keep you from having to redefine the constants for each application that uses the class, because they become part of the COM component itself. Where goes the class, so go its enumerations.

Events defined for a class are formal messages sent from an object instance to its application. The application can implement an event handler to respond to these messages in whatever manner deemed necessary.

Note
Visual Basic and COM define events as part of a class, alongside properties and methods. One might assume then that we can define events on an interface, thereby making them available to classes implementing the interface. Although this is a reasonable assumption and a desirable feature, Visual Basic and COM do not support this. As such, do not plan to use events in conjunction with interface implementation.

Component Coupling

With the flexibility to place COM classes into components and then have these components reference each other, it can become easy to create an environment of high coupling. *Coupling* occurs when we create a reference from a COM class in one component to the interface of a COM class in another component. Because components are different physical entities, this has the effect of hooking the two components together relative to distribution. Wherever we distribute a component that references other components, we also must distribute all the referenced components, all their referenced components, and so on. One reason for coupling is that we might not properly group functionality into common components. Functionality that represents a single subpart of the overall business application might be a good candidate for a single component. Alternatively, functionality that represents similar design patterns might belong in a single component.

> **Tip**
>
> It is important during the analysis and design phases to group components based on similar functionality. Although we invariably need to create system-level classes for use by other classes, we should try to minimize the creation of a chain of component references. These chains lead to administration and maintenance issues after the application is in production.

Another issue that leads to coupling is that we try to over-modularize the application by placing small snippets of subparts into components. Beyond the coupling aspects, each ActiveX DLL has a certain amount of overhead to load and retain in memory. Placing functionality in ten components when two would suffice adds unnecessary performance overhead and complexity to your application.

From a performance perspective, we can look at the time necessary to initialize the two scenarios. There are two initialization times to look at: the first is the time required to initialize the component, and the second is the time required to initialize the object. Remembering that a component in the COM world is a specialized DLL, we can infer that some initialization time is associated with the DLL. When Visual Basic must load an ActiveX DLL, it must go through a process of "learning" what objects are defined in the component in terms of properties, methods, and events. In the two scenarios, the 10-DLL case will have five times the load time of the 2-DLL case, assuming negligible differences in the aggregate learning time of the objects within the components.

From a complexity perspective, the more components created means more work on the development team. One of the problematic issues with any object-oriented or interface implementation project is that of recompilation and distribution when something changes, especially in the early development phases of the application. For example, if the definition of a core class referenced throughout the project changes, it is much easier to recompile the two components versus the ten. As you might already know from multitiered development in the DCOM environment, propagating such seemingly simple changes across tiers can be very difficult. Thus, appropriate minimization of the number of components up front is desirable.

We are not trying to say that you should place all your functionality into one component—this leads to its own set of problems. The moral of the story is that one should not force modularity purely for the sake of doing so. You should find an appropriate balance that can come only from experience in developing these sorts of systems. The framework presented in Part II is a good starting point for understanding where these lines of balance should be drawn.

When we need to provide a superset of functionality based on classes in separate components, there is a tendency to have one class directly reference the other to do this. In this case, we can put the new functionality on an existing class or we can implement a new class within one of the components to handle this. Remember that the tenant of CBD is ultimately a high level of modularity. If we design our components well, there might be other applications that need the base functionality afforded by one component, but not that of the secondary component or the bridging functionality binding them together. If we design our components in the manner just discussed, we must distribute both components just to get to the little bit of functionality that we need in one.

Tip
To minimize coupling between loosely related components, it is always better to build a third component to provide the bridge between the two components. In this manner, each can be distributed independent of the other.

Figure 3.11 shows tight coupling, whereas Figure 3.12 shows its bridged counterpart.

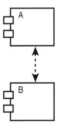

Figure 3.11   A graphical representation of tight coupling.

In Figure 3.11, it should be clear that components A and B must travel together wherever they go. An application that only needs component A must bring along component B as well. An application that uses component A might go through test, debug, and redistribution whenever component B changes, although it is not using it.

In Figure 3.12, we show components A and B bridged together by component C. In this implementation, both A and B can be used singularly in applications, whereas applications that need the bridged functionality can use component C to provide this.

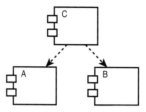

Figure 3.12   A graphical representation of bridged coupling.

Summary

We have learned some of the important concepts of object orientation and component-based development in this chapter. We have also learned how Microsoft's Visual Basic and the Component Object Model implement these concepts and how we can begin to use them to build modular, flexible applications. In the next chapter, we turn our attention to understanding the Relational Database Management system because it is the foundation for the information storage and retrieval component of our application. We will also begin laying the groundwork for good database design techniques, specifically as they pertain to our framework.

4

The Relational Database Management System

ALTHOUGH THE COM MODEL IS GOOD for defining and implementing classes in the form of binary reusable components, it offers nothing in the form of persistence or the long-term storage of object state. By *state*, we mean the values of the properties at any given moment in time. Perhaps this is something that Microsoft will address in a future release of the COM standard, but until then, a common solution to this problem is to store and retrieve data using a relational database management system (RDBMS).

Object-oriented databases are beginning to make their way into mainstream application development. Although they provide a solution to the issue of object persistence, object-oriented databases are still a relatively minor player. This is partly because they have proprietary programming interfaces, limited scalability, and in some cases, worse performance. Relational database management systems (RDBMS), on the other hand, have been around for many years and represent one of the most robust server-side pieces of software available. Many existing internal and external applications, whether they are mainframe- or PC-based, most likely use some form of an RDBMS as their data storage device. As such, we will be using an RDBMS in our framework architecture as well.

One of the greatest challenges faced when developing any application that interacts with an RDBMS is how to provide a mapping between the database, the business objects, and the user interface. There are several different theories on how to accomplish this, but the prevalent models involve taking a data-centric, a user-centric, or a business-centric view.

Data-Centric Database Design

The data-centric view defines the database structure independently of any other considerations. Following this model, we can sacrifice functionality in our business and data layers, severely impeding our ability to cleanly implement the application.

The data-centric view sometimes presents itself simply because of the organization of the development team. On many teams, there is a database expert focused on data integrity, normalization, and performance. This person might care about nothing else. Many database design decisions come about strictly because of what the database expert perceives to be best for the application. In some cases, this works adversely to the rest of the development team from an implementation and flexibility standpoint. For example, the database designer might want to have all database access take the form of stored procedures, disallowing any direct manipulation by dynamic SQL calls generated by the application. The reasoning behind this, in the database expert's mind, is to protect the integrity of the database from developers who do not necessarily understand the database structure. It might also come about simply because of territorial infringement issues. Using this model, we must code specific data access procedures on each business object because the calling convention will be different depending on the properties defined. It is extremely difficult to define a generic database layer using this approach or using a polymorphic method on the class.

From our examples in the last chapter, let us define how we can implement a RetrieveProperties method on CBond using a stored procedure approach (see Listing 4.1).

Listing 4.1   **The *RetrieveProperties* Method on *CBond* Using Stored Procedure Approach**

```
'From CBond
Public Sub RetrieveProperties(ByVal ObjectId As Long, _
ByRef FaceValue As Currency, _
ByRef CouponRate As Single, _
ByRef BondTerm As Intger, _
ByRef BondType As EnumBondType, _
ByRef Name As String)
Dim rs As ADODB.Recordset
cmd.CommandText = "sp_RetrieveBond"
```

```
cmd.CommandType = adCmdStoredProc
Call cmd.Parameters.Append(cmd.CreateParameter("ObjectId", _
 adInteger, _
 adParamInput, _
 ObjectId))
Call cmd.Parameters.Append(cmd.CreateParameter("FaceValue", _
 adCurrency, _
 adParamOutput, _
 FaceValue))
Call cmd.Parameters.Append(cmd.CreateParameter("CouponRate", _
 adSingle, _
 adParamOutput, _
 CouponRate))
Call cmd.Parameters.Append(cmd.CreateParameter("BondTerm", _
 adInteger, _
 adParamOutput, _
 BondType))
Call cmd.Parameters.Append(cmd.CreateParameter("BondType", _
 adInteger, _
 adParamOutput, _
 BondType))
Call cmd.Parameters.Append(cmd.CreateParameter("Name", _
 adVarChar, _
 adParamOutput, _
 Name))
Set cmd.ActiveConnection = cnn ' global connection for COM lib
Call cmd.Execute
Set cmd = Nothing
End Sub
```

Now imagine having to write a `RetrieveProperties` method on a `CPerson` class. Because the properties on such a class are different from our `CBond` class, we cannot implement a polymorphic procedure for the `RetrieveProperties` method across various classes. This means a significant amount of coding overhead during the initial development phase, followed by more issues during maintenance. Similarly, our overall code base will be bloated because we have not effectively followed good object-oriented design principles, simply because the database expert wanted to use stored procedures versus a dynamic SQL approach.

In terms of extensibility, suppose that we need to add a new field to the database to support a new property on a business object. The stored procedures driving this business object will need updating along with the business object code. Because we will be changing the `RetrieveProperties` method, we will be changing an interface on the class, which means that we will need to modify, recompile, and redeploy the applications using this class to make this change.

User-Centric Database Design

The user-centric view defines the database by how we present the information to the user. This is probably the worst approach to use in defining a database and is akin to the issues with data-bound controls. Most likely, these sorts of interfaces are simple master/detail type screens, with little to no data normalization on the information making up the detail portion.

Business-Centric Database Design

Because object-orientation enables us to model the real world, and the business layer is the realization of that model, we should be able to follow a business-centric view during database design. This is precisely what we have done because it is simple when we have a good object model. In so doing, we guarantee that the database structure closely follows the business object structure.

Table Orientation

In an RDBMS, information is stored in tables. Each table defines a series of columns that make up an individual data record. We call these records *rows*. A single database can have an unlimited number of tables (or at least a maximum number defined by the database vendor). All data insertions, updates, and deletions occur at a single table at the row level. We can relate tables using the primary/foreign key pairs on the tables. These keys are special columns that we use solely to enforce relationships between rows in one table and rows in other tables. We define a primary key on a table as the unique identifier for a given row. External tables that reference the primary key on a given table use foreign keys on the external table. We can retrieve data from a single table or join multiple tables to give us a broader data set. We can predefine these joins using a database view that looks and acts like a table with retrieval-only properties.

An important concept in RDBMS theory is that of data normalization. The fundamental principal of normalization is to eliminate redundant information. This not only improves capacity utilization, but it also ensures that we do not have multiple copies of the same information floating around within the database. For example, if we were to define an AccountPerson table and a LoanPerson table to coincide with Figure 3.5 from Chapter 3, we might have a duplicate record for a given person. If we have to make an address change, we might remember to do it in one of the tables and not the other. With this example, we begin to see a similarity between RDBMS normalization and object-orientation in that any given entity should exist only once, just as in the real world.

Mapping Tables and Objects

With our wonderful object-orientation and RDBMS worlds at our disposal, a problem arises when it comes to marrying the two together. We call this the impedance mismatch problem, where we have to programmatically map objects into our database structure. Tables are row- and column-based; classes are object- and property-based.

Our mapping process is actually simple. We create a table for every class and define columns of the appropriate data type for each property. Thus, a class maps to a table and properties map to columns, with a table row representing an object instance. In the case of an inheritance relationship, we map all subclasses of a base class to a single table, with a `ClassType` field to indicate the particular subclass. In this mode, we must ensure that there are columns defined to represent all properties across the subclasses. Although this might create "empty" column conditions on some rows, it is a much more efficient approach. Our data layer will know which columns are safe to ignore during our insert and update processing.

We handle object relationships with primary/foreign key pairs. In our `CAccount` and `CPerson` association example, we would have tables `Table_Account` and `Table_Person` defined. Following this object relationship, `Table_Account` would have a column (foreign key) known as `Person_Id` to reference the `Id` column (primary key) of `Table_Person`. In this mode, we reference the associated object from the object that makes the association. We sometimes refer to this as downward referencing.

In a collection-oriented relationship, such as our `CPortfolio` and `CIBonds` example, we make our relationships in an upward fashion. Because these are one-to-many ownership relationships, we must place foreign keys on the owned object to point back to its owner's primary key. In this example, we would define tables `Table_Portfolio` and `Table_Bond` for the class tables. On `Table_Bond`, we place a `Portfolio_Id` column to reference the portfolio that "owns" this bond. Again, we will design our data layer with these conventions in mind so it will know how to react accordingly.

Object Identifiers (OIDs)

In our framework, there is an integer-based `Id` field on every table. We define it to be the primary key on the table. Good database design practice says that a primary key should have no business meaning. The reason for this is to minimize the impact of a change in business processes on the database. If we define a column solely to serve as the OID and primary key, we insulate it from any change brought about by business process changes, meaning that our table relationships are forever preserved.

For example, suppose you had developed a system that used a 10-digit part number string as its primary key on a table. Now suppose that through mergers and acquisitions this part number changes to a 15-digit part number loosely based on the formats from the combined companies. To accommodate this change, you not only have to update your primary table with the new numbers, but also update every table that references the primary table with this key. This level of work also includes the expansion of the effected fields and the synchronization of the values in all tables, a task that can grow to be quite complex.

Another benefit of the approach of using a single Id field as the primary key is that of overall database size. On SQL Server, an integer field requires four bytes of storage space. In the preceding example, the 10-digit part number required 10 bytes of space, and the expanded version required 15 bytes. Let us assume from the preceding example that the primary table has 10,000 records. Let us also assume that an additional 50,000 records among 10 other tables reference this primary table. In the 10-digit scenario, the key values alone would consume 585KB of space in the database, whereas the 15-digit version would jump to 879KB. In the Id-based approach, the keys require only 234KB of space. These numbers might seem small given the relatively low cost of storage space, but it should be easy to extrapolate this 73% reduction in key storage space across a much larger data set.

OID Generation

With the need of OIDs in mind, we must be able to generate unique OID values in an efficient fashion. Some developers prefer to create a single table with a single row that does nothing other than track the last OID value used. In this mode, our OID values are unique across a database when they only need to be unique within a table. This has the effect of under-utilizing the key storage capacity of the long integer field by disbursing its values across all tables. To solve this problem, some developers have modified the previous approach by creating a last used row for each table. Although this does solve the under-utilization problem, it forces a database read followed by an update (to increment the key value) for each row inserted elsewhere in the database. This is in conjunction with the overhead associated with the data row access in the target table.

To further circumvent this issue, some developers have resorted to a multi-key approach in OID generation. Here, we generate a session-based identifier from a database table as in the previous example. The application is then responsible for iterating through a low value used in conjunction with the high value. Although this approach satisfies the read/update issue of OID generation, it leaves holes in the key sequence, again under-utilizing the capacity of the underlying integer data type.

A third approach to OID generation is to have an insert trigger on the table calculate the next Id value and perform an update with the appropriate value. For performance and uniqueness reasons, this technique relies on there being a unique clustered index on the Id column. Such an index has the property that the Id value is unique across all rows and that the RDBMS physically orders the rows according to their logical sort order based on the index. Database administrators normally apply these types of indexes to the primary key, with the intent of improving search times on the most commonly used index. Just prior to our row insert, we perform an SQL query to get the maximum current `Id` value, increment it by one, and use the result as our new OID. There are some issues with this approach. The most problematic is that, to ensure concurrency, a lock must be placed on the table from the time the SQL statement to generate the `Id` is executed until the update has completed. For high transaction situations, this can create significant deadlock issues that can force one or more client operations to fail at the expense of others.

In our model, we are relying on the underlying capabilities of the `Identity` column type, also known as an `AutoNumber` field in Access. The `Identity` type is a special column that is based on the integer type, but one in which SQL Server automatically increments with each row insertion. Until version 2.1 of ADO, there was no reliable way to retrieve this value from the server so it could be used to programmatically formulate the necessary relationships to other tables in the database. With the 2.1 release, we are able to retrieve these values as long as triggers do not insert additional rows into other tables with `Identity` columns. A complete discussion of this issue can be found on Microsoft's KnowledgeBase in an article titled "Identity and Auto-Increment Fields in ADO 2.1 and Beyond."

Note

It is important to note that for the sample code accompanying the text to work on the provided Access database, the Microsoft Jet OLE DB Provider 4.0 must be used in conjunction with the Microsoft Jet 4.0 version database. Both are installed by Microsoft Access 2000.

The primary issue with this approach is that currently it is guaranteed to work only with SQL Server and Jet 4.0 databases. The insert trigger issue might also present a problem if the development team cannot move the functionality implemented by these triggers to the Application tier.

Referential Integrity

Most, if not all, RDBMS systems have some mechanism for defining referential integrity (RI). When we speak of RI, we mean that the database server makes sure that we do not cause invalid primary/foreign key pair references in the database. For example, in the `Table_Portfolio` example, when we delete a row in table, we should also delete every referenced row in `Table_Bonds`. There are several ways to accomplish this. Most RDBMS servers have declarative RI, where we formally define the primary/foreign key pairs and the server takes care of RI natively. Although this is efficient, on many servers, the names of the columns must be unique across the entire database, meaning we cannot implement a standard naming convention across all the tables as discussed in the previous section.

An issue arises with this approach when we might want to nullify a foreign key column when its parent row is deleted, versus simply deleting the row with the foreign key. In the `CSerializedAutomobile` and `CSerializedEngine` example from Chapter 3, "Objects, Components, and COM," we might not want to delete the engine when we delete the automobile. By nullifying the foreign key, we simply indicate that no automobile owns the engine.

Another issue arises in that we might want to perform more than just RI during a delete process, such as inactivating an account if we delete all its transactions or providing complex validation logic. In these cases, we will be using database triggers to perform this work. A database trigger is a programming hook provided by the vendor that allows us to write code for the insert, update, and delete events of a given database row. Part of this logic could be to abort the transaction if something is not valid.

Tip
For maximum flexibility and maintainability and the issues with declarative RI, we should consolidate our RDBMS side logic into triggers.

Data Localization

When we begin discussing an enterprise scale application, geographies invariably enter the picture. During our analysis phases, we will find that we need to manage some data at a global corporate level while we need to manage other data at the local site level. Because of this, we need a mechanism to ensure that every site has suitable access to the global data. In SQL Server 6.5, joins can occur only across tables located on the server. Joins that cross servers cannot be accomplished. Therefore, we need a local copy of the global data if we need to join our local data to it.

To accomplish this, we have to set up a replication environment where we maintain global data in a master server and then copy it at periodic intervals to the local servers. We determine the frequency of replication and required server connection mode by the need for real-time data at the remote sites. If we need real-time access, replication cycles in one- or five-minute intervals over a WAN are required. If we need near–real-time response, we can get by with an hourly cycle over a WAN or dial-up connection. If we need only periodic synchronization, a daily cycle over a WAN or dial-up is sufficient.

What is important about global data is that we should try to maintain it at the master server level. Although it is possible to enable bidirectional replication, it is extremely painful to keep global data synchronized if we are generating global data at the local level. It is also difficult to ensure that there are not any OID collisions. Because we are generating OID values based on the `Id` field of a table in a site-based server we might have to go to a multi-key approach where we include a `Site_Id` column on every table.

Locking

With an RDBMS system, we are concerned with data locking. At one level, we want to ensure that two users are not trying to update the same row simultaneously. Fortunately, the RDBMS takes care of this for us in conjunction with our lock settings controlled through the data access library (ADO). In SQL Server 6.5 and later, locking occurs at the page level, which means not only the row being altered is locked, but also every row on the same data page as the locked row. This can cause some issues in high-volume situations. We will provide workarounds to this problem in Chapter 10, "Adding an ActiveX Control to the Framework."

When we instantiate an object, we retrieve the state information from the RDBMS. Only during this retrieval process is the row locked because we return our database connection to the pool when we are finished. After this happens, there are no safeguards to prevent another user from instantiating another editable copy of the object. Because of this, we must provide an object-locking mechanism. We will discuss such details in Chapter 10.

Performance Tuning

One of the significant issues faced in enterprise applications is the performance of the system as the number of records managed by the underlying RDBMS grows. One of the most difficult problems to tackle is the fact that as the composition of the data changes, what was once an optimal query path suddenly becomes suboptimal. A specific manifestation of this issue is related to the fact that the SQL Server query optimizer, just like the optimizers of many RDBMS products, relies on indexes and the statistics on those indexes to determine an optimal query plan. SQL Server does not specifically update these statistics automatically, so over time the optimizer can begin making inefficient query plans as the database becomes more populated. A few weeks or months after the launch date of the application, the performance of the RDBMS can noticeably degrade because of incorrect assumptions made by the query optimizer when the development team originally defined these views. It is a common misconception that the degradation is due to an increasing user load when it might simply be a sign that the RDBMS is ready for tuning.

For example, SQL Server's goal in query optimization is to generate an initial working table based on one or more of the WHERE clause conditions. From there, it joins this working result set to the table that should produce the next-smallest result of the remaining tables, creating yet a new result set in the process. This process of joining repeats for all remaining tables, with a scan through the final result to return the rows that satisfy the conditions of the WHERE clause. The optimizer relies on table indexes and their associated statistics to make these decisions. If these statistics do not properly reflect the underlying data or indexes on the data, the query optimizer can produce a very large initial result set or choose an inefficient index.

For example, assume that one of the conditions in the WHERE clause produces a working result set of 10,000 rows. If the optimizer incorrectly picks an inefficient index because of stale statistics, it might spend a significant amount of time retrieving these rows, although it thinks it is being efficient. Worse, the optimizer might have forgone an initial working result set that would have produced only five rows because of bad statistics.

Although this is a simple concept to grasp, what is difficult about it is how SQL Server can determine that one condition will produce the five-row result set while the other will produce the 10,000-row result set. SQL Server will not know how many rows a given condition will generate until it actually performs the query; by that time, it is too late. Instead, SQL Server tries to use index statistics as an approximation of result set size and row-selection efficiency. To do this, it first makes a list of which indexes it can use based on the columns in the indexes and the columns in the WHERE clause and join portions of the query. For each possible index, it looks at a statistic known as *average row hits* to estimate how many rows will need examining to find a specific row using this index. A unique clustered index on the primary key of the table will have this value set to 2, whereas other indexes on the table might be in the thousands. SQL Server will also express this value as a percentage of the total rows in the table that it must examine to select a row. It will also provide a subjective, textual rating.

For example, in the unique clustered index case, the percentage is 0.00% for very good selectivity, while another index might have a percentage of 5% and a rating of very poor selectivity. You can access this information for an index by clicking the Distribution button in the Manage Indexes dialog box in the SQL Enterprise Manager.

Note

Indexes with selectivity indexes greater than 5% should be considered for removal from the RDBMS because they add little value but have some maintenance overhead.

Using the efficiencies of all available indexes combined with the relative table sizes, SQL Server proceeds to pick the order in which it will filter and join to arrive at the result set. There is little you can do other than to provide SQL Server with good indexes, fresh statistics, and occasional optimizer hints when it comes to performance tuning. Because of this, database tuning can seem like an art more than a science. Following several essential steps can provide a method to the madness:

1. Verify that you have indexes on all columns that are participating as part of a table join operation. Normally, these should be the primary and foreign keys of each table, with one index for the primary key columns and another for the foreign key columns.

2. Verify that you have indexes on one or more columns that are participating in the WHERE clause. These are sometimes known as covering indexes.

3. Rebuild the indexes used by the queries in question to have them placed on sequential pages in the database. This will also update the statistics on the index.

4. Verify the results using an SQL query window within Enterprise Manager with the Show Query Plan option turned on. You might still need to override the SQL Server query plan optimizer using optimizer hints.

After you have gotten through the initial tuning phase of your RDBMS, you still must periodically repeat the last few steps to maintain optimal efficiencies. In the long run, you might need to re-tweak certain queries by adding or modifying indexes and repeating the steps. Many production SQL Server implementations use the Task Manager to schedule weekly or monthly re-indexing operations during off-peak load times. You can accomplish this by selecting the Execute as Task button when rebuilding an index from the Manage Indexes dialog box within the Executive Manager.

Summary

This chapter covered the basics of an RDBMS system. Specifically, we talked about simple database design techniques and methods for mapping objects to tables for the purpose of persistence. We have also talked about some of the issues related to generating an OID value and returning that value to the client application so we can maintain the proper table references in the database. We also touched on secondary issues such as data replication, locking, and performance tuning to address the scalability and accessibility issues associated with enterprise applications.

In the next chapter, we will begin discussing the issues involved with creating a distributed application. We will focus our efforts on how we can place objects on different machines and make them communicate through Distributed COM (DCOM) technologies. We will also explore some of the tradeoff decisions that must be made relative to moving data efficiently between machines.

Distribution Considerations

REGARDLESS OF THE TECHNOLOGY CHOSEN FOR communication between distributed objects—in our case DCOM—there are some basic considerations relative to how objects are instantiated and how information travels between the tiers of the system. Although the distribution mechanism itself handles most of the headaches, there are still some areas for trade-off decision-making. It is prudent for the system architect and development team to be aware of the options available to them and their associated issues before making what will be a long-term decision.

Data Marshalling

An important concept to understand is that object orientation is a development and programming convenience, as we said earlier, to manage complexity. Although there might be standard ways to diagram classes in terms of properties and methods, each object-oriented environment can internally implement object-orientation differently. Thus, there is not a standard way to pass an object over a network boundary. The foundation on which DCOM resides, the Remote Procedure Call (RPC) mechanism, itself is not object-oriented, but procedural. From our DCOM overview, we know that for objects to "move" around the network, the distribution engine must first convert them into a data stream that fits nicely into the packet structure of the network transport protocol.

A process known as *data marshalling* executes this conversion process. The counter-activity, known as *de-marshaling*, converts the marshaled data back into an object on the receiving end. The COM engine has an auto marshaller that is good at providing this functionality in the background, so in most cases, you do not have to worry about the details of handling this yourself. For complex objects, you can override the auto marshaller by implementing a specific `IMarshal` interface on your COM class. Alternatively, you can programmatically move the state data of your object into an intermediate format that is much easier for the auto marshaller to deal with, a concept known as pre-marshalling. We will discuss several pre-marshalling techniques later, because we will exploit this method for our architecture.

Remote Activation

One of the most important design considerations relative to a distributed architecture is how objects are instantiated and how data is transferred between the two sides of a DCOM boundary that spans a network connection.

In the DCOM world, remote objects are instantiated on the server side of the boundary with an object reference pointer sent back to the client. In this mode, DCOM creates a proxy process on the client that looks and feels just like a COM object to the client process. DCOM then creates a stub process on the server that communicates with the client-side proxy and the server-side COM object requested by the client. Because the remote object physically resides on the server, DCOM sends all method calls and property accesses through this proxy/stub pair over the network, using RPC as discussed earlier.

The calling convention for this mode might look something like in Listing 5.1.

Listing 5.1 **Instantiating a Remote DCOM Object to Pull Properties**

```
Sub LoadPerson(Id as Long)
 Dim Person As CPerson
 100 Set Person = CreateObject("OfficeLibServer.CPerson","MTS-HOU05")
 105 Call Person.Load(Id)
 110 txtLastName.Text = Person.LastName
 115 txtFirstName.Text = Person.FirstName
 ...
 195 txtDomainName.Text = Person.DomainName
End Sub
```

On line 100, the object is created on the remote server `"MTS-HOU05"` and the resulting object reference is sent back to the client and set to the `Person` object reference. At this point, DCOM has created the proxy and stub. On line 105, we call the `Load` method of the `Person` object to populate the state from the data store. DCOM must marshal the `Id` parameter during this call. By line 110, our `Person` object is instantiated and its state has been set from the data store. We begin moving the data from the object into our UI elements for presentation to the user. Each of the property accesses result in a trip through the proxy/stub layer to the server, because that is where the object is physically living. DCOM must also call the marshaller into action for each of these property accesses.

An equivalent subroutine to save the object back to the data store might be as shown in Listing 5.2.

Listing 5.2 **Instantiating a Remote DCOM Object to Push Properties**

```
Sub SavePerson(Id as Long)
 Dim Person As CPerson
 100 Set Person = CreateObject("OfficeLibServer.CPerson","MTS-HOU05")
 105 Person.Id = Id
 110 Person.LastName = txtLastName.Text
 115 Person.FirstName = txtFirstName.Text
 ...
 195 Person.DomainName = txtDomainName.Text
 200 Person.Save
End Sub
```

Again, each property access requires the same proxy/stub layer traversal and passes through the marshaller.

Although this simple example might seem trivial, we only need to imagine an application with five to ten objects per UI form and a user base of several hundred to see the implications of this approach. There will be many server round trips through the proxy/stub layer to perform relatively simple tasks. One common way to solve some of the round-tripping overhead is to bundle all the individual property accesses into batch methods.

The same LoadPerson subroutine when re-written with a batch call might look something like Listing 5.3.

Listing 5.3 **An Optimized DCOM Call That Pulls Properties as a UDT**

```
Sub LoadPerson(Id as Long)
 Dim Person As CPerson
 Dim PersonData As PersonDataType
 100 Set Person = CreateObject("OfficeLibServer.CPerson","MTS-HOU05")
 105 Call Person.Load(Id)
 110 Call Person.SetStateToUDT(PersonData)
 115 txtLastName.Text = PersonData.LastName
 120 txtFirstName.Text = PersonData.FirstName
 ...
 195 txtDomainName.Text = PersonData.DomainName
End Sub
```

In this incarnation, the subroutine puts the state data of the entire `Person` object into a User Defined Type (UDT) and sets the object state in a single call, a method we will discuss later in this chapter. Because of the single method call, only one pass through the proxy/stub layer is required, as well as a single pass through the marshaller. This results in a more efficient use of network bandwidth and better response time over slower networks.

A similarly developed `SavePerson` subroutine might look like Listing 5.4.

Listing 5.4   **An Optimized DCOM Call That Pushes Properties as a UDT**

```
Sub SavePerson(Id as Long)
 Dim Person As CPerson
 Dim PersonData As PersonDataType
 100 Set Person = CreateObject("OfficeLibServer.CPerson","MTS-HOU05")
 105 PersonData.Id = Id
 110 PersonData.LastName = txtLastName.Text
 115 PersonData.FirstName = txtFirstName.Text
 ...
 195 PersonData.DomainName = txtDomainName.Text
 200 Call Person.SetStateFromUDT(PersonData)
 210 Person.Save(Id)
End Sub
```

Again, by using a UDT in a single call, we are making judicious use of network and system resources.

Structured Data-Passing Techniques

As might have become apparent by now, one of the primary issues to solve when implementing distributed objects is how to optimally communicate object state information between the tiers. We have already discussed using a UDT as a mechanism to pass a structured data packet that represents the state of all properties. By doing this, we can accommodate the setting or getting of all properties with a single call across the DCOM boundary. The next sections expand on this technique with several alternatives that are commonly used to solve this problem.

Disconnected Recordsets

The disconnected recordset approach to pass structured data is the one recommended by Microsoft and many books on the subject matter. The reason for this recommendation is that it offers a flexible and programmer-friendly mechanism to transfer information. In this mode, the server creates a recordset on the server and sends it to the client. The client can then move the information from the recordset into an object, or can work with the recordset directly. This recordset, if sourced by the server, might be the direct result of a database query, or it might be the result of programmatic activity on the server to explicitly build it.

The `LoadPerson` subroutine written with a recordset passing convention would look like Listing 5.5.

Listing 5.5   **An Optimized DCOM Call That Pulls Properties as an ADO Recordset**

```
Sub LoadPerson(Id as Long)
 Dim Person As CPerson
 Dim rsPersonData As ADOR.RecordSet
 100 Set Person = CreateObject("OfficeLibServer.CPerson","MTS-HOU05")
 105 Call Person.Load(Id)
 110 Call Person.SetStateToRS(rsPersonData)
 115 txtLastName.Text = rsPersonData.Fields.Item("LastName").Value
 120 txtFirstName.Text = rsPersonData.Fields.Item("FirstName").Value
 ...
 195 txtDomainName.Text = rsPersonData.Fields.Item("DomainName").Value
End Sub
```

The implementation of the `SetStateToRS` method on `CPerson` might look something like Listing 5.6.

Listing 5.6   **An Optimized DCOM Call That Pushes Properties as an ADO Recordset**

```
Public Sub SetStateToRS(ByRef rsRet as ADOR.RecordSet)
 100 If Not rsState Is Nothing Then
   ' NOTE: rsState is a private member of this class
 110 rsState.MoveFirst
 115 Set rsRet = rsState
 140 Else
 145 Set rsRet = Nothing
 150 End If
End Sub
```

In the case of collections of objects, we can return the information for the multiple objects with the single call. The need for this might arise quite frequently when we talk about the detail side of a master/detail relationship. In this case, the return parameter would still be the recordset, but it would have a row for each object instance. The client-side object is responsible for iterating through each row.

Although the recordset approach is programmatically simple on both sides of the DCOM boundary, there are several issues with its use. The first issue is with the overhead in the form of metadata that must accompany the actual data during the transfer. For example, in addition to the actual result set, each recordset has a Fields collection to describe the column layout of the information. Each `Field` object in this collection has information about the column name, its data type, and two collections of attributes and properties. Additionally, if a database query creates the recordset, there is extra information associated with the SQL grammar and database connection used to generate the result set. Marshalling must occur on all this extra overhead data in conjunction with the actual data before sending it across the DCOM boundary. Because of this overhead, the use of a recordset to send information across processes is expensive. Additionally, it appears that the recordset custom marshaller is pre-marshalling the information before marshalling. With these overhead issues, it appears that ADO recordsets recover this extra cost somewhere above 10,000 records.

Note

For result sets above 10,000 records, ADO recordsets are the most efficient method for sending information across a DCOM boundary. In such cases, you should consider redesigning an application that needs to send so many records across a DCOM boundary.

Another potential issue is that the client side not only must have the ADO library installed (or its lighter-weight ADOR sibling), but its version must be compatible with the version running on the server. Because this is a technology just entering widespread use, expect Microsoft to make revisions over time and include such revisions in their full range of products. Confounding this issue is that the names Microsoft uses for the primary DLLs to support ADO and ADOR are the same, regardless of the version. For example, the ADO library is found in a DLL called MSADO15.DLL whether it is version 1.5, 2.0, or 2.1; the same is true for MSADOR15.DLL. Although the libraries are backward compatible with each other, you might have ADO or ADOR upgraded on your client machine as part of some other installation process without it becoming evident to you. If you start using some of the newer properties, you might experience difficulty when deploying to an MTS machine with older libraries installed. Worse, it can take you several days to determine the source of the problem because the filenames for the libraries are the same across versions.

As of the writing of this book, Microsoft has gone through three revisions (1.5, 2.0, and 2.1) of ADO, whereas 2.5 is currently in beta. In addition, because ADO might actually interface with ODBC to get to the database server, it too will need installing and administering on the client side.

Tip

Do not use ADO on the client unless you are prepared to maintain it and potentially distribute and maintain ODBC across the user base.

Property Bags

Microsoft developed the PropertyBag object to support the saving of design time settings for ActiveX controls created in Visual Basic. Although we can extrapolate their use to support structured information communication, they are still just a collection of name/value pairs. In one sense, however, we can think of a PropertyBag as a portable collection with one important caveat. The PropertyBag has a Contents property that converts the name/value pairs into an intermediate byte array that then converts directly to a string representation. On the receiving end of the DCOM boundary, another PropertyBag object can use this string to re-create the byte array and subsequently set its Contents property, effectively re-creating the information.

The `LoadPerson` subroutine written with a PropertyBag passing convention would look like Listing 5.7.

Listing 5.7   **An Optimized DCOM Call That Pulls Properties as a PropertyBag**

```
Sub LoadPerson(Id as Long)
 Dim Person As CPerson
 Dim pbPersonData As New PropertyBag
 Dim sData As String
 Dim baData() As Byte
 100 Set Person = CreateObject("OfficeLibServer.CPerson","MTS-HOU05")
 105 Call Person.Load(Id)
 110 Call Person.SetStateToPBString(sData)
 115 baData = sData
 120 pbPersonData.Contents = baData
 125 txtLastName.Text = pbPersonData.ReadProperty("LastName")
 130 txtFirstName.Text = pbPersonData.ReadProperty("FirstName")
 ...
 195 txtDomainName.Text = pbPersonData.ReadProperty("DomainName")
End Sub
```

Although the marshalling aspect of the string generated by the Contents property is of minimal concern, creating a PropertyBag is more expensive than other options in terms of speed and information bloat. If we assume that an ADO recordset is the original source of most information, we will have to traverse the entire recordset programmatically in VB to move the data into the PropertyBag.

The implementation of the `SetStateToPBString` method on `CPerson` might look something like Listing 5.8.

Listing 5.8   **An Optimized DCOM Call That Pushes Properties as a PropertyBag**

```
Public Sub SetStateToPBString(ByRef sRet as String)
 Dim pb As New PropertyBag
 Dim rsField As ADOR.Field
 Dim ba() As Byte
 100 If Not rsState Is Nothing Then
  ' NOTE: rsState is a private global member of this class
 110 rsState.MoveFirst
 115 For Each rsField In rsState.Fields
 120  pb.WriteProperty rsField.Name, rsField.Value
 125 Next
 130 ba = pb.Contents
 135 sRet = ba
 140 Else
 145 sRet = ""
 150 End If
End Sub
```

In the preceding example, a significant amount of programmatic overhead is associated with building the return string. First, we must create the PropertyBag object. Second, we must traverse the recordset's Fields collection (line 115). For each iteration, we add the current field/value pair to the bag (line 120). After we complete the traversal, we create the byte array (line 130) and create the final return string (line 135).

This process is complicated further if there are multiple records requiring a collection or array of Contents strings. In this case, the return parameter would be an array of strings representing individual property bags, each re-creating the field name metadata that corresponds to a particular value.

User-Defined Types

User-Defined Types (UDTs) are simple in concept in that they follow the structural definition common to many procedural languages. In Visual Basic, we define a UDT using a `Type...End Type` block in the declaration section of a code module.

A sample UDT definition corresponding to the `CPerson` class might look something like Listing 5.9.

Listing 5.9   **The PersonDataType UDT**

```
Public Type PersonDataType
 Id As Long
 LastName As String
 FirstName As String
 MiddleIntital As String
 EmployeeNumber As String
 OfficePhone As String
 OfficeFax As String
```

```
    Pager As String
    RoomNumber As String
    DepartmentId As Long
    UserName As String
    DomainName As String
End Type
```

To reiterate here, the `LoadPerson` subroutine with a UDT passing convention would look like Listing 5.10.

Listing 5.10 **An Optimized DCOM Call That Pulls Properties as a UDT**

```
Sub LoadPerson(Id as Long)
 Dim Person As CPerson
 Dim PersonData As PersonDataType
100 Set Person = CreateObject("OfficeLibServer.CPerson","MTS-HOU05")
105 Call Person.Load(Id)
110 Call Person.SetStateToUDT(PersonData)
115 txtLastName.Text = PersonData.LastName
120 txtFirstName.Text = PersonData.FirstName
 ...
195 txtDomainName.Text = PersonData.DomainName
End Sub
```

The implementation of the `SetStateToUDT` method on `CPerson` might look something like Listing 5.11.

Listing 5.11 **Moving Data from an ADO Recordset to a UDT**

```
Public Sub SetStateToUDT(ByRef udtRet as PersonDataType)
100 If Not rsState Is Nothing Then
 ' NOTE: rsState is a private global member of this class
105 rsState.MoveFirst
110 If Not rsState Is Nothing
115 With udtRet
120   .Id = rsState.Fields.Item("Id").Value
125   .LastName = rsState.Fields.Item("LastName").Value
130   .FirstName = rsState.Fields.Item("FirstName").Value
135   .MiddleInitial = rsState.Fields.Item("MiddleInitial").Value
140   ' code to copy the remainder of the field values into the UDT
195   .DomainName = rsState.Fields.Item("DomainName").Value
200 End With
210 Else
 ' code to set every member of the UDT to an
 ' appropriate zeroed state
215 End If
End Sub
```

The UDT approach is simple and easily managed because the type definition is visible to both the client and server sides of the boundary when it is declared Public within a public class module on the server. As in the case of the other options discussed so far, we might need to handle multiple records as an array of the UDT type. This is still an efficient approach because only data travels across the boundary. No metadata describing the data is necessary because it is inherent in the type definition.

With all the benefits of UDTs, it might be difficult to understand why any other approach might be necessary. At issue is the only major drawback to a UDT—it cannot be supported by VBScript. At first glance, this might seem insignificant until we remember that the basis for Active Server Pages is VBScript. With more application functionality moving to the IIS server, this becomes a crippling limitation.

Variant Arrays

Variant arrays are the most flexible and the simplest form of data transfer across a DCOM boundary. Although it does require the development of some indexing structures to handle them effectively, such development is relatively minor when viewed against the long-term benefits.

The `LoadPerson` subroutine written with a variant passing convention would look like Listing 5.12.

Listing 5.12   **An Optimized DCOM Call That Pulls Properties as a Variant Array**

```
Sub LoadPerson(Id as Long)
 Dim Person As CPerson
 Dim vData As Variant
 Dim vFields As Variant
 Dim diFields as Scripting.Dictionary
 Dim i as Integer
100 Set Person = CreateObject("OfficeLibServer.CPerson","MTS-HOU05")
105 Call Person.Load(Id)
110 Call Person.SetStateToVariant(vFields,vData)
115 If IsArray(vData) Then
120 Set diFields = CreateObject("Scripting.Dictionary")
125 For i = LBound(vFields) To UBound(vFields)
130   diFields.Add vFields(i), CStr(i)
135 Next I
140 txtLastName.Text = vData(diFields.Item("LastName"),0)
145 txtFirstName.Text = vData(diFields.Item("FirstName"),0)
...
195 txtDomainName.Text = vData(diFields.Item("DomainName"),0)
200 End Ff
End Sub
```

In the preceding example, we are receiving two return parameters from the `SetStateToVariant` method: `vFields` and `vData`. The former is a variant array of string values representing the field names. The ordinal position of the values in this array corresponds to the same ordinal positions in the `vData` array, which is the actual data being returned. So that we can more easily manage the data array, we create a Dictionary object keyed on the field name so that we can index into it. ASP again drives an implementation decision to use the Dictionary object instead of a standard VBA Collection object, which VBScript does not support. Regardless of whether we are returning data for single or multiple rows, `vData` will always be a two-dimensional array, hence the second index dimension on lines 140–195. This directly relates to the use of the `GetRows` functionality on the ADO recordset to generate the variant array.

The implementation of the `SetStateToVariant` method on `CPerson` might look something like Listing 5.13.

Listing 5.13 **An Optimized DCOM Call That Pushes Properties as a Variant Array**

```
Public Sub SetStateToVariant(ByRef vFields As Variant, ByRef vData As Variant)
 Dim rsField As ADOR.Field
 Dim i as Integer
 100 If Not rsState Is Nothing Then
  ' NOTE: rsState is a private global member of this class
 105 rsState.MoveFirst
 110 If Not rsState Is Nothing
 115 vData = rsState.GetRows
 115 ReDim vFields(0 to rsState.Fields.Count - 1)
 120 i = 0
 115 For Each rsField In rsState.Fields
 120  vFields(i) = rsField.Name
 125  i = i + 1
 125 Next
 210 Else
 215 vData = vbEmpty
 220 vFields = vbEmpty
 215 End If
End Sub
```

The variant array approach is simple and fast. It also represents the utmost in flexibility because neither the server nor the client requires UDT definitions. As in the case of the other options discussed so far, we might need to handle multiple records. The variant array approach handles this naturally because it is a two-dimensional array with the first dimension representing the field and the second indicating the row. The metadata needed to describe the data is simply an ordered list of string values that apply to the entire data set.

If we consider that most data originates as a database query, Microsoft must realize something here because they provide a highly optimized method in the form of the `GetRows` method. Although the method must be performing a memory copy, the internal structure of the recordset must be similar to that of the variant array that it generates. We can make this inference from the fact that even for large recordsets, the `GetRows` method returns quickly. The auto marshaller then processes this resulting array quickly for passage across the DCOM boundary. This approach is not only of minimal cost in performance and of overhead, but it also represents the best solution in flexibility in supporting both the typed VB language and the variant-based VBScript within ASP.

XML

Although we will cover XML (eXtensible Markup Language) in detail in Chapter 13, "Interoperability," it is important to note that although it is usable as a cross-process communication mechanism, it is the one with the highest cost. Because of this, we relegate it to boundaries that cross platforms or applications rather than simple cross-process communication within a platform. In these cases, the boundary might cross over the Internet, something that DCOM does not handle cleanly.

XML is simply a textual stream of data, similar in style to the HTML pages that your browser pulls down from the Internet and renders on-the-fly to present to you. What differentiates XML from HTML is that XML represents data, whereas HTML represents content and format. Because XML is capable of representing complex object hierarchies within the confines of a textual stream, it is easy to see how we can employ it as a communication vehicle.

A simple XML stream corresponding to the `CPerson` class might look something like Listing 5.14.

Listing 5.14   **A Simple XML Stream**

```
<?xml version="1.0"?>
<!DOCTYPE Person [
<!ELEMENT Person EMPTY>
<!ATTLIST Person
   Id PCDATA #REQUIRED
   LastName PCDATA #REQUIRED
   FirstName PCDATA #REQUIRED
   MiddleInitial PCDATA #REQUIRED
   EmployeeNumber PCDATA #REQUIRED
   OfficePhone PCDATA #REQUIRED
   OfficeFax PCDATA #REQUIRED
   Pager PCDATA #REQUIRED
   RoomNumber PCDATA #REQUIRED
   DepartmentId PCDATA #REQUIRED
   UserName PCDATA #REQUIRED
   DomainName PCDATA #REQUIRED
```

```
>
]>
<Person Id="1234"
  LastName="Smith"
  FirstName="Joe"
  MiddleInitial="M"
  EmployeeNumber="5678"
  OfficePhone="(212) 555-5555"
  OfficeFax="(212) 555-5556"
  Pager="(212) 555-5557"
  RoomNumber="13256"
  DepartmentId="52"
  UserName="JMSmith"
  DomainName="XYZCORP"
/>
```

The LoadPerson subroutine rewritten using an XML strategy and the Microsoft XML parser would look like Listing 5.15.

Listing 5.15   **An Optimized DCOM Call That Pulls Properties as XML**

```
Sub LoadPerson(Id as Long)
 Dim Person As CPerson
 Dim sXMLData As String
 Dim i as Integer, j as Integer
 Dim XMLDoc As New MSXML.DOMDocument
 Dim XMLNode As MSXML.IXMLDOMNode
 Dim XMLAttribute As MSXML.IXMLDOMAttribute
100 Set Person = CreateObject("OfficeLibServer.CPerson","MTS-HOU05")
105 Call Person.Load(Id)
110 Call Person.SetStateToXML(sXMLData)
115 Call XMLDoc.loadXML(sXMLData)
120 If XMLDoc.parseError.errorCode = 0 Then
125 For i = 0 to XMLNode.childNodes.length-1
130  Set XMLNode = XMLNode.childNodes.item(i)
135  If XMLNode.nodeType = MSXML.NODE_ELEMENT Then
140  For j = 0 to XMLNode.attributes.length-1
145   With XMLNode.attributes.item(j)
150    Select Case .baseName
     Case "Id"
155     lPersonId = .value
     Case "LastName"
160     txtLastName.Text = .value
     Case "FirstName"
165     txtFirstName.Text = .value
...
     Case "DomainName"
195     txtDomainName.Text = .value
200    End Select
205  Next j
```

continues

Listing 5.15   **Continued**

```
210  End If
215 Next i
220 End If
End Sub
```

Although it is easy to generate an XML text stream to represent structured information, there is a relatively high cost in doing so. As can be seen by the preceding code
example, there is also a high cost on the receiving end to parse the XML stream and
to use the resulting data to set the state of an object. Additionally, as can be seen from
the sample XML definition, there is a high ratio of metadata to data in this format,
especially when we are only communicating the state for a single object.

The implementation of the `SetStateToXML` method on `CPerson` might look something
like Listing 5.16.

Listing 5.16   **An Optimized DCOM Call That Pushes Properties as XML**

```
Public Sub SetStateToXML(ByRef sXML As String)
 Dim rsField As ADOR.Field
 Dim XMLStream As New Stream ' MDAC 2.5 only
100 If Not rsState Is Nothing Then
  ' NOTE: rsState is a private global member of this class
105 rsState.MoveFirst
110 If Not rsState Is Nothing
   rsState.Save XMLStream, adPersistXML
   sXML = XMLStream.ReadText
210 Else
215 sXML = ""
215 End If
End Sub
```

The `LoadPerson` subroutine written using an XML strategy and the ADO recordset's
capability to load an XML stream would look like Listing 5.17.

Listing 5.17   **Tight Integration Between ADO Recordset and ADO**

```
Sub LoadPerson(Id as Long)
 Dim Person As CPerson
 Dim sXML As String
 Dim rsPersonData As New ADOR.RecordSet
 Dim XMLStream As New Stream ' MDAC 2.5 only
100 Set Person = CreateObject("OfficeLibServer.CPerson","MTS-HOU05")
105 Call Person.Load(Id)
110 Call Person.SetStateToXML(sXMLData)
115 Stream.WriteText sXML
120 rsPersonData.Open Stream, "Provider=MSPersist;", , , adCmdFile
```

```
125 If Not (rsPersonData.BOF or rsPersonData.EOF) Then
130 RsPersonData.MoveFirst
135 txtLastName.Text = rsPersonData.Fields.Item("LastName").Value
140 txtFirstName.Text = rsPersonData.Fields.Item("FirstName").Value
...
195 txtDomainName.Text = rsPersonData.Fields.Item("DomainName").Value
200 End If
End Sub
```

From this example, it is clear that the ADO recordset approach to XML streaming is more programmatically friendly, and we can assume that it is less costly from a performance perspective than the MSXML approach. Although the ADO recordset can support XML, the memory stream-based version is available only with ADO 2.5, which is in beta at the time of this writing. With the ADO 2.1 release, the only manner in which XML streaming can be accomplished is by saving the recordset to a file in XML format and then re-reading the file back into a string variable.

If the file-based approach is used, then both the client and server sides of the DCOM boundary must deal with temporary file management issues in addition to the extra overhead of file access. If the Stream object is used instead, then everything happens in memory, which is both more efficient and faster. Nonetheless, the same issues associated with using an ADO recordset on the client concern us here as well. As programming-unfriendly as it can be, it is much easier to install and administer the MSXML parser on the client than is ADO.

Comparative Costs—A Technical Overview

Because it is difficult to find objective data covering the various forms of cross-process communication, we will try to provide a comparative testing methodology and summary here that you can replicate in your environment. To test the various methods, we have devised a method that considers various factors of the distributed communication process. In this test, we assume that all data originates from an ADO query and therefore is held constant across all communication modes.

Thus, we are concerned with the remainder of the micro-level timing parameters that make up the total time. These micro-level elements include the following:

- The time to package the data, if any, into a form suitable for transfer (pre-marshalling).
- The time to marshal/transfer/de-marshal the data.
- The time to move the data into client-side elements.

Methodology

The best test environment is that of your own corporate infrastructure, including clients, servers, and the underlying network connecting them. One critical factor is to perform the testing first under light network loads. It is common sense that a corporate network is most heavily loaded in the morning, after lunch, and just before closing time because people sift through their emails at these times of day. After you have developed your test bed during the evening hours and weekends, you can validate your findings during the peak times to make sure the relative timings are still valid.

It is also important to understand what your performance requirements really are. To a user on a 56Kbps dial-up modem connection, minor timing differences might be negligible. On the other end of the spectrum, a 100Mbps network will expose underlying performance issues in your architecture. It is also important to understand your user base. If you can guarantee the proper installation and administration of ADO on the client, then ADO recordset–based approaches might be sufficient. If, on the other hand, a thin-client, IIS/ASP approach is used, a lightning-fast, variant-array approach is probably more suitable.

To test in your environment, create a collection of *n* simple objects of the same class within the context of an MTS component. Each object should consist of various randomly generated data types, such as strings, integers, floating points, and dates. Create a disconnected recordset from the collection, followed by a variant array created from the recordset (using the `GetRows` function). From a client-side component, repeatedly request the data set to be sent to the client under several scenarios. The exact same data set should be sent with each test run. Average the total time for each scenario and divide by the number of requests to determine the average time.

The scenarios are as follows:

1. As a collection of native objects.
2. As the native ADO recordset.
3. As the variant array created from the ADO recordset (one `GetRows` call per test run).
4. As a variant array created from the ADO recordset with each request (*n* `GetRows` calls per test run).

Under many environments up to about 10,000 records, you might find that scenarios 1 and 3 are the fastest and on par with each other. Scenario 4 is the next fastest, but about 100 times slower than 1 and 3. Scenario 3 is the worst performer, about 500 times slower than 1 and 3.

Microsoft Transaction Server

We have spent a significant amount of time in the last several chapters talking about DCOM, remote activation, and distribution considerations. Underlying all this is the use of MTS in the server side of these discussions. Although MTS is not a requirement for implementing DCOM, it makes things significantly easier. Several of the reasons that we use MTS are for its DCOM hosting capability coupled with its sophisticated object and database connection pooling. It also makes the DCOM administrative process much easier.

Using MTS

One of the most important things to remember is that the development team must be using Windows NT Workstation or Server as its development platform. The reason for this is that MTS runs only on these platforms, so for many debugging purposes, this will simplify things. We will call this the local MTS when we refer to debugging activities. If we are using an MTS instance on another machine—whether we are talking about debug or production modes—we refer to it as the remote MTS.

Tip

When in development, it is important to have the remote MTS as physically nearby as possible. You will need to go to it often, so don't put it on the 12th floor if you are in the basement, unless you want to ensure that you are getting sufficient exercise during coding sessions.

Note

Walking to the snack machine does not constitute an acceptable form of exercise.

How you structure the directories and component packages within MTS is important. If you do not already have a standard structure within your organization, consider employing the ones presented here.

MTS Packages

In MTS, DCOM components run within the context of a package. A package is a unit of management for MTS relative to security, lifetime, and so on. Each package can contain one or more components, whether they belong to one or multiple applications. Although it is possible to place all your DCOM components into a single package on MTS, it is easier to manage the development and maintenance aspects of the application base if you group components under some logical mechanism. This package is the unit of distribution for the components of your distributed application. Fixing a class in one of the components in the package means a redistribution of the entire package.

You may create a package that groups the components driving one of the subparts of the application. You might alternatively decide to group based on a similar set of functionality that the components provide. The reason that such grouping is important is that after a developer begins working on a single component within a package, other components within the package are not available to other developers.

Tip

It is prudent to align your development team and MTS package layout, or vice-versa, as much as possible. After the application begins coming together, you might have one developer waiting on another to complete his or her work if their components are co-mingled in the same package.

Summary

This chapter has addressed the issues associated with communication between distributed objects. Several widely used techniques can be used to pass object state information between tiers: user-defined types, ADO disconnected recordsets, PropertyBags, variant arrays, and XML. Each technique has its own advantages and disadvantages, although our framework will follow the variant array approach in future chapters.

The next chapter covers the development fundamentals and design goals for enterprise applications. It lays the final groundwork for our work in Part II, "Implementation of an Enterprise Framework."

6

Development Fundamentals and Design Goals of an Enterprise Application

ALTHOUGH A RICH SET OF DEVELOPMENT TOOLS and technologies are at our disposal, they sit before us with minimal structure. We are free to do with them what we please. Although this level of flexibility is important, we must decide on a standard approach to implementation when we begin using these tools. The importance of standardization spans both small and large development teams. Standardization creates consistent implementation techniques, nomenclatures, and methodologies that become the underlying fabric and texture of your application. Standardization also forces a best-practice implementation that, in turn, promotes the fundamental stability of the application. If one development team member reviews a piece of work by another team member, it should make some reasonable level of sense or it should provide the information for another developer to understand it relatively quickly. Similarly, when you look at the code six to twelve months from now in a maintenance mode, you should be able to re-acclimate yourself to it quickly.

In this chapter, I will outline some of the fundamental design and implementation decisions that we must make, regardless of which part of the application is under construction. In the process of outlining this, I will provide some sample techniques or argue for one approach over another. This chapter covers Visual Basic 6.0, Microsoft Transaction Server (MTS) 2.0, Internet Information Server (IIS) 4.0, and Structured Query Language (SQL) Server.

Visual Basic

We will begin by taking a look at some of the capabilities of the Visual Basic programming language. A thorough understanding of these concepts will allow you to utilize the language to its full extent.

Option Explicit

Visual Basic has the capability to force or ignore compile-time type checking. We can only assume that Microsoft chose to allow this for flexibility purposes, although it has such significant consequences that perhaps Microsoft should consider eliminating this option in future releases, or at least making it the default option. It is important to note before proceeding that this topic differs slightly from the discussions on runtime versus compile-time type checking in Chapter 3, "Objects, Components, and COM." In the current chapter, the reference to type checking is relative to variable declarations versus the object binding methods discussed before. Unless it is told otherwise, Visual Basic will implicitly dimension variables upon first use. If Visual Basic does this, it has no other option but to dimension the variables as variant data types. As previously discussed, the use of these data types reduces application performance because Visual Basic must perform extra steps when assigning values to, and accessing the values from, variables of the variant type.

It just so happens that this implicit declaration of variables is the default mode for Visual Basic. To switch this behavior, an `Option Explicit` statement is required at the beginning of the declaration section of every module. In this mode, Visual Basic will generate a compile-time error if it encounters a variable in the source code that has not been declared in the current scope.

There are other important reasons to use the `Option Explicit` mode and not allow Visual Basic to implicitly declare each variable as variant. When assigning a value to a variant type variable, Visual Basic must make some assumptions as to the intrinsic underlying type of the variable. If the value being assigned is the result of a function of a known type, Visual Basic's job is relatively easy. For example, the statement `ThisDate = Now()` tells Visual Basic that the underlying type of `ThisDate`, which is implicitly a variant if it has not been declared in the current scope, is a date because that is the type returned by the `Now` function. It is important to understand that a variant data type has both data and a data-type descriptor. Within the first few bytes of the storage allocated for the variant variable is information defining this type information. The `VbVarType` enumeration defined under Visual Basic for Applications (VBA) provides the list of these types. If the `VarType` function were performed on `ThisDate`, it would return `vbDate`.

If Visual Basic cannot determine the underlying data type, it must make some assumptions that might not correlate with the assumptions you would make. For example, consider the following function:

```
Public Function Add(PartOne, PartTwo) As Variant
 Add = PartOne + PartTwo
End Function
```

The preceding example compiles without issue because it is syntactically correct. Visual Basic considers the command-line parameters as variant types because they have not been explicitly declared as any explicit type. When Visual Basic performs the addition in the first line, it has to determine at runtime whether the underlying storage values are of some type of numeric or string format. Depending on whether two numbers, two strings, or a string and a number are passed in, the return value will be either a number or a string.

If, when we call the Add function elsewhere in the code, and a specific result type is expected, problems will arise at runtime if Visual Basic expects something else. For example, consider the following:

```
Public Sub DoSomething(A, B)
 C = Add(A, B)
 D = C * 5
End Sub
```

Again, the preceding example will compile without issue. If the data types of parameters of A and B are always numeric, we have no issue. The assignment of D will fail, however, if either parameter, A or B, is of a string type. This problem arises when the user of the DoSomething routine is unaware of what is happening within in it. Although this is a trivial example given for exposition, the manifestations of these issues can become complex in real-world situations.

In essence, by following an implicit data type approach, you are allowing both Visual Basic and your development team to make possibly incompatible assumptions throughout your code base. Although you will catch many of these issues during the development and debug stages, your team will spend non–value-added time tracking them down and fixing them. Worse still, your team might not catch all these issues and they can escape into production, where the cost to fix them can affect you in terms of additional time (which is measurable) and lowered customer satisfaction (which is immeasurable). Remember that being penny-wise might result in being dollar-foolish here. Although many would argue that not setting Option Explicit is acceptable development practice for small-scale applications, it is inappropriate when building robust enterprise applications. The following is an example of its implementation:

```
Option Explicit
Private mName As String
Private mAddress As String
```

Enumerations

Component Object Model (COM) defines enumerations as their own first-class entity, making them shareable across all the classes defined within the COM component and visible to users of the component. Visual Basic does not have a mechanism to natively support the definition of enumerations. To do so would mean that a new type of code module would have to be developed to support them. If enumerations are placed in a standard code module (*bas* module), they become visible to the classes defined in the component but invisible to anything externally. To solve this, the developer must place the enumeration definitions within any public class module defined in the component. This technique has the effect of making the enumeration visible both internally and externally to the component. Although the choice of which class module within the component is used to define the enumeration does not matter, a good practice is to place it in one of the classes that will be using it. In essence, one of the class modules is acting as a gracious host for the enumeration definition, so it makes sense that the class that needs it should be the one that defines it. Although this makes no sense, Microsoft has taken this approach to enable COM development within Visual Basic. If you look at the bigger picture, this quirky enumeration implementation is a relatively minor issue.

Enumerations can be used in place of global constants that are used by more than one component. In the `CBond` example in Chapter 4, "The Relational Database Management System," we defined a `BondType` field with possible values of `CouponBond`, `DiscountBond`, and `ConsolBond`. A code sample for these definitions using constants would be as follows:

```
' in global.bas of Bonds.DLL
' Public Const COUPON_BOND As Integer = 1
' Public Const DISCOUNT_BOND As Integer = 2
' Public Const CONSOL_BOND As Integer = 3

' in global.bas of PortfolioManager.EXE
' Public Const COUPON_BOND As Integer = 1
' Public Const DISCOUNT_BOND As Integer = 2
' Public Const CONSOL_BOND As Integer = 3
```

What should be apparent is that these types of constants must be defined in both the component itself and the application that uses the component. Furthermore, the definitions in both places must be synchronized as changes are made to the `CBond` class.

If instead we use an enumeration, changes made during code development or maintenance activities will have minimal impact. Changes in the enumeration defined in the component become immediately and automatically visible to the applications using the component. For completeness, you should realize that simple recompilations of the component and its host applications must be performed when changing enumeration values. For highly modular applications, this can lead to a significant number of recompilation steps.

The same set of values, defined as an enumeration, would be as follows:

```
' in CBond.cls
Public Enum EnumBondTypes
 btCouponBond = 1
 btDiscountBond = 2
 btConsolBond = 3
End Enum
```

One of the greatest benefits from a productivity standpoint is that using enumerations enables the Visual Basic IntelliSense feature, in many situations, to prompt you with the list of possible values as you are editing your code. Furthermore, you can usually select from this list with just a few keystrokes. Figure 6.1 shows how this prompting mechanism works.

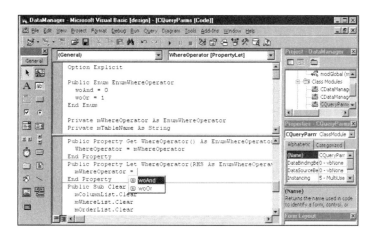

Figure 6.1   The code completion function of the Visual Basic IntelliSense editor for enumerations.

This not only saves the time to remember or look up the particular constant name, but also the time required typing it into the editor. This might seem like trivial savings, but over the course of many hours of code development, it can actually produce some significant savings.

With so many positive aspects to using enumerations, you should be acutely cognizant of one of its major drawbacks in the component-based world. As you begin debugging your MTS components, Visual Basic will require that you compile them using the Binary Compatibility option. This has the effect of freezing the Globally Unique Identifier (GUID) values for each component that has this option set. Without this option set, Visual Basic can generate new GUID values as necessary during the code modification and recompilation process, keeping everything synchronized between the components transparently to the developer. The COM engine uses these GUID values to identify the various components in the system.

After a component is compiled with this option, any changes to class interfaces or enumerations force the developer to break compatibility, which means generation of a new GUID and a forced recompilation of each component that references the changed component. Each of these components referencing the original component must also break compatibility in the process, generating more new GUID values. This occurs whether the change in the original component would have had any impact on the current component's functionality. This process repeats until all components in the referencing chain are recompiled. In a highly layered environment, this can be very frustrating. After an application is placed into a production mode, changing an enumeration in a component running on an MTS server can force a recompilation of all components such that the application must be redistributed all the way back to the client. This runs counter to one of the main goals of a distributed architecture: being able to make simple changes on the application tier without affecting the client.

Note

You should seriously consider whether to use enumerations on the application and data tiers or whether a set of constants would be more appropriate. Only when you are 99.99% sure that an enumeration on these tiers would not change over the lifetime of the application should you consider using one.

Naming Conventions

As is evident in the biblical story of the Tower of Babel, things are much more efficient when we are using a common language. We will extrapolate this here and apply it to the importance of developing standardized naming conventions for various parts of your code.

Variables

It is easy to clearly understand the data type associated with a variable if you are within the declaration section of a code module, `Function`, `Sub`, or `Property` block. However, you quickly lose focus of that if that section is no longer physically visible on the screen within the editor. One method the industry has adopted, sometimes referred to as Hungarian notation, is to prefix the variable name with something to indicate its data type. Examples include an *i* to designate integer types, an *l* for long, an *s* for string, a *b* for boolean, an *o* for object, a *c* for class, an *sng* for single, a *dt* for date, and so on. Similarly, we also want to use suffixes that have some sort of embedded meaning reflecting their use. Examples include `LastName`, `FirstName`, `HomePhoneNumber`, `Balance`, and so on. By combining these prefixes and suffixes, we can derive useful variable names. For example, `sLastName` tells us that that the variable is a string used to store a value representing a last name.

Functions and Subroutines

Function naming might not seem like something with which we should concern our-selves. Again, we would argue that standardization is vital to making it easier for developers to be able to grasp what an area of code is trying to accomplish with minimal effort. It is important to understand that most functions and subroutines do something. More precisely, some type of action is performed. That said, each function and subroutine should contain a verb fragment in its name, such as `Delete`, `Create`, `Make`, `Run`, `Do`, `Get`, and so on. Likewise, there should be a receiver of the action, such as `Report`, `Query`, and so on. If there is a series of functions or subroutines that provide similar functionality, their names should provide some indication of the difference. For example, rather than having two names like `SetStateOne` and `SetStateTwo`, we would prefer to name them `SetStateFromVariant` and `SetStateFromXML`.

Many developers over the years have chosen to abbreviate or shorten functional names to the point where they are cryptic. A quick glance at the functions defined within the Windows Application Programming Interface (API) will provide you with some great examples. The reasoning behind this is that as names become more descriptive, their length increases, making it more time-consuming to fully type them out in the editor. This is especially true in a procedural-based language. This same problem does not exist in the Visual Basic editor for long method and property names because the IntelliSense feature will help complete the code with minimal keystrokes.

Files

As you add files to your project, Visual Basic attempts to name each one for you, depending upon its intended use. Classes would be named `Class1.cls`, `Class2.cls`, `Class3.cls`, and so on if you allowed Visual Basic to handle it. Forms and basic modules will follow an identical pattern. The framework presented in Part II will be following the approach shown in Table 6.1.

Table 6.1 **File/Source Naming Conventions**

Item Type	Item Name	Filename
Forms	FrmXYZ	frmXYZ.frm
Class Modules	Csomething	CSomething.cls
Basic Modules	BasSomething	basSomething.bas
User Control	CtlSomething	ctlSomething.ctl
Project Names - EXE	MyApplication	MyApplication.exe
Project Names - DLL	LibSomething	LibSomething.dll

Commenting Conventions

Any general-purpose programming course will stress the need for comments. Although comments are vital to good programming, these courses tend go overboard. Most courses insist that you place a nice block of comments at the beginning of each function or subroutine to explain the inputs and outputs. However, if proper naming conventions were followed, the need for many of the comments is diminished. In one sense, the code should document itself as much as possible through these conventions. It is painful to follow code that has more comments than code.

Although it would be wonderful if such a minimalist approach were sufficient for all code, there still exists a need to ensure that code written today can still be understood six months from now when maintenance or enhancement phases are started. Some of the areas that need particular attention are the areas in which business logic is being implemented. In many cases, this is a step-based process, so it makes sense to make a comment like the following:

```
' Step 1 - Check that start date is less than end date
... code
' Step 2 - Get a list of transactions between start and end dates
... code
' Step 3 - etc.
```

Whatever the approach, make sure that it is followed consistently by all developers. Do not make it so burdensome that your team begins skipping proper commenting during late-hour coding sessions.

Property Lets and Gets

In the COM API, properties are implemented as special types of functions known in the object-orientation world as mutator and accessor functions. The former name implies a change in the state of the object—in this case, the property to which a new value is assigned. In the latter case, the state of the object is returned, or accessed. In Visual Basic, these special functions take the form of Property Let and Property Get statements. For properties that are object references, the Let statement is replaced with a Set statement. The Get statement returns the value of the property, whereas the Let/Set statement assigns a value to the property. For example, an OpenDate property might be implemented as in the following:

```
Private mOpenDate As Date ' in class declarations section
Public Property Get OpenDate As Date
 OpenDate = mOpenDate
End Property
Public Property Let OpenDate(RHS As Date)
 If IsDate(RHS) Then
  mOpenDate = RHS
 Else
  Err.Raise vbObjectError + ERR_BAD_DATE
```

```
    End If
End Property
```

Visual Basic does not require explicit programming of the `Get` and `Let`/`Set` functions because declaring public variables in the declaration section of the class module will have the same effect. The reason that you should formally program property `Get` and `Let`/`Set` statements is so there is a place for validation logic. Whether this logic is implemented today is irrelevant because you are protecting against the need for future change by putting the framework in place today. The use of `Get` and `Let`/`Set` statements also imparts standardization throughout the code base, an important feature in multi-developer environments. The maintenance teams will thank you as well because they will not have to break compatibility to add functionality under a `Get` or `Let`/`Set` statement in the future. As discussed in the enumeration section, breaking compatibility necessitates the recompilation of all the code that uses that component, which might lead to redistribution.

The use of a private variable to store the state of a non-derived property—one that is not calculated by its accessor function but is retrieved from a static variable—is common among object-oriented languages. In many cases, normal Hungarian notation requirements are relaxed by prefixing the variable with the letter *m* to designate *member*. This approach loses visibility to the underlying data type. This is a common naming convention used throughout Visual Basic code development, and it is the default mechanism used in the code generated by the Visual Modeler, which is discussed later in this chapter in the section titled "Modeling Tools." Some developers do not like the loss of data type visibility by the convention, so an indication of the underlying variable type can be added back in. For example, the private variable `mOpenData` for the `OpenDate` property can be named `mdtOpenDate`. This is a matter of preference. Again, just be sure to standardize across your development team.

As mentioned earlier, the accessor function can be implemented in a mode that does not simply reference a private variable, but instead derives itself from other information and functionality available to the statement. Examples include using a case statement to select among several values or using a logic set traversed with `If...Then...Else` blocks. Another example of a derived property is one that calculates its final result, such as a property named `TotalCost` that is the sum of several other properties defined on the class.

Registry-Based Configuration

As we develop our solutions, there inevitably are times when our applications need some form of configuration information. A configured approach is preferred over a "hard-coded" one as a means to ensure flexibility. This configuration information might be the name of the MTS server used by the application, publication path names to Web servers whose content is generated by the application, application login names, or simply general-purpose information needed by the application.

The Win32 system has a Registry that is just the place to store this information. In most cases, the standard Visual Basic functions of `GetSetting` and `SetSetting` can be used to perform this Registry access. These functions place Registry keys in a specific, Visual Basic area of the Registry. In some cases, an application might be integrating with other applications and will need access to the full Registry.

Collection Classes

Collections are some of the most fundamental classes in the framework presented in Part II. Everywhere there is a one-to-many relationship in the model there will be a collection class in the code. Visual Basic already provides a `Collection` class, but the framework creates its own collection, employing the Visual Basic version to do most of the dirty work. The reason for this is that, as a developer, I might want to add more business-specific functionality onto a collection class than is available on the Visual Basic version. For example, I might have a `CAccount` class that contains a `CTransactionItems` collection of `CTransactionItem` objects. Aside from the standard `Add`, `Item`, `Remove`, and `Count` methods and properties available on the Visual Basic collection, we might want to add a method called `CalculateBalance`. This method will loop through the collection, adding debits and credits to the account along the way to produce a result.

It is important to get into the habit of defining all collection classes in this manner, even if you do not plan to extend the standard collection with business functionality. Although it might not seem necessary today, a week or a month from now you might realize that you do and it will be much more difficult to put in. It is relatively trivial to set up a collection class in this manner, especially when the code generation tools discussed later in the "Modeling Tools" section are used.

Inheritance and Polymorphism Using Interfaces

As discussed in Chapter 3, interfaces are the fundamental mechanism of inheritance and polymorphism in the COM world. Again, it is important to understand the difference between polymorphism and inheritance at the source code versus runtime level. Inheritance and polymorphism at the source code level means a recompile of the code to add a new variation of a base class. Although there are several issues with this approach, the constant recompile, debug, and redistribution is what causes headaches for both the developers and end users.

In discussing polymorphism through COM interfaces, examples routinely use simple, real-world examples such as dogs or modes of transportation. Microsoft even uses dinosaurs in its own literature to make the same points. Although these are good primers on interfaces, there is much more that can and should be done with them to build flexible applications.

When using interfaces to implement polymorphism at the runtime level, a single component can constitute one or more variations of a base class, simply by implementing the COM interface defining the class one or more times. Similarly, a single COM interface can be implemented in multiple components, with each implementation providing its own behavior variation. Thus, if a new variation of a base class is needed, it is simply a matter of adding an interface implementation to a new or existing component. This is useful if a segregation of functionality is required.

An example might be when an application has a basic file import process that supports a multitude of file formats. Some customers might need one set of importers, while others might need a completely different set. Rather than place all importers in the same component, they can be separated out into logical groups and implemented in several components. Adding support for new importers can require creation of a new component or modification of an existing component. If you bind these components to the client application in a configurable manner, then the application does not have to be recompiled and redistributed with each release of a new importer. Instead, a new or existing component is distributed and changes are made to the configuration information. In essence, the application can be configured in an a la carte fashion using this technique.

Modeling Tools

If you begin to explore all the extras that come with Visual Basic Enterprise Edition, you will find two modeling tools: One is the Class Builder Utility and the other is the Visual Modeler. Both enable you to formally define classes and class hierarchies with subsequent code generation. The idea is that using either of these tools reduces much of the basic coding of class properties and methods and enforces a certain standard coding style implicitly with what it generates.

Class Builder Utility

The Class Builder Utility is the simpler tool, but there are several issues and limitations with it. The Class Builder Utility enables you to define new classes in terms of properties, methods, and events using a simple dialog. After the definitions are made, the utility creates the necessary class modules and generates the skeleton code to support the properties and methods just defined. To access this utility, you must first add it using the Add-In Manager in Visual Basic. Figure 6.2 shows the Class Builder Utility being used to edit properties on a class, while Figure 6.3 shows it being used to edit methods.

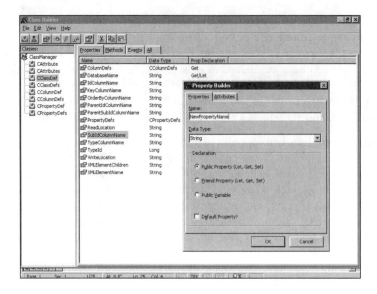

Figure 6.2   The Class Builder Utility—Property Editor.

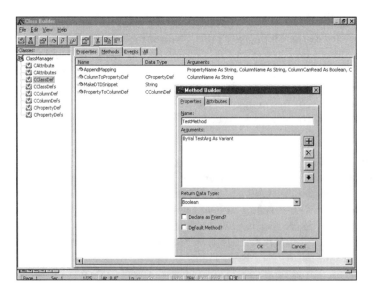

Figure 6.3   The Class Builder Utility—Methods Editor.

The first issue is that as you are going through and adding property names, this utility does not enable you to add a property named Name. This just happens to be one of the most frequently used property names in object-oriented design. To circumvent this issue, you must name your property something else and then edit the generated code.

The second issue is that the Class Builder Utility does not enable you to override the Add method on the collection classes that it generates, using the long calling convention that we spoke of earlier. This can lead to broken compatibility issues when making changes to the underlying class that we are collecting.

The third issue is that the Class Builder Utility does not enable you to make a collection containing another collection, a design requirement that can occasionally surface within the application.

The fourth issue is that the Class Builder Utility does not generate any code with the Option Explicit statement, so you will have to go back and add this information yourself.

The fifth issue is that the Class Builder Utility does not support the definition or implementation of interfaces within your design. As discussed earlier, we should be taking advantage of the features of object-orientation to make our application more robust and skewed toward the expectations of enterprise-level users.

Overall, the Class Builder Utility is inferior to the Visual Modeler that Microsoft has also bundled with Visual Basic. It is perfectly legitimate to ask why Microsoft has chosen to bundle two similar utilities. The answer is that the Visual Modeler only comes with the Enterprise Edition of Visual Basic, because it is really the product of another company (Rational Software) to which Microsoft must pay royalties. The Class Builder Utility, on the other hand, ships with lesser editions of Visual Basic as a simple productivity utility in those editions.

Visual Modeler

The Visual Modeler is a much more sophisticated and powerful tool that we should use for any large-scale application development. The functionality of this tool extends far beyond the simple class-building mechanism as in the Class Builder Utility. It represents a complete modeling tool that enables you to plan your application across a three-tiered deployment model using the standardized UML notation. It is highly flexible in how it generates its code, allowing the user to set many of the generation options. It also allows for reverse engineering, whereby you can make changes in the source code and have the model easily updated. It also exhibits none of the issues outlined in the Class Builder Utility case. To access the Visual Modeler, you must first add the Visual Modeler Menus add-in using the Add-In Manager in Visual Basic. Figure 6.4 shows the Visual Modeler in action, while Figure 6.5 shows it being used to edit properties on a class and Figure 6.6 shows it being used to edit methods.

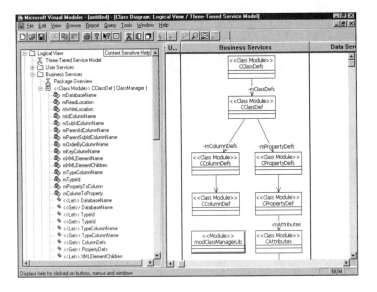

Figure 6.4   The Visual Modeler.

Figure 6.5   The Visual Modeler Properties Editor.

The Visual Modeler not only has the capability to generate source code from the model information, it also has the capability to reverse-engineer the model from the code. This latter feature is important when changes are made in the code in terms of properties and methods that must be annotated back into the model. This is crucial when multiple developers are working on the same component but only one copy of the model exists. During standard code check-in processes, a single individual can be responsible for updating the model to reflect the most recent changes.

Figure 6.6   The Visual Modeler Methods Editor.

Another important feature is that the Visual Modeler is fully aware of COM interface implementation, and can even generate code to support this concept, if modeled appropriately.

Because of the rich feature set and the fact that the framework presented in Part II, "Implementation of an Enterprise Framework," will be using interface implementation, the Visual Modeler will be used exclusively in the course of development activities throughout the remainder of the book.

SQL Server

Setting up an RDBMS such as SQL Server presents the development team and database administrator (DBA) with several decision points. Although many of the administrative tasks are not necessarily crucial to the operation of a given framework, some database design decisions must be made to coincide with the application architecture being implemented.

Logins

The configuration of SQL Server offers many options related to setting up user logins and mapping security rights to users. SQL Server provides both standard and integrated security models. In the former model, user logins are created on the server as in most other RDBMSs. In the latter model, users are implicitly logged in using their standard Windows NT login. These NT logins must then be mapped to SQL Server user groups, which then define the various levels of access to the underlying entities on the server. Although this might be acceptable for a small user base, this process of mapping NT to SQL Server users can become administratively burdensome for a large user base. In the framework in Part II, a decision has been made to provide a common application login to the server and to administer user rights programmatically.

Although this adds a bit more development complexity throughout the application, it offers more flexibility and moves security off the data tier and into a service tier. It is important to note that the database is still protected from malicious individuals through this common login, as long as login names and passwords are safely hidden.

Views

In the framework presented in Part II, views will be defined that join the underlying tables in the manners needed by the application data objects. Although this join logic can be provided as part of the ad hoc SQL that is being issued to the database by the application, a performance hit is associated with this technique. When views are created in SQL Server, the SQL is parsed into an efficient format known as a normalized query tree. This information is stored in the database in a system table know as *sysprocedures*. Upon the first access of the view after the SQL Server has started, this query tree is placed into an in-memory procedure cache for quicker performance. Using this tree, SQL Server must only generate a query plan based on the current index statistics to access the information. In the ad hoc approach, SQL Server must first compile the SQL into the normalized query tree before generating the query plan. After SQL Server has satisfied the ad hoc request, it discards the query tree because it has no basis for knowing which queries might be used again in the near future. Management of such a cache can degrade performance more than improve it in highly loaded situations. Because these ad hoc query trees cannot be cached, there is a high likelihood of degraded performance over the view approach.

Keys and Indexes

As will be further discussed in Chapter 9, "A Two-Part, Distributed Business Object," each table will be created with a specific Id field to designate its primary key. Furthermore, foreign keys will be defined on child tables that will reference this primary key for table joins. Because of this architecture, a unique clustered index will be defined on each Id field. This will not only ensure that keys are unique, but also that the rows in the database are consistent between their physical and logical order. Because new Id values will be generated sequentially as rows are added, there will not be a performance hit associated with maintaining this index. Likewise, an index will be placed on each foreign key in the table because it is often used as part of the WHERE clause of the SQL statements generated by this framework.

Indexes will also be added to the fields that are designated to be part of the name uniqueness pattern. An example of such a pattern may be when an application needs to guarantee that there are not two rows with the same values in the FirstName, LastName, MiddleInitial, and SocialSecurityNumber fields. Although a unique index can be implemented to force the RDBMS to generate name uniqueness violations, the resulting error messages returned from the server will not be sufficient to inform the user of the problem. In this case, the application will receive a "Unique index xyz had been violated" message from the server, which is non-informative to the user and will most likely generate a hotline call. Instead, a better choice is not to make this a unique index but instead handle the name uniqueness pattern in the INSERT and UPDATE triggers where an explicit and much more descriptive error message can be generated. Here, an error can be raised that reads "The First Name, Last Name, Middle Initial, and Social Security Number must be unique," which tells the user exactly what the issue is without the need for a hotline call. This is one of the deviations from an academically pure n-tier model, in that this represents a portion of the business logic that resides on the RDMBS. It is important to note that not all tables will need this name uniqueness pattern; therefore, this type of index will not need implementation on all tables.

Stored Procedures

The use of stored procedures in the framework presented in Part II is limited to performance-sensitive areas of the application. Although many system architects are proponents of using stored procedures for handling the CRUD (Create, Retrieve, Update, and Delete) processing, it has already been discussed how this limits flexibility and requires more redistribution of the code when object definitions change. A slight performance hit will be taken in exchange for such flexibility in this architecture. If, in your analysis you determine that this performance is more important than flexibility, switch over to stored procedures.

Triggers

As mentioned earlier, we will be using triggers to enforce our name uniqueness pattern requirements. We will also be using triggers to enforce referential integrity explicitly, rather than allowing the RDBMS to do it implicitly. The reasoning for this was discussed the "Referential Integrity" section of Chapter 4.

Binary Fields

It is important to note that the framework presented in this book does not support the use of binary large object (BLOB) or text fields. SQL Server includes these data types as a means to store large amounts of binary or textual data. Because most of the aggregate and query functionality becomes limited on these data types, there is little impetus for having them in an RDBMS to begin with. For these types of fields, in most cases, it is much more efficient to place them on a file server and to simply store in the database a path to their location. This is the recommended approach followed by the framework presented in Part II.

Internet Information Server (IIS) and Visual InterDev

IIS has been chosen as the framework Web server for the reasons as outlined in Chapter 1, "An Introduction to the Enterprise." Visual InterDev has been chosen as our tool for editing Active Server Pages (ASP). With the ASP application model, we have several options as to how we might structure our application, which we will discuss here.

Global Configurations

For the same reasons as those outlined in the previous Registry-based configuration discussion, application variables within the `global.asa` file will be used to control such configuration settings on the IIS machine. Some sample settings might be MTS server names, administrator `mailto:` addresses, and so on.

Stylesheets

Although not an IIS-specific feature, stylesheets are used extensively to control the look and feel of the Web site portion of the framework discussed in Part II. This allows for easy modifications to the formatting aspects of the application over time, which can include font formats as well as colors. In cases where an MTS object is generating a complex HTML stream directly, most of the formatting tasks can be driven by the stylesheet. This enables minor format changes to be made without having to recompile the object.

Include Files

If you dig through the IIS documentation, you might find it difficult to learn anything about the notion of server-side include files. The framework in Part II will be using include files to help modularize the Web site portion of the application. For example, the script code to check the user's login status is in one include file. The script code to generate the header and footer parts of each page is also implemented as include files. If the header or footer needs changing, it can be made in just those places versus the potential hundreds of pages that would otherwise be affected.

Creating an IIS Service Layer Component

The framework discussed in Part II will have its own IIS-specific service-layer component that will be used across multiple ASP pages. One set of functionality will be to provide the user login and verification services that must be handled. Several utility functions will also be implemented that will enable extraction of information from the object state information needed to generate the ASP page.

This service-layer component will be used also to gain access to functionality provided in Visual Basic that is missing in VBScript. Examples include string and date formatting functions.

Business Layer

ASP will be used as a simple scripting tool to glue MTS components together in the form of a cohesive application. In the framework, IIS is used as a surrogate for the user interface layer in the form of the HTML pages sent back to the client browser. Business-layer activities will not be performed on the IIS server, but instead will be relegated to the business-layer components in MTS. Stated another way, no direct business-layer logic will be embedded with ASP script. Instead, ASP will call the appropriate functionality found within a business-layer object running within MTS.

This notion is difficult to grasp and is one of our major divergences from a traditional viewpoint. Although ASP can directly access databases through ADO, it does so in a scripting context that is inefficient. It is important to remember that everything is a variant data type in this environment, that the ASP page must be compiled with every access, and that it is run in an interpreted, rather than compiled, format. MTS offers not only resource pooling, but also the capability to run components in a compiled binary format. Even if the functionality to be delivered is only to the intranet portion of the application, it is more prudent to place it in a business-layer component under MTS. Resorting to MTS is a minor issue because the infrastructure to do so is already in place since other parts of the application are already using it.

Indeed, Microsoft must have recognized these issues, making the integration between IIS and MTS highly efficient when the two are running on the same physical server.

Microsoft Transaction Server (MTS)

As we have mentioned many times over, MTS forms the core of the application framework discussed in Part II. Although there are many ways in which to configure MTS and install components, some practices enable efficient development, debug, and deployment activities.

Directories

In MTS, you will need a place to put the ActiveX DLL files that will be loaded as DCOM processes. You might also have a series of ActiveX DLL files to support these DCOM libraries, but are themselves in-process COM servers. When moving component packages, you will need a location to which you can export the necessary files for both the clients and servers.

A possible directory structure for a server named MTS-HOU05 and an application named MOJO might be as follows:

```
MTS-HOU05\D$\MTS\MOJO\INPROC
MTS-HOU05\D$\MTS\MOJO\DCOM
MTS-HOU05\D$\MTS\MOJO\EXPORTS
```

You might choose to share the `MTS-HOU05\D$\MTS\MOJO` directory as simply `MTS-HOU05\MOJO`. Obviously, you want to limit access to this directory to administrative use only.

The `INPROC` directory is where service layer components reside on the server. These are the components required by the MTS components, but they are not MTS components themselves. You will need a mechanism to register these components on the server using a program, such as REGSVR32.EXE or some other remote registration utility. At some point, when your application reaches a production phase, you can build an installer to install and register these components more efficiently.

The `DCOM` directory is where the MTS objects reside on the server. You should copy your ActiveX DLL files to this location, and then import them into a package on the MTS server. This process will be discussed in more detail in Chapter 9.

The `EXPORTS` directory is where you export the packages so that you can move them to other MTS servers. This process will also generate the client-side installers needed by the application. Again, this topic will be discussed this topic in more detail in Chapter 9.

Debugging

It is important to perform development on a computer with an NT Workstation or Server installed because you can run an instance of MTS on these configurations and step through your code during component debug. Although this method does not represent a pure debugging model in that issues on the MTS server in compiled mode might not be visible in debug mode, it does help to identify many of the possible issues that will arise.

As the component count increases in an application, it becomes harder to debug on a development machine. The reason for this is that the entire MTS structure must be re-created and/or synchronized on the local machine just to debug a single component that might be of interest. This means that if 10 developers are running local MTS instances for debug purposes, then all 10 developers must constantly pull the components under development from the other nine development machines over to their machines. This becomes more pronounced as the number of changes being made increases or the application gets closer to production release. Because of these issues, it is sometimes better to maintain one or two remote MTS instances that are run for debug purposes. Unfortunately, this solution creates its own problems in that it can become very difficult to debug an application on a remote MTS machine.

For those issues that are difficult to find in debug mode on a development machine, a developer can take advantage of the NT event log to write out debug or exception information. The ERL variable becomes very important when debugging MTS components in this mode. This little-known variable tracks the last line number encountered before an exception occurred. By writing this information out to the event log along with the error information, the location of errors can be more easily pinpointed in the source. An important thing to note is that the Visual Basic functionality used to write to the event log works only when the component is running in compiled mode, so do not expect to see events being logged while you are stepping through the code.

One important thing to remember about the event log is that when it fills up, MTS stops for all components. With this in mind, the event log should not be used to write out volumes of data such as the value of a variable within a loop that repeats 100 times. The event viewer application is available under the Administrative Tools section of the Start menu. Be sure to switch the log view mode from System to Application when looking for information logged from the application.

Figure 6.7 shows the Event Viewer and an event written to the event log from within Visual Basic.

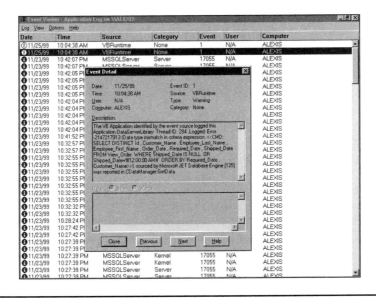

Figure 6.7   The Event Viewer and a VB logged event.

Design Goals

As we work our way through the framework beginning with the next chapter, we must have some basic design goals to drive our efforts. Our overarching goal is to follow an n-tier, distributed approach. Figure 6.8 shows an overview of where Part II will head with this architecture.

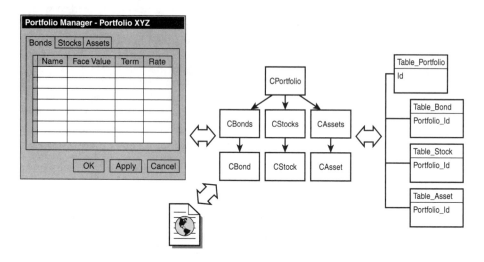

Figure 6.8   Our guidepost of where we are headed.

User Interface

We want to offer our users a simple Web browser interface where it is appropriate. Many of our users will need only simple data retrieval services, so this allows us to project our application to the widest possible audience. Still, we must also preserve our ability to provide a rich user interface for the more complex, entry-intensive tasks. These users will be fewer in number, but they will be responsible for the vast majority of the information going into the system. We do not want to penalize them by unnecessarily forcing them to use a Web browser for input purposes. The issues with a Web browser interface, as a data entry mechanism, is that we want to provide user input validation as soon as possible, as well as a high level of responsiveness from our application. These are two things we cannot easily achieve using a browser and client-side scripting code. If we must use the browser as the user-interface delivery vehicle, then we want the ability to use ActiveX controls as needed. If we are smart in our design, we should be able to use the same ActiveX controls in both the Visual Basic client and Web browser.

For the rich client, we want to preserve the user interface metaphors that users have already become accustomed to from using Windows (95, 98, NT4), such as the Explorer, Finder, tabbed dialogs, and so on.

Business Logic

We want to keep our business logic in one place so that it is easier to maintain over time. We want the same business objects supporting our Visual Basic client as our Web browser. We do not want client-side business logic muddled up in our Web pages. We do not want business logic muddled up in our ASP pages.

Database Server

We want to preserve the ability to switch out RDBMS vendors at any point in time; therefore, we must minimize the use of any one server-vendor's proprietary functionality.

Summary

This chapter has provided an overview of the design goals and development fundamentals that will be followed from this point forward. It has done so with a very broad brush, first covering the development technologies (Visual Basic, SQL Server, IIS, and MTS). For each of these technologies, you learned a series of best practices and common pitfalls as a preparation going forward so it will be more clear why a particular design or implementation decision is being made. This was followed by a discussion of specific design goals for the application as a whole, and then broken down into the User, Business, and Data layers of the system. A discussion on modeling tools, specifically comparing the Class Builder Utility to the Visual Modeler, was also provided.

Next, you learn the long-awaited implementation of the framework that we have spent so much time building up to. Chapter 7, "The ClassManager Library," introduces the concept of metadata-driven class definitions and provides the initial building block for the application framework.

II

Implementation of an Enterprise Framework

7

The ClassManager Library

WITH THE COMPLETION OF PART I AND ITS overview material, we can now turn our attention to the presentation and development of the framework for which you bought this book. This presentation starts with one of the core components of the business layer—the ClassManager Library. This ActiveX DLL library is primarily responsible for managing the metadata necessary to map class definitions to database tables.

Remembering the section titled "Mapping Tables and Objects" in Chapter 4, "The Relational Database Management System," there is a need in an object-based application to persist state information to the database. A technique was discussed that mapped classes to tables and properties to the columns in those tables. The ClassManager Library presented in this chapter provides the necessary objects to implement this mapping and class definition process.

In addition to defining the mapping between objects and tables, the ClassManager library enables developers to define arbitrary attributes at the property level. These attributes can be used to track any form of additional metadata needed by the application, such as validation rule parameters, XML tag names and so on. Examples of both types of additional metadata will be shown; the XML tag name information is particularly important for topics discussed in Chapter 13, "Interoperability."

Design Theory

The underlying design goal of the ClassManager library is to provide the definition mechanism necessary to drive both the CRUD (Create, Retrieve, Update, and Delete) capabilities and the simple property-level validation required by the business and data layers. The overarching design goal is to provide a generic solution that can easily be modified through metadata changes at the business layer and schema changes on the RDMBS when support for new properties is needed. To do this with a minimal level of effort, we will place this library on the application tier running on MTS. This particular library is not itself an MTS object, but provides a service to the business objects running on MTS.

Many object-oriented languages have a facility known as reflection, which means that the runtime environment has access to the type information of the classes currently running. In essence, the code can see pieces of itself and understand the class definitions defined by the code. Unfortunately, Visual Basic is not one of those languages. Lack of runtime-type information indicates that this information must be provided explicitly in a programmatic fashion. Such is the goal behind this chapter.

Implementation

To provide this metadata-oriented definition process, we need to create several Visual Basic classes.

The first requirement is to create one class to support the definition of a database column, and another to support the definition of an object property. For the former, we will create a class called CColumnDef, while for the latter, we will create one called CPropertyDef. To augment the CPropertyDef class, we will create a CAttribute class to allow us to add other important metadata to our property definitions. The second requirement is to provide a mechanism to link a column to a property. After these base classes have been established, a class known as CClassDef is defined to pull everything together and provide the core functionality of the library. As discussed in Chapter 4, "The Relational Database Management System," we perform a one-to-one mapping of a class to a database table. In the case of class inheritance, all subclasses are mapped to the same table and use a ClassType field within the definition to designate the specific implementation.

The CColumnDef Class

The CColumnDef class is simple, containing only properties. See Figure 7.1 for the Unified Modeling Language (UML) representation.

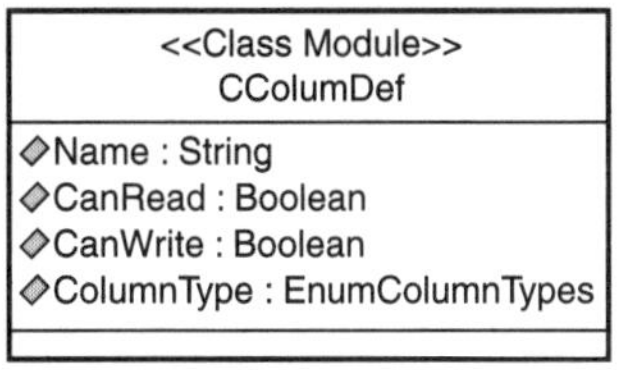

```
              <<Class Module>>
                 CColumnDef
  ◇Name : String
  ◇CanRead : Boolean
  ◇CanWrite : Boolean
  ◇ColumnType : EnumColumnTypes
```

Figure 7.1   The CColumnDef class in the UML graphical model.

Properties

The Name property is used to provide the name of the column within the RDMBS system. The CanRead property indicates whether the column can be read from the database, whereas the CanWrite property determines whether the column can be written to. The CanRead property is used in conjunction with the ReadLocation property on the CClassDef to generate the SQL column list for data retrieval purposes. Similarly, the CanWrite property is used in conjunction with the WriteLocation property on CClassDef to generate the SQL column list for data updates. The CClassDef class is discussed in more detail in the "CClassDef" section later in this chapter.

We must explicitly provide both a CanRead and CanWrite indicator for a given column versus using a singular approach because there are times when we might want to read without writing, or vice-versa. If we are storing a foreign key reference to another table, we must be able to read columns from the referenced tables within the context of a view, but we will not want to write those same columns back out. Only the column with the foreign key reference can be written to in this case.

We also define a ColumnType property to help us during the SQL generation process in our data layer. Sometimes, the system cannot explicitly determine an underlying data type in order for the appropriate SQL grammar to be generated to support a given database request. For example, a property might be defined as a string type, but the underlying column in the database, for whatever reason, is an integer. In this case, when building an SQL WHERE clause using this property, a VarType performed on the property would infer a string, causing the SQL generator logic to place quotes around it in the SQL statement. The RDBMS would generate an error because the column is an integer. Thus, for robustness, we provide a mechanism to explicitly define a particular column type.

Building this CColumnDef class using the Visual Modeler is rather straightforward. Start the Visual Modeler from the Start menu of Windows (95/98/NT) under the Programs, Visual Studio 6.0 Enterprise Tools, Microsoft Visual Modeler submenus. When Visual Modeler starts, expand the Logical View node, followed by the Business Services node in the tree view. Right-click the Business Services node followed by New, followed by Class, as shown in Figure 7.2.

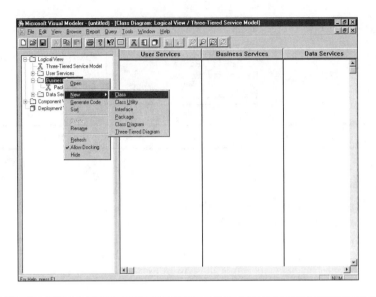

Figure 7.2   Defining a new class in the Visual Modeler.

When you tell Visual Modeler to create a new class, a new child node is added to the Business Services node, a UML graphical symbol for a class is placed into the right-hand view under the Business Services column, and the newly added node is placed into edit mode so the class name can be entered. Figure 7.3 shows the Visual Modeler after the new class has been named `CColumnDef`.

To add property definitions to the `CColumnDef` class, simply right-click the CColumnDef node and select New, Property. Again, a new child node is added with the name of NewProperty, this time to the CColumnDef node, and a property name `NewProperty` is added to the graphical representation. There is also a symbol that looks like a lock with a blue rectangle at an angle. The blue rectangle signifies that this is a property. A purple rectangle signifies a method. The lock indicates that the property is private, whereas a key indicates protected mode (or Friend mode in Visual Basic parlance); a hammer indicates implementation mode, and a rectangle by itself indicates public mode.

Public mode indicates that the property will be visible both internal and external to the component; protected mode means that it will be visible to all classes within the component but not visible external to the component; private mode means it will be visible within the class itself but not visible elsewhere; and implementation mode is similar in meaning to private mode. The Visual Modeler can be used to generate C++ code, and the Rational Rose product on which it is based can generate for Java as well; both are true object-oriented languages with multilevel inheritance. In these cases, the protected and private modes take on expanded meanings because visibility is now concerned with the subclassing. This explains why the implementation and private modes are similar for Visual Basic.

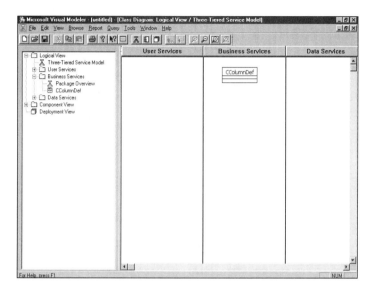

Figure 7.3   The `CColumnDef` class created within Visual Modeler.

Turning back to the Visual Modeler, the `NewProperty` property is renamed `Name`. Double-clicking the new `Name` property node launches the Property Specifications dialog. The Type field is set to `String`, and the Export Control selection is set to `Public`. There is also a Documentation field in which you can enter text that describes the property. If this is done, the information will be placed above the property implementation in the generated code as commented text. At this point, this information does not make it into the COM property help field that is displayed by the object browser. The end result of these edits appears in Figure 7.4.

As you continue to add the properties to complete the `CColumnDef` class, you might begin thinking that this is too tedious a process and that it just might be easier to manually type the code. If this is the case, there is a faster way to enter these properties than what was just described. Double-click the CColumnDef node to launch the Class Specifications dialog box. Click the Properties tab to show a list of all the currently defined properties. Right-click this list to bring up a menu with an Insert option. Select this option to insert a new property into the list in an edit mode. After you enter the name, if you slowly double-click the icon next to the property name, a graphical list box of all the visibility modes appears, as shown in Figure 7.5. If you do the same in the Type column, a list of available data types appears as well, as shown in Figure 7.6.

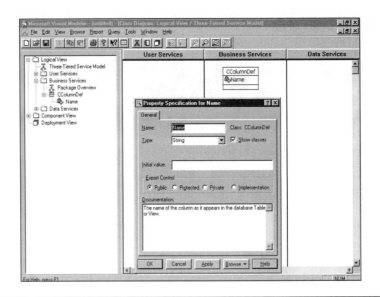

Figure 7.4   The `Name` property added to the `CColumnDef` class within Visual Modeler.

Figure 7.5   Changing the visibility of a property in the Class
Specification dialog in the Visual Modeler.

To add the `ColumnType` property, follow the same procedure as for the other properties. Because the Visual Modeler has no way to define an enumeration for generation (they can only be reverse engineered from an ActiveX DLL), you will have to manually enter the name of the enumeration in the Type field. After the code is generated, the enumeration must be manually entered into the source.

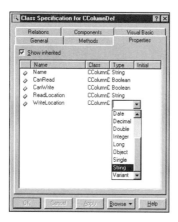

Figure 7.6 Changing the data type of a property in the
Class Specification dialog in the Visual Modeler.

To generate code for this class, several other pieces of information must be defined.
The first is a component to contain this class. To do this, right-click the Component
View folder, select New, and then select Component. Enter ClassManager for the
component name. Double-click the ClassManager node to launch the Component
Specification dialog. From this dialog, select ActiveX for the Stereotype field. This tells
the Visual Modeler to generate an ActiveX DLL for the component. The Language
field should be set to Visual Basic. The last item before generation is to assign the class
to this newly created component. The easiest way to accomplish this is to drag the
CColumnDef node and drop it onto the ClassManager node. From this point, code
generation can occur.

Right-click the CColumnDef node and select GenerateCode to launch the Code
Generation Wizard. Step through this wizard until the Preview Classes step appears,
as indicated in the title bar of the dialog. Select the CColumnDef class in the list and
click the Preview button. The wizard switches into Class Options mode, as shown in
Figure 7.7. From this wizard, set the Instancing Mode to MultiUse. In the Collection
Class field, enter the name CColumnDefs. Anything other than the word Collection in
this field will tell the Visual Modeler to generate a collection class for this class.

Click the Next button in the wizard to go to the Property Options step. Select the
CanRead property in the list, and then check the Generate Variable, Property Get, and
Property Let options. This tells the Visual Modeler to generate a private variable
named mCanRead, followed by the Property Let and Property Get statements. This
activity is summarized in the text box at the bottom of the screen. Repeat this for
every property in the list. For the ColumnType property that is defined as
EnumColumnType, the Visual Modeler only allows for the property Set and Get options.
After generation, this Set will have to be changed to a Let in the source code. The
results of this step are shown in Figure 7.8.

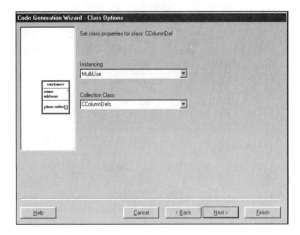

Figure 7.7   The Class Options step of the Code Generation Wizard (Preview Classes subwizard) in the Visual Modeler.

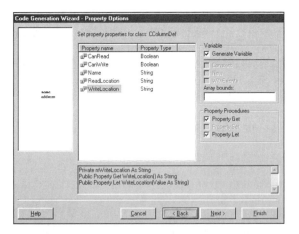

Figure 7.8   The Property Options step of the Code Generation Wizard (Preview Classes subwizard) in the Visual Modeler.

Click the Next button in the wizard to go to the Role Options. Skip over this for now. Click the Next button again to go to the Methods Options step. Because no methods are defined on this class, the list is empty. Click the Finish button to return to the Preview Classes step of the wizard. If multiple classes were being generated, you would preview each class in the manner just described. Click the Next button to get to the General Options step. Deselect the Include Debug Code and Include Err.Raise in All Generated Methods options. Click the Finish button, and the wizard first prompts for a model name and then launches Visual Basic. The result of this generation effort is shown in Figure 7.9.

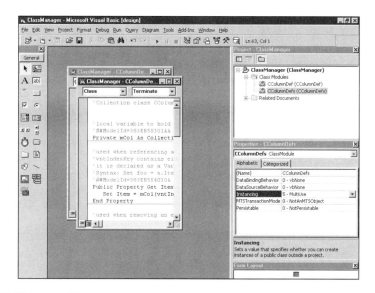

Figure 7.9   The code generated in Visual Basic by the Visual Modeler.

Notice that a `Form1` is generated by the Visual Modeler. This is actually a by-product of the automation steps in Visual Basic. When you return to the Visual Modeler, the wizard is on the Delete Classes step with this `Form1` selected in the Keep These Classes list. Click it to move it to the Delete These Classes list. Click OK to delete it from the project and display a summary report of the Visual Modeler's activities.

To add the enumeration for the `ColumnType` property, go to the Visual Basic class module for the `CColumnDef` class and manually enter the enumeration as shown in the following code fragment:

```
Public Enum EnumColumnType
 ctNumber = 0
 ctString = 1
 ctDateTime = 2
End Enum
```

Listing 7.1 provides the code to implement the `CColumnDef` class. The comments generated by the Visual Modeler have been omitted for the sake of brevity.

Listing 7.1   **The *CColumnDef* Class**

```
Option Base 0
Option Explicit

Public Enum EnumColumnType
 ctNumber = 0
 ctString = 1
 ctDateTime = 2
End Enum

Private mName As String
Private mCanRead As Boolean
Private mCanWrite As Boolean
Private mReadLocation As String
Private mWriteLocation As String
Private mColumnType As EnumColumnType

Public Property Get ColumnType() As EnumColumnType
    Set ColumnType = mColumnType
End Property

Public Property Let ColumnType(ByVal Value As EnumColumnType)
    Let mColumnType = Value
End Property

Public Property Get WriteLocation() As String
   Let WriteLocation = mWriteLocation
End Property

Public Property Let WriteLocation(ByVal Value As String)
    Let mWriteLocation = Value
End Property

Public Property Get ReadLocation() As String
   Let ReadLocation = mReadLocation
End Property

Public Property Let ReadLocation(ByVal Value As String)
    Let mReadLocation = Value
End Property

Public Property Get CanWrite() As Boolean
   Let CanWrite = mCanWrite
End Property

Public Property Let CanWrite(ByVal Value As Boolean)
    Let mCanWrite = Value
End Property

Public Property Get CanRead() As Boolean
   Let CanRead = mCanRead
End Property
```

```
Public Property Let CanRead(ByVal Value As Boolean)
    Let mCanRead = Value
End Property

Public Property Get Name() As String
   Let Name = mName
End Property

Public Property Let Name(ByVal Value As String)
    Let mName = Value
End Property
```

Listing 7.2 shows the code generated by the Visual Modeler for the CColumnDefs class, again with comments omitted.

Listing 7.2   **The *CColumnDefs* Collection Class**

```
' declarations section
Option Explicit
Private mCol As Collection

' code section
Public Property Get Item(vntIndexKey As Variant) As CColumnDef
  Set Item = mCol(vntIndexKey)
End Property

Public Sub Remove(vntIndexKey As Variant)
  mCol.Remove vntIndexKey
End Sub

Public Sub Add(Item As CColumnDef, _
               Optional Key As String, _
               Optional Before As Variant, _
               Optional After As Variant)
  If IsMissing(Key) Then
    mCol.Add Item
  Else
    mCol.Add Item, Key
  End If
End Sub

Public Property Get Count() As Long
  Count = mCol.Count
End Property

Public Property Get NewEnum() As IUnknown
  Set NewEnum = mCol.[_NewEnum]
End Property

Private Sub Class_Initialize()
```

continues

Listing 7.2 **Continued**

```
  Set mCol = New Collection
End Sub

Private Sub Class_Terminate()
  Set mCol = Nothing
End Sub
```

We should point out several things about how the Visual Modeler generates collection classes. The first is that it generates a NewEnum property that has a bizarre bit of code in the form of the following statement:

```
Set NewEnum = mCol.[_NewEnum]
```

This syntax enables users of this collection class to use a special COM iteration construct to iterate through the elements in a collection. For example, consider the following code fragment:

```
For Each ColumnDef In ColumnDefs
  ' ...
Next
```

According to Microsoft, this is faster than using a standard iteration method as the following code fragment demonstrates:

```
For i = 1 To ColumnDefs.Count
  Set ColumnDef = ColumnDefs.Item(i)
  ' ...
Next i
```

The second item to notice is that the Visual Modeler has declared a private variable mCol of type Collection to use as the underlying storage mechanism. In this case, however, it does not instantiate the variable until the Class_Initialize event, and it does not destroy it until the Class_Terminate event. This generation mode can be overridden in the Visual Modeler based on the preference of the development team. One school of thought says that the code size will be smaller using this technique because Visual Basic will not allocate space for the mCol variable at compile time, but rather at runtime. Conversely, the object will take longer to instantiate because it must allocate memory for this variable at runtime during startup. The preference of this book is to use the default mode of Visual Modeler.

The **CAttributeItem** Class

Before we can define our CPropertyDef class, we must first define a simple CAttributeItem class and its associated CAttributeItems collection class. CAttributeItem has a simple Name and Value property. These attributes will be used to allow extra information needed by the application to be added to the property definition information. This approach provides for a significant amount of flexibility over time because a developer can just add another property to the `CAttributeItems` collection without forcing any changes to the interface of a class. The Visual Modeler can once again be used to generate the `CAttributeItem` class and its associated `CAttributeItems` collection class. Listing 7.3 shows the code for the `CAttributeItem` class.

Listing 7.3 **The *CAttribute* Class**

```
' declarations section
Option Explicit
Private mName As String
Private mValue As Variant

' code section
Public Property Get Value() As Variant
  If IsObject(mValue) Then
    Set Value = mValue
  Else
    Let Value = mValue
  End If
End Property

Public Property Let Value(ByVal Value As Variant)
  Let mValue = Value
End Property

Public Property Get Name() As String
  Let Name = mName
End Property

Public Property Let Name(ByVal Value As String)
  Let mName = Value
End Property
```

Although there is nothing overly exciting Listing 7.3, one area in particular deserves closer investigation. Looking at the code generated by the Visual Modeler for the `Property Get` statement for the `Value` property shows that it is implemented slightly differently than what has been seen in the past. Because we have declared the property as a variant type, it can contain an object reference and therefore needs the `Set` construct in these cases. The `IsObject` function enables Visual Basic to check whether the variant contains an object reference so that the code can react accordingly.

Again, we now need to use the Visual Modeler to generate a collection class for `CAttributeItem`. The complete code listing will not be shown because it differs only slightly from the code generated in the `CColumnDefs` case. However, several changes have been made to the `Add` method, as shown in the following code fragment:

```
Public Sub Add(Name As String, Value As Variant)
  Dim ThisAttribute As New CAttribute

  ThisAttribute.Name = Name
  ThisAttribute.Value = Value

  ' for this collection, we want to replace values if their key
  ' already exists
  If KeyExists(mCol, ThisAttribute.Name) Then
   Call mCol.Remove(ThisAttribute.Name)
  End If
  mCol.Add ThisAttribute, ThisAttribute.Name
End Sub
```

Because we will be adding only name-value pairs to this collection, a lot of programming time and overhead is needed to create an AttributeItem object, set its properties, and pass it into the add method. Instead, we are just passing in the name-value pairs, allowing the Add method to perform the instantiation. In addition, the Add method checks for the existence of the key in the collection before attempting to add a new item. If the key exists, it removes the previous element and replaces it with the new one. This implementation decision to check first, rather than letting mCol raise an error, is made because duplicates here will be from a programming issue and not from a data entry issue by an end user. Therefore, there is little concern with replacement, and this method makes the code more robust. The KeyExists function referenced by the Add method is a public function inside a basic code module in the component. This function is simple to implement and will be used throughout all components in this framework, so the following code fragment is presented:

```
Public Function KeyExists(c As Collection, sKey As String) As Boolean
 On Error GoTo KeyNotExists
 c.Item (sKey)
 KeyExists = True
 Exit Function
KeyNotExists:
 KeyExists = False
End Function
```

The CPropertyDef Class

The CPropertyDef class, like its CColumnDef cousin, is composed only of simple properties. Figure 7.10 shows the UML representation for this class.

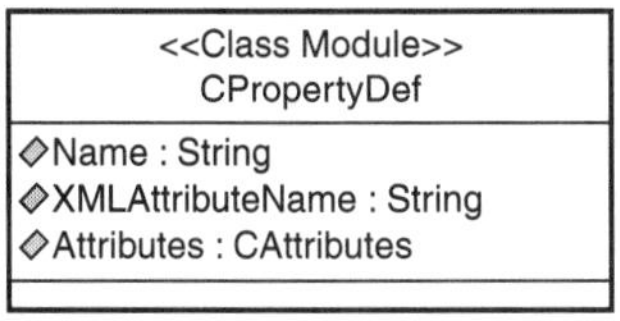

Figure 7.10   The CPropertyDef class in the UML graphical model.

Properties

Here, the Name property is used to identify the name that will be used to refer to this property throughout the business and user layers. Although the Name property here can exactly match the Name property on its mapped CColumnDef object, it does not have to do so. The only other property is AttributeItems, which as discussed previously, is used as a freeform mechanism to store additional information related to a property. We can use this information throughout the business layer, and we can pass it to the user layer if necessary. The flexibility exists to add whatever information at a property level is needed by the application. Some examples of standard items that could be simple property validation might include PropertyType, ListId, MinimumValue, MaximumValue, DefaultValue, and Decimals. In this framework, a standard XMLAttributeName property for XML generation is defined, a topic covered in Chapter 13. Once again, the Visual Modeler is used to define both a CPropertyDef class and its associated CPropertyDefs collection class. Listing 7.4 provides the code to implement the CPropertyDef class.

Listing 7.4   **The *CPropertyDef* Class**

```
' declarations section
Option Explicit
Public Enum EnumPropertyTypes
 ptString = 0
 ptInteger = 1
 ptReal = 2
 ptDate = 3
 ptList = 4
End Enum

Private mName As String
Private mAttributes As CAttributeItems

Public Property Get Attributes() As CAttributeItems
  Set Attributes = mAttributes
End Property

Public Property Get Name() As String
  Let Name = mName
```

continues

Listing 7.4 **Continued**

```
End Property

Public Property Let Name(ByVal Value As String)
  Let mName = Value
End Property

Private Sub Class_Initialize()
 Set mAttributes = New CAttributeItems
End Sub

Private Sub Class_Terminate()
 Set mAttributes = Nothing
End Sub
```

Looking at the code, you will see that we have done a few things differently than before. First, only a `Property Get` statement has been created for the `Attributes` property. The corresponding `Property Set` statement has been omitted because this subordinate object is being managed directly by the `CPropertyDef` class, so there is no reason for any external code to set its value to something other than the internal, private `mAttributes` variable. Doing so would potentially wreak havoc on the application; therefore, access to it is protected under the principle of encapsulation and data hiding that was talked about in Chapter 3, "Objects, Components, and COM." In addition, you will note that the contained objects are instantiated in the `Class_Initialize` event as was done for collections earlier in the chapter. The same reasoning applies here.

Because the `CPropertyDefs` collection class is not changed from the code generated by the Visual Modeler, the listing is omitted here.

The `CClassDef` Class

Now that the `CColumnDef` and `CPropertyDef` classes and their supporting collection classes have been created, it is time to generate the `CClassDef` class, which is responsible for pulling everything together to drive the metadata model. Figure 7.11 shows the UML representation for this class.

Properties

To provide the class-to-RDBMS mapping, both the name of the table that we will be using to save object state information and the name of the view that will be used to retrieve object state information must be known to the application. The mapping technique was discussed in detail in Chapter 4. To meet these needs, the properties `WriteLocation` and `ReadLocation` are defined.

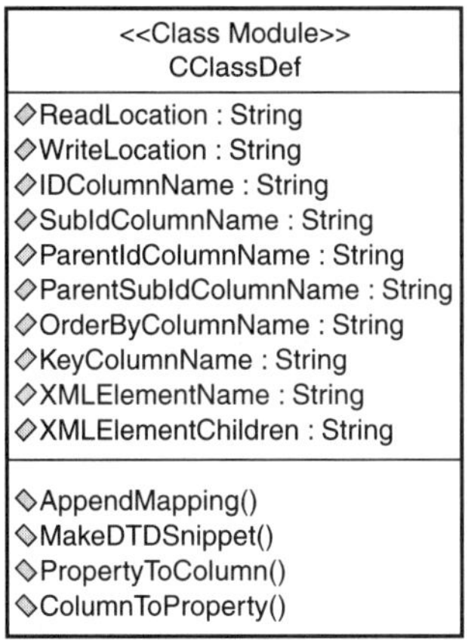

```
            <<Class Module>>
               CClassDef
 ◇ReadLocation : String
 ◇WriteLocation : String
 ◇IDColumnName : String
 ◇SubIdColumnName : String
 ◇ParentIdColumnName : String
 ◇ParentSubIdColumnName : String
 ◇OrderByColumnName : String
 ◇KeyColumnName : String
 ◇XMLElementName : String
 ◇XMLElementChildren : String

 ◇AppendMapping()
 ◇MakeDTDSnippet()
 ◇PropertyToColumn()
 ◇ColumnToProperty()
```

Figure 7.11   The `CClassDef` class in the UML graphical model.

After the names of the table and views have been defined, the columns that act as the primary keys on the table must be defined. Recall from Chapter 4 that these keys also serve as the Object Identifier (OID) values for an object instance. This framework can support two-column keys, or OIDs; so, the properties `IdColumnName` and `SubIdColumnName` are defined. The framework assumes that an empty value for `SubIdColumnName` indicates that only a single key is used. The response of the framework when `IdColumnName` is empty is not defined.

If the particular class that is being defined by an instance of the `CClassDef` class is the child in a parent-child–style relationship, the columns that represent the foreign keys to the table containing the parent object instances must be defined as well. The properties `ParentIdColumnName` and `ParentSubIdColumnName` are defined for just this purpose. The data layer, discussed in Chapter 8, "The DataManager Library," will use this information during its SQL generation process for retrieval statements. Similarly, for a parent-child–style relationship, there can be many child objects as in the case of a one-to-many or master-detail relationship. In these cases, the developer might need to order the items in a particular way, so an `OrderByColumnName` property is defined. If more than one column is required, a comma-separated list of column names on which to sort can be provided. These columns do not necessarily have to appear in the `ColumnDefs` property that we will discuss shortly.

If one-level inheritance structure is being created (through an interface implementation), we must be able to discern which subclass of the base class a given record in the database represents. Therefore, the properties `TypeColumnName` and `TypeId` have been defined to drive this. If a value for `TypeColumnName` is defined, then the framework assumes that an inheritance structure is in force and handles data retrieval, inserts, and updates accordingly.

There are many instances where we want to reference an object by a human-friendly name rather than by its OID, such as in an object browser, explorer, or lookup mechanism. To support this, a property called KeyColumnName is defined to indicate which column to use for this purpose. In this case, the KeyColumnName must correspond to a ColumnDef in the ColumnDefs collection.

To support the XML functionality discussed in Chapter 13, we must define the information necessary to generate an XML Document Type Definition (DTD) for the class. The properties XMLElementName and XMLElementChildren are defined for this purpose. These properties are used in conjunction with the MakeDTDSnippet method defined on the class and discussed in the "Methods" section, later in this chapter.

Finally, the CClassDef class contains a property of type PropertyDefs and another of type ColumnDefs. Because these two sets of definitions are built programmatically at runtime, these two properties store the column and property definition information for use by the business and data layers. In addition to these two properties, two other properties are implemented to help map between ColumnDef objects and PropertyDef objects. They are called PropertyToColumn and ColumnToProperty, both of which are implemented as simple Visual Basic Collection classes. The keying mechanism of the collection will be used to help provide this mapping.

Once again, the Visual Modeler can be used to implement both the CClassDef class and CClassDefs collection class. Be sure to use the same model that has been used throughout this chapter so that there is visibility to the PropertyDefs and ColumnDefs collection classes.

Listing 7.5 provides the code to implement the properties of the CClassDef class.

Listing 7.5   **Properties of the *CClassDef* Class**

```
' declarations section
Option Explicit
Private mReadLocation As String
Private mWriteLocation As String
Private mIdColumnName As String
Private mSubIdColumnName As String
Private mParentIdColumnName As String
Private mParentSubIdColumnName As String
Private mOrderByColumnName As String
Private mTypeColumnName As String
Private mTypeId As Long
Private mKeyColumnName As String
Private mXMLElementName As String
Private mXMLElementChildren As String
Private mPropertyToColumn As Collection
Private mColumnToProperty As Collection
Private mPropertyDefs As CPropertyDefs
Private mColumnDefs As CColumnDefs
```

```
' code section
Public Property Get ColumnDefs() As CColumnDefs
  Set ColumnDefs = mColumnDefs
End Property

Public Property Get PropertyDefs() As CPropertyDefs
  Set PropertyDefs = mPropertyDefs
End Property

Public Property Get XMLElementChildren() As String
  Let XMLElementChildren = mXMLElementChildren
End Property

Public Property Let XMLElementChildren(ByVal Value As String)
  Let mXMLElementChildren = Value
End Property

Public Property Get XMLElementName() As String
  Let XMLElementName = mXMLElementName
End Property

Public Property Let XMLElementName(ByVal Value As String)
  Let mXMLElementName = Value
End Property

Public Property Get TypeId() As Long
  Let TypeId = mTypeId
End Property

Public Property Let TypeId(ByVal Value As Long)
  Let mTypeId = Value
End Property

Public Property Get TypeColumnName() As String
  Let TypeColumnName = mTypeColumnName
End Property

Public Property Let TypeColumnName(ByVal Value As String)
  Let mTypeColumnName = Value
End Property

Public Property Get KeyColumnName() As String
  Let KeyColumnName = mKeyColumnName
End Property

Public Property Let KeyColumnName(ByVal Value As String)
  Let mKeyColumnName = Value
End Property

Public Property Get OrderByColumnName() As String
  Let OrderByColumnName = mOrderByColumnName
End Property
```

continues

Listing 7.5   **Continued**

```
Public Property Let OrderByColumnName(ByVal Value As String)
  Let mOrderByColumnName = Value
End Property

Public Property Get ParentSubIdColumnName() As String
  Let ParentSubIdColumnName = mParentSubIdColumnName
End Property

Public Property Let ParentSubIdColumnName(ByVal Value As String)
  Let mParentSubIdColumnName = Value
End Property

Public Property Get ParentIdColumnName() As String
  Let ParentIdColumnName = mParentIdColumnName
End Property

Public Property Let ParentIdColumnName(ByVal Value As String)
  Let mParentIdColumnName = Value
End Property

Public Property Get SubIdColumnName() As String
  Let SubIdColumnName = mSubIdColumnName
End Property

Public Property Let SubIdColumnName(ByVal Value As String)
  Let mSubIdColumnName = Value
End Property

Public Property Get IdColumnName() As String
  Let IdColumnName = mIdColumnName
End Property

Public Property Let IdColumnName(ByVal Value As String)
  Let mIdColumnName = Value
End Property

Public Property Get WriteLocation() As String
  Let WriteLocation = mWriteLocation
End Property

Public Property Let WriteLocation(ByVal Value As String)
  Let mWriteLocation = Value
End Property

Public Property Get ReadLocation() As String
  Let ReadLocation = mReadLocation
End Property

Public Property Let ReadLocation(ByVal Value As String)
  Let mReadLocation = Value
End Property
```

```
Private Sub Class_Initialize()
  Set mPropertyToColumn = New Collection
  Set mColumnToProperty = New Collection
End Sub

Private Sub Class_Terminate()
  Set mPropertyToColumn = Nothing
  Set mColumnToProperty = Nothing
End Sub
```

Methods

Four methods are defined on the `CClassDef` class to implement creation of the meta-data model at runtime. The first of these is `AppendMapping`, a method that is responsible for creating `ColumnDef` and `PropertyDef` instances, adding them to the necessary collections, and providing the mapping between the two. Listing 7.6 provides the code listing for this method.

Listing 7.6   **The *AppendMapping* Method of the *CClassDef* Class**

```
Public Sub AppendMapping(PropertyName As String, _
                         ColumnName As String, _
                         ColumnCanRead As Boolean, _
                         ColumnCanWrite As Boolean, _
                         ColumnType As EnumColumnType, _
                         XMLAttributeName As String)
  Dim ColumnDef As New CColumnDef
  Dim PropertyDef As New CPropertyDef
  Dim AttributeItem As CAttributeItem

  On Error GoTo ErrorTrap

100  ColumnDef.Name = ColumnName
105  ColumnDef.CanRead = ColumnCanRead
110  ColumnDef.CanWrite = ColumnCanWrite
120  ColumnDef.ColumnType = ColumnType
125  mColumnDefs.Add ColumnDef, ColumnDef.Name

130  PropertyDef.Name = PropertyName

135  Call PropertyDef.Attributes.Add("XMLAttributeName", XMLAttributeName)

140  mPropertyDefs.Add PropertyDef, PropertyDef.Name

145  mColumnToProperty.Add PropertyDef, ColumnName

150  mPropertyToColumn.Add ColumnDef, PropertyName

  Exit Sub
```

continues

Listing 7.6   **Continued**

```
ErrorTrap:
    '1.  Details to EventLog
    Call WriteNTLogEvent("CClassDef:AppendMapping", Err.Number,
                         Err.Description, Err.Source)
    '2.  Generic to client - passed back on error stack
    Err.Raise Err.Number, "CClassDef:AppendMapping",
    Err.Description & " [" & Erl & "]"
    End Sub
```

In an effort to minimize the mapping creation process in the business layer, only the minimal information needed to create a column and property, and subsequently generate a mapping, is passed into the method. This information is all that is needed to drive the basic architecture. If additional information is needed by your implementation of this framework, then the AppendMapping method can be modified, although the recommended approach is to utilize the Attributes property on the PropertyDef class. The reasoning behind this is so that flexibility going forward is preserved by not having to modify the AppendMapping method.

The AppendMapping method is self-explanatory up until line 145, where the actual mappings are created. It is here that the keying feature of a Collection is used to provide the bidirectional mappings. For the private mColumnToProperty collection, the PropertyDef object is added, keyed on the column name. For the private mPropertyToColumn collection, the opposite is performed and the ColumnDef object is added, keyed on the property name. Rather than provide direct access to these underlying collections, two methods to expose this mapping facility in a cleaner fashion are implemented. These methods are PropertyToColumnDef and ColumnToPropertyDef. The code for these two methods is provided in Listing 7.7.

Listing 7.7   **The *PropertyToColumnDef* and *ColumnToPropertyDef* Methods of the *CClassDef* Class**

```
Public Function PropertyToColumnDef(PropertyName As String) As CColumnDef
On Error GoTo NotFound
  Set PropertyToColumnDef = mColumnDefs.Item(PropertyName)
  Exit Function
NotFound:
  Set PropertyToColumnDef = Nothing
End Function

Public Function ColumnToPropertyDef(ColumnName As String) As CPropertyDef
On Error GoTo NotFound
  Set ColumnToPropertyDef = mPropertyDefs.Item(ColumnName) Exit Function
NotFound:
  Set ColumnToPropertyDef = Nothing
End Function
```

Finally, the `MakeDTDSnippet` method that will be used in the XML DTD generation facility of the framework is implemented. Although a detailed discussion of this functionality will be deferred until Chapter 13, I'll make a few comments. The code is provided in Listing 7.8.

Listing 7.8 **The *MakeDTDSnippet* Method of the *CClassDef* Class**

```
Public Function MakeDTDSnippet() As String
 Dim sXML As String
 Dim PropertyDef As CPropertyDef

  Call Append(sXML, "<!ELEMENT" & vbTab)
  Call Append(sXML, XMLElementName & " ")
  Call Append(sXML, XMLElementChildren & ">" & vbCrLf)
  Call Append(sXML, "<!ATTLIST" & vbTab & XMLElementName & vbCrLf)
 Call Append(sXML, "<!ATTLIST" & vbTab & XMLElementName & vbCrLf)
 For Each PropertyDef In PropertyDefs
  If PropertyDef.XMLAttributeName <> "" Then
        Call Append(sXML, vbTab & XMLAttributeName)
        Call Append(sXML, " CDATA #REQUIRED" & vbCrLf)
  End If
 Next
 Call Append(sXML, ">" & vbCrLf)
 MakeDTDSnippet = sXML
End Function
```

Looking at the `For Each PropertyDef In PropertyDefs` statement in the preceding code, we can see a use of the strange `Item.[_NewEnum]` syntax that the Visual Modeler generates for collection classes. An `Append` method has also been defined within the basic code module for this component to facilitate the appending of information to a string.

Using the `ClassManager` Component

Now that we have completely defined our class manager component, it is time to put it to work. Figure 7.12 shows the completed class hierarchy for the `ClassManager` library.

Suppose that we want to define the persistence information for the example using bonds discussed in Chapter 3. Table 7.1 provides the property and column information from that example.

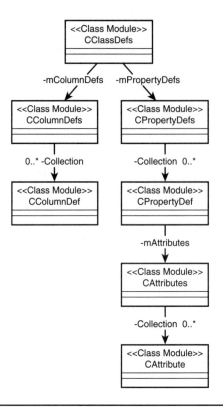

Figure 7.12 The ClassManager library in the UML graphical model.

Table 7.1   **Meta Information for the *CBond* Class Example**

Property Name	Column Name	Readable	Writeable
Id	Id	Yes	No
Name	Name	Yes	Yes
FaceValue	Face_Value	Yes	Yes
CouponRate	Coupon_Rate	Yes	Yes
BondTerm	Bond_Term	Yes	Yes
BondType	Bond_Type	Yes	Yes

Recalling this CBond example from Chapter 3, a class inheritance structure has been defined as shown in Figure 7.13.

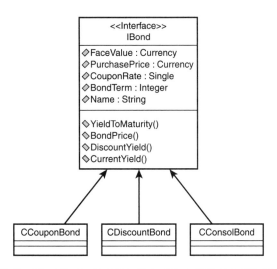

Figure 7.13   The bond inheritance structure.

To implement the CBond object structure, a new ActiveX DLL called BondLibrary is created in Visual Basic. Class modules for IBond, CDiscountBond, CConsolBond, and CCouponBond are added, and a reference to the ClassManager DLL is set.

Because this example follows an interface implementation mechanism, and the metadata for all subclasses is identical except for the TypeId property, it is more efficient to implement the majority of the mapping functionality in the IBond class. Each subclass implementing IBond will delegate most of this mapping functionality to Ibond. The subclass implementing the specific functionality will simply set the TypeId property. For example, using the information from Table 7.1, the initialization code for IBond in shown in Listing 7.9. Listings 7.10, 7.11, and 7.12 provide the specific initialization code needed by the CDiscountBond, CCouponBond, and CConsolBond classes, respectively.

Listing 7.9   **The *CClassDef* Instantiation code for *IBond***

```
Option Explicit
' declarations section
Private mClassDef As CClassDef
' code section
Private Sub Class_Initialize()
  Set mClassDef = New CClassDef
  With mClassDef
   .ReadLocation = "dbo.fdb.Table_Bond"
   .WriteLocation = "dbo.fdb.Table_Bond"
   .IdColumnName = "Id"
   .KeyColumnName = "Name"
   .TypeColumnName = "Bond_Type"
```

continues

Listing 7.9   **Continued**

```
    .AppendMapping "Id", "Id", True, False, ctNumber, "OID"
    .AppendMapping "Name", "Name", True, True, ctString, "Name"
    .AppendMapping "FaceValue", "Face_Value", True, False, ctNumber, "FaceValue"
    .AppendMapping "CouponRate", "Coupon_Rate", True, False,
                   ctNumber, "CouponRate"
    .AppendMapping "BondTerm", "Bond_Term", True, False, ctNumber, "BondTerm"
    .AppendMapping "BondType", "Bond_Type", True, False, ctNumber, "BondType"
  End With
End Sub
```

Listing 7.10   **The *CDiscountBond* Initialization Code Relative to *CClassDef***

```
Option Explicit
' declarations section
Private mIBondObject As IBond
' code section
Private Sub Class_Initialize()
 Set mIBondObject = New IBond
 mIBondObject.ClassDef.TypeId = 1
End Sub
```

Listing 7.11   **The *CCouponBond* Initialization Code Relative to *CClassDef***

```
Option Explicit
' declarations section
Private mIBondObject As IBond
' code section
Private Sub Class_Initialize()
 Set mIBondObject = New IBond
 mIBondObject.ClassDef.TypeId = 2
End Sub
```

Listing 7.12   **The *CConsolBond* Initialization Code Relative to *CClassDef***

```
Option Explicit
' declarations section
Private mIBondObject As IBond
' code section
Private Sub Class_Initialize()
 Set mIBondObject = New IBond
 mIBondObject.ClassDef.TypeId = 3
End Sub
```

The previous set of code listings shows the initialization process that provides the complete population of a ClassDef object for a given subclass. For example, looking at Listing 7.12, you can see that when a CConsolBond object is instantiated, the first statement in its Class_Initialize event instantiates an IBond object, which transfers control to the IBond object initialization routine. This routine proceeds to populate the vast majority of the ClassDef object. After returning to the initialization routine of CConsolBond, the only property left to set is the TypeId associated with the subclass.

Summary

This chapter has developed the first major component of the framework, the ClassManager. This component is responsible for managing the metadata that describes class definitions and the object-to-table mappings needed for object persistence. In development of this component, the Visual Modeler was used extensively to generate both the base classes and their collection class counterparts.

In the next chapter, attention turns to defining the second core component, the DataManager. This component will be used to interact with the database on behalf of the application. It will use information found in the ColumnDefs collection, defined in the CClassDef class, as one of its primary tools for generating the appropriate SQL needed to accomplish the tasks required by the application.

8

The DataManager Library

N OW THAT WE HAVE DEFINED AND IMPLEMENTED the ClassManager components, the capability exists to create class definitions programmatically through metadata. This component also provides the infrastructure to define the mappings of classes to tables and properties to columns within an RDBMS. Now, we need a mechanism to interact with the database itself. This mechanism, aptly called DataManager, is also an ActiveX DLL residing in the data services layer and is enlisted by the business layer. Its design is such that it is the sole interface into the database by the application. The business services layer is the only one, by design, that can enlist it into action because the user services layer does not have visibility to it. Although this library physically runs on the MTS machine, it does not run under an MTS package. Instead, the business layer running under an MTS package calls this library into action directly as an in-process COM component.

Design Theory

The goal in creating the DataManager component is to provide a library that can handle all interactions with a Relational Database Management System (RDBMS) on behalf of the application. The majority of these requests are in the form of basic CRUD (Create, Retrieve, Update, and Delete) processing that makes up a significant portion of any application. *Create* processing involves implementing the logic to create a new row in the database, copy the object state information into it, and generate a unique Object Identifier (OID) for the row and object. *Retrieve* processing involves formulating the necessary SQL SELECT statement to retrieve the desired information. *Update* processing involves implementing the logic to retrieve a row from the database for a given OID, copying the object state information into it and telling the RDMS to commit the changes back to the row. *Delete* processing involves formulating the necessary SQL DELETE statement to delete a specific row from the database based on a given OID.

In addition, stored procedure-calling capability might be needed as well to implement business functionality on the RDBMS. Such capability might also be needed to augment the standard CRUD routines if there are performance issues with the generic approach. Nonetheless, this framework attempts to remain as generic as possible and utilize just the core CRUD routines that will be implemented.

For the Retrieve and Delete portions of CRUD, an SQL composer is implemented. An SQL composer is nothing more than a generator that can take minimal information and create a valid SQL statement from it. The information used by the composer logic is taken directly from the metadata in a ClassDef object. Pieces of the composer logic that is used by the retrieve and delete methods are also used to assist in the create and update portions of CRUD. Abstracting this composition logic in the DataManager component in such a manner allows the application to automatically adapt to database changes. For example, as new column names are added to support new properties, existing functionality in the DataManager component is not broken. Because all database access is driven through the metadata in a ClassDef object, the DataManager component never must be redeveloped to support changes in the object hierarchy or database schema.

Although this approach is very flexible, the dynamic SQL generation implemented by the composer logic does have compilation overhead that repeats with every database transaction. As discussed in Chapter 6, "Development Fundamentals and Design Goals of an Enterprise Application," SQL Server views are precompiled and cached in a manner similar to stored procedures; thus, much of the overhead associated with the compilation process does not exist on retrievals from views. Assuming that the highest percentage of database activity on many applications is in retrievals and those retrievals are from views, the penalty from dynamic SQL generation might be negligible. On high-volume objects though, this might not be acceptable. On some database servers (although not on SQL Server 6.x), the system caches dynamic SQL statements so that it does not have to recompile. A significant amount of such dynamic SQL can overflow the cache and degrade overall database performance. In either case—high-volume objects or caching of dynamically generated SQL statements—a stored-procedure approach might be necessary.

Implementation

As in the previous chapters, the implementation discussion starts by defining a few core functions and helper classes, the latter of which allow for cleaner communication between the business and data layers.

Component-Level Functions

First, several core functions are defined within the context of a basic code module that is used by all classes within the component. The first function is a generic `RaiseError` function (see Listing 8.1), whose purpose is to wrap outbound errors with information to indicate that the source was within this component—an approach that will be adopted with many of the server-side components to be implemented in future chapters.

Listing 8.1   **A Core *RaiseError* Function Defined Within the DataManager Component**

```
Public Sub RaiseError(ErrorNumber As Long, _
                      Source As String, _
                      Description As String)
   Err.Raise ErrorNumber, _
             "[CDataManager]" & Source, _
             CStr(ErrorNumber) & " " & Description
End Sub
```

The second is a function (see Listing 8.2) to write error messages to the NT event log, called aptly `WriteNTLogEvent`. This is important for libraries running on a remote server, as discussed in the "Debugging" section in Chapter 6.

Listing 8.2   **The *WriteNTEventLog* Function**

```
Public Sub WriteNTLogEvent(ProcName As String, _
                           ErrNumber As Long, _
                           ErrDescription As String, _
                           ErrSource As String)
   Dim sMsg As String

   sMsg = "Error " & ErrNumber & " (" & ErrDescription & "), sourced by " & _
          ErrSource & " was reported in " & ProcName
   App.StartLogging "", vbLogToNT
   App.LogEvent sMsg, vbLogEventTypeWarning ' will only write in compiled mode
   Debug.Print sMsg ' will only write in run-time mode
End Sub
```

As can be seen from the code in Listing 8.2, two messages are actually written. One message is to the NT event log, which can occur only when the component is running in non-debug mode. The other message is to the debug window, which can only occur when the component is running in debug mode.

The CStringList Class

Because SQL statements are composed of lists of strings, a CStringList class is implemented to help manage this information. This class is used to store the individual string values that make up the select column list, the order by column list, and the where clause list necessary to formulate an SQL select statement. Figure 8.1 shows a Unified Modeling Language (UML) representation of the CStringList class.

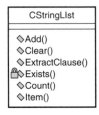

Figure 8.1   The CStringList class in the UML graphical model.

Methods

The CStringList class is straightforward in its design and implementation. The CStringList is modeled on the collection class metaphor, with the exception that the Add method has been modified to handle multiple strings at a time. Additionally, the Item method returns a string versus an object, as has otherwise been the case to this point. Several other methods have been added as well. A Clear method removes all the strings from the internal collection. An ExtractClause method formats the collection of strings into a single string separated by a delimiter character provided to the method. Additionally, a private method Exists has been created for use by the Add method to check to see whether a string already exists in the collection. The reason for this is so that errors are not raised because of an inadvertent programming error that attempts to add a duplicate key to the internal collection. Standard Count and Item methods are provided as well for iteration purposes, consistent with collection design. The code listing for CStringList is shown in Listing 8.3.

Listing 8.3   **Method Implementations for *CStringList***

```
Option Explicit
Private mCol As Collection

Public Sub Add(ParamArray StringItems() As Variant)
```

```vb
  Dim i As Integer
  For i = LBound(StringItems) To UBound(StringItems)
   If Not Exists(CStr(StringItems(i))) Then
    mCol.Add CStr(StringItems(i)), CStr(StringItems(i))
   End If
  Next i
End Sub

Private Sub Class_Initialize()
 Set mCol = New Collection
End Sub

Private Sub Class_Terminate()
 Set mCol = Nothing
End Sub

Public Sub Clear()
 Dim i As Integer
 For i = 1 To mCol.Count
  mCol.Remove 1
 Next i
End Sub

Public Function Count() As Integer
 Count = mCol.Count
End Function

Public Function Item(Index) As String
 Item = mCol.Item(Index)
End Function

Public Function ExtractClause(Delimiter As String) As String
 Dim i As Integer
 Dim s As String
 If mCol.Count > 0 Then
  For i = 1 To mCol.Count - 1
   s = s & mCol.Item(i) & " " & Delimiter & " "
  Next i
  s = s & mCol.Item(i)
 Else
  s = ""
 End If
 ExtractClause = s
End Function

Private Function Exists(SearchString As String) As Boolean
 On Error GoTo ErrorTrap
 Call mCol.Item(SearchString)
 Exists = True
 Exit Function
ErrorTrap:
 Exists = False
End Function
```

The `Add` method has been designed to accept multiple string values through a `ParamArray` parameter named `StringItems`. The method iterates through the individual strings in this `StringItems` array, adding them one at a time to the internal collection. A calling convention to this method might look like the following:

```
StringList.Add("Id","Name","Address1","Address2")
```

This design technique allows for a dynamically sized parameter list, making it easier to build the string list from the calling code.

The `ExtractClause` is implemented to help quickly turn the list of strings stored in the internal collection into a delimited version of itself. This is needed by the composer logic to create the `select`, `from`, and `where` predicates needed for the SQL statements. Continuing with the preceding example, a call to the `ExtractClause` method is simply

```
StringList.ExtractClause(",")
```

This call would produce the string `"Id , Name , Address1 , Address 2"` as its result.

The `CQueryParms` Class

With the capability to create lists of strings in tidy `CStringList` objects, attention turns to defining the parameters necessary to form an SQL query to support CRUD processing. To generate a retrieve or delete statement, the table name (or possible view name) as well as the row specification criteria must be known. Furthermore, for the `select` statement, the list of columns and optionally an order by list needs to be known. A `CQueryParms` class is defined to accommodate these requirements. Figure 8.2 shows a UML representation of the `CQueryParms` class.

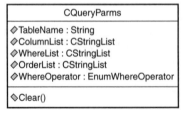

CQueryParms
◇TableName : String
◇ColumnList : CStringList
◇WhereList : CStringList
◇OrderList : CStringList
◇WhereOperator : EnumWhereOperator
◈Clear()

Figure 8.2   The `CQueryParms` class in the UML graphical model.

Properties

The `CQueryParms` class has a simple `TableName` property, along with three other properties that are instances of the `CStringList` class. These properties are `ColumnList`, `WhereList`, and `OrderList`. If a list of `where` conditions are used, a mechanism to tell

the composer logic how to concatenate them together must be defined; therefore, a
WhereOperator property is defined for this purpose.

Note

This framework does not support complex concatenation of where clauses in the CRUD processing
because it occurs relatively infrequently and because implementation of such support would be extremely
difficult. Anything that requires this level of complexity is usually outside the capabilities of basic CRUD,
and instead within the realm of the business logic domain. For these types of queries, a secondary path-
way on CDataManager is provided that can accept ad hoc SQL.

The code required to support these properties appears in Listing 8.4.

Listing 8.4   *CQueryParms* **Properties**

```
Public Enum EnumWhereOperator
 woAnd = 0
 woOr = 1
End Enum

Private mTableName As String
Private mColumnList As CStringList
Private mWhereList As CStringList
Private mOrderList As CStringList
Private mWhereOperator As EnumWhereOperator

Public Property Get TableName() As String
 TableName = mTableName
End Property

Public Property Let TableName(RHS As String)
 mTableName = RHS
End Property

Public Property Get ColumnList() As CStringList
 Set ColumnList = mColumnList
End Property

Public Property Get WhereList() As CStringList
 Set WhereList = mWhereList
End Property

Public Property Get OrderList() As CStringList
 Set OrderList = mOrderList
End Property

Public Property Get WhereOperator() As EnumWhereOperator
 WhereOperator = mWhereOperator
End Property
```

continues

Listing 8.4   **Continued**

```
Public Property Let WhereOperator(RHS As EnumWhereOperator)
 mWhereOperator = RHS
End PropertyWith

Private Sub Class_Initialize()
 Set mColumnList = New CStringList
 Set mWhereList = New CStringList
 Set mOrderList = New CStringList
End Sub

Private Sub Class_Terminate()
 Set mColumnList = Nothing
 Set mWhereList = Nothing
 Set mOrderList = Nothing
End Sub
```

Methods

Because `CQueryParms` is primarily a data container, its only method is `Clear`, which simply calls the `Clear` method of its `ColumnList`, `WhereList`, and `OrderList` properties.

```
Public Sub Clear()
 mColumnList.Clear
 mWhereList.Clear
 mOrderList.Clear
End Sub
```

The `CDataManager` Class

With these two base helper classes (`CStringList` and `CQueryParms`) defined, we can turn our attention to the implementation of the `CDataManager` class itself. Figure 8.3 shows a UML representation of `CDataManager`.

Properties

The `CDataManager` class is relatively property-free, save for a simple `Timeout` setting (see Listing 8.5). This property enables the developer to override the standard timeout setting if we think it will be exceeded. This property first checks to see if the instance has connected to the database, as would be the case if this property were set before the `DoConnect` method, discussed in the next section, is called. Although we can raise an error at this point, this framework has not implemented it in this manner.

Figure 8.3   The CDataManager class in the UML graphical model.

Listing 8.5   *CDataManager* **Properties**

```
Private mTimeout As Long

Public Property Let Timeout(RHS As Long)
 mTimeout = RHS
 If Not cnn Is Nothing Then
  cnn.CommandTimeout = RHS
 End If
End Property

Public Property Get Timeout() As Long
 Timeout = mTimeout
End Property
```

Methods

Because the underlying data repository is an RDBMS, and because Active Data Objects (ADO) is used to access it, we need to define methods that enable the class to connect to, and disconnect from, the database. These methods are called DoConnect and DoDisconnect, respectively, and they are shown in Listing 8.6. It is assumed that the business layer provides some form of direction on how to connect through a ConnectString parameter that follows ADO syntactical requirements.

Listing 8.6   **The** *DoConnect* **and** *DoDisconnect* **Methods on** *CDataManager*

```
Private cnn As ADODB.Connection

Public Function DoConnect(ConnectString As String) As Boolean
 On Error GoTo DoConnectErr

 Set cnn = New ADODB.Connection
```

continues

Listing 8.6   **Continued**

```
' do not change the cursor to server side
' in the following statement.
' there is a bug during insert
' operations when ODBC is used in
' conjunction with server side cursors...
cnn.CursorLocation = adUseClient
Call cnn.Open(ConnectString)
DoConnect = True
Exit Function

DoConnectErr:
  Call RaiseError(Err.Number, _
                 "CDataManager:DoConnect Method", _
                 Err.Description)
  DoConnect = False
End Function

Public Function DoDisconnect() As Boolean
  On Error GoTo DoDisconnectErr

  Call cnn.Close
  DoDisconnect = True
  Exit Function

DoDisconnectErr:
  Call RaiseError(Err.Number, _
                 "CDataManager:DoDisconnect Method", _
                 Err.Description)
  DoDisconnect = False
End Function
```

The DoConnect method is straightforward, following the requirements of ADO to set up a Connection object. One item to note is that the connection object's CursorLocation property is set to adUseClient because there are bugs if an ODBC provider is used, versus a native OLEDB provider. The DoDisconnect method is equally straightforward, requiring no further comment.

After a connection has been established, the capability to interact in CRUD fashion with the database exists using one of four methods. The first two methods, GetData and DeleteData, implement the retrieve and delete functionality, respectively. The second two methods, GetInsertableRS and GetUpdatableRS, are helpers to the business layer to implement the create and update functionality, respectively. The GetData, DeleteData, and GetUpdatableRS methods each take a CQueryParms object as an argument to provide the necessary information for the composer logic within the methods. The logic within the GetInsertableRS needs only a table name, so it does not require the CQueryParms object. A fifth method, ExecuteSQL, is implemented to accept ad hoc SQL statements for execution. This SQL statement can be the name of a stored procedure that does not have any OUT arguments defined. If the need to support such a stored procedure exists, a new method will have to be added to the CDataManager class.

The GetData method returns a Recordset object that can contain zero or more records. The GetData code is shown in Listing 8.7.

Listing 8.7   **The *GetData* Method of *CDataManager***

```
Public Function GetData(QueryParms As CQueryParms) As ADODB.Recordset
Dim rs As ADODB.Recordset
Dim rsField As ADODB.Field
Dim strColumns As String
Dim strWhere As String
Dim strOrder As String
Dim SQL As String
Dim i As Integer
Dim strWhereOperator As String

On Error GoTo GetDataErr

If QueryParms.TableName = "" Then
 Err.Raise dmeErrorNoTableName + vbObjectError, "", _
          LoadResString(dmeErrorNoTableName)
End If

  strWhereOperator = IIf(QueryParms.WhereOperator = woAnd, "AND", "OR")
  strColumns = QueryParms.ColumnList.ExtractClause(",")
  strWhere = QueryParms.WhereList.ExtractClause(strWhereOperator)
  strOrder = QueryParms.OrderList.ExtractClause(",")

 If strColumns = "" Then
  Err.Raise dmeErrorNoFromClause + vbObjectError, "", _
          LoadResString(dmeErrorNoFromClause)
 End If

 If strWhere = "" Then
  Err.Raise dmeErrorNoWhereClause + vbObjectError, "", _
  LoadResString(dmeErrorNoWhereClause)
 End If

 strWhere = " WHERE " & strWhere
 If strOrder <> "" Then strOrder = " ORDER BY " & strOrder

125 SQL = "SELECT DISTINCT " & strColumns & _
          " FROM " & QueryParms.TableName & " " & _
          strWhere & " " & strOrder

 Set rs = ExecuteSQL(SQL)

130 If Not (rs.EOF Or rs.BOF) Then
  Set GetData = rs
```

continues

Listing 8.7   **Continued**

```
  Set rs = Nothing
 Else
  Set GetData = Nothing
 End If

 Exit Function

GetDataErr:
 If Erl >= 125 Then
  '1. Details to EventLog
  Call WriteNTLogEvent("CDataManager:GetData", _
                  Err.Number, _
                  Err.Description & " <<CMD: " & SQL & ">>", _
                  Err.Source & " [" & Erl & "]")
   '2. Generic to client
   Err.Raise Err.Number, "CDataManager:GetData", _
            Err.Description & " <<CMD: " & SQL & ">>" & " [" & Erl & "]"
 Else
   '1. Details to EventLog
   Call WriteNTLogEvent("CDataManager:GetData",_
                  Err.Number, _
                  Err.Description, _
                  Err.Source & " [" & Erl & "]")

   '2. Generic to client
   Err.Raise Err.Number, "CDataManager:GetData", _
                  Err.Description & " [" & Erl & "]"
 End If

End Function
```

The GetData method starts by checking to make sure that the TableName property has been set, and then proceeds to expand the CStringList properties of the CQueryParm object. After these expanded strings are built, checks are made to ensure that there are FROM and WHERE clauses. If any violations of these conditions are found, errors are raised and the method is exited. The order by list is optional, so no checks for this property are made.

After all the necessary information has been expanded and validated, the method proceeds to form an SQL statement from the pieces. A DISTINCT keyword is placed in the statement to ensure that multiple identical rows are not returned, a condition that can happen if malformed views are in use. Although this offers some protection, it also limits the processing of Binary Large Object (BLOB) columns that cannot support this keyword. If your application requires BLOB support, you must implement specific functionality in addition to the framework presented.

After the SQL statement is ready, it is simply passed off to the `ExecuteSQL` method that will be discussed at the end of this section. To check for the existence of records, the `If Not(rs.EOF Or rs.BOF)` syntax is used. Although a `RecordCount` property is available on the `Recordset` object, it is not always correctly populated after a call, so the previous convention must be used for robustness.

Several other items to note relate to error handling. From the code, you can see that an error enumeration is used with a resource file providing the error messages. The purpose of this is to make it easier to modify the error messages without recompiling the code, as well as reducing the overall compiled code size. This also allows for multi-language support if so required by your application. The Visual Basic Resource Editor add-in can be used for this purpose. Figure 8.4 shows the Edit String Tables dialog that is used to build the resource file.

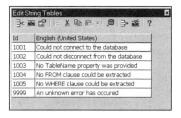

Figure 8.4   The Resource Editor.

The other item to note is that the error-handling routine has been designed to operate differently based on the line number at which the error occurred. For line items greater than 125, the SQL has been generated. Thus, it might be helpful to see the potentially offending SQL statement in the error stream for debugging purposes. Otherwise, the absence of an SQL statement in the error stream indicates that the error occurred prior to SQL formation.

The `DeleteData` method works in a fashion similar to `GetData`, and is able to delete one or more rows from the database. This method expects that the `TableName` and `WhereList` properties on the `CQueryParms` argument object have been populated. All other properties are ignored. This method proceeds to extract the `WHERE` clause and ensure that it has information, similar to the checking performed in the `GetData` method. In this case, the existence of `WHERE` clause information is vital, or else the resulting SQL statement will delete all rows in the table—a lesson learned the hard way. Again, the necessary SQL `DELETE` statement is generated and passed off to the `ExecuteSQL` method. The `DeleteData` code is shown in Listing 8.8.

Listing 8.8   **The *DeleteData* Method of *CDataManager***

```
Public Function DeleteData(QueryParms As CQueryParms) As Boolean
 Dim rs As ADODB.Recordset
 Dim strWhere As String
 Dim sSQL As String
 Dim strWhereOperator As String

 On Error GoTo ErrorTrap

 If QueryParms.TableName = "" Then
  Err.Raise dmeErrorNoTableName + vbObjectError, "", _
           LoadResString(dmeErrorNoTableName)
 End If

 StrWhereOperator = IIf(QueryParms.WhereOperator = woAnd, "AND", "OR")
 strWhere = QueryParms.WhereList.ExtractClause(strWhereOperator)

 If strWhere = "" Then
  Err.Raise dmeErrorNoWhereClause + vbObjectError, "", _
           LoadResString(dmeErrorNoWhereClause)
 End If

 strWhere = " WHERE " & strWhere
125 SQL = "DELETE FROM " & QueryParms.TableName & strWhere
 Set rs = ExecuteSQL(SQL)

ExitFunction:
 Exit Function
ErrorTrap:
  If Erl >= 125 Then
    '1.  Details to EventLog
    Call WriteNTLogEvent("CDataManager:DeleteData", _
                         Err.Number, _
                         Err.Description & " <<CMD: " & SQL & ">>", _
                         Err.Source & " [" & Erl & "]")

    '2.  Generic to client
    Err.Raise Err.Number, "CDataManager:DeleteData", _
           Err.Description & " <<CMD: " & SQL & ">>" & " [" & Erl & "]"
  Else
    '1.  Details to EventLog
    Call WriteNTLogEvent("CDataManager:DeleteData", _
                         Err.Number, Err.Description, _
                         Err.Source & " [" & Erl & "]")

    '2.  Generic to client
    Err.Raise Err.Number, "CDataManager:DeleteData", _
           Err.Description & " [" & Erl & "]"
  End If
End Function
```

Now that the two simpler components of CRUD have been implemented, attention turns to the more complex Create and Update portions of the acronym. Although the dynamic SQL generation process can be followed as in the previous two methods, there are issues with this approach. Specifically, there are concerns with how to handle embedded quotes in the SQL data. Rather than dealing with this issue in INSERT and UPDATE statements, it is easier to work with Recordset objects.

The GetInsertableRS is defined to support creates, requiring only a TableName parameter. The code for GetInsertableRS is shown in Listing 8.9.

Listing 8.9   **The *GetInsertableRS* Method on *CDataManagers***

```
Public Function GetInsertableRS(TableName As String) As ADODB.Recordset
Dim rs As ADODB.Recordset
Dim SQL As String

On Error GoTo ErrorTrap

SQL = "select * from " & TableName & " where Id = 0"
'should populate with an empty row, but all column definitions

Set rs = ExecuteSQL(SQL)
Set GetInsertableRS = rs
Set rs = Nothing
Exit Function

ErrorTrap:
Call RaiseError(Err.Number, "CDataManager:UpdateData Method", Err.Description)
End Function
```

This method forms a simple SQL SELECT statement of the form "SELECT * FROM TableName WHERE Id=0". This has the effect of creating an empty Recordset object that has all the columns of the underlying table. This empty Recordset object is passed back to the business layer to receive the object state information. The business layer calls the Update method on the Recordset object, retrieves the auto-generated OID field generated by SQL Server, and sets the value in the object.

Update processing is done in a similar fashion, except that a CQueryParms object is required as an argument. This CQueryParms object exactly matches the criteria set forth in the GetData case, except that the TableName property must be the underlying table rather than a view. Because the composition logic to retrieve an updateable Recordset object is the same as that already implemented in the GetData method, the GetUpdatableRS method taps in to it simply by passing the CQueryParm object through to it and passing the result back out. The simple code for GetUpdatableRS is given in Listing 8.10.

Listing 8.10 **The *GetUpdatableRS* Method on *CDataManager***

```
Public Function GetUpdatableRS(QueryParms As CQueryParms) As ADODB.Recordset
 On Error GoTo ErrorTrap
 Set GetUpdatableRS = GetData(QueryParms)
 Exit Function

ErrorTrap:
 Call RaiseError(Err.Number, _
                 "CDataManager:GetUpdatableRS Method", _
                 Err.Description)
 End Function
```

The final data access method of the CDataManager class is the ExecuteSQL method that is used by each of the other four CRUD components. This method is also exposed to the outside world for use directly by the business layer if something beyond normal CRUD processing must be accomplished. As stated several times in this chapter already, an example might include the one-shot execution of a stored procedure. As discussed in Chapter 13, "Interoperability," these types of needs arise when integrating to legacy systems that do not follow the framework outlined here. The code for the ExecuteSQL method is shown in Listing 8.11.

Listing 8.11 **The *ExecuteSQL* Method on *CDataManager***

```
Public Function ExecuteSQL(SQL As String, _
                          Optional CursorMode As CursorTypeEnum, _
                          Optional LockMode As LockTypeEnum) As ADODB.Recordset
 Dim rs As New ADODB.Recordset

  If IsMissing(CursorMode) Then
    CursorMode = adOpenKeyset
  End If

  If IsMissing(LockMode) Then
    LockMode = adLockOptimistic
  End If

  rs.Open SQL, cnn, CursorMode, LockMode, adCmdText
  Set ExecuteSQL = rs
End Function
```

The ExecuteSQL method can accept simply an SQL statement as an argument, or it can be more finely controlled through the use of two optional parameters to control the cursor and lock types used by the query. Although the default values are acceptable for most situations, there might be times when these values need to be adjusted for performance or concurrency reasons.

With all the effort that has gone into creating the CDataManager class, you might dread having to manually create the collection class associated with this CDataManager class. Even though the Visual Modeler was not used to create the CDataManager class, it can still be used to generate a collection class. To do this, the DataManager component must be reverse engineered. Follow these steps to do so:

1. First, click the DataManager component in Visual Basic's Project Explorer window.

2. Next, select the Add-Ins menu, Visual Modeler, Reverse Engineering Wizard.

3. In the Selection of a Model dialog box that appears, click the New button. This will start the Visual Modeler and launch the Reverse Engineering Wizard dialog.

4. Click the Next button to arrive at the Selection of Project Items step, as shown in Figure 8.5.

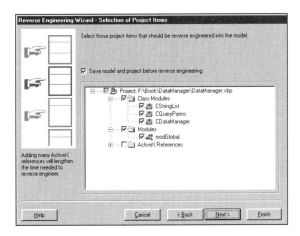

Figure 8.5   The Reverse Engineering Wizard, Selection of Project Items step in the Visual Modeler.

5. Leaving the default items selected, click the Next button to arrive at the Assignment of Project Items step. Drag each project item onto the Data Services logical package to make the appropriate layer assignment.

6. Click once again on the Next button to bring up a summary of the activities that the Visual Modeler is about to perform, along with an estimated time to complete.

7. Click the Finish button to start the reverse engineering process. Upon completion, a summary step appears. When you close the wizard, the newly reverse-engineered classes appear under the Data Services folder of the tree view on the left side of the Visual Modeler screen.

8. Right-click the `CDataManager` class, and then select the Generate Code menu item to launch the Code Generation Wizard discussed in Chapter 7, "The ClassManager Library."

9. On the Class Options step of the Preview step, give the collection class the name `CDataManagers`. The only other changes in this preview process are to deselect any of the Generate Variable options in the wizard to prevent regeneration of existing properties.

10. When generation is complete, be sure to move all the members in the Delete These Members list to the Keep These Members List during the Delete Members in Class step of the wizard.

Although this might seem a bit cumbersome, it is much faster to generate collection classes in this manner when you are familiar with the Visual Modeler.

Summary

In this chapter, we built the data-layer component `DataManager` that implements the business layer's interface into the RDBMS. This component also provides the SQL composition necessary to enable row creation, retrieval, update and deletion using metadata from the `ClassManager` component.

The next chapter introduces and implements the multipart business object paradigm. It uses both the `DataManager` and `ClassManager` components as its foundation, and also incorporates the distribution topics covered in Chapter 5, "Distribution Considerations." The next chapter also implements the first component that is run under the control of Microsoft Transaction Server.

9

A Two-Part, Distributed Business Object

W E HAVE SPENT A SIGNIFICANT AMOUNT of time getting ready for this chapter. The multi-part business object defined here represents impurity at its finest, not only in how we define our business layer, but also in how we make it work across the client and application tiers of the system. Before we delve into the subject matter, be prepared to become slightly upset when we split our "pure" business object into two "impure" components. Also be prepared for further distress when we remove many of the business-specific methods on our classes and move them onto an application-specific surrogate class. Our reasoning for breaking with traditional object-oriented design theory has to do with our goal of maximum reuse and performance in a distributed object world. Hopefully, we will make our decision factors clear as we work our way through this chapter.

Design Theory

If we analyze the drawbacks of a pure layer-to-tier mapping, the most obvious issue is that of round trip calls that must be made between the user layer that receives the user input and the business layer that validates the input. Well-designed applications should be capable of providing validation to the user as soon as possible. If the entire business layer resides on a middle tier, then even simple property validation becomes programmatically tedious. To accomplish this, the client must move one or more of the object properties into the chosen transport structure, make a validation request with this information over the DCOM boundary, wait for a response, and handle the results accordingly. This technique represents a significant amount of effort and bandwidth to find out that the user entered an invalid date of "June 31, 1999." This is even more frustrating if the client is sitting in Singapore and the server is sitting in Texas over a WAN connection. Thus, it would be advantageous to move some of this simple functionality to the client tier without having to move the entire business layer with it.

Thus, we base our design goals for a multi-part business object upon our desire to have as much business functionality in a centrally controlled location as possible. These design goals include the following:

- Provide fast response time to user validation over a potentially slow network connection.
- Make our business layer functionality available to the widest range of consumers, whether they connect by a Visual Basic (VB) client or an Active Server Pages (ASP)-driven Web interface.
- Give the capability to add support for new business objects in as straightforward a manner as possible.
- Build our client as thin as possible without sacrificing an efficient interface in the process.

How do we make such a split in the business object? The most obvious solution is to move the property level validation over to the client tier while leaving the core business logic and data layer interfaces on the application tier. In fact, this is exactly what this framework does. Although this approach does not necessarily represent a new concept, we take it a bit further with our architecture. If we simply make the split and nothing more, we create two halves of a business object—one that lives on the application tier and one that lives on the client tier. This approach can lead to some duplication of similar functionality across the two halves of the business object. To avoid such duplication, we define our business class on the client tier and implement basic property-level validation. On the application tier, we implement a single business application class that can serve the CRUD (Create, Retrieve, Update, and Delete) requirements of all business classes implemented on the client, in essence creating a pseudo object-request broker. To do this, we use metadata defined using our ClassManager component developed in the previous chapter. We use this same application tier component as a surrogate to implement application-level business logic. Thus, we have created a user-centric component (the object that resides on the client) and a business-centric component (the application-tier component).

From this point forward, we use a modified version of the Northwind database that ships with Visual Basic as the example for our architecture. Figure 9.1 shows the object model for this database.

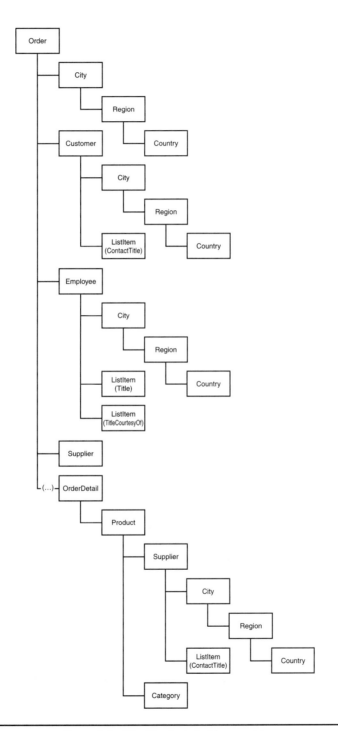

Figure 9.1   The Northwind object model.

The modifications we have made to the database include normalization and the implementation of our database development standards to support our architecture. We have created a ListItem object to provide a lookup mechanism for simple data normalization purposes. We have also made objects out of the city, region, and country entities. The reasons for doing this are for normalization and a desire to preserve future flexibility. At some point in the future, we might want to extend our application to track information specific to a city, region, or country. An example might be a country's telephone dialing prefix. By having an object instead of a simple text field that stores the country name, we can simply add the DialingPrefix property to the definition for the country class.

We can define a business layer component called NWServer that runs on a server-based tier. For congruence, let us call the client-side mate to this component NWClient. Although we can implement NWServer directly with minimal issue, if we were to implement a second and then third such application tier component for other applications, we would see that there is a significant amount of similar functionality between them. The major difference is just in the setup of the ClassDefs collection used to store the metadata for our classes. This being the case, we define an interface definition that we call IAppServer, primarily to deliver the CRUD functionality needed by our business objects. Through several specific methods implemented on IAppServer, we can generate the object state information necessary to instantiate existing user-centric business objects defined within NWClient (that is, from the application server to client). Going the other direction (from the client to the application server), IAppServer can also create new instances, receive state information necessary to update existing object instances, and delete instances of business objects on behalf of NWClient. Figure 9.2 shows the server side of this set of components.

Implementation

Because we have already spent a lot of effort in building helper classes in previous chapters, our server-side component of the business layer does not need any additional direct helper classes of its own. We define the data-centric form of the multi-part business object first in terms of an interface definition IAppServer. This interface implements the majority of the functionality necessary to implement CRUD processing using our ClassManager and DataManager libraries. By subsequently implementing this interface on a class called CNWServer, we gain access to that functionality.

COM purity would have us define an enumeration to identify our class types that we are implementing on the server side. The real world tells us that binary compatibility issues down the road will have us rolling the dice too many times with each series of recompilations of the server, so we stick to using constants. Although we still force a recompile whenever we add a new class type to our server, VB is not going to see any changes in the enumeration that would otherwise break compatibility. Breaking compatibility across the DCOM boundary forces us to redeploy server- and client-side components. Another benefit of the constant approach is that it enables us to build the

IAppServer component for use by many applications, where an enumeration would force us to have to reimplement the CRUD functionality in a cut-and-paste fashion.

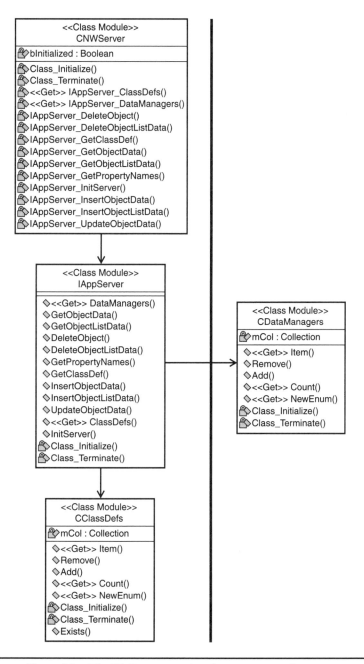

Figure 9.2   The UML representation for IAppServer and NWServer.

An MTS Primer

Before going into the details of our `IAppServer` and `CNWServer` classes, we must spend a few paragraphs talking about Microsoft Transaction Server (MTS) and the features we are interested in for our framework. Although we can easily drop any ActiveX DLL into MTS, we cannot take advantage of its transactional features and object pooling mechanisms unless we program specifically for them.

The `ObjectControl` Interface

Implementation of the `ObjectControl` interface allows our MTS-hosted object to perform the necessary initialization and cleanup activities as it is activated and deactivated. To do this, we simply implement the `Activate` and `Deactivate` methods of this interface. The interface also defines a method called `CanBePooled`, which should simply return `False`. Microsoft put this last method in without implementing anything in MTS that actually uses it. For future compatibility safety, leave it set to `False`. The following code shows the use of the simple implementation of these methods:

```
Private Sub ObjectControl_Activate()
  Set ObjCtx = GetObjectContext
End Sub

Private Function ObjectControl_CanBePooled() As Boolean
  ObjectControl_CanBePooled = False
End Function

Private Sub ObjectControl_Deactivate()
  Set ObjCtx = Nothing
End Sub
```

The `Activate` and `Deactivate` methods can be viewed similarly to the `Class_Initialize` and `Class_Terminate` events in non-MTS objects. These methods are called as objects are activated and deactivated. Although we will not be maintaining state in our MTS objects, the `Activate` event would be the mechanism used to reestablish state. Similarly, the `Deactivate` event can be used to restore the object back to the state in which you found it.

The `ObjectContext` Class

The `ObjectContext` class is defined in the Microsoft Transaction Server Type Library (`mtxas.dll`). As the name implies, the `ObjectContext` is an object that accesses the current object's context. *Context*, in this case, provides information about the current object's execution environment within MTS. This includes information about our parent and, if used, the transaction in which we are running. A *transaction* is a grouping mechanism that allows a single object or disparate set of objects to interact with a database in a manner such that all interactions must complete successfully or every interaction is rolled back.

Examples of transactional processing include a series of database insertions that must all complete successfully for the entire set to be valid. For example, suppose we are inserting information for a customer and its associated billing address using a CCustomer class and a CAddress class. Let us also assume that an address must be present for the customer to be valid. Suppose the CCustomer object inserts its state into the database without issue. Next, the CAddress object attempts to insert itself into the database, but it fails. The CAddress object has no mechanism to know what dependent inserts have happened before it to signal to them that there was a problem. However, by grouping all such interactions within the context of a transaction, any downstream failure will signal to MTS to roll back all interactions within the same transaction that have happened up to the point of failure.

To create an instance of an ObjectContext class, an MTS object must call the GetObjectContext function that is also defined in the MTS Type Library. By performing the GetObjectContext function, we are requesting MTS to either create a transaction on our behalf or enlist us into the existing transaction of our parent object. In either case, MTS starts monitoring our interactions with the database. Within Visual Basic, we can set our transaction mode for a class within the class properties page. The specific property is MTSTransactionMode, which can take on values of NotAnMTSObject, NoTransactions, RequiresTransactions, UsesTransactions, and RequiresNewTransactions. Table 9.1 provides the uses of these property settings.

Table 9.1   **The Property Settings for *MTSTransactionMode***

Property Setting	Description
NotAnMTSObject	The class does not support Transaction Server. No object context is created for this class.
NoTransactions	The class does not support transactions and does not run within the scope of a transaction. An object context is created but no transaction is created.
RequiresTransactions	The class requires transactions. When an object is created, it inherits the transaction of its parent. If no parent transaction exists then one is created.
UsesTransactions	The class can use transactions. When an object is created, it inherits the transaction of its parent. If no parent transaction exists, one is not created.
RequiresNewTransactions	The class must use its own transaction. When an object is created, a new transaction is created.

If we want to create any further MTS objects from within our existing MTS object that can access our transaction, we must use the CreateInstance method of the ObjectContext class to do so.

For an object to force a rollback of the transaction, the SetAbort method of ObjectContext must be called. This tells MTS to start the rollback process. This method call also has the caveat that the object that calls the SetAbort method is immediately deactivated. Likewise, ObjectContext contains a SetComplete method that signals to MTS that the object has completed successfully. Again, a call to this method immediately deactivates the object.

Database Connection Pooling

MTS is capable of sharing a database connection across multiple objects, even if those connections are not created directly from MTS objects. The reason for this latter statement is that MTS is not performing the work necessary to enable pooling. Instead, the OLE DB provider or the ODBC resource dispenser takes ownership of this task. In either case, this pooling is based simply on the connection string. If a connection with a given connection string has been used before, and that database connection is inactive, then the existing connection is used. If the database connection is either in use or non-existent then a new connection is created.

For ODBC version 3.x, pooling is controlled at the database driver level through a CPTimeout registry setting. Values greater than zero tell the ODBC driver to keep the driver in the connection pool for the specified number of seconds.

IAppServer/CNWServer

We will build out our application side classes, IAppServer and CNWServer, in a parallel fashion. In some cases, we will implement methods on IAppServer and provide hooks into it by simply calling into an IAppServer object instantiated on CNWServer. In other cases, the methods on IAppServer are simply abstract in nature and will require full implementation by our CNWServer class with no calls into IAppServer.

Getting Started

To start our development of our IAppServer and CNWServer classes, we must first create two new ActiveX DLL projects within Visual Basic. The first project will be called AppServer, and the second will be called NWServer. We define our IAppServer class within our AppServer project. Likewise, we define in our NWServer the CNWServer class that implements IAppServer. Both the IAppServer and NWServer components will be hosted in MTS, so our normal programming model for interface implementation will change somewhat as we go through our development. To start with, for our CNWServer object to create a reference to an IAppServer object, it must use a CreateObject statement, and it must do so within the Activate event of the ObjectControl rather than the Class_Initialize event. The following code shows this new initialization mechanism:

```
Private Sub ObjectControl_Activate()
  Set ObjCtx = GetObjectContext
  Set mIAppServer = ObjCtx.CreateInstance("AppServer.IAppServer")
End Sub

Private Function ObjectControl_CanBePooled() As Boolean
  ObjectControl_CanBePooled = False
End Function

Private Sub ObjectControl_Deactivate()
  Set mIAppServer = Nothing
  Set ObjCtx = Nothing
End Sub
```

Note that we are using the `CreateInstance` method of the `ObjectContext` object to create our `IAppServer` object. This is because we want to enlist `IAppServer` in our transaction.

Our next step is to define the set of classes supported by the `CNWServer` component. We first do this by adding a basic code module with class-type constants to our `NWServer` project. These constants will be used as indexes into our class definitions. They also will form the common language with the `CNWClient` class. If we are using SourceSafe, we can share this file between both the client and application tiers; otherwise, we must create matching copies of the file. The following listing shows the constant definitions for the Northwind application:

```
Public Const CT_CATEGORY As Integer = 1
Public Const CT_CITY As Integer = 2
Public Const CT_COUNTRY As Integer = 3
Public Const CT_CUSTOMER As Integer = 4
Public Const CT_EMPLOYEE As Integer = 5
Public Const CT_LIST_ITEM As Integer = 6
Public Const CT_ORDER As Integer = 7
Public Const CT_ORDER_DETAIL As Integer = 8
Public Const CT_PRODUCT As Integer = 9
Public Const CT_REGION As Integer = 10
Public Const CT_SHIPPER As Integer = 11
Public Const CT_SUPPLIER As Integer = 12
```

To create the class definitions, we must define an abstract method `InitServer` on `IAppServer` and provide its implementation on `CNWServer`. This method is responsible for defining and connecting to each `CDataManager` object required by `NWServer` (one `DataManager` object is required for each database). This method will be called before any external activity to ensure that the object context is valid and the databases are defined and connected. Listing 9.1 shows the implementation of the `InitServer` method for our `NWServer` class.

Listing 9.1   **The *InitServer* Method Implemented on *CNWServer***

```
Private Function IAppServer_InitServer() As Boolean
  Dim DataManager As CDataManager
  Dim ClassDef As CClassDef
  Dim ConnectString As String

  On Error GoTo NoInit
  If ObjCtx Is Nothing Then
    Set ObjCtx = GetObjectContext
    Set mIAppServer = ObjCtx.CreateInstance("AppServer.IAppServer")
  End If

  If mIAppServer.DataManagers.Count = 0 Then

    Set DataManager = New CDataManager

    ConnectString = GetSetting("Northwind", "Databases", "NWIND", "")
    If ConnectString = "" Then GoTo NoInit
    If Not DataManager.DoConnect(ConnectString) Then GoTo NoInit

    Call mIAppServer.DataManagers.Add(DataManager, "NWIND")
  End If

Init:
  IAppServer_InitServer = True
  Exit Function

NoInit:
    IAppServer_InitServer = False
    '1.  Details to EventLog
    Call WriteNTLogEvent("NWServer:InitServer", Err.Number, _
                         Err.Description, Err.Source)
    '2.  Generic to client - passed back on error stack
    Err.Raise Err.Number, "NWServer:InitServer", _
                         Err.Description & " [" & Erl & "]"
    ObjCtx.SetAbort
End Function
```

Although the code in Listing 9.1 looks relatively simple, there are several very important elements to it. First, notice the `If ObjCtx Is Nothing Then` statement. We must perform this check here because the `ObjCtx` might be invalid at this point. As we will see later in this chapter, some of the methods on `IAppServer` and `CNWServer` call other internal methods to perform database updates or inserts. When those methods complete, the `SetComplete` method must be called to indicate to MTS that the transaction can be committed. Calling `SetComplete` invalidates our object context, so we must reestablish it here.

Also notice that if we enter into the error-handling region of the code at the bottom, we call the `SetAbort` method of the object context. The reason for this call is so we can signal to MTS that something went awry and we cannot participate in the transaction. We call it last because it immediately passes control to the `Deactivate` method on the object control, and our error-handling activities would not complete otherwise.

Also notice that we are retrieving the connection strings for the database from the registry. These connection strings correspond to the ADO `ConnectString` property on the `Connection` object. At this point, we have created a DSN to the `NWND2.MDB` database; therefore, the `ConnectString` parameter is set to `"Provider=MSDASQL;DSN=NORTHWIND"`. For a DSN-less version, we can have a connection string that looks something like

```
"Provider=Microsoft.Jet.OLEDB.4.0;Data Source=F: \NWServer\Nwind2.mdb"
```

The second abstract method to implement is `GetClassDef`. The `GetClassDef` method is responsible for defining the `CClassDef` object for each class type implemented by the system. Rather than defining all class types at the initialization of the object, we build them in a Just-In-Time (JIT) fashion, as we need them. We implement this method as a simple case statement switched on the class type constant. If we have not defined the requested class type yet, we build and save it. Subsequent requests within the same object activation session are then much faster. This technique enables us to balance between fast initialization and fast response time. The code for the `GetClassDef` method for `NWAppServer` appears in Listing 9.2.

Listing 9.2   **The *GetClassDef* Method Implemented on *CNWServer***

```
Private Function IAppServer_GetClassDef(ByVal ClassId As Integer) As CClassDef
Dim ClassDef As CClassDef

  Call IAppServer_InitServer
  If Not mIAppServer.ClassDefs.Exists(CStr(ClassId)) Then

    Select Case ClassId

      Case CT_CATEGORY
        Set ClassDef = New CClassDef
        With ClassDef
          .DatabaseName = "NWIND"
          .ReadLocation = "Table_Category"
          .WriteLocation = "Table_Category"
          .IdColumnName = "Id"
          .OrderByColumnName = "Name"

          .AppendMapping "Id", "Id", True, False, "ID"
          .AppendMapping "Name", "Name", True, True, "NAME"
          .AppendMapping "Description", "Description", True, True, _
                         "DESCRIPTION"
```

continues

Listing 9.2 **Continued**

```
    End With
    Call mIAppServer.ClassDefs.Add(ClassDef, CStr(CT_CATEGORY))

Case CT_CITY
  Set ClassDef = New CClassDef
  With ClassDef
    .DatabaseName = "NWIND"
    .ReadLocation = "Table_City"
    .WriteLocation = "Table_City"
    .IdColumnName = "Id"
    .ParentIdColumnName = "Region_Id"
    .OrderByColumnName = "Name"

    .AppendMapping "Id", "Id", True, False, "ID"
    .AppendMapping "RegionId", "Region_Id", True, True, "REGION_ID"
    .AppendMapping "Name", "Name", True, True, "NAME"
  End With
  Call mIAppServer.ClassDefs.Add(ClassDef, CStr(CT_CITY))

Case CT_COUNTRY
  Set ClassDef = New CClassDef
  With ClassDef
    .DatabaseName = "NWIND"
    .ReadLocation = "Table_Country"
    .WriteLocation = "Table_Country"
    .IdColumnName = "Id"
    .OrderByColumnName = "Name"

    .AppendMapping "Id", "Id", True, False, "ID"
    .AppendMapping "Name", "Name", True, True, "NAME"
  End With
  Call mIAppServer.ClassDefs.Add(ClassDef, CStr(CT_COUNTRY))

Case CT_CUSTOMER
  Set ClassDef = New CClassDef
  With ClassDef
    .DatabaseName = "NWIND"
    .ReadLocation = "View_Customer"
    .WriteLocation = "Table_Customer"
    .IdColumnName = "Id"
    .OrderByColumnName = "Company_Name"

    .AppendMapping "Id", "Id", True, False, "ID"
    .AppendMapping "CustomerCode", "Customer_Code", True, True, _
                   "CUSTOMER_CODE"
    .AppendMapping "CompanyName", "Company_Name", True, True, _
                   "COMPANY_NAME"
    .AppendMapping "ContactName", "Contact_Name", True, True, _
                   "CONTACT_NAME"
    .AppendMapping "ContactTitleId", "Contact_Title_Id", True, True, _
                   "CONTACT_TITLE_ID"
```

```
        .AppendMapping "ContactTitle", "Contact_Title", True, False, _
                      "CONTACT_TITLE"
        .AppendMapping "Address", "Address", True, True, "ADDRESS"
        .AppendMapping "PostalCode", "Postal_Code", True, True, "POSTAL_CODE"
        .AppendMapping "CountryId", "Country_Id", True, False, "COUNTRY_ID"
        .AppendMapping "Country", "Country", True, False, "COUNTRY"
        .AppendMapping "RegionId", "Region_Id", True, False, "REGION_ID"
        .AppendMapping "Region", "Region", True, False, "REGION"
        .AppendMapping "CityId", "City_Id", True, True, "CITY_ID"
        .AppendMapping "City", "City", True, False, "CITY"
        .AppendMapping "Phone", "Phone", True, True, "PHONE"
        .AppendMapping "Fax", "Fax", True, True, "FAX"
    End With
    Call mIAppServer.ClassDefs.Add(ClassDef, CStr(CT_CUSTOMER))

  Case CT_EMPLOYEE
    Set ClassDef = New CClassDef
    With ClassDef
      .DatabaseName = "NWIND"
      .ReadLocation = "View_Employee"
      .WriteLocation = "Table_Employee"
      .IdColumnName = "Id"
      .OrderByColumnName = "Last_Name, First_Name"

      .AppendMapping "Id", "Id", True, False, "ID"
      .AppendMapping "LastName", "Last_Name", True, True, "LAST_NAME"
      .AppendMapping "FirstName", "First_Name", True, True, "FIRST_NAME"
      .AppendMapping "TitleId", "Title_Id", True, True, "TITLE_ID"
      .AppendMapping "Title", "Title", True, False, "TITLE"
      .AppendMapping "TitleOfCourtesyId", "Title_Of_Courtesy_Id", _
                    True, True, "TITLE_OF_COURTESY_ID"
      .AppendMapping "TitleOfCourtesy", "Title_Of_Courtesy", _
                    True, False, "TITLE_OF_COURTESY"
      .AppendMapping "BirthDate", "Birth_Date", True, True, "BIRTH_DATE"
      .AppendMapping "HireDate", "Hire_Date", True, True, "HIRE_DATE"
      .AppendMapping "Address", "Address", True, True, "ADDRESS"
      .AppendMapping "PostalCode", "Postal_Code", True, True, "POSTAL_CODE"
      .AppendMapping "HomePhone", "Home_Phone", True, True, "HOME_PHONE"
      .AppendMapping "Extension", "Extension", True, True, "EXTENSION"
      .AppendMapping "Notes", "Notes", True, True, "NOTES"
      .AppendMapping "ReportsToId", "Reports_To_Id", _
                    True, True, "REPORTS_TO_ID"
      .AppendMapping "ReportsToLastName", "Reports_To_Last_Name", _
                    True, False, "REPORTS_TO_LAST_NAME"
      .AppendMapping "ReportsToFirstName", "Reports_To_First_Name", _
                    True, False, "REPORTS_TO_FIRST_NAME"
      .AppendMapping "CountryId", "Country_Id", True, False, "COUNTRY_ID"
      .AppendMapping "Country", "Country", True, False, "COUNTRY"
      .AppendMapping "RegionId", "Region_Id", True, False, "REGION_ID"
      .AppendMapping "Region", "Region", True, False, "REGION"
      .AppendMapping "CityId", "City_Id", True, True, "CITY_ID"
```

continues

Listing 9.2 **Continued**

```
                  .AppendMapping "City", "City", True, False, "CITY"
                End With
                Call mIAppServer.ClassDefs.Add(ClassDef, CStr(CT_EMPLOYEE))

          Case CT_LIST_ITEM
            Set ClassDef = New CClassDef
            With ClassDef
              .DatabaseName = "NWIND"
              .ReadLocation = "Table_List"
              .WriteLocation = "Table_List"
              .IdColumnName = "Id"
              .ParentIdColumnName = "List_Id"
              .OrderByColumnName = "Sort"

              .AppendMapping "Id", "Id", True, False, "ID"
              .AppendMapping "ListId", "List_Id", True, True, "LIST_ID"
              .AppendMapping "Item", "Item", True, True, "ITEM"
              .AppendMapping "Sort", "Sort", True, True, "SORT"
            End With
            Call mIAppServer.ClassDefs.Add(ClassDef, CStr(CT_LIST_ITEM))

          Case CT_ORDER
            Set ClassDef = New CClassDef
            With ClassDef
              .DatabaseName = "NWIND"
              .ReadLocation = "View_Order"
              .WriteLocation = "Table_Order"
              .IdColumnName = "Id"

              .AppendMapping "Id", "Id", True, False, "ID"
              .AppendMapping "CustomerId", "Customer_Id", True, True, "CUSTOMER_ID"
              .AppendMapping "CustomerName", "Customer_Name", _
                             True, False, "CUSTOMER"
              .AppendMapping "EmployeeId", "Employee_Id", True, True, "EMPLOYEE_ID"
              .AppendMapping "EmployeeLastName", "Employee_Last_Name", _
                             True, False, "EMPLOYEE_LAST_NAME"
              .AppendMapping "EmployeeFirstName", "Employee_First_Name", _
                             True, False, "EMPLOYEE_FIRST_NAME"
              .AppendMapping "OrderDate", "Order_Date", True, True, "ORDER_DATE"
              .AppendMapping "RequiredDate", "Required_Date", _
                             True, True, "REQUIRED_DATE"
              .AppendMapping "ShippedDate", "Shipped_Date", _
                             True, True, "SHIPPED_DATE"
              .AppendMapping "ShipperId", "Shipper_Id", True, True, "SHIPPER_ID"
              .AppendMapping "ShipperName", "Shipper_Name", _
                             True, False, "SHIPPER_NAME"
              .AppendMapping "FreightCost", "Freight_Cost", _
                             True, True, "FREIGHT_COST"
              .AppendMapping "ShipToName", "Ship_To_Name", _
                             True, True, "SHIP_TO_NAME"
```

```
      .AppendMapping "ShipToAddress", "Ship_To_Address", _
                     True, True, "SHIP_TO_ADDRESS"
      .AppendMapping "ShipToPostalCode", "Ship_To_Postal_Code", _
                     True, True, "SHIP_TO_POSTAL_CODE"
      .AppendMapping "ShipToCountryId", "Ship_To_Country_Id", _
                     True, False, "SHIP_TO_COUNTRY_ID"
      .AppendMapping "ShipToCountry", "Ship_To_Country", _
                     True, False, "SHIP_TO_COUNTRY"
      .AppendMapping "ShipToRegionId", "Ship_To_Region_Id", _
                     True, False, "SHIP_TO_REGION_ID"
      .AppendMapping "ShipToRegion", "Ship_To_Region", _
                     True, False, "SHIP_TO_REGION"
      .AppendMapping "ShipToCityId", "Ship_To_City_Id", _
                     True, True, "SHIP_TO_CITY_ID"
      .AppendMapping "ShipToCity", "Ship_To_City", _
                     True, False, "SHIP_TO_CITY"
   End With
   Call mIAppServer.ClassDefs.Add(ClassDef, CStr(CT_ORDER))

Case CT_ORDER_DETAIL
   Set ClassDef = New CClassDef
   With ClassDef
      .DatabaseName = "NWIND"
      .ReadLocation = "View_Order_Detail"
      .WriteLocation = "Table_Order_Detail"
      .IdColumnName = "Id"
      .ParentIdColumnName = "Order_Id"
      .OrderByColumnName = "Id"

      .AppendMapping "Id", "Id", True, False, "ID"
      .AppendMapping "OrderId", "Order_Id", True, True, "ORDER_ID"
      .AppendMapping "ProductId", "Product_Id", True, True, "PRODUCT_ID"
      .AppendMapping "Product", "Product", True, False, "PRODUCT"
      .AppendMapping "Supplier", "Supplier", True, False, "SUPPLIER"
      .AppendMapping "UnitPrice", "Unit_Price", True, True, "UNIT_PRICE"
      .AppendMapping "Discount", "Discount", True, True, "DISCOUNT"
   End With
   Call mIAppServer.ClassDefs.Add(ClassDef, CStr(CT_ORDER_DETAIL))

Case CT_PRODUCT
   Set ClassDef = New CClassDef
   With ClassDef
      .DatabaseName = "NWIND"
      .ReadLocation = "View_Product"
      .WriteLocation = "Table_Product"
      .IdColumnName = "Id"
      .OrderByColumnName = "Name"

      .AppendMapping "Id", "Id", True, False, "ID"
      .AppendMapping "Name", "Name", True, True, "NAME"
      .AppendMapping "SupplierId", "Supplier_Id", _
                     True, True, "SUPPLIER_ID"
```

continues

Listing 9.2 **Continued**

```
            .AppendMapping "Supplier", "Supplier", True, False, "SUPPLIER"
            .AppendMapping "CategoryId", "Category_Id", _
                        True, True, "CATEGORY_ID"
            .AppendMapping "Category", "Category", True, False, "CATEGORY"
            .AppendMapping "QuantityPerUnit", "Quantity_Per_Unit", _
                        True, True, "QUANTITY_PER_UNIT"
            .AppendMapping "UnitPrice", "Unit_Price", _
                        True, True, "UNIT_PRICE"
            .AppendMapping "UnitsInStock", "Units_In_Stock", _
                        True, True, "UNITS_IN_STOCK"
            .AppendMapping "UnitsOnOrder", "Units_On_Order", _
                        True, True, "UNITS_ON_ORDER"
            .AppendMapping "ReorderLevel", "Reorder_Level", _
                        True, True, "REORDER_LEVEL"
            .AppendMapping "IsDiscontinued", "Is_Discontinued", _
                        True, True, "IS_DISCONTINUED"

        End With
        Call mIAppServer.ClassDefs.Add(ClassDef, CStr(CT_PRODUCT))

    Case CT_REGION
      Set ClassDef = New CClassDef
      With ClassDef
        .DatabaseName = "NWIND"
        .ReadLocation = "Table_Region"
        .WriteLocation = "Table_Region"
        .IdColumnName = "Id"
        .ParentIdColumnName = "Country_Id"
        .OrderByColumnName = "Name"

        .AppendMapping "Id", "Id", True, False, "ID"
        .AppendMapping "CountryId", "Country_Id", True, True, "COUNTRY_ID"
        .AppendMapping "Name", "Name", True, True, "NAME"
      End With
      Call mIAppServer.ClassDefs.Add(ClassDef, CStr(CT_REGION))

    Case CT_SHIPPER
      Set ClassDef = New CClassDef
      With ClassDef
        .DatabaseName = "NWIND"
        .ReadLocation = "Table_Shipper"
        .WriteLocation = "Table_Shipper"
        .IdColumnName = "Id"
        .OrderByColumnName = "Company_Name"

        .AppendMapping "Id", "Id", True, False, "ID"
        .AppendMapping "CompanyName", "Company_Name", _
                    True, True, "COMPANY_NAME"
        .AppendMapping "Phone", "Phone", True, True, "PHONE"
      End With
```

```
            Call mIAppServer.ClassDefs.Add(ClassDef, CStr(CT_SHIPPER))

        Case CT_SUPPLIER
          Set ClassDef = New CClassDef
          With ClassDef
            .DatabaseName = "NWIND"
            .ReadLocation = "View_Supplier"
            .WriteLocation = "Table_Supplier"
            .IdColumnName = "Id"
            .OrderByColumnName = "Company_Name"

            .AppendMapping "Id", "Id", True, False, "ID"
            .AppendMapping "CompanyName", "Company_Name", _
                           True, True, "COMPANY_NAME"
            .AppendMapping "ContactName", "Contact_Name", _
                           True, True, "CONTACT_NAME"
            .AppendMapping "ContactTitleId", "Contact_Title_Id", _
                           True, True, "CONTACT_TITLE_ID"
            .AppendMapping "ContactTitle", "Contact_Title", _
                           True, False, "CONTACT_TITLE"
            .AppendMapping "Address", "Address", True, True, "ADDRESS"
            .AppendMapping "CountryId", "Country_Id", True, False, "COUNTRY_ID"
            .AppendMapping "Country", "Country", True, False, "COUNTRY"
            .AppendMapping "RegionId", "Region_Id", True, False, "REGION_ID"
            .AppendMapping "Region", "Region", True, False, "REGION"
            .AppendMapping "CityId", "City_Id", True, True, "CITY_ID"
            .AppendMapping "City", "City", True, False, "CITY"
            .AppendMapping "PostalCode", "Postal_Code", _
                           True, True, "POSTAL_CODE"
            .AppendMapping "Phone", "Phone", True, True, "PHONE"
            .AppendMapping "Fax", "Fax", True, True, "FAX"
          End With
          Call mIAppServer.ClassDefs.Add(ClassDef, CStr(CT_SUPPLIER))
      End Select
    End If
    Set IAppServer_GetClassDef = mIAppServer.ClassDefs.Item(CStr(ClassId))
  End Function
```

Although this appears to be a significant amount of code for one method, it represents the core of the application framework. Let us look at one of the class types, say CT_SUPPLIER. We start by creating a new CClassDef object and setting its DatabaseName, ReadLocation, and WriteLocation properties. We then proceed to state that its IdColumnName is simply Id and that we want to have our OrderByColumnName as the Company_Name column. We then define our property and column definitions using the AppendMapping method. If we look more closely at the ContactTitleId and ContactTitle property definitions, we see that the CanWrite property of the latter is False. This is because the ContactTitle is a field in the database view (ReadLocation) but not in the table (WriteLocation). We have also put XML tags into the AppendMapping call, which we will use in Chapter 13, "Interoperability."

We define all our other methods as part of IAppServer. Components implementing the IAppServer interface need only call into these methods to gain access to the functionality. The first method that we define is GetPropertyNames, which returns an array of the property names for a given class type. This function is important for both our NWClient and our ASP consumers because it is the basis for indexing into variant data arrays. The code for GetPropertyNames appears in Listing 9.3.

Listing 9.3   **The *GetPropertyNames* Method on *IAppServer***

```
Public Function GetPropertyNames(ByVal ClassId As Integer) As Variant
  Dim pn As Variant
  Dim ClassDef As CClassDef
  Dim PropertyDef As CPropertyDef
  Dim i As Integer

  On Error GoTo ErrorTrap
  Set ClassDef = ClassDefs.Item(ClassId)

  ReDim pn(1 To ClassDef.PropertyDefs.Count)
  i = 1
  For Each PropertyDef In ClassDef.PropertyDefs
    pn(i) = PropertyDef.Name
    i = i + 1
  Next
  GetPropertyNames = pn

  Exit Function
ErrorTrap:
    '1.  Details to EventLog
    Call WriteNTLogEvent("IAppServer:GetPropertyNames", _
                      Err.Number, Err.Description, Err.Source)
    '2.  Generic to client - passed back on error stack
    Err.Raise Err.Number, "IAppServer:GetPropertyNames", _
                      Err.Description & " [" & Erl & "]"
End Function
```

This method simply iterates through the PropertyDefs collection of the class type defined for the requested class type. Remember that we have already defined this information using the GetClassDef method of CNWServer. Our implementation of this method on CNWServer is as follows:

```
Private Function IAppServer_GetPropertyNames(ByVal ClassId As Integer) _
              As Variant
  Call IAppServer_GetClassDef(ClassId)
  IAppServer_GetPropertyNames = mIAppServer.GetPropertyNames(ClassId)
End Function
```

We now turn our attention to hooking into our CRUD processing routines, which we so cleverly built into our CDataManager library. We start with data retrieval by defining two public methods, GetObjectData and GetObjectListData. The

GetObjectData method requires that we pass in a class type, an ObjectId, and an ObjectSubId. It returns a list of property names and the actual object data. We declare these two return parameters as variants because of the need to support ASP, whose underlying VBScript engine supports only this data type. GetObjectData proceeds to build a CQueryParms object, moving the associated ReadLocation property of the CClassDef object into the TableName property of the CQueryParms object. Similarly, we iterate through the ColumnDefs collection of the CClassDef object to build the ColumnList property of the CQueryParm object.

Next, the WhereList is built using the ObjectId and ObjectSubId values passed in, combined with the IdColumnName and SubIdColumnName fields of the CClassDef object. After the CQueryParm object is complete, we call the GetData method of a CDataManager object to retrieve the data from the database. If data is returned, then the fields collection of the resultset is iterated with a call to the ColumnToPropertyDef method of the class definition to generate the PropertyNames array that are sent back. Finally, we make a call to the GetRows method of the recordset to generate the Data return parameter. The code for the GetData method is provided in Listing 9.4.

Listing 9.4   **The *GetObjectData* Method on *IAppServer***

```
Public Sub GetObjectData(ByVal ClassId As Integer, _
                         ByVal ObjectId As Long, _
                         ByVal ObjectSubId As Long, _
                         PropertyNames As Variant, _
                         Data As Variant, _
                         Errors As Variant)
  Dim ClassDef As CClassDef
  Dim DataManager As CDataManager
  Dim ColumnDef As CColumnDef
  Dim QueryParms As New CQueryParms
  Dim rs As ADODB.Recordset
  Dim rsField As ADODB.Field
  Dim vData As Variant
  Dim i As Integer

  On Error GoTo ErrorTrap

  Set ClassDef = mClassDefs.Item(ClassId)
  Set DataManager = mDataManagers.Item(ClassDef.DatabaseName)
  QueryParms.TableName = ClassDef.ReadLocation
  For Each ColumnDef In ClassDef.ColumnDefs
    If ColumnDef.CanRead Then
      QueryParms.ColumnList.Add ColumnDef.Name
    End If
  Next
  If ObjectId > 0 Then
    QueryParms.WhereList.Add (ClassDef.IdColumnName & "=" & _
                        CStr(ObjectId))
  End If
```

continues

Listing 9.4   **Continued**

```
If ObjectSubId > 0 Then
  QueryParms.WhereList.Add (ClassDef.SubIdColumnName & "=" & _
                              CStr(ObjectSubId))
End If
Set rs = DataManager.GetData(QueryParms)
If Not rs Is Nothing Then
  ReDim PropertyNames(0 To QueryParms.ColumnList.Count - 1)
  i = 0
  For Each rsField In rs.Fields
    PropertyNames(i) = ClassDef.ColumnToPropertyDef(rsField.Name).Name
    i = i + 1
  Next
  vData = rs.GetRows
Else
  vData = vbEmpty
End If
Data = vData
Exit Sub

ErrorTrap:
  '1.  Details to EventLog
  Call WriteNTLogEvent("IAppServer:GetObjectData", Err.Number, _
                      Err.Description, Err.Source)
  '2.  Generic to client - passed back on error stack
  Err.Raise Err.Number, "IAppServer:GetObjectData", _
                      Err.Description & " [" & Erl & "]"
End Sub
```

As you can see, the overall method is straightforward because we are relying heavily on our `DataManager` component to perform the bulk of the data access for us. From our `CNWServer` component, the implementation of this method looks like Listing 9.5.

Listing 9.5   **The *GetObjectData* Method Implemented on *CNWServer***

```
Private Sub IAppServer_GetObjectData(ByVal ClassId As Integer, _
                                     ByVal ObjectId As Long, _
                                     ByVal ObjectSubId As Long, _
                                     PropertyNames As Variant, _
                                     Data As Variant, _
                                     Errors As Variant)
  Call IAppServer_GetClassDef(ClassId)
  Call mIAppServer.GetObjectData(ClassId, ObjectId, ObjectSubId, _
                                 PropertyNames, Data, Errors)
End Sub
```

In the previous method implementation, we first call the `GetClassDef` method to make sure the class definitions for the requested class type have been generated. Next, we simply call into our `GetObjectData` method on our `IAppServer` object instance to complete the call.

If we need to retrieve a list of objects, as in a master-detail relationship, we define a `GetObjectListData` method. Again, we pass in a class type and expect in return `PropertyNames` and `Data` arrays. In this case, we also add `ParentId` and `ParentSubId` parameters to the list. Again, we form a `CQueryParms` object, setting its `TableName` and `ColumnList` properties as we did in the `GetData` case. However, in the `GetObjectListData` case, we construct our `Where` clause using the `ParentIdColumnName` in conjunction with the `ParentId` value, and the `ParentSubIdColumnName` in conjunction with the `ParentSubId` value. We also copy the `OrderByColumnName` property of our `CClassDef` object to our `OrderList` property of our `CQueryParms` object. Finally, we call the `GetData` method on the appropriate `CDataManager` object, generating the `PropertyNames` and `Data` arrays as in the `GetObjectData` case. The code for the `GetObjectListData` method is provided in Listing 9.6.

Listing 9.6   **The *GetObjectListData* Method on *IAppServer***

```
Public Sub GetObjectListData(ByVal ClassId As Integer, _
                             ByVal ParentId As Long, _
                             ByVal ParentSubId As Long, _
                             PropertyNames As Variant, _
                             Data As Variant, _
                             Errors As Variant)
    Dim ClassDef As CClassDef
    Dim DataManager As CDataManager
    Dim ColumnDef As CColumnDef
    Dim QueryParms As New CQueryParms
    Dim rs As ADODB.Recordset
    Dim rsField As ADODB.Field
    Dim vData As Variant
    Dim vErrors As Variant
    Dim i As Integer

    On Error GoTo ErrorTrap

    Set ClassDef = mClassDefs.Item(ClassId)
    Set DataManager = mDataManagers.Item(ClassDef.DatabaseName)

    QueryParms.TableName = ClassDef.ReadLocation
    For Each ColumnDef In ClassDef.ColumnDefs
      If ColumnDef.CanRead Then
        QueryParms.ColumnList.Add ColumnDef.Name
      End If
    Next

    If ParentId > 0 Then
```

continues

Listing 9.6   **Continued**

```
    QueryParms.WhereList.Add _
      (ClassDef.ParentIdColumnName & "=" & CStr(ParentId))
  End If
  If ParentSubId > 0 Then
    QueryParms.WhereList.Add _
      (ClassDef.ParentSubIdColumnName & "=" & CStr(ParentSubId))
  End If
  If ClassDef.OrderByColumnName <> "" Then
    QueryParms.OrderList.Add ClassDef.OrderByColumnName
  End If

  Set rs = DataManager.GetData(QueryParms)
  If Not rs Is Nothing Then
    ReDim PropertyNames(0 To QueryParms.ColumnList.Count - 1)
    i = 0
    For Each rsField In rs.Fields
      PropertyNames(i) = ClassDef.ColumnToPropertyDef(rsField.Name).Name
      i = i + 1
    Next
    vData = rs.GetRows
  Else
    vData = vbEmpty
  End If
  Data = vData
  Exit Sub

ErrorTrap:
    '1.  Details to EventLog
    Call WriteNTLogEvent("IAppServer:GetObjectListData", Err.Number, _
                         Err.Description, Err.Source)
    '2.  Generic to client - passed back on error stack
    Err.Raise Err.Number, "IAppServer:GetObjectListData", _
                         Err.Description & " [" & Erl & "]"
End Sub
```

Again, you should be able to see that this method is straightforward, with the CDataManager object performing the bulk of the work. Again, our CNWServer component hooks into this component in a straightforward fashion as shown in Listing 9.7.

Listing 9.7   **The *GetObjectListData* Method Implemented on *CNWServer***

```
Private Sub IAppServer_GetObjectListData(ByVal ClassId As Integer, _
                                         ByVal ParentId As Long, _
                                         ByVal ParentSubId As Long, _
                                         PropertyNames As Variant, _
                                         Data As Variant, _
                                         Errors As Variant)
```

```
    If Not bInitialized Then IAppServer_InitServer
    Call IAppServer_GetClassDef(ClassId)
    Call mIAppServer.GetObjectListData(ClassId, ParentId, ParentSubId, _
                                       PropertyNames, Data, Errors)
End Sub
```

Now that we can retrieve individual objects or lists of objects, we turn our attention to the deletion of objects. To delete an object or list of objects from the system, we define DeleteObject and DeleteObjectList methods on IAppServer. As you might surmise, DeleteObject deletes a single object, whereas DeleteObjectList deletes a list of objects based on a master-detail or parent-child relationship.

DeleteObject takes a ClassId parameter along with an ObjectId and ObjectSubId. The class type is used to look up the CClassDef object so that we can build the appropriate CQueryParms object. In this case, we use the WriteLocation property of the CClassDef object to set the TableName property of the CQueryParms object. We use the ObjectId and ObjectSubId in conjunction with the IdColumnName and SubIdColumnName properties to form the WhereList object of the CQueryParms object. We then pass this CQueryParms object off to the DeleteData method of our CDataManager object, which performs the delete. The code for DeleteObject follows in Listing 9.8.

Listing 9.8   **The *DeleteObject* Method on *IAppServer***

```
Public Sub DeleteObject(ByVal ClassId As Integer, _
                        ByVal ObjectId As Long, _
                        ByVal ObjectSubId As Long, _
                        Errors As Variant)
  Dim ClassDef As CClassDef
  Dim DataManager As CDataManager
  Dim QueryParms As New CQueryParms

  On Error GoTo ErrorTrap

  Set ClassDef = mClassDefs.Item(ClassId)
  Set DataManager = mDataManagers.Item(ClassDef.DatabaseName)
  QueryParms.TableName = ClassDef.WriteLocation
  If ObjectId > 0 Then
    QueryParms.WhereList.Add (ClassDef.IdColumnName & "=" & _
                              CStr(ObjectId))
  End If
  If ObjectSubId > 0 Then
    QueryParms.WhereList.Add (ClassDef.SubIdColumnName & "=" & _
                              CStr(ObjectSubId))
  End If
  QueryParms.WhereOperator = woAnd
  Call DataManager.DeleteData(QueryParms)
  ObjCtx.SetComplete
  Exit Sub
```

continues

Listing 9.8   **Continued**

```
ErrorTrap:
    '1.  Details to EventLog
    Call WriteNTLogEvent("IAppServer:DeleteObject", Err.Number, _
                          Err.Description, Err.Source)
    '2.  Generic to client - passed back on error stack
    Err.Raise Err.Number, "IAppServer:DeleteObject", _
                          Err.Description & " [" & Erl & "]"
    ObjCtx.SetAbort
End Sub
```

Note that we have introduced the use of the object context in this method with the
`SetComplete` and `SetAbort` calls. The reason for this is that we are altering the state of
the database with this call, so it should operate within a transaction. Our previous
methods have been simple retrievals that do not require transactional processing.

Again, we implement this in `CNWServer` in a straightforward fashion as shown in
Listing 9.9.

Listing 9.9   **The *DeleteObject* Method Implemented on *CNWServer***

```
Private Sub IAppServer_DeleteObject(ByVal ClassId As Integer, _
                            ByVal ObjectId As Long, _
                            ByVal ObjectSubId As Long, _
                            Errors As Variant)
    On Error GoTo ErrorTrap
    Call IAppServer_GetClassDef(ClassId)
    Call mIAppServer.DeleteObject(ClassId, ObjectId, ObjectSubId, Errors)
    ObjCtx.SetComplete
    Exit Sub
ErrorTrap:
    ObjCtx.SetAbort
End Sub
```

Notice that we have taken our wrapping approach a little further with this method,
with the implementation of the `SetComplete` and `SetAbort` methods as well. This is
because our transaction has been completed or aborted by our enlisted `IAppServer`
object, so we must follow suit as well. Although technically this is not required because
one abort is sufficient, it is good programming practice to follow as the system
becomes more complex.

If you handle your referential integrity on the RDBMS, then nothing else must be
done here. If, on the other hand, you want the business layer to manage this functionality, you can modify this `DeleteObject` method to do just this using a `Case` statement.
Such a modification might look like the code shown in Listing 9.10.

Listing 9.10   **The Modified *DeleteObject* Method Implemented on *CNWServer***

```
Private Sub IAppServer_DeleteObject(ByVal ClassId As Integer, _
                                    ByVal ObjectId As Long, _
                                    ByVal ObjectSubId As Long, _
                                    Errors As Variant)
  On Error GoTo ErrorTrap

  Call IAppServer_GetClassDef(ClassId)
  Select Case ClassId
    Case CT_CATEGORY
      Call IAppServer_GetClassDef(CT_PRODUCT)
      If Not mIAppServer.IsReferenced(ObjectId, ObjectSubId, _
                                    CT_PRODUCT, "CategoryId", "") Then
        Call mIAppServer.DeleteObject(CT_CATEGORY, ObjectId, _
                                    ObjectSubId, Errors)
      End If
    Case CT_CITY
      Call IAppServer_GetClassDef(CT_ORDER)
      If Not mIAppServer.IsReferenced(ObjectId, ObjectSubId, _
                                    CT_ORDER, "ShipToCityId", "") Then
        GoTo NoDelete
      End If
      Call IAppServer_GetClassDef(CT_CUSTOMER)
      If Not mIAppServer.IsReferenced(ObjectId, ObjectSubId, _
                                    CT_CUSTOMER, "CityId", "") Then
        GoTo NoDelete
      End If
      Call IAppServer_GetClassDef(CT_EMPLOYEE)
      If Not mIAppServer.IsReferenced(ObjectId, ObjectSubId, _
                                    CT_EMPLOYEE, "CityId", "") Then
        GoTo NoDelete
      End If
      Call IAppServer_GetClassDef(CT_SUPPLIER)
      If Not mIAppServer.IsReferenced(ObjectId, ObjectSubId, _
                                    CT_SUPPLIER, "CityId", "") Then
        GoTo NoDelete
      End If
      Call IAppServer_GetClassDef(CT_REGION)
      If Not mIAppServer.IsReferenced(ObjectId, ObjectSubId, _
                                    CT_REGION, "CityId", "") Then
        GoTo NoDelete
      End If
      Call mIAppServer.DeleteObject(CT_CITY, ObjectId, ObjectSubId, Errors)
    Case CT_REGION
      Call IAppServer_GetClassDef(CT_CITY)
      If Not mIAppServer.IsReferenced(ObjectId, ObjectSubId, _
                                    CT_CITY, "RegionId", "") Then
        Call mIAppServer.DeleteObjectListData(CT_REGION, ObjectId, _
                                    ObjectSubId, Errors)
      End If
```

continues

Listing 9.10   **Continued**

```
    Case CT_CUSTOMER
      Call IAppServer_GetClassDef(CT_ORDER)
      If Not mIAppServer.IsReferenced(ObjectId, ObjectSubId, _
                                  CT_ORDER, "CustomerId", "") Then
        Call mIAppServer.DeleteObject(CT_CUSTOMER, ObjectId, _
                                  ObjectSubId, Errors)
      End If
    Case CT_EMPLOYEE
      Call IAppServer_GetClassDef(CT_ORDER)
      If Not mIAppServer.IsReferenced(ObjectId, ObjectSubId, _
                                  CT_ORDER, "EmployeeId", "") Then
        Call mIAppServer.DeleteObject(CT_EMPLOYEE, ObjectId, _
                                  ObjectSubId, Errors)
      End If
    Case CT_ORDER
      Call IAppServer_GetClassDef(CT_ORDER_DETAIL)
      Call mIAppServer.DeleteObjectListData(CT_ORDER_DETAIL, ObjectId, _
                                      ObjectSubId, Errors)
      Call mIAppServer.DeleteObject(ClassId, ObjectId, _
                                  ObjectSubId, Errors)
    Case CT_PRODUCT
      Call IAppServer_GetClassDef(CT_ORDER)
      If Not mIAppServer.IsReferenced(ObjectId, ObjectSubId, _
                                  CT_ORDER, "ProductId", "") Then
        Call mIAppServer.DeleteObject(CT_PRODUCT, ObjectId, _
                                  ObjectSubId, Errors)
      End If
    Case CT_SHIPPER
      Call IAppServer_GetClassDef(CT_ORDER)
      If Not mIAppServer.IsReferenced(ObjectId, ObjectSubId, _
                                  CT_ORDER, "ShipperId", "") Then
        Call mIAppServer.DeleteObject(CT_ORDER, ObjectId, _
                                  ObjectSubId, Errors)
      End If
    Case CT_SUPPLIER
      Call IAppServer_GetClassDef(CT_SUPPLIER)
      If Not mIAppServer.IsReferenced(ObjectId, ObjectSubId, _
                                  CT_PRODUCT, "SupplierId", "") Then
        Call mIAppServer.DeleteObject(CT_SUPPLIER, ObjectId, _
                                  ObjectSubId, Errors)
      End If
    Case Else
      Call IAppServer_GetClassDef(ClassId)
      Call mIAppServer.DeleteObject(ClassId, ObjectId, _
                                  ObjectSubId, Errors)
  End Select
  ObjCtx.SetComplete
  Exit Sub
```

```
NoDelete:
ErrorTrap:
  ObjCtx.SetAbort
End Sub
```

In this modified version of the DeleteObject method on CNWServer, we perform a
Select Case statement to determine what sort of action we should take given the
ClassId. In most cases, we simply want to ensure that the record we are about to
delete is not being referenced anywhere. For this purpose, we have defined an
IsReferenced method on our IAppServer. This approach moves all referential integrity
functionality to the business layer and away from the RDBMS. This has the effect of
enabling us to develop for multiple RDBMSes, but at the cost of lower performance
because the data must move from the RDBMS to the MTS component for the verification to take place. If you do not need this added flexibility then putting the referential integrity on the RDBMS might be easier to implement and more performance
beneficial. The code for the IsReferenced method appears in Listing 9.11.

Listing 9.11   **The *IsReferenced* Method on *IAppServer***

```
Public Function IsReferenced(ObjectId As Long, _
                             ObjectSubId As Long, _
                             TargetClassId As Integer, _
                             TargetPropertyName As String, _
                             TargetSubPropertyName As String) As Boolean
    Dim ClassDef As CClassDef
    Dim DataManager As CDataManager
    Dim rs As ADODB.Recordset
    Dim rsField As ADODB.Field
    Dim QueryParms As New CQueryParms

    On Error GoTo ErrorTrap

    Set ClassDef = mClassDefs.Item(TargetClassId)
    Set DataManager = mDataManagers.Item(ClassDef.DatabaseName)
    QueryParms.TableName = ClassDef.WriteLocation

    QueryParms.ColumnList.Add "Count(*)"
    If ObjectId > 0 And TargetPropertyName <> "" Then
      QueryParms.WhereList.Add _
        ClassDef.PropertyToColumnDef(TargetPropertyName).Name & "=" & ObjectId
    End If
    If ObjectSubId > 0 And TargetSubPropertyName <> "" Then
      QueryParms.WhereList.Add _
        ClassDef.PropertyToColumnDef(TargetSubPropertyName).Name & _
          "=" & ObjectSubId
    End If

    Set rs = DataManager.GetData(QueryParms)
```

continues

Listing 9.11   **Continued**

```
  If Not rs Is Nothing Then
    rs.MoveFirst
    IsReferenced = rs.Fields.Item(0).Value > 0
  Else
    IsReferenced = True ' better safe than sorry
  End If
  ObjCtx.SetComplete
  Exit Function

ErrorTrap:
    '1.  Details to EventLog
    Call WriteNTLogEvent("IAppServer:IsReferenced", Err.Number, _
                         Err.Description, Err.Source)
    '2.  Generic to client - passed back on error stack
    Err.Raise Err.Number, "IAppServer:IsReferenced", _
                          Err.Description & " [" & Erl & "]"
    ObjCtx.SetAbort
End Function
```

We implement the IsReferenced method similar to our other CRUD methods in that
we build a CQueryParms object, populate our WhereList, and make a call to GetData.
However, the major difference here is that our ColumnList contains a "count(*)"
clause versus a standard column list. We retrieve this value to determine whether any
records exist that reference a given ObjectId and ObjectSubId. Note that we have
added the SetAbort and SetComplete calls on our object context for the IsReferenced
method. The reason for this is that if we have an issue determining whether an object
is referenced, we do not want a delete being performed on the database.

Our DeleteObjectList method builds a CQueryParms object using the same
WriteLocation to TableName copy. For the WhereList, we use the ParentIdColumnName
and ParentSubIdColumnName properties of the CClassDef in conjunction with the
ParentId and ParentSubId values. Again, the DeleteData method of CDataManager
handles the dirty work. The code for DeleteObjectList appears in Listing 9.12.

Listing 9.12   **The *DeleteObjectList* Method on *IAppServer***

```
Public Sub DeleteObjectList(ByVal ClassId As Integer, _
                            ByVal ParentId As Long, _
                            ByVal ParentSubId As Long, _
                            Errors As Variant)
  Dim ClassDef As CClassDef
  Dim DataManager As CDataManager
  Dim QueryParms As New CQueryParms

  On Error GoTo ErrorTrap

  Set ClassDef = mClassDefs.Item(ClassId)
```

```
    Set DataManager = mDataManagers.Item(ClassDef.DatabaseName)
    QueryParms.TableName = ClassDef.WriteLocation
    If ParentId > 0 Then
      QueryParms.WhereList.Add _
        (ClassDef.ParentIdColumnName & "=" & ParentId)
    End If
    If ParentSubId > 0 Then
      QueryParms.WhereList.Add _
        (ClassDef.ParentSubIdColumnName & "=" & ParentSubId)
    End If
    QueryParms.WhereOperator = woAnd
    Call DataManager.DeleteData(QueryParms)
    ObjCtx.SetComplete
    Exit Sub

ErrorTrap:
    '1.  Details to EventLog
    Call WriteNTLogEvent("IAppServer:DeleteObjectList", Err.Number, _
                        Err.Description, Err.Source)
    '2.  Generic to client - passed back on error stack
    Err.Raise Err.Number, "IAppServer:DeleteObjectList", _
                        Err.Description & " [" & Erl & "]"
    ObjCtx.SetAbort
End Sub
```

On `CNWServer`, we call into `DeleteObjectList` in the following manner:

```
Private Sub IAppServer_DeleteObjectList(ByVal ClassId As Integer, _
                                        ByVal ParentId As Long, _
                                        ByVal ParentSubId As Long, _
                                        Errors As Variant)
  Call IAppServer_GetClassDef(ClassId)
  Call mIAppServer.DeleteObjectList(ClassId, ParentId, ParentSubId, Errors)
  ObjCtx.SetComplete
  Exit Sub
ErrorTrap:
  ObjCtx.SetAbort
End Sub
```

Again, we simply verify that we have defined the `CClassDef` object for the given `ClassId`. We then call the `DeleteObjectList` method on our `mIAppServer` object.

▶ **Note**

In our framework, to delete an object with contained objects or collections of objects, we must call the `DeleteObject` and/or `DeleteObjectList` methods explicitly for each of these contained items. We finish with a call to `DeleteObject` for the parent object.

With retrievals and deletes out of the way, we turn our attention to inserts and updates. As before, we have the capability to handle single objects or collections of objects, the latter being for a master-detail or parent-child–style relationship. Our `InsertObjectData` function looks similar in calling convention to our `GetObjectData` method, except that now we are receiving a variant array of object state information. The first step of the `InsertObjectData` function is to call the `GetInsertableRS` method of the `CDataManager` object. We then use the `PropertyNames` array to loop through the `Data` variant array, moving values into the associated recordset fields. We use our `PropertyDefToColumn` mapping here to assist us in this process. We also check to ensure that we do not overwrite fields with the `CanWrite` property set to `False`. If we have validation functionality in place, we would perform that checking here as well.

After all the data has been moved into the updateable recordset, we have a choice on how we generate our primary key value. One option is to retrieve a value for the primary key before the insert, while another is to allow the RDBMS to generate the key. In the first case, we can create a method on our `CDataManager` object to do this, or we can implement it on our `IAppServer`. This method can be called something like `GetNextKey` with a parameter of `ClassId` or `TableName`. How it is implemented will depend on how you choose to define your keys. In the case of the RDBMS generating the key, an `AutoNumber` type column (in the case of Microsoft Access) or an `Identity` type column (in the case of SQL Server) is used that will automatically generate the next integer sequence. For our purposes, we will be allowing the RDBMS to generate our keys, but you can change this to suit your needs.

The code for `InsertObjectData` appears in Listing 9.13.

Listing 9.13 **The *InsertObjectData* Method on *IAppServer***

```
Public Sub InsertObjectData(ByVal ClassId As Integer, _
                            ByVal PropertyNames As Variant, _
                            ByVal Data As Variant, _
                            Errors As Variant, _
                            ObjectId As Long, _
                            ObjectSubId As Long)
    Dim ClassDef As CClassDef
    Dim DataManager As CDataManager
    Dim l As Long
    Dim rs As ADODB.Recordset
    Dim rsField As ADODB.Field
    Dim i As Integer
    Dim lRet As Long
    Dim pName as String

    On Error GoTo ErrorTrap
```

```
    Set ClassDef = mClassDefs.Item(ClassId)
    Set DataManager = mDataManagers.Item(ClassDef.DatabaseName)
    Set rs = DataManager.GetInsertableRS(ClassDef.WriteLocation)
    rs.AddNew

    For i = LBound(PropertyNames) To UBound(PropertyNames)
      pName = PropertyNames(i)
      With ClassDef
        If .ColumnDefs.Item(.PropertyToColumnDef(pName).Name).CanWrite Then
          Set rsField = rs.Fields(.PropertyToColumnDef(pName).Name)
          If rsField.Type = adLongVarBinary Or rsField.Type = adLongVarChar Then
            ' requires chunk operations
          Else
            If IsEmpty(Data(i, 0)) Then
              rsField.Value = vbEmpty
            Else
              rsField.Value = Data(i, 0)
            End If
          End If
        End If
      End If
    Next i

    rs.Update
    ' the following code only works for certain combinations of
    ' drivers and database engines (see MS KnowledgeBase)

    ' note that if there are triggers that fire and insert additional records
    ' with Identity/Autonumber columns, this number retrieved below
    ' will be wrong.
    If ClassDef.IdColumnName <> "" Then
      ObjectId = rs.Fields(ClassDef.IdColumnName)
    End If

    If ClassDef.SubIdColumnName <> "" Then
      ObjectSubId = rs.Fields(ClassDef.SubIdColumnName)
    End If

    ObjCtx.SetComplete
    Exit SubErrorTrap:
      '1.  Details to EventLog
      Call WriteNTLogEvent("IAppServer:InsertObjectData", _
                           Err.Number, Err.Description, Err.Source)
      '2.  Generic to client - passed back on error stack
      Err.Raise Err.Number, "IAppServer:InsertObjectData", _
                           Err.Description & " [" & Erl & "]"
      ObjCtx.SetAbort
End Sub
```

From our CNWServer class, the implementation of this method looks like Listing 9.14.

Listing 9.14   **The *InsertObjectData* Method Implemented on *CNWServer***

```
Private Sub IAppServer_InsertObjectData(ByVal ClassId As Integer, _
                                        ByVal PropertyNames As Variant, _
                                        ByVal Data As Variant, _
                                        Errors As Variant, _
                                        ObjectId As Long, _
                                        ObjectSubId As Long)
    Call IAppServer_GetClassDef(ClassId)
    Call mIAppServer.InsertObjectData(ClassId, PropertyNames, Data, Errors, _
                            ObjectId, ObjectSubId)
    ObjCtx.SetComplete
    Exit Sub
ErrorTrap:
    ObjCtx.SetAbort
End Sub
```

Likewise, we have our `InsertObjectListData` method to insert objects based on a parent object (see Listing 9.15). Here, we pass in a `PropertyNames` array along with the
variant array of data elements. The `Data` array is two-dimensional because we are
inserting more than one object. The layout of this array mimics the layout produced
by the `GetRows` method of a recordset object. We also pass in our `ClassId`, `ParentId`,
and `ParentSubId` values. The first activity we perform is to delete the previous list
using the `DeleteObjectList` method. We then proceed to obtain a recordset to work
with using the `GetInsertableRS` method as before. We follow a similar process to
move the information from the variant array into the recordset, performing validation
if we have implemented such functionality. We call the `UpdateBatch` method of the
recordset object to commit the data to the database. Because object lists are the child
part of a parent-child relationship, we do not need to know the ID values that the
database is generating here.

Listing 9.15   **The *InsertObjectListData* Method on *IAppServer***

```
Public Sub InsertObjectListData(ByVal ClassId As Integer, _
                                ByVal ParentId As Long, _
                                ByVal ParentSubId As Long, _
                                ByVal PropertyNames As Variant, _
                                ByVal Data As Variant, _
                                Errors As Variant)
    Dim ClassDef As CClassDef
    Dim DataManager As CDataManager
    Dim rs As ADODB.Recordset
    Dim rsField As ADODB.Field
    Dim i As Integer, j As Integer
    Dim pName As String

    On Error GoTo ErrorTrap
```

```
    Set ClassDef = mClassDefs.Item(ClassId)
    Set DataManager = mDataManagers.Item(ClassDef.DatabaseName)

    Call DeleteObjectList(ClassId, ParentId, ParentSubId, Errors)

    Set rs = DataManager.GetInsertableRS(ClassDef.WriteLocation)
    For i = LBound(Data, 2) To UBound(Data, 2)
      rs.AddNew
      For j = LBound(PropertyNames) To UBound(PropertyNames)
        pName = PropertyNames(j)
        With ClassDef
          If .ColumnDefs.Item(.PropertyToColumnDef(pName).Name).CanWrite Then
            Set rsField = rs.Fields(.PropertyToColumnDef(pName).Name)
            If rsField.Type = adLongVarBinary Or _
              rsField.Type = adLongVarChar Then
              ' chunk operations required
            Else
              If IsEmpty(Data(j, i)) Then
                rsField.Value = vbEmpty
              Else
                rsField.Value = Data(j, i)
              End If
            End If
          End If
        End With
      Next j
    Next i
    Call rs.UpdateBatch
    ObjCtx.SetComplete
    Exit Sub
ErrorTrap:
    '1. Details to EventLog
    Call WriteNTLogEvent("IAppServer:InsertObjectListData", Err.Number, _
                      Err.Description, Err.Source)
    '2. Generic to client - passed back on error stack
    Err.Raise Err.Number, "IAppServer:InsertObjectListData", _
                      Err.Description & " [" & Erl & "]"
    ObjCtx.SetAbort
End Sub
```

From our CNWServer class, the implementation of this method looks like Listing 9.16.

Listing 9.16 **The *InsertObjectListData* Method Implemented on *CNWServer***

```
Private Sub IAppServer_InsertObjectListData(ByVal ClassId As Integer, _
                                        ByVal ParentId As Long, _
                                        ByVal ParentSubId As Long, _
                                        ByVal PropertyNames As Variant, _
                                        ByVal Data As Variant, _
                                        Errors As Variant)
```

continues

Listing 9.16   **Continued**

```
   Call IAppServer_GetClassDef(ClassId)
   Call mIAppServer.InsertObjectListData(ClassId, _
                                         ParentId, _
                                         ParentSubId, _
                                         PropertyNames, _
                                         Data, _
                                         Errors)
    ObjCtx.SetComplete
    Exit Sub
ErrorTrap:
    ObjCtx.SetAbort
End Sub
```

Our last component of CRUD is that of update. Here, we only provide a mechanism to update a single object. As in the insert case, this method calls the `GetUpdateableRS` method of the appropriate `CDataManager` object. Again, we form a `CQueryParm` object to help us make the appropriate call by first setting the `TableName` property from the `ReadLocation` of the `CClassDef` object. We loop through the `ColumnDefs` property of the `CClassDef` object, adding the columns, whose `CanWrite` property is set to `True`, to the `ColumnList` property of the `CQueryParm` object. We also add both the `IdColumnName` and `SubIdColumnName` to the `ColumnList` to ensure that OLE DB has the necessary keys for the update that is to follow. If we do not do this, OLE DB is not able to perform the update. Remember that the `Add` method of our `CStringList`, which forms our `ColumnList`, is designed to ignore duplicates, so we are safe in adding these two columns without first checking to see if they have already been added.

After we have called our `GetUpdateableRS` method in our `CDataManager` object, we can proceed to move data from the variant-array–based `Data` parameter into the recordset, using our `PropertyNames` array and the `PropertyToColumnDef` method of the `CClassDef` object. Again, if we are implementing server-side validation, we perform the necessary validation in this process, raising any errors back in the `Errors` array. The code for `UpdateObjectData` appears in Listing 9.17.

Listing 9.17   **The *UpdateObjectData* Method on *IAppServer***

```
Public Sub UpdateObjectData(ByVal ClassId As Integer, _
                            ByVal PropertyNames As Variant, _
                            ByVal Data As Variant, _
                            Errors As Variant, _
                            ObjectId As Long, _
                            ObjectSubId As Long)
    Dim ClassDef As CClassDef
    Dim DataManager As CDataManager
    Dim rs As ADODB.Recordset
    Dim rsField As ADODB.Field
    Dim i As Integer
```

```
   Dim QueryParms As New CQueryParms
   Dim ColumnDef As CColumnDef
   Dim pName As String

   On Error GoTo ErrorTrap

   Set ClassDef = mClassDefs.Item(ClassId)
   Set DataManager = mDataManagers.Item(ClassDef.DatabaseName)
   QueryParms.TableName = ClassDef.WriteLocation
   For Each ColumnDef In ClassDef.ColumnDefs
     If ColumnDef.CanWrite Then
       QueryParms.ColumnList.Add ColumnDef.Name
     ElseIf ClassDef.IdColumnName = ColumnDef.Name Then
       QueryParms.ColumnList.Add ColumnDef.Name
     ElseIf ClassDef.SubIdColumnName = ColumnDef.Name Then
       QueryParms.ColumnList.Add ColumnDef.Name
     End If
   Next

   If ObjectId > 0 Then
     QueryParms.WhereList.Add (ClassDef.IdColumnName & "=" & _
                              CStr(ObjectId))
   End If
   If ObjectSubId > 0 Then
     QueryParms.WhereList.Add (ClassDef.SubIdColumnName & "=" & _
                              CStr(ObjectSubId))
   End If

   Set rs = DataManager.GetUpdatableRS(QueryParms)
   For i = LBound(PropertyNames) To UBound(PropertyNames)
     pName = PropertyNames(i)
     With ClassDef
       If .ColumnDefs.Item(.PropertyToColumnDef(pName).CanWrite Then
         Set rsField = rs.Fields(.PropertyToColumnDef(pName))
         If rsField.Type = adLongVarBinary Or rsField.Type = adLongVarChar Then
           ' requires chunk operations
         Else
           If IsEmpty(Data(i, 0)) Then
             rsField.Value = vbEmpty
           Else
             rsField.Value = Data(i, 0)
           End If
         End If
       End If
     End With
   Next i
   rs.Update
   ObjCtx.SetComplete
   Exit Sub
ErrorTrap:
    '1. Details to EventLog
```

continues

Listing 9.17 **Continued**

```
    Call WriteNTLogEvent("IAppServer:UpdateObjectData", _
                        Err.Number, Err.Description, Err.Source)
    '2.  Generic to client - passed back on error stack
    Err.Raise Err.Number, "IAppServer:UpdateObjectData", _
                        Err.Description & " [" & Erl & "]"
    ObjCtx.SetAbort
End Sub
```

From our `CNWServer` class, the implementation of this method looks like Listing 9.18.

Listing 9.18 **The *UpdateObjectData* Method Implemented on *CNWServer***

```
Private Sub IAppServer_UpdateObjectData(ByVal ClassId As Integer, _
                                        ByVal PropertyNames As Variant, _
                                        ByVal Data As Variant, _
                                        Errors As Variant, _
                                        ObjectId As Long, _
                                        ObjectSubId As Long)
    Call IAppServer_GetClassDef(ClassId)
    Call mIAppServer.UpdateObjectData(ClassId, _
                                    PropertyNames, _
                                    Data, _
                                    Errors, _
                                    ObjectId, _
                                    ObjectSubId)
    ObjCtx.SetComplete
    Exit Sub
ErrorTrap:
    ObjCtx.SetAbort
End Sub
```

Finally, we want to give our system the added flexibility of querying for individual objects or lists of objects. This becomes important as we build our ASP-based reporting engine in Chapter 11, "A Distributed Reporting Engine." To implement this, we define a method `QueryObjectListData`, which looks similar to a standard `GetObjectListData` call, except we have replaced the `ParentId` and `ParentSubId` parameters with a `Criteria` array and a `Sort` array.

We implement our `QueryObjectListData` method by once again building a `CQueryParm` object. We copy the `ReadLocation` of our `CClassDef` object over to our `TableName` property name of the `CQueryParm` object. We then create our `ColumnList`, as in our other cases. Next, we form the `WhereList` from our `Criteria` array, which is an array of arrays. Each inner array contains three elements: `PropertyName`, `Operator`, and `Value`. We then build our `OrderByList` from the `Sort` array and call our `CDataManager` with the `GetData` method. We perform our normal `PropertyName` array creation, as well as the `GetRows` call. The code for `QueryObjectListData` appears in Listing 9.19.

Listing 9.19   **The *QueryObjectListData* Method on *IAppServer***

```
Public Sub QueryObjectListData(ByVal ClassId As Integer, _
                               ByVal Criteria As Variant, _
                               ByVal Sort As Variant, _
                               ByRef PropertyNames As Variant, _
                               Data As Variant, _
                               Errors As Variant)
  Dim ClassDef As CClassDef
  Dim DataManager As CDataManager
  Dim ColumnDef As CColumnDef
  Dim QueryParms As New CQueryParms
  Dim rs As ADODB.Recordset
  Dim rsField As ADODB.Field
  Dim vData As Variant
  Dim i As Integer
  Dim p As String

  On Error GoTo ErrorTrap

  Set ClassDef = mClassDefs.Item(ClassId)
  Set DataManager = mDataManagers.Item(ClassDef.DatabaseName)

  QueryParms.TableName = ClassDef.ReadLocation
  For Each ColumnDef In ClassDef.ColumnDefs
    If ColumnDef.CanRead Then
      QueryParms.ColumnList.Add ColumnDef.Name
    End If
  Next

  If IsArray(Criteria) Then
    ' Criteria(i)(0) = PropertyName
    ' Criteria(i)(1) = Operator
    ' Criteria(i)(2) = Value

    For i = LBound(Criteria, 1) To UBound(Criteria, 1)
      p = Criteria(i)(0)
      If IsNumeric(Criteria(i)(2)) Then
        QueryParms.WhereList.Add ClassDef.PropertyToColumnDef(p).Name & _
                             Criteria(i)(1) & Criteria(i)(2)
      Else
        QueryParms.WhereList.Add ClassDef.PropertyToColumnDef(p).Name & _
                             Criteria(i)(1) & "'" & Criteria(i)(2) & "'"
      End If
    Next i
    QueryParms.WhereOperator = woAnd
  End If

  If IsArray(Sort) Then
    For i = LBound(Sort) To UBound(Sort)
      QueryParms.OrderList.Add _
        ClassDef.PropertyToColumnDef(CStr(Sort(i))).Name
```

continues

Listing 9.19   **Continued**

```
   Next i
 End If

 Set rs = DataManager.GetData(QueryParms)

 If Not rs Is Nothing Then
   ReDim PropertyNames(0 To QueryParms.ColumnList.Count - 1)
   i = 0
   For Each rsField In rs.Fields
     PropertyNames(i) = ClassDef.ColumnToPropertyDef(rsField.Name).Name
     i = i + 1
   Next
   vData = rs.GetRows
 Else
   vData = vbEmpty
 End If

 Data = vData
 Exit Sub
ErrorTrap:
   '1.  Details to EventLog
   Call WriteNTLogEvent("IAppServer:QueryObjectListData", Err.Number, _
                     Err.Description, Err.Source)
   '2.  Generic to client - passed back on error stack
   Err.Raise Err.Number, "IAppServer:QueryObjectListData", _
                     Err.Description & " [" & Erl & "]"
End Sub
```

From our `CNWServer` class, the implementation of this method is provided in
Listing 9.20.

Listing 9.20   **The *QueryObjectListData* Method Implemented on *CNWServer***

```
Private Sub IAppServer_QueryObjectListData(ByVal ClassId As Integer, _
                                   ByVal Criteria As Variant, _
                                   ByVal Sort As Variant, _
                                   PropertyNames As Variant, _
                                   Data As Variant, _
                                   Errors As Variant)
   Call IAppServer_GetClassDef(ClassId)
   Call mIAppServer.QueryObjectListData(ClassId, _
                               Criteria, _
                               Sort, _
                               PropertyNames, _
                               Data, _
                               Errors)
End Sub
```

IAppClient/CNWClient

With our server-side IAppServer and CNWServer classes in place, we can move from the application tier to the user tier and build the client-side mates. In a similar fashion to the server side, we define an interface called IAppClient. Unlike IAppServer though, our implementing class CNWClient is responsible for implementing all methods defined by IAppClient. Our NWClient ActiveX DLL that contains CNWClient is responsible for defining a class for each class type of the library that is to be exposed to the client application. This definition takes the form of Visual Basic class modules, which define the same properties spelled out in the CClassDef on the server side. Our first order of business is to define an InitClient method that connects to the DCOM object using the passed-in server name. We always override our InitClient method with code similar to that shown for the CNWClient implementation in Listing 9.21.

Listing 9.21   **The *InitClient* Method Implemented on *CNWClient***

```
' From the declarations section
Option Explicit
Implements IAppClient
Private mIAppClient As IAppClient
Private NWServer As CNWServer

Private Sub IAppClient_InitClient(Server As String)
    Set NWServer = CreateObject("NWServer.CNWServer", Server)
    Set mIAppClient.AppServer = NWServer
    Call mIAppClient.AppServer.InitServer
End Sub
```

The InitClient method uses the CreateObject construct to create an instance of the CNWServer object. We use this rather than a New operator because this is the only mechanism that creates a DCOM object on a remote computer. The server name that is passed in is the same as the computer name of the machine running MTS which has a package installed that hosts the CNWServer class.

Now that we can connect to the DCOM client, we turn our attention to defining two more interfaces in the same ActiveX library as IAppClient. These two interfaces are IAppObject and IAppCollection, both of which we use to implement our final objects and collection of objects, respectively. Our IAppCollection contains a collection of IAppObjects. On our IAppObject, we define the methods of SetStateToVariant and SetStateFromVariant that we must override in our implementations. These methods are responsible for converting between native objects and variant Data arrays. We also define an IsValid method to help us check for validity across properties. Finally, we define properties Id and SubId used during our CRUD processing that we will be implementing. The interface definition for IAppObject appears in Listing 9.22.

Listing 9.22   **The *IAppObject* Interface Definition**

```
Option Explicit
Private mId As Long
Private mSubId As Long
Private mClassId As Integer
Private mIsLoaded As Boolean
Private mIsDirty As Boolean

Public Sub SetStateToVariant(PropertyNames As Collection, Data As Variant)
  ' override this method
End Sub

Public Sub SetStateFromVariant(PropertyNames As Collection, Data As Variant, _
                               Optional RowIndex As Integer)
  ' override this method
End Sub

Public Function IsValid() As Boolean
  ' override this method
End Function

Public Property Get Id() As Long
  Id = mId
End Property

Public Property Let Id(RHS As Long)
  mId = RHS
End Property

Public Property Get SubId() As Long
  SubId = mSubId
End Property

Public Property Let SubId(RHS As Long)
  mSubId = RHS
End Property

Public Property Get ClassId() As Long
  ClassId = mClassId
End Property

Public Property Let ClassId(RHS As Long)
  mClassId = RHS
End Property

Public Property Let IsLoaded(RHS As Boolean)
  mIsLoaded = RHS
End Property

Public Property Get IsLoaded() As Boolean
  IsLoaded = mIsLoaded
End Property
```

```
Public Property Let IsDirty(RHS As Boolean)
  mIsDirty = RHS
End Property

Public Property Get IsDirty() As Boolean
  IsDirty = mIsDirty
End Property
```

Our IAppCollection interface is a bit more complicated, but it implements many of the methods itself. This method also contains a SetStateFromVariant method to convert a two-dimensional variant Data array into a collection of objects. We also define a SetStateToVariant method for the reverse process. The other methods and properties are those required to implement a collection, including Item, Add, Count, and NewEnum. The interface definition for IAppCollection appears in Listing 9.23.

Listing 9.23   **The *IAppCollection* Interface Definition**

```
Option Explicit
Private mCol As Collection
Private mClassId As Integer
Private mIsLoaded As Boolean
Private mIsDirty As Boolean

Public Sub SetStateFromVariant(PropertyNames As Collection, Data As Variant)
  ' override this method
End Sub

Public Sub SetStateToVariant(PropertyNames As Collection, Data As Variant)
  ' override this method
End Sub

Public Property Get Item(vntIndexKey As Variant) As IAppObject
  Set Item = mCol(vntIndexKey)
End Property

Public Sub Add(AppObject As IAppObject, vntKey As Variant)
  mCol.Add AppObject, vntKey
End Sub

Public Property Get Count() As Long
  Count = mCol.Count
End Property

Public Property Get NewEnum() As IUnknown
  Set NewEnum = mCol.[_NewEnum]
End Property
```

continues

Listing 9.23   **Continued**

```
Private Sub Class_Initialize()
  Set mCol = New Collection
End Sub

Private Sub Class_Terminate()
  Set mCol = Nothing
End Sub

Public Property Get ClassId() As Long
  ClassId = mClassId
End Property

Public Property Let ClassId(RHS As Long)
  mClassId = RHS
End Property

Public Property Let IsLoaded(RHS As Boolean)
  mIsLoaded = RHS
End Property

Public Property Get IsLoaded() As Boolean
  IsLoaded = mIsLoaded
End Property

Public Property Let IsDirty(RHS As Boolean)
  mIsDirty = RHS
End Property

Public Property Get IsDirty() As Boolean
  IsDirty = mIsDirty
End Property
```

Again, we must override the `SetStateFromVariant` and `SetStateToVariant` methods for each class implementing this interface.

Now that we can connect to the DCOM client and we have our `IAppObject` and `IAppCollection` interfaces defined, we turn our attention to the data retrieval methods of `LoadObject` and `LoadCollection`. As you might guess, we will be calling the corresponding `GetObjectData` and `GetObjectDataList` methods on our `CNWServer` object.

We call `LoadObject` with a `ClassId` and an `Id`/`SubId` pair. It returns an `IAppObject` reference. Within the `LoadObject` method, we dimension a variable of each class type, along with an `IAppObject` object. We perform a `Select Case` statement to determine which object to create based on the `ClassId`. After we have identified the correct class type, we call the `GetObjectData` method of our `CNWServer` class. The code for `LoadObject` for our `CNWClient` class appears in Listing 9.24.

Listing 9.24   **The *LoadObject* Method Implemented on *CNWClient***

```
Private Function IAppClient_LoadObject(ClassId As Integer, _
                                       Id As Long, _
                                       SubId As Long) As _
                                       AppClient.IAppObject
   Dim AppObject As IAppObject
   Dim Order As COrder
   Dim CityItem As CCityItem
   Dim CategoryItem As CCategoryItem
   Dim CountryItem As CCountryItem
   Dim RegionItem As CRegionItem
   Dim CustomerItem As CCustomerItem
   Dim EmployeeItem As CEmployeeItem
   Dim ProductItem As CProductItem
   Dim ShipperItem As CShipperItem
   Dim SupplierItem As CSupplierItem
   Dim Data As Variant
   Dim Errors As Variant
   Dim PropertyNames() As String


   On Error GoTo ErrorTrap

   Select Case ClassId
     Case CT_ORDER
       Set Order = New COrder
       Set AppObject = Order
     Case CT_CATEGORY
       Set CategoryItem = New CCategoryItem
       Set AppObject = CategoryItem
     Case CT_CITY
       Set CityItem = New CCityItem
       Set AppObject = CityItem
     Case CT_COUNTRY
       Set CountryItem = New CCountryItem
       Set AppObject = CountryItem
     Case CT_REGION
       Set RegionItem = New CRegionItem
       Set AppObject = RegionItem
     Case CT_CUSTOMER
       Set CustomerItem = New CCustomerItem
       Set AppObject = CustomerItem
     Case CT_EMPLOYEE
       Set EmployeeItem = New CEmployeeItem
       Set AppObject = EmployeeItem
     Case CT_PRODUCT
       Set ProductItem = New CProductItem
       Set AppObject = ProductItem
     Case CT_SHIPPER
       Set ShipperItem = New CShipperItem
       Set AppObject = ShipperItem
```

continues

Listing 9.24 **Continued**

```
   Case CT_SUPPLIER
     Set SupplierItem = New CSupplierItem
     Set AppObject = SupplierItem
   Case Else
     GoTo SkipLoadObject
 End Select

 Call mIAppClient.AppServer.GetObjectData(ClassId, Id, SubId, _
                                   PropertyNames, Data, Errors)
 If IsArray(Data) Then
   AppObject.SetStateFromVariant(MakePropertyIndex(PropertyNames), Data
 End If
 Set IAppClient_LoadObject = AppObject

SkipLoadObject:
 Exit Function
ErrorTrap:
 Err.Raise ERR_CANNOT_LOAD + vbObjectError, "CNWClient:LoadObject", _
           LoadResString(ERR_CANNOT_LOAD) & "[" & Err.Description & "]"
End Function
```

As can be seen from the previous code sample, we must dimension each class type. We then perform a `Select Case` statement on the `ClassId`, creating the specific object instance of the requested class. We then set the instance of the generic `AppObject` variable to our specific instance of an object that has implemented the `IAppObject` interface. From there, we fall through to the `GetObjectData` method of our `CAppServer` variable. If the method returns a non-empty `Data` variable, we call the generic `SetStateFromVariant` method of our `AppObject` to move the information from the variant data array into the property values of the specific object. We then return our `AppObject` to the calling routine. The reason for the use of `AppObject` is to prevent the late binding that can slow performance. Using this approach can make our code base more modular.

To illustrate a specific implementation of the `SetStateFromVariant` method of an `IAppObject`, we offer the code for our `COrder` class in Listing 9.25.

Listing 9.25 **The *COrder* Class That Implements *IAppObject***

```
Option Explicit

Implements IAppObject

Private mCustomerId As Long 'local copy
Private mCustomerName As String 'local copy
Private mEmployeeId As Long 'local copy
Private mEmployeeLastName As String 'local copy
Private mEmployeeFirstName As String 'local copy
```

```vb
Private mOrderDate As Date 'local copy
Private mRequiredDate As Date 'local copy
Private mShippedDate As Date 'local copy
Private mShipperId As Long 'local copy
Private mShipperName As String 'local copy
Private mFreightCost As Double 'local copy
Private mShipToName As String 'local copy
Private mShipToAddress As String 'local copy
Private mShipToPostalCode As String 'local copy
Private mShipToCountry As String 'local copy
Private mShipToRegion As String 'local copy
Private mShipToCityId As Long 'local copy
Private mShipToCity As String 'local copy
Private mIAppObject As IAppObject

Private Property Let IAppObject_Id(RHS As Long)
  mIAppObject.Id = RHS
End Property

Private Property Get IAppObject_Id() As Long
  IAppObject_Id = mIAppObject.Id
End Property

Private Property Let IAppObject_SubId(RHS As Long)
  mIAppObject.SubId = RHS
End Property

Private Property Get IAppObject_SubId() As Long
  IAppObject_SubId = mIAppObject.SubId
End Property

Public Property Let ShipToCity(ByVal RHS As String)
    mShipToCity = RHS
End Property

Public Property Get ShipToCity() As String
    ShipToCity = mShipToCity
End Property

Public Property Let ShipToCityId(ByVal RHS As Long)
    mShipToCityId = RHS
End Property

Public Property Get ShipToCityId() As Long
    ShipToCityId = mShipToCityId
End Property

Public Property Let ShipToRegion(ByVal RHS As String)
    mShipToRegion = RHS
End Property
```

continues

Listing 9.25   **Continued**

```
Public Property Get ShipToRegion() As String
    ShipToRegion = mShipToRegion
End Property

Public Property Let ShipToCountry(ByVal RHS As String)
    mShipToCountry = RHS
End Property

Public Property Get ShipToCountry() As String
    ShipToCountry = mShipToCountry
End Property

Public Property Let ShipToPostalCode(ByVal RHS As String)
    mShipToPostalCode = RHS
End Property

Public Property Get ShipToPostalCode() As String
    ShipToPostalCode = mShipToPostalCode
End Property

Public Property Let ShipToAddress(ByVal RHS As String)
    mShipToAddress = RHS
End Property

Public Property Get ShipToAddress() As String
    ShipToAddress = mShipToAddress
End Property

Public Property Let ShipToName(ByVal RHS As String)
    mShipToName = RHS
End Property

Public Property Get ShipToName() As String
    ShipToName = mShipToName
End Property

Public Property Let FreightCost(ByVal RHS As Double)
    mFreightCost = RHS
End Property

Public Property Get FreightCost() As Double
    FreightCost = mFreightCost
End Property

Public Property Let ShipperName(ByVal RHS As String)
    mShipperName = RHS
End Property

Public Property Get ShipperName() As String
    ShipperName = mShipperName
End Property
```

```
Public Property Let ShipperId(ByVal RHS As Long)
    mShipperId = RHS
End Property

Public Property Get ShipperId() As Long
    ShipperId = mShipperId
End Property

Public Property Let ShippedDate(ByVal RHS As Date)
    mShippedDate = RHS
End Property

Public Property Get ShippedDate() As Date
    ShippedDate = mShippedDate
End Property

Public Property Let RequiredDate(ByVal RHS As Date)
    mRequiredDate = RHS
End Property

Public Property Get RequiredDate() As Date
    RequiredDate = mRequiredDate
End Property

Public Property Let OrderDate(ByVal RHS As Date)
    mOrderDate = RHS
End Property

Public Property Get OrderDate() As Date
    OrderDate = mOrderDate
End Property

Public Property Let EmployeeFirstName(ByVal RHS As String)
    mEmployeeFirstName = RHS
End Property

Public Property Get EmployeeFirstName() As String
    EmployeeFirstName = mEmployeeFirstName
End Property

Public Property Let EmployeeLastName(ByVal RHS As String)
    mEmployeeLastName = RHS
End Property

Public Property Get EmployeeLastName() As String
    EmployeeLastName = mEmployeeLastName
End Property

Public Property Let EmployeeId(ByVal RHS As Long)
    mEmployeeId = RHS
End Property
```

continues

Listing 9.25   **Continued**

```
Public Property Get EmployeeId() As Long
    EmployeeId = mEmployeeId
End Property

Public Property Let CustomerName(ByVal RHS As String)
    mCustomerName = RHS
End Property

Public Property Get CustomerName() As String
    CustomerName = mCustomerName
End Property

Public Property Let CustomerId(ByVal RHS As Long)
    mCustomerId = RHS
End Property

Public Property Get CustomerId() As Long
    CustomerId = mCustomerId
End Property

Private Sub IAppObject_SetStateFromVariant(PropertyNames As Collection, _
                                       Data As Variant, _
                                       Optional RowIndex As Integer)
  If IsMissing(RowIndex) Then RowIndex = 0
  mIAppObject.Id = Data(PropertyNames("Id"), RowIndex)
  CustomerId = _
    GetValue(Data(PropertyNames("CustomerId"), RowIndex), vbLong)
  CustomerName = _
    GetValue(Data(PropertyNames("CustomerName"), RowIndex), vbString)
  EmployeeId = _
    GetValue(Data(PropertyNames("EmployeeId"), RowIndex), vbLong)
  EmployeeLastName = _
    GetValue(Data(PropertyNames("EmployeeLastName"), RowIndex), vbString)
  EmployeeFirstName = _
    GetValue(Data(PropertyNames("EmployeeFirstName"), RowIndex), vbString)
  OrderDate = _
    GetValue(Data(PropertyNames("OrderDate"), RowIndex), vbDate)
  RequiredDate = _
    GetValue(Data(PropertyNames("RequiredDate"), RowIndex), vbDate)
  ShippedDate = _
    GetValue(Data(PropertyNames("ShippedDate"), RowIndex), vbDate)
  ShipperId = _
    GetValue(Data(PropertyNames("ShipperId"), RowIndex), vbLong)
  ShipperName = _
    GetValue(Data(PropertyNames("ShipperName"), RowIndex), vbString)
  FreightCost = _
    GetValue(Data(PropertyNames("FreightCost"), RowIndex), vbDouble)
  ShipToName = _
    GetValue(Data(PropertyNames("ShipToName"), RowIndex), vbString)
```

```
    ShipToAddress = _
      GetValue(Data(PropertyNames("ShipToAddress"), RowIndex), vbString)
    ShipToPostalCode = _
      GetValue(Data(PropertyNames("ShipToPostalCode"), RowIndex), vbString)
    ShipToCountry = _
      GetValue(Data(PropertyNames("ShipToCountry"), RowIndex), vbString)
    ShipToRegion = _
      GetValue(Data(PropertyNames("ShipToRegion"), RowIndex), vbString)
    ShipToCityId = _
      GetValue(Data(PropertyNames("ShipToCityId"), RowIndex), vbLong)
    ShipToCity = _
      GetValue(Data(PropertyNames("ShipToCity"), RowIndex), vbString)
End Sub
```

As you can see from the code, we have defined all our properties using Let and Get statements. If we choose, this technique allows us to provide to the client instant feedback about data validation. We also define an IsValid method on IAppObject, which performs validation across properties. If we look at the SetStateFromVariant method, we see that we have received a PropertyNames collection. This collection is a list of integers keyed on property names. The numeric values correspond to column positions in the Data array for a given property. We also receive an optional RowIndex parameter in case this Data array is the result of a multirow resultset.

We have also defined a simple helper function called GetValue to help us trap null values and convert them to a standard set of empty values. The simple code for this appears in Listing 9.26.

Listing 9.26   **The *GetValue()* Function**

```
Public Function GetValue(Data As Variant, _
                         Optional vbType As VbVarType) _
                         As Variant
  If Not IsMissing(vbType) Then
    Select Case vbType
      Case vbString
        GetValue = IIf(IsNull(Data), "", Data)
      Case vbDate
        GetValue = IIf(IsNull(Data), vbEmpty, Data)
      Case Else
        GetValue = IIf(IsNull(Data), 0, Data)
    End Select
  Else
    GetValue = IIf(IsNull(Data), vbEmpty, Data)
  End If
End Function
```

We call our `LoadCollection` method with a `ClassId` and a `ParentId/ParentSubId` pair. Within the `LoadCollection` method, we dimension a variable of each collection class type along with an `IAppCollection` object. We perform a `Select Case` statement to determine which collection to create based on the `ClassId`. After we have identified the correct class type, we call the `GetObjectListData` method of our `CNWServer`. The code for `LoadCollection` for our `CNWClient` object appears in Listing 9.27.

Listing 9.27 **The *LoadCollection* Method Implemented on *CNWClient***

```
Private Function IAppClient_LoadCollection(ClassId As Integer, _
                                           ParentId As Long, _
                                           ParentSubId As Long) _
                                           As AppClient.IAppCollection
    Dim AppCollection As IAppCollection
    Dim ListItems As CListItems
    Dim OrderDetailItems As COrderDetailItems
    Dim CategoryItems As CCategoryItems
    Dim CityItems As CCityItems
    Dim CountryItems As CCountryItems
    Dim RegionItems As CRegionItems
    Dim CustomerItems As CCustomerItems
    Dim EmployeeItems As CEmployeeItems
    Dim ProductItems As CProductItems
    Dim ShipperItems As CShipperItems
    Dim SupplierItems As CSupplierItems

    Dim Data As Variant
    Dim Errors As Variant
    Dim PropertyNames() As String

    On Error GoTo ErrorTrap

    Select Case ClassId
      Case CT_LIST_ITEM
        Set ListItems = New CListItems
        Set AppCollection = ListItems
      Case CT_ORDER_DETAIL
        Set OrderDetailItems = New COrderDetailItems
        Set AppCollection = OrderDetailItems
      Case CT_CATEGORY
        Set CategoryItems = New CCategoryItems
        Set AppCollection = CategoryItems
      Case CT_CITY
        Set CityItems = New CCityItems
        Set AppCollection = CityItems
      Case CT_COUNTRY
        Set CountryItems = New CCountryItems
        Set AppCollection = CountryItems
      Case CT_REGION
        Set RegionItems = New CRegionItems
        Set AppCollection = RegionItems
```

```
      Case CT_CUSTOMER
        Set CustomerItems = New CCustomerItems
        Set AppCollection = CustomerItems
      Case CT_EMPLOYEE
        Set EmployeeItems = New CEmployeeItems
        Set AppCollection = EmployeeItems
      Case CT_PRODUCT
        Set ProductItems = New CProductItems
        Set AppCollection = ProductItems
      Case CT_SHIPPER
        Set ShipperItems = New CShipperItems
        Set AppCollection = ShipperItems
      Case CT_SUPPLIER
        Set SupplierItems = New CSupplierItems
        Set AppCollection = SupplierItems
      Case Else
        GoTo SkipLoadCollection
    End Select

    Call mIAppClient.AppServer.GetObjectListData(ClassId, _
                                                 ParentId, _
                                                 ParentSubId, _
                                                 PropertyNames, _
                                                 Data, _
                                                 Errors)
    If IsArray(Data) Then
      AppCollection.SetStateFromVariant(MakePropertyIndex(PropertyNames), Data
    End If
    Set IAppClient_LoadCollection = AppCollection

SkipLoadCollection:
  Exit Function
ErrorTrap:
  Err.Raise ERR_CANNOT_LOAD + vbObjectError, "CNWClient:LoadCollection", _
            LoadResString(ERR_CANNOT_LOAD) & "[" & Err.Description & "]"
End Function
```

We define `LoadCollection` in a manner similar to `LoadObject`, except that we dimension collection classes and an `AppCollection` of type `IAppCollection`. We also call `GetObjectListData` on our `CAppServer` object, and we define a `SetStateFromVariant` on our `IAppCollection` interface. The code for our `COrderDetailItems` collection appears in Listing 9.28.

Listing 9.28 **The *COrderDetailItems* Collection**

```
Option Explicit

Implements IAppCollection
Dim mIAppCollection As IappCollection
```

continues

Listing 9.28   **Continued**

```
Private Sub Class_Initialize()
  Set mIAppCollection = New IAppCollection
End Sub

Private Sub Class_Terminate()
  Set mIAppCollection = Nothing
End Sub

Private Sub IAppCollection_Add_
  (AppObject As AppClient.IAppObject, vntKey As Variant)
  Call mIAppCollection.Add(AppObject, vntKey)
End Sub

Private Property Get IAppCollection_Count() As Long
  IAppCollection_Count = mIAppCollection.Count
End Property

Private Property Get IAppCollection_Item_
  (vntIndexKey As Variant) As AppClient.IAppObject
  Set IAppCollection_Item = mIAppCollection.Item(vntIndexKey)
End Property

Private Property Get IAppCollection_NewEnum() As stdole.IUnknown
  Set IAppCollection_NewEnum = IAppCollection.NewEnum
End Property

Private Sub IAppCollection_SetStateFromVariant(PropertyNames As Collection,_
    Data As Variant)
  Dim AppObject As IAppObject
  Dim OrderDetailItem As COrderDetailItem
  Dim i As Integer

  For i = LBound(Data, 2) To UBound(Data, 2)
    Set OrderDetailItem = New COrderDetailItem
    Set AppObject = OrderDetailItem
    Call AppObject.SetStateFromVariant(PropertyNames, Data, i)
    Call IAppCollection_Add(AppObject, CStr(OrderDetailItem.Id))
  Next i
End Sub

Private Property Get IAppCollection_ClassId() As Long
  IAppCollection_ClassId = mIAppCollection.ClassId
End Property

Private Property Let IAppCollection_ClassId(RHS As Long)
  mIAppCollection.ClassId = RHS
End Property

Private Property Get IAppCollection_IsDirty() As Boolean
  IAppCollection_IsDirty = mIAppCollection.IsDirty
End Property
```

```
Private Property Let IAppCollection_IsDirty(RHS As Boolean)
  mIAppCollection.IsDirty = RHS
End Property

Private Property Let IAppCollection_IsLoaded(RHS As Boolean)
  mIAppCollection.IsLoaded = RHS
End Property

Private Property Get IAppCollection_IsLoaded() As Boolean
  IAppCollection_IsLoaded = mIAppCollection.IsLoaded
End Property

Private Function IAppCollection_IsValid(Errors As Variant) As Boolean
  Dim i As Integer
  Dim AppObject As IAppObject
  IAppCollection_IsValid = True

  For i = 1 To mIAppCollection.Count
    Set AppObject = mIAppCollection.Item(i)
    IAppCollection_IsValid = IAppCollection_IsValid And _
                             AppObject.IsValid(Errors)
  Next i

End Function
Private Sub IAppCollection_Remove(vntIndexKey As Variant)
  Call mIAppCollection.Remove(vntIndexKey)
End Sub
```

The Add, Count, Item, and NewEnum methods tap directly into the mIAppCollection variable for functionality. Similarly, the IsLoaded, IsDirty, and ClassId properties are inherited from our mIAppCollection variable. The only methods that we override are the SetStateFromVariant and IsValid methods. In the SetStateFromVariant method, we loop through the Data array a row at a time. For each row, we instantiate our specific COrderDetailItem, set a generic IAppObject reference to it, and call the SetStateFromVariant method on the generic object reference. After the state has been set, we add the IAppObject reference onto the collection. We proceed for all rows of the Data array.

The SetStateFromVariant method for COrderDetailItem appears in Listing 9.29.

Listing 9.29   **The *SetStateFromVariant* Method Implemented on *COrderDetailItem***

```
Private Sub IAppObject_SetStateFromVariant(PropertyNames As Collection, _
                                           Data As Variant, _
                                           Optional RowIndex As Integer)
  If IsMissing(RowIndex) Then RowIndex = 0
  mIAppObject.Id = Data(PropertyNames("Id"), RowIndex)
  OrderId = GetValue(Data(PropertyNames("OrderId"), RowIndex), vbLong)
  ProductId = GetValue(Data(PropertyNames("ProductId"), RowIndex), vbLong)
```

continues

Listing 9.29 **Continued**

```
    Product = GetValue(Data(PropertyNames("Product"), RowIndex), vbString)
    Supplier = GetValue(Data(PropertyNames("Supplier"), RowIndex), vbString)
    UnitPrice = GetValue(Data(PropertyNames("UnitPrice"), RowIndex), vbDouble)
    Discount = GetValue(Data(PropertyNames("Discount"), RowIndex), vbDouble)
    IAppObject_IsDirty = False
End Sub
```

We implement all left-side variables on the object as `Property Let/Get` statements. We do not present the code for all objects here in the chapter, but the implementations are included in the code for the chapter.

We now define the delete portion of CRUD on the client side. Here, we define `DeleteObject` and `DeleteCollection` methods. Because of simplicity, we can implement the `DeleteObject` functionality in our `IAppClient` class and call into it from our `CNWClient` implementation. Within the `IAppClient` implementation of the `DeleteObject` method, we pass in our desired `ClassId`, `Id`, and `SubId` values. We then pass this information off to the `DeleteObject` method of our `IAppServer` object. The code for the `DeleteObject` method appears in Listing 9.30.

Listing 9.30 The *DeleteObject* **Method Implemented on** *CNWClient*

```
Public Sub DeleteObject(ClassId As Integer, Id As Long, SubId As Long, _
                        Errors As Variant)
    On Error GoTo ErrorTrap
    If Id > 0 Then
        Call mIAppServer.DeleteObject(ClassId, Id, SubId, Errors)
    End If
    Exit Sub
ErrorTrap:
    Err.Raise ERR_CANNOT_DELETE + vbObjectError, "IAppClient:DeleteObject", _
              LoadResString(ERR_CANNOT_DELETE) & "[" & Err.Description & "]"
End Sub
```

As you can see, this method implementation is straightforward. The call into this method from `CNWClient` appears in Listing 9.31.

Listing 9.31 The *DeleteObject* **Method on** *CNWClient*

```
Private Sub IAppClient_DeleteObject(ClassId As Integer, Id As Long, _
                                    SubId As Long, Errors As Variant)
    Call mIAppClient.DeleteObject(ClassId, Id, SubId, Errors)
End Sub
```

Likewise, we implement a `DeleteCollection` method that substitutes a `ParentId` and `ParentSubId` in its parameter list. The code for the `DeleteCollection` method appears in Listing 9.32.

Listing 9.32 **The *DeleteCollection* Method on *CNWClient***

```
Public Sub DeleteCollection(ClassId As Integer, ParentId As Long, _
                            ParentSubId As Long, Errors As Variant)
  On Error GoTo ErrorTrap
  If ParentId > 0 Then
    Call mIAppServer.DeleteObjectList(ClassId, ParentId, ParentSubId, Errors)
  End If
  Exit Sub
ErrorTrap:
  Err.Raise ERR_CANNOT_DELETE + vbObjectError, "IAppClient:DeleteCollection", _
            LoadResString(ERR_CANNOT_DELETE) & "[" & Err.Description & "]"
End Sub
```

Again, the CNWClient implementation is simple, as follows:

```
Private Sub IAppClient_DeleteCollection(ClassId As Integer, _
                                        ParentId As Long, _
                                        ParentSubId As Long, _
                                        Errors As Variant)
  Call mIAppClient.DeleteCollection(ClassId, ParentId, ParentSubId, Errors)
End Sub
```

Our attention now turns to the data insertion activity. We define an InsertObject method that takes ClassId and AppObject parameters with the latter being a return value. Again, we must dimension a variable of every supported class type. Using a Select Case statement, we instantiate our specific object reference and set it to the generic AppObject. We fall through to a block of code that creates the necessary property index for a subsequent call to the SetStateToVariant method of our generic AppObject. We then call the InsertObjectData method on our AppServer object to perform the insert. We expect the method to return ObjectId and ObjectSubId parameters, which we set to our Id and SubId properties of our AppObject. The code for the InsertObject method on CNWClient appears in Listing 9.33.

Listing 9.33 **The *InsertObject* Method Implemented on *CNWClient***

```
Private Sub IAppClient_InsertObject(ClassId As Integer, _
                                    AppObject As AppClient.IAppObject)
  Dim ObjectId As Long, ObjectSubId As Long
  Dim Order As COrder
  Dim CityItem As CCityItem
  Dim CategoryItem As CCategoryItem
  Dim CountryItem As CCountryItem
  Dim RegionItem As CRegionItem
  Dim CustomerItem As CCustomerItem
  Dim EmployeeItem As CEmployeeItem
  Dim ProductItem As CProductItem
  Dim ShipperItem As CShipperItem
  Dim SupplierItem As CSupplierItem
  Dim Data As Variant
```

continues

Listing 9.33   **Continued**

```
        Dim Errors As Variant
        Dim PropertyNames As Variant
        Dim PropertyIndex As Collection

        On Error GoTo ErrorTrap

        Select Case ClassId
          Case CT_ORDER
            Set Order = AppObject
          Case CT_CATEGORY
            Set CategoryItem = AppObject
          Case CT_CITY
            Set CityItem = AppObject
          Case CT_COUNTRY
            Set CountryItem = AppObject
          Case CT_REGION
            Set RegionItem = AppObject
          Case CT_CUSTOMER
            Set CustomerItem = AppObject
          Case CT_EMPLOYEE
            Set EmployeeItem = AppObject
          Case CT_PRODUCT
            Set ProductItem = AppObject
          Case CT_SHIPPER
            Set ShipperItem = AppObject
          Case CT_SUPPLIER
            Set SupplierItem = AppObject
          Case Else
            GoTo SkipInsertObject
        End Select

        PropertyNames = mIAppClient.AppServer.GetPropertyNames(ClassId)
        Set PropertyIndex = MakePropertyIndex(PropertyNames)
        ReDim Data(1 To PropertyIndex.Count, 0)
        Call AppObject.SetStateToVariant(PropertyIndex, Data)
        Call mIAppClient.AppServer.InsertObjectData(ClassId, PropertyNames, _
                                          Data, Errors, _
                                          ObjectId, ObjectSubId)

        AppObject.Id = ObjectId
        AppObject.SubId = ObjectSubId

SkipInsertObject:
      Exit Sub
ErrorTrap:
      Err.Raise ERR_CANNOT_INSERT + vbObjectError, _
            "CNWClient:InsertObject", _
            LoadResString(ERR_CANNOT_INSERT) & "[" & Err.Description & "]"
      End Sub
```

The `InsertCollection` method follows a similar pattern whereby an `AppCollection` is passed in on the parameter list along with `ParentId` and `ParentSubId` values. Again, we dimension a variable of each type, setting the appropriate value in a `Select Case` statement. We fall through to a block of code that creates the necessary property index for a subsequent call to the `SetStateToVariant` method of the collection. We follow this by a call to our `InsertObjectListData` method of our `AppServer` object. The code for the `InsertCollection` method of `CNWClient` appears in Listing 9.34.

Listing 9.34   **The *InsertCollection* Method Implemented on *CNWClient***

```
Private Sub IAppClient_InsertCollection(ClassId As Integer, _
                     ParentId As Long, _
                     ParentSubId As Long, _
                     AppCollection As AppClient.IAppCollection, _
                     Errors As Variant)
    Dim ListItems As CListItems
    Dim OrderDetailItems As COrderDetailItems
    Dim CategoryItems As CCategoryItems
    Dim CityItems As CCityItems
    Dim CountryItems As CCountryItems
    Dim RegionItems As CRegionItems
    Dim CustomerItems As CCustomerItems
    Dim EmployeeItems As CEmployeeItems
    Dim ProductItems As CProductItems
    Dim ShipperItems As CShipperItems
    Dim SupplierItems As CSupplierItems

    Dim Data As Variant
    Dim PropertyNames As Variant
    Dim PropertyIndex As Collection

    On Error GoTo ErrorTrap

  Select Case ClassId
     Case CT_LIST_ITEM
       Set ListItems = AppCollection
     Case CT_ORDER_DETAIL
       Set OrderDetailItems = AppCollection
     Case CT_CATEGORY
       Set CategoryItems = AppCollection
     Case CT_CITY
       Set CityItems = AppCollection
     Case CT_COUNTRY
       Set CountryItems = AppCollection
     Case CT_REGION
       Set RegionItems = AppCollection
     Case CT_CUSTOMER
       Set CustomerItems = AppCollection
     Case CT_EMPLOYEE
       Set EmployeeItems = AppCollection
```

continues

Listing 9.34   **Continued**

```
      Case CT_PRODUCT
        Set ProductItems = AppCollection
      Case CT_SHIPPER
        Set ShipperItems = AppCollection
      Case CT_SUPPLIER
        Set SupplierItems = AppCollection
      Case Else
        GoTo SkipInsertCollection
    End Select

    PropertyNames = mIAppClient.AppServer.GetPropertyNames(ClassId)
    Set PropertyIndex = MakePropertyIndex(PropertyNames)
    ReDim Data(1 To PropertyIndex.Count, 1 To AppCollection.Count)
    Call AppCollection.SetStateToVariant(PropertyIndex, Data)
    Call mIAppClient.AppServer.InsertObjectListData(ClassId, _
                                                    ParentId, _
                                                    ParentSubId, _
                                                    PropertyNames, _
                                                    Data, _
                                                    Errors)

SkipInsertCollection:
  Exit Sub
ErrorTrap:
  Err.Raise ERR_CANNOT_INSERT + vbObjectError, "CNWClient:InsertCollection", _
          LoadResString(ERR_CANNOT_INSERT) & "[" & Err.Description & "]"
End Sub
```

For our `OrderDetailItems` collection, we simply hook into the `SetStateToVariant`
method of our `IAppCollection` interface. The simple code on `CNWClient` follows:

```
Private Sub IAppCollection_SetStateToVariant(PropertyNames As Collection, _
                                             Data As Variant)
  Call mIAppCollection.SetStateToVariant(PropertyNames, Data)
End Sub
```

Our `UpdateObject` method is similar in calling convention to our `InsertObject`
method. Here, we pass in our generic `AppObject` reference in conjunction with a
`ClassId`. Again, we dimension a variable of each class type for which we plan to provide update functionality. We use a `Select Case` statement to identify the class type,
creating our specific reference followed by a setting to our generic `AppObject` reference. We fall through to a block of code that creates the necessary property index for a
subsequent call to the `SetStateToVariant` method of our generic `AppObject`. We then
call the `UpdateObjectData` method on our `AppServer` object to perform the insert. The
code for the `UpdateObject` method on `CNWClient` appears in Listing 9.35.

Listing 9.35   **The *UpdateObject* Method Implemented on *CNWClient***

```
Private Sub IAppClient_UpdateObject(ClassId As Integer, _
                                   AppObject As AppClient.IAppObject)
  Dim ObjectId As Long, ObjectSubId As Long
  Dim Order As COrder
  Dim CityItem As CCityItem
  Dim CategoryItem As CCategoryItem
  Dim CountryItem As CCountryItem
  Dim RegionItem As CRegionItem
  Dim CustomerItem As CCustomerItem
  Dim EmployeeItem As CEmployeeItem
  Dim ProductItem As CProductItem
  Dim ShipperItem As CShipperItem
  Dim SupplierItem As CSupplierItem
  Dim Data As Variant
  Dim Errors As Variant
  Dim PropertyNames As String
  Dim PropertyIndex As Collection

  On Error GoTo ErrorTrap

  ObjectSubId = 0
  Select Case ClassId
    Case CT_ORDER
      Set Order = AppObject
    Case CT_CATEGORY
      Set CategoryItem = AppObject
    Case CT_CITY
      Set CityItem = AppObject
    Case CT_COUNTRY
      Set CountryItem = AppObject
    Case CT_REGION
      Set RegionItem = AppObject
    Case CT_CUSTOMER
      Set CustomerItem = AppObject
    Case CT_EMPLOYEE
      Set EmployeeItem = AppObject
    Case CT_PRODUCT
      Set ProductItem = AppObject
    Case CT_SHIPPER
      Set ShipperItem = AppObject
    Case CT_SUPPLIER
      Set SupplierItem = AppObject
    Case Else
      GoTo SkipUpdateObject
  End Select

  ObjectId = AppObject.Id
  ObjectSubId = AppObject.SubId
  PropertyNames = mIAppClient.AppServer.GetPropertyNames(ClassId)
  Set PropertyIndex = MakePropertyIndex(PropertyNames)
```

continues

Listing 9.35   **Continued**

```
    Call AppObject.SetStateToVariant(PropertyIndex, Data)
    Call mIAppClient.AppServer.UpdateObjectData(ClassId, PropertyNames, _
                                        Data, Errors, _
                                        ObjectId, ObjectSubId)

SkipUpdateObject:
  Exit Sub
ErrorTrap:
  Err.Raise ERR_CANNOT_UPDATE + vbObjectError, _
            "CNWClient:UpdateObject", _
            LoadResString(ERR_CANNOT_UPDATE) & "[" & Err.Description & "]"
End Sub
```

Our SetStateToVariant method does the reverse of our SetStateFromVariant
method by moving the state information of the object into a variant array. The code
for our COrder object appears in Listing 9.36.

Listing 9.36   **The *SetStateToVariant* Method Implemented on *COrder***

```
Private Sub IAppObject_SetStateToVariant(PropertyNames As Collection, _
                                        Data As Variant, _
                                        Optional RowIndex As Integer)
    If IsMissing(RowIndex) Then RowIndex = 0
    Data(PropertyNames("Id"), RowIndex) = mIAppObject.Id
    Data(PropertyNames("CustomerId"), RowIndex) = CustomerId
    Data(PropertyNames("EmployeeId"), RowIndex) = EmployeeId
    Data(PropertyNames("OrderDate"), RowIndex) = OrderDate
    Data(PropertyNames("ShippedDate"), RowIndex) = ShippedDate
    Data(PropertyNames("RequiredDate"), RowIndex) = RequiredDate
    Data(PropertyNames("ShipperId"), RowIndex) = ShipperId
    Data(PropertyNames("FreightCost"), RowIndex) = FreightCost
    Data(PropertyNames("ShipToName"), RowIndex) = ShipToName
    Data(PropertyNames("ShipToAddress"), RowIndex) = ShipToAddress
    Data(PropertyNames("ShipToPostalCode"), RowIndex) = ShipToPostalCode
    Data(PropertyNames("ShipToCityId"), RowIndex) = ShipToCityId
End Sub
```

We assume that the calling function has already dimensioned our Data array to the
appropriate size. We start by creating a variant array of the same size as the number of
property names. We again use the PropertyNames collection to index into the appropriate element of the Data array to set the state value.

Finally, we implement our LoadQueryCollection method. Again, because this is for
programmatic use, we do not need a high level of sophistication in its implementation.
Here, we take our ClassId, along with WhereClause and OrderClause arrays, and
return an IAppCollection. Again, we dimension variables of our specific collections

and use a `Select Case` statement to set our specific reference. We pass the `WhereClause` and `OrderClause` parameters through to the `QueryObjectListData` method of our `AppServer`. This call returns `Data` and `PropertyNames` arrays. Again, we pass these values into our `SetStateFromVariant` method to retrieve our final collection. The code for our `LoadQueryCollection` method appears in Listing 9.37.

Listing 9.37   **The *LoadQueryCollection* Method on *CNWClient***

```
Private Function IAppClient_LoadQueryCollection(ClassId As Integer, _
                                       WhereClause As Variant, _
                                       OrderClause As Variant) _
                                       As AppClient.IAppCollection
    Dim AppCollection As IAppCollection
    Dim ListItems As CListItems
    Dim OrderDetailItems As COrderDetailItems
    Dim CategoryItems As CCategoryItems
    Dim CityItems As CCityItems
    Dim CountryItems As CCountryItems
    Dim RegionItems As CRegionItems
    Dim CustomerItems As CCustomerItems
    Dim EmployeeItems As CEmployeeItems
    Dim ProductItems As CProductItems
    Dim ShipperItems As CShipperItems
    Dim SupplierItems As CSupplierItems
    Dim Orders As COrders

    Dim Data As Variant
    Dim Errors As Variant
    Dim PropertyNames() As String

    On Error GoTo ErrorTrap

    Select Case ClassId
      Case CT_LIST_ITEM
        Set ListItems = New CListItems
        Set AppCollection = ListItems
      Case CT_ORDER
        Set Orders = New COrders
        Set AppCollection = Orders
      Case CT_ORDER_DETAIL
        Set OrderDetailItems = New COrderDetailItems
        Set AppCollection = OrderDetailItems
      Case CT_CATEGORY
        Set CategoryItems = New CCategoryItems
        Set AppCollection = CategoryItems
      Case CT_CITY
        Set CityItems = New CCityItems
        Set AppCollection = CityItems
```

continues

Listing 9.37   **Continued**

```
        Case CT_COUNTRY
          Set CountryItems = New CCountryItems
          Set AppCollection = CountryItems
        Case CT_REGION
          Set RegionItems = New CRegionItems
          Set AppCollection = RegionItems
        Case CT_CUSTOMER
          Set CustomerItems = New CCustomerItems
          Set AppCollection = CustomerItems
        Case CT_EMPLOYEE
          Set EmployeeItems = New CEmployeeItems
          Set AppCollection = EmployeeItems
        Case CT_PRODUCT
          Set ProductItems = New CProductItems
          Set AppCollection = ProductItems
        Case CT_SHIPPER
          Set ShipperItems = New CShipperItems
          Set AppCollection = ShipperItems
        Case CT_SUPPLIER
          Set SupplierItems = New CSupplierItems
          Set AppCollection = SupplierItems
        Case Else
          GoTo SkipQueryCollection
      End Select

      Call mIAppClient.AppServer.QueryObjectListData(ClassId, WhereClause, _
                                         OrderClause, PropertyNames, _
                                         Data, Errors)
      If IsArray(Data) Then
        AppCollection.SetStateFromVariant(MakePropertyIndex(PropertyNames), Data
      End If
      Set IAppClient_LoadQueryCollection = AppCollection

  SkipQueryCollection:
    Exit Function
  ErrorTrap:
    Err.Raise ERR_CANNOT_LOAD + vbObjectError, _
            "CNWClient:LoadQueryCollection", LoadResString(ERR_CANNOT_LOAD) & _
            "[" & Err.Description & "]"

  End Function
```

What We Have Accomplished

We have covered a significant amount of material in this chapter to introduce and
define the multi-part business object. Because it might be all jumbled at this point, the
simple diagram in Figure 9.3 shows what we have done.

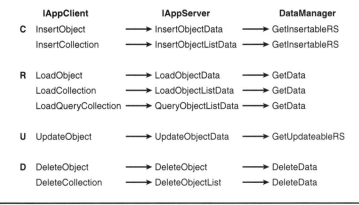

Figure 9.3 The relationship between the parts of the business layer.

Installing Components into MTS

Now that we have completed our AppServer and NWServer components, we must install them into MTS so that our AppClient and NWClient can access them. Components within MTS are placed into groups called packages. One package can host multiple components, but one component can reside within only one package. A package is an administration convenience when installing and transferring these components between MTS machines and creating client-side installation routines to access these components.

Creating the Package

To start our installation process, we must start the MTS Explorer. From within the MTS Explorer, open the Packages Installed folder under the My Computer folder, as shown in Figure 9.4. This assumes that we are running the MTS Explorer on the same computer that will host our MTS components.

From the Packages folder, right-click, select New, and then Package. This brings up the Package Wizard dialog as shown in Figure 9.5.

From the Package Wizard, select the Create an Empty Package button. In the Create Empty Package dialog that appears, type the name of our package, in this case Northwind Traders. Click on the Next button, which takes us to the Set Package Identity page of the wizard. Next, select the Interactive User option and click the Next button. Note that this option can be changed later after the package is installed.

Click the Finish button to complete the process. We now see that our new package has been added in the MTS Explorer, as shown in Figure 9.6.

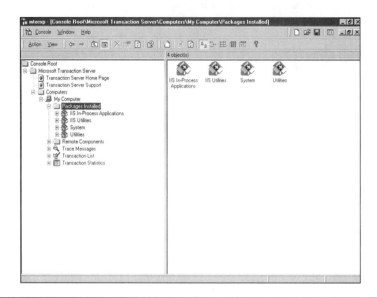

Figure 9.4   Navigating to the Packages folder in MTS.

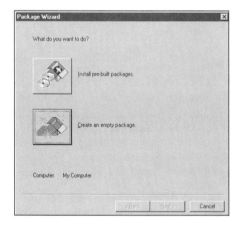

Figure 9.5   Launching the Package Wizard.

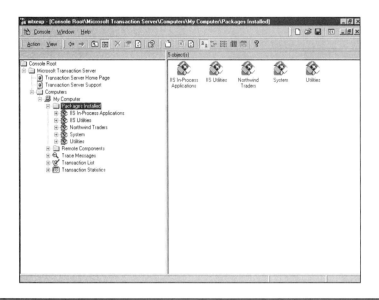

Figure 9.6   The newly added Northwind Traders package.

To add our `AppServer` and `NWServer` components to the package, we first must expand the Northwind Traders package to gain visibility to the Components folder. This appears in Figure 9.7.

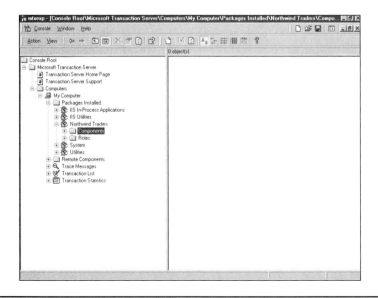

Figure 9.7   Navigating to the Components folder.

If we right-click on the Components folder, and then select New, Component, the Component Wizard appears as shown in Figure 9.8.

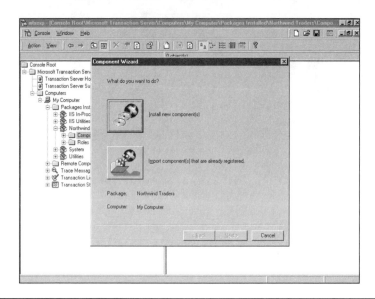

Figure 9.8 Launching the Component Wizard.

From the first page of the Component Wizard, select the Install New Component(s) option. From the Install Components dialog, click the Add Files button. From there we browse to our directory with our AppServer component and click on the Open button. Click on the Add Files button once again and select the NWServer component. After both files have been selected, our dialog looks like Figure 9.9.

We click on the Finish button to add our components to the package. If we take a look at our MTS Explorer, we will see that the two new components appear under the Components folder and in the right pane. This is shown in Figure 9.10.

Creating Client-Side Stubs

With our components now running inside MTS, we must make them accessible to our client machines. The easiest way to do this is to use MTS to create an Export Package. This package not only creates a client-side installer, it also creates a file necessary to move a package from one MTS machine to another.

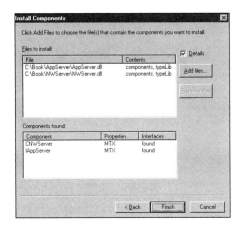

Figure 9.9 Adding components to the package.

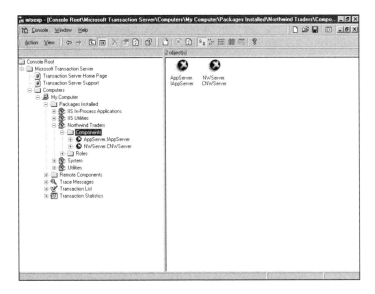

Figure 9.10 Our newly added components.

To create the export package, we right-click on the Northwind Traders package in the MTS Explorer and select the Export menu item. The Export Package dialog appears as shown in Figure 9.11.

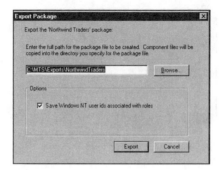

Figure 9.11   Exporting our package.

We enter the name of the path to which we want to export, and click the Export button. Upon completion of this process, MTS has created a NorthwindTraders.Pak file in the directory that we specified. It has also placed a copy of AppServer.DLL and NWServer.DLL into the same directory as the PAK file. Additionally, a subdirectory named Clients has been created that contains a file named NorthwindTraders.exe. This executable program is the setup program that sets the appropriate registry settings on the client machine to enable remote access. If we were to look at our references to our AppServer and NWServer components within Visual Basic after running this installer, it would look something like Figure 9.12.

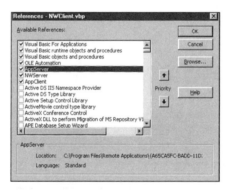

Figure 9.12   Our remote components installed on our client.

From Figure 9.12, you can see how the file reference to our AppServer component is now set to C:\Program Files\Remote Applications\{A65CA5FC-BADD-11D3...}. The client-side installer set up this directory and remapped our AppServer reference to it via the registry. It also modified the registry to inform the DCOM engine that this component runs on a remote server.

Moving the Package

Each time we install a component into an MTS server, a new GUID is generated for that component. If we want to move our package to another MTS machine without generating a new GUID, we must import into the new MTS machine the PAK file we generated in the previous section. By doing this, our client applications do not need to be recompiled with the new GUID, but instead simply point to the new MTS server.

To import a PAK file, we simply right-click on our Packages folder on the target MTS server and select the New menu item. From the Package Wizard that appears, we select the Install Pre-Built Package option. On the Select Packages page, we browse to the PAK file we created and select it. We click the Next button to arrive at the Set Package Identity page, where we once again choose the Interactive User option. We click the Next button once again, and enter the target location of where the files should be installed. We click the Finish button to complete the process.

Summary

In this chapter, we discussed the heart of our application framework—the multipart distributed business object. In so doing we have abstracted as much functionality into several interfaces on both the client and server sides so that build-out of our specific application is as easy as possible. We have also provided that build-out for our sample Northwind application.

We also talked about some of the fundamentals of MTS. At one level, we looked at the programming model that must be used to take full advantage of its transactional and object pooling features. We also looked at how to deploy our MTS objects from both a server- and client-side perspective.

In the next chapter, we will complete the last layer of the system, the user layer. We will look at building reusable ActiveX controls that interface tightly with our multipart distributed business object that we built in this chapter.

10

Adding an ActiveX Control to the Framework

U SER INTERFACE DESIGN CAN TAKE on many different forms based on the many different views on the subject. Indeed, such topics can be the subject matter of a book in itself. In Part I, "An Overview of Tools and Technologies," we discussed how the central design issue for an enterprise system is focused first on the business layer and how the data and user layers are a natural outgrowth of this within our framework. We also demonstrated the manifestation of the business and data layers in Chapter 8, "The DataManager Library," and Chapter 9, "A Two-Part, Distributed Business Object;" so now let us turn our attention to the user layer.

Design Theory

Although we can define our user layer directly using Visual Basic forms, we have chosen to implement our user interface with ActiveX controls that are subsequently placed into these forms. The reason for this is that it gives us the added flexibility of placing these elements into an (IE) Internet Explorer-based browser, enabling us to provide a rich interface that cannot be provided with simple HTML form elements. Our design also enables us to transparently place these same controls into any other environment that enables the use of ActiveX control hosting. The ultimate benefit derived from this architecture is that we can place our controls in any VBA-enabled application, giving us powerful integration opportunities.

To start our design, we must define our basic user interface metaphors. The entry point into an application can vary, but here we follow a simple Microsoft Explorer approach. Other approaches can include the Microsoft Outlook version, a simple Single Document Interface (SDI) or a Multiple Document Interface (MDI) interface. We use the Explorer here because it maps easily to an object-oriented framework and is simpler to build for the sake of exposition. For our individual dialogs, we are following a simple tabbed dialog approach, again because of the natural mapping to object orientation.

Implementation

This section discusses the details of building the Explorer- and Tabbed Dialog-style interfaces necessary for our application framework.

Our Explorer interface is covered first. This interface mechanism is more generically called an *outliner* because it is especially well suited for representing an object hierarchy or set of hierarchies. This representation enables us to build a navigational component for the user to quickly browse to an area of the system in which he is particularly interested. It is easy to extend the infrastructure provided by our outliner to implement an object selection mechanism, as well.

Our Tabbed Dialog interface is covered next. This interface has a more generic name, often referred to as a *property page*. It is well suited to represent an object within our system. Through the browsing mechanism provided by the outliner, we can choose a particular object that interests us and open it up for viewing and potential editing.

The Explorer Interface

The initial development of our Explorer interface is easy because Visual Basic provides a wizard to do most of the dirty work. For our Explorer, we have chosen not to implement any menus but instead to rely solely on a toolbar. After we have used Visual Basic's wizard to create an Explorer application, we create a new User Control project named NWExplorer and copy over the objects and code. Before copying, we delete the common dialog control that Visual Basic creates because we will not be using it. In the target User Control project, we must set a component reference to the Microsoft Windows Common Controls 6.0 control. We then create a Standard EXE project, called Northwind, and add a form with the name frmNorthWind. We set a component reference to our newly created NWExplorer component and drop it onto frmNorthWind. We show the end result of this effort in Figure 10.1, albeit after we have implemented the NWExplorer control that is to follow.

We are using the Explorer control not only for navigational purposes through our various objects but also for the implementation of simple add and delete functionality. We also take advantage of the fact that the TreeView component of the Explorer natively understands the object hierarchy that we can use to help us maintain our parent/child relationships more efficiently. For example, in managing our country, region, and city object hierarchies, it is much easier for the user to click on a region node and have a pop-up menu with the option of adding a new city to it. The counter-option to this would be to have a dialog with multiple `ComboBox` controls, managing the loading between them based on inputs from the others. For example, choosing a new country would reload a region `ComboBox`. Choosing a new region would reload a city `ComboBox`.

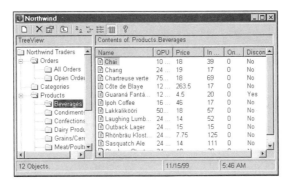

Figure 10.1   The Northwind Explorer entry point.

Many third-party Explorer-style controls are on the market, many of which you might prefer to use rather than one implemented in these examples. We do not intend for the code samples that follow to constitute a complete coverage of the design theory of an Explorer control. Instead, our goal is to discuss how to use our client components covered in the last chapter to complete the application. As such, we do not spend any time going over the code that Visual Basic generates to implement the Explorer. Instead, we focus on the code that we are adding to hook this Explorer code into our `IAppClient`, `IAppCollection`, and `IAppObject` components created in Chapter 9, "A Two-Part, Distributed Business Object."

The first item to discuss is another interface, which, in this case, we define to support our Explorer control. We use this interface, which we call `IExplorerItem`, to help us manage the information necessary to manage the `TreeView` and `ListView` controls that make up the Explorer. It is convenient that Microsoft defines the `Tag` property of a `TreeView` `Node` object as a `Variant` so that we can use this to hold a reference to an `IExplorerItem` object associated with the node. We use this bound reference to help us determine the actions that the `NWExplorer` control must take relative to user interaction. As with most of our interface definitions, the majority of the properties are common and thus implemented by `IExplorerItem`. However, there is one property that we must override for our specific implementation.

Creating a Client-Side Common Support Library

To start with, we create a new ActiveX DLL in which to put our `IExplorerItem` interface definition. Because we must create several other client-side classes to help drive these ActiveX controls and the application in general, we call this project `AppCommon`. This library constitutes our system layer on the client tier. We will be adding other classes to this DLL throughout this chapter.

The properties on `IExplorerItem` are straightforward. They include several Boolean-based properties to indicate how the state management for the toolbar should be handled, as well as how the `TreeView` of the Explorer can be traversed. Specifically, we call these properties `CanAdd`, `CanDelete`, `CanUpdate`, and `CanGoUp`. We also have several other properties to handle how a given node of the `TreeView` component appears. These properties include `Caption`, `ImageIndex`, and `ImageIndexExpanded`. These latter two properties represent indexes into the image lists associated with the `TreeView` and `ListView` controls. We have populated our image lists with simple open and closed folder icons, but you can add images that correspond directly to the type of object related to a given node. If both large and small icons are to be used, it is assumed that two image lists are set up in a parallel manner. Next, we have a property, `Loaded`, to tell us whether we have already loaded our child nodes so that we potentially do not repeat a long-running load. We also define two other properties to hold references to either `IAppObject` or `IAppCollection` objects. The use of these latter properties becomes apparent later in the chapter.

The only property that we override on `IExplorerItem` is `Mode`. It is here that we add our application-specific information. To implement this property, we must first create a `CNWExplorerItem` class within our `NWExplorer` user control project. We must also define a set of constants to represent our Explorer-type items. For our Northwind application, we place these constants into a code module within the NWExplorer project. We define these constants as follows in Listing 10.1.

Listing 10.1 **Constants Defined Within Our *NWExplorer* User Control Project**

```
Public Const EIT_INIT = -1
Public Const EIT_ROOT = 0
Public Const EIT_CATEGORY = 1
Public Const EIT_CRC = 2
Public Const EIT_CUSTOMER = 3
Public Const EIT_EMPLOYEE = 4
Public Const EIT_LISTITEM = 5
Public Const EIT_ORDER_ROOT = 6
Public Const EIT_ORDER = 7
Public Const EIT_PRODUCT = 8
Public Const EIT_SHIPPER = 9
Public Const EIT_SUPPLIER = 10
Public Const EIT_ORDER_ALL = 11
Public Const EIT_ORDER_OPEN = 12
Public Const EIT_PRODUCT_ROOT As Integer = 13
```

```
Public Const EIT_PRODUCT_CATEGORY As Integer = 14
Public Const EIT_COUNTRY_ROOT As Integer = 15
Public Const EIT_COUNTRY_REGION_ROOT As Integer = 16
Public Const EIT_COUNTRY_REGION_CITY As Integer = 17
Public Const EIT_ADMIN = 100
Public Const EIT_ALL = 999
```

You might notice that many of the names look conspicuously close to our class type constants, whereas others look a little different. These constants are purely arbitrary because we tie them to our CT_xxx constants logically in our code. We use the EIT_INIT, EIT_ROOT, EIT_CRC, EIT_ADMIN, and EIT_ALL constants for control purposes. We demonstrate their use in code samples that follow. Note that our Explorer not only provides navigation for the Northwind system but also selection functions for the various dialogs we will be creating. This is the reason for the EIT_ALL constant. We can place this control in Explorer mode by setting the SelectMode property to EIT_ALL, while any other setting constitutes a selection mode for a particular class.

Back to the implementation of our Mode property on CNWExplorerItem, it looks like the code in Listing 10.2.

Listing 10.2   **The Implementation of the *Mode* Property Within Our**
CNWExplorerItem **Class**

```
Public Property Let IExplorerItem_Mode(ByVal RHS As Integer)
  With mIExplorerItem
    Select Case RHS
      Case EIT_ROOT
        .Caption = "Northwind Traders"
        .ImageIndex = IML16_FOLDER
        .ImageIndexExpanded = IML16_FOLDER
        .CanAdd = False
        .CanDelete = False
        .CanUpdate = False
        .CanGoUp = False

      Case EIT_ADMIN
        .Caption = "Administration"
        .ImageIndex = IML16_FOLDER
        .ImageIndexExpanded = IML16_FOLDER
        .CanAdd = False
        .CanDelete = False
        .CanUpdate = False
        .CanGoUp = True

      Case EIT_COUNTRY_ROOT
        .Caption = "Countries"
        .ImageIndex = IML16_FOLDER
```

continues

Listing 10.2 **Continued**

```
          .ImageIndexExpanded = IML16_FOLDER
          .CanAdd = True
          .CanDelete = True
          .CanUpdate = True
          .CanGoUp = True

     Case EIT_COUNTRY_REGION_ROOT
          .Caption = "Regions"
          .ImageIndex = IML16_FOLDER
          .ImageIndexExpanded = IML16_FOLDER
          .CanAdd = True
          .CanDelete = True
          .CanUpdate = True
          .CanGoUp = True

     Case EIT_COUNTRY_REGION_CITY
          .Caption = "Cities"
          .ImageIndex = IML16_FOLDER
          .ImageIndexExpanded = IML16_FOLDER
          .CanAdd = False
          .CanDelete = False
          .CanUpdate = False
          .CanGoUp = True

     Case EIT_COUNTRY
          .Caption = "Country"
          .ImageIndex = IML16_FOLDER
          .ImageIndexExpanded = IML16_FOLDER
          .CanAdd = True
          .CanDelete = True
          .CanUpdate = True
          .CanGoUp = True

     Case EIT_REGION
          .Caption = "Country"
          .ImageIndex = IML16_FOLDER
          .ImageIndexExpanded = IML16_FOLDER
          .CanAdd = True
          .CanDelete = True
          .CanUpdate = True
          .CanGoUp = True

     Case EIT_CITY
          .Caption = "Country"
          .ImageIndex = IML16_FOLDER
          .ImageIndexExpanded = IML16_FOLDER
          .CanAdd = True
          .CanDelete = True
          .CanUpdate = True
          .CanGoUp = True
```

```
Case EIT_LISTITEM
  .Caption = "Lists"
  .ImageIndex = IML16_FOLDER
  .ImageIndexExpanded = IML16_FOLDER
  .CanAdd = False
  .CanDelete = False
  .CanUpdate = False
  .CanGoUp = True

Case EIT_CATEGORY
  .Caption = "Categories"
  .ImageIndex = IML16_FOLDER
  .ImageIndexExpanded = IML16_FOLDEROPEN
  .CanAdd = True
  .CanDelete = True
  .CanUpdate = True
  .CanGoUp = False

Case EIT_PRODUCT
  .Caption = "Products"
  .ImageIndex = IML16_FOLDER
  .ImageIndexExpanded = IML16_FOLDEROPEN
  .CanAdd = True
  .CanDelete = True
  .CanUpdate = True
  .CanGoUp = False

Case EIT_PRODUCT_ROOT
  .Caption = "Products"
  .ImageIndex = IML16_FOLDER
  .ImageIndexExpanded = IML16_FOLDEROPEN
  .CanAdd = False
  .CanDelete = False
  .CanUpdate = False
  .CanGoUp = True

Case EIT_PRODUCT_CATEGORY
  .Caption = "Products Categories"
  .ImageIndex = IML16_FOLDER
  .ImageIndexExpanded = IML16_FOLDEROPEN
  .CanAdd = True
  .CanDelete = True
  .CanUpdate = True
  .CanGoUp = True

Case EIT_EMPLOYEE
  .Caption = "Employees"
  .ImageIndex = IML16_FOLDER
  .ImageIndexExpanded = IML16_FOLDEROPEN
  .CanAdd = True
```

continues

Listing 10.2 **Continued**

```
              .CanDelete = True
              .CanUpdate = True
              .CanGoUp = False

          Case EIT_CUSTOMER
            .Caption = "Customers"
            .ImageIndex = IML16_FOLDER
            .ImageIndexExpanded = IML16_FOLDEROPEN
            .CanAdd = True
            .CanDelete = True
            .CanUpdate = True
            .CanGoUp = False

          Case EIT_ORDER_ROOT
            .Caption = "Orders"
            .ImageIndex = IML16_FOLDER
            .ImageIndexExpanded = IML16_FOLDEROPEN
            .CanAdd = False
            .CanDelete = False
            .CanUpdate = False
            .CanGoUp = True

          Case EIT_ORDER_OPEN
            .Caption = "Open Orders"
            .ImageIndex = IML16_FOLDER
            .ImageIndexExpanded = IML16_FOLDEROPEN
            .CanAdd = True
            .CanDelete = True
            .CanUpdate = True
            .CanGoUp = True

          Case EIT_ORDER_ALL
            .Caption = "All Orders"
            .ImageIndex = IML16_FOLDER
            .ImageIndexExpanded = IML16_FOLDEROPEN
            .CanAdd = True
            .CanDelete = True
            .CanUpdate = True
            .CanGoUp = True

          Case EIT_SUPPLIER
            .Caption = "Suppliers"
            .ImageIndex = IML16_FOLDER
            .ImageIndexExpanded = IML16_FOLDEROPEN
            .CanAdd = True
            .CanDelete = True
            .CanUpdate = True
            .CanGoUp = False
```

```
    Case EIT_SHIPPER
      .Caption = "Shippers"
      .ImageIndex = IML16_FOLDER
      .ImageIndexExpanded = IML16_FOLDEROPEN
      .CanAdd = True
      .CanDelete = True
      .CanUpdate = True
      .CanGoUp = False
    End Select
    .Mode = RHS
End Property
```

As you can see from the previous code sample, we are simply setting the various properties based on the type of Explorer item we are creating.

Although the startup process for the Northwind application is not complicated, it helps to have a flowchart to help us through our discussion. We show this in Figure 10.2.

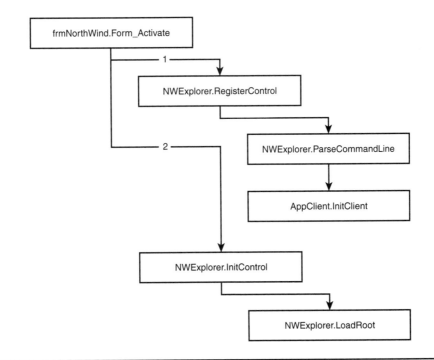

Figure 10.2   The Northwind Explorer startup process.

The code for our `Activate` event for `frmNorthWind` appears in Listing 10.3.

Listing 10.3   **The *Activate* Event on Our *frmNorthWind* Form**

```
Private Sub Form_Activate()
Dim Server As String
Dim SecurityKey As String
Dim sCMD As String
  ' should make this a registry setting or command line parameter
  Server = "NORTHWIND"
  If bLoading Then
    With NWExplorer
       sCMD = "server=" & Server & "&" & "securitykey=" & CStr(SecurityKey)
      .RegisterControl sCMD
      .SelectMode = EIT_ALL
      Call .InitControl
    End With
    bLoading = False
  End If
End Sub
```

From the flowchart, we initially follow Path 1, which has us calling the
`RegisterControl` method of our `NWExplorer` user control. We format our `CommandLine`
parameter in a manner similar to an HTML-form post command line. More specifically, the format is defined as `"var1=value1&var2=value2"`. Using this method, we can
arbitrarily define and communicate parameters that are of interest. For our example,
we pass in `Server` and `SecurityKey` parameters. This latter parameter is used by the
security mechanism that is discussed in Chapter 15, "Concluding Remarks." We use
this strange calling approach to simplify the integration of our ActiveX controls with
our IE browser. The code for the `RegisterControl` method appears in Listing 10.4.

Listing 10.4   **The *RegisterControl* Method of Our *NWExplorer* User Control**

```
Public Sub RegisterControl(CommandLine As String)
  Call ParseCommandLine(CommandLine)
  Call AppClient.InitClient(Server)
End Sub
```

As can be seen in the preceding listing, our `RegisterControl` method immediately
calls a `ParseCommandLine` method that splits out the string and sets control-level properties based on the information passed. These properties include `Server`, `SecurityKey`,
and `BrowserMode`. The code for our `ParseCommandLine` method on the `NWExplorer`
control appears in Listing 10.5.

Listing 10.5   **The *ParseCommandLine* Method of Our *NWExplorer* User Control**

```
Public Sub ParseCommandLine(ByVal CommandLine As String)
  Dim Args() As String
  Dim ArgValue() As String
```

```
  Dim i As Integer, j As Integer

  If Left(CommandLine, 1) = Chr(34) Then
    CommandLine = Mid(CommandLine, 2)
  End If
  If Right(CommandLine, 1) = Chr(34) Then
    CommandLine = Left(CommandLine, Len(CommandLine) - 1)
  End If

For i = LBound(Args) To UBound(Args)
    ArgValue = Split(Args(i), "=")
    Select Case UCase(ArgValue(0))
      Case "SERVER"
        Server = ArgValue(1)
      Case "SECURITYKEY"
        SecurityKey = ArgValue(1)
      Case "BROWSERMODE"
        Select Case UCase(ArgValue(1))
          Case "TRUE", "Y", "YES"
            BrowserMode = True
          Case Else
            BrowserMode = False
        End Select
    End Select
  Next i
End Sub
```

After this method completes, the `RegisterControl` method proceeds to call the `InitClient` method on our `AppClient` object of the control. This object is initially instantiated as `CNWClient` and then mapped to `AppClient`, which is an instance of `IAppClient`. We define both of these variables to be global in scope relative to the user control and instantiate them on the `UserControl_Initialize` event, as seen in Listing 10.6.

Listing 10.6   **The Implementation of the *Initialize* Event on Our *NWExplorer* User Control**

```
Private Sub UserControl_Initialize()
  Set NWClient = New CNWClient
  Set AppClient = NWClient
  lvListView.View = lvwReport
  tbToolBar.Buttons(LISTVIEW_MODE3).Value = tbrPressed
End Sub
```

The `InitClient` method attempts to establish the connection to the remote MTS object running on the server that we identified with our "`Server=`" portion of the command line.

After we have completed Path 1, we fall back to our `Form_Activate` method of `frmNorthWind` and proceed down Path 2. Now, we call the `InitControl` method of our `NWExplorer` control, which then calls our `LoadRoot` method. This final method is responsible for setting up the `TreeView`, binding its nodes to the necessary `IExplorerItem` objects. From that point on, we are ready to respond to user interaction. Our `LoadRoot` method follows in Listing 10.7.

Listing 10.7   **The *LoadRoot* and Supporting Methods in Our *NWExplorer* User Control**

```
Private Sub LoadRoot()
Dim oNode As Node, oRootNode As Node
Dim oChildNode As Node, oDummyNode As Node
Dim ExplorerItem As IExplorerItem
Dim NWExplorerItem As CNWExplorerItem
Dim i As Integer

On Error GoTo ExitSub

  With tvTreeView.Nodes
    .Clear

    'root item.
    Set NWExplorerItem = New CNWExplorerItem
    Set ExplorerItem = NWExplorerItem
    ExplorerItem.Mode = EIT_ROOT
    With ExplorerItem
      Set oRootNode = .Add(, , , .Caption, .ImageIndex, .ImageIndex)
    End With
    oRootNode.ExpandedImage = ExplorerItem.ImageIndexExpanded
    Set oRootNode.Tag = ExplorerItem

    If SelectMode = EIT_ALL Or SelectMode = EIT_ORDER_ROOT Then
        Set NWExplorerItem = New CNWExplorerItem
        Set ExplorerItem = NWExplorerItem
        ExplorerItem.Mode = EIT_ORDER_ROOT
        Set oNode = AddNode(oRootNode, ExplorerItem)

        Set NWExplorerItem = New CNWExplorerItem
        Set ExplorerItem = NWExplorerItem
        ExplorerItem.Mode = EIT_ORDER_ALL
        Set oChildNode = AddNode(oNode, ExplorerItem)

        Set NWExplorerItem = New CNWExplorerItem
        Set ExplorerItem = NWExplorerItem
        ExplorerItem.Mode = EIT_ORDER_OPEN
        Set oChildNode = AddNode(oNode, ExplorerItem)
    End If
```

```
If SelectMode = EIT_ALL Or SelectMode = EIT_CATEGORY Then
    Set NWExplorerItem = New CNWExplorerItem
    Set ExplorerItem = NWExplorerItem
    ExplorerItem.Mode = EIT_CATEGORY
    Set oNode = AddNode(oRootNode, ExplorerItem)
End If

If SelectMode = EIT_ALL Or SelectMode = EIT_PRODUCT_ROOT Then
    Set NWExplorerItem = New CNWExplorerItem
    Set ExplorerItem = NWExplorerItem
    ExplorerItem.Mode = EIT_PRODUCT_ROOT
    Set oNode = AddNode(oRootNode, ExplorerItem)
    Set oChildNode = .Add(oNode, tvwChild, , "DUMMY", 0, 0)
End If

If SelectMode = EIT_ALL Or SelectMode = EIT_EMPLOYEE Then
    Set NWExplorerItem = New CNWExplorerItem
    Set ExplorerItem = NWExplorerItem
    ExplorerItem.Mode = EIT_EMPLOYEE
    Set oNode = AddNode(oRootNode, ExplorerItem)
End If

If SelectMode = EIT_ALL Or SelectMode = EIT_CUSTOMER Then
    Set NWExplorerItem = New CNWExplorerItem
    Set ExplorerItem = NWExplorerItem
    ExplorerItem.Mode = EIT_CUSTOMER
    Set oNode = AddNode(oRootNode, ExplorerItem)
End If

If SelectMode = EIT_ALL Or SelectMode = EIT_SHIPPER Then
    Set NWExplorerItem = New CNWExplorerItem
    Set ExplorerItem = NWExplorerItem
    ExplorerItem.Mode = EIT_SHIPPER
    Set oNode = AddNode(oRootNode, ExplorerItem)
End If

If SelectMode = EIT_ALL Or SelectMode = EIT_SUPPLIER Then
    Set NWExplorerItem = New CNWExplorerItem
    Set ExplorerItem = NWExplorerItem
    ExplorerItem.Mode = EIT_SUPPLIER
    Set oNode = AddNode(oRootNode, ExplorerItem)
End If

If SelectMode = EIT_ALL Or SelectMode = EIT_COUNTRY_ROOT Then
    Set NWExplorerItem = New CNWExplorerItem
    Set ExplorerItem = NWExplorerItem
    ExplorerItem.Mode = EIT_COUNTRY_ROOT
    Set oNode = AddNode(oRootNode, ExplorerItem)
    Set oChildNode = .Add(oNode, tvwChild, , "DUMMY", 0, 0)
End If
```

continues

Listing 10.7   **Continued**

```
  End With

'initial settings....
  Set tvTreeView.SelectedItem = oRootNode
  CurrentNode = oRootNode
  Call SetListViewHeader(EIT_INIT)
  oRootNode.Expanded = True

  If SelectMode <> EIT_ALL Then
    ' preselect the first child node
    CurrentNode = CurrentNode.Child
    tvTreeView.SelectedItem = CurrentNode
    Call tvTreeView_NodeClick(CurrentNode)
  End If

ExitSub:
    Exit Sub
End Sub

Private Function AddNode(ANode As Node, ExplorerItem As IExplorerItem) As Node
  Dim oNode As Node

  With ExplorerItem
    Set oNode = tvTreeView.Nodes.Add(ANode, tvwChild, , .Caption, _
                                    .ImageIndex, .ImageIndexExpanded)
    oNode.ExpandedImage = .ImageIndexExpanded
  End With

  Set oNode.Tag = ExplorerItem
  Set AddNode = oNode
End Function
```

The `Expand` and `NodeClick` events of the `TreeView` are responsible for driving the navigational aspects of the Explorer control. In either of these events, we call a `LoadChildren` method to process the event. The code for `LoadChildren` appears in Listing 10.8.

Listing 10.8   **The *LoadChildren* Method on Our *NWExplorer* User Control to Handle Events Generated by the User**

```
Private Const TRE_NODECLICK As Integer = 0
Private Const TRE_EXPAND As Integer = 1
Private Const LVW_DBLCLICK As Integer = 2

Private Function LoadChildren(oTreeNode As Node, iEventType As Integer)
        As Boolean
Dim i As Integer
Dim sCriteria As String
Dim oItem As ListItem
```

```
Dim oNode As Node, ChildNode As Node, oDummyNode As Node
Dim NWExplorerItem As CNWExplorerItem
Dim ExplorerItem As IExplorerItem
Dim iMode As Integer

Dim CategoryItems As CCategoryItems
Dim CategoryItem As CCategoryItem
Dim CountryItem As CCountryItem
Dim CountryItems As CCountryItems
Dim RegionItem As CRegionItem
Dim RegionItems As CRegionItems
Dim CityItem As CCityItem
Dim CityItems As CCityItems
Dim AppCollection As IAppCollection
Dim AppObject As IAppObject

On Error GoTo ErrorTrap

Screen.MousePointer = vbHourglass

  If TypeOf oTreeNode.Tag Is IExplorerItem Then

    ' check for our dummy node...we put it there to get the +
    If Not oTreeNode.Child Is Nothing Then
      If oTreeNode.Child.Text = "DUMMY" Then
        tvTreeView.Nodes.Remove (oTreeNode.Child.Index)
      End If
    End If

    Set ExplorerItem = oTreeNode.Tag
    iMode = ExplorerItem.Mode
    Select Case iMode
      Case EIT_PRODUCT_ROOT
        If Not ExplorerItem.Loaded Then
          ExplorerItem.Loaded = True
          Set CategoryItems = AppClient.LoadCollection(CT_CATEGORY, 0, 0)
          Set AppCollection = CategoryItems
          For i = 1 To AppCollection.Count
            Set CategoryItem = AppCollection.Item(i)
            Set NWExplorerItem = New CNWExplorerItem
            Set ExplorerItem = NWExplorerItem
            ExplorerItem.Mode = EIT_PRODUCT_CATEGORY
            ExplorerItem.AppObject = CategoryItem
            Set oNode = tvTreeView.Nodes.Add(oTreeNode, tvwChild, , _
                                             CategoryItem.Name, _
                                             IML16_FOLDER, IML16_FOLDEROPEN)
            Set oNode.Tag = ExplorerItem
          Next
        End If

      Case EIT_COUNTRY_ROOT
        If Not ExplorerItem.Loaded Then
```

continues

Listing 10.8   **Continued**

```
        ExplorerItem.Loaded = True
        Set CountryItems = AppClient.LoadCollection(CT_COUNTRY, 0, 0)
        Set AppCollection = CountryItems
        For i = 1 To AppCollection.Count
          Set CountryItem = AppCollection.Item(i)
          Set NWExplorerItem = New CNWExplorerItem
          Set ExplorerItem = NWExplorerItem
          ExplorerItem.Mode = EIT_COUNTRY_REGION_ROOT
          ExplorerItem.AppObject = CountryItem
          Set oNode = tvTreeView.Nodes.Add(oTreeNode, tvwChild, , _
                                          CountryItem.Name, _
                                          IML16_FOLDER, IML16_FOLDEROPEN)
          Set ChildNode = tvTreeView.Nodes.Add(oNode, tvwChild, , _
                                          "DUMMY", 0, 0)
          Set oNode.Tag = ExplorerItem
        Next
      End If

    Case EIT_COUNTRY_REGION_ROOT
      If Not ExplorerItem.Loaded Then
        ExplorerItem.Loaded = True
        Set AppObject = ExplorerItem.AppObject
        Set RegionItems = AppClient.LoadCollection(CT_REGION, _
                                                  AppObject.Id, _
                                                  AppObject.SubId)
        Set AppCollection = RegionItems
        For i = 1 To AppCollection.Count
          Set RegionItem = AppCollection.Item(i)
          Set NWExplorerItem = New CNWExplorerItem
          Set ExplorerItem = NWExplorerItem
          ExplorerItem.Mode = EIT_COUNTRY_REGION_CITY
          ExplorerItem.AppObject = RegionItem
          Set oNode = tvTreeView.Nodes.Add(oTreeNode, tvwChild, , _
                                          RegionItem.Name, _
                                          IML16_FOLDER, IML16_FOLDEROPEN)
          Set ChildNode = tvTreeView.Nodes.Add(oNode, tvwChild, , _
                                          "DUMMY", 0, 0)
          Set oNode.Tag = ExplorerItem
        Next
      End If


  End Select

  If iEventType = TRE_NODECLICK Or iEventType = LVW_DBLCLICK Then
    CurrentListViewMode = iMode
    If Not oTreeNode.Child Is Nothing Then
      ' transfer child nodes
      Set oNode = oTreeNode.Child
```

```
                i = oNode.FirstSibling.Index
                Set oItem = lvListView.ListItems.Add(, , oNode.FirstSibling.Text, _
                                            IML32_FOLDER, IML16_FOLDER)
                Set oItem.Tag = oNode.FirstSibling

                While i <> oNode.LastSibling.Index
                    Set ChildNode = tvTreeView.Nodes(i)
                    Set oItem = lvListView.ListItems.Add(, , ChildNode.Next.Text, _
                                            IML32_FOLDER, IML16_FOLDER)
                    Set oItem.Tag = ChildNode.Next
                    i = tvTreeView.Nodes(i).Next.Index
                Wend
                RaiseEvent ItemSelectable(False)
            Else
                Call LoadDetail
            End If
        End If
    End If

ExitFunction:
    Screen.MousePointer = vbDefault
    LoadChildren = ErrorItems.Count = 0
    Exit Function

ErrorTrap:
    Call HandleError(Err.Number, Err.Source, Err.Description)
    Resume Next
End Function
```

The parameters for this method include the `Node` object that received the event and the event type indicated by `iEventType`. We define three constants that let us know what type of event generated this method call so that we can handle it appropriately. We define them as `TRE_NODECLICK`, `TRE_EXPAND`, and `LVW_DBLCLICK`. We first ensure that the `Tag` property of the `Node` object contains a reference to an `IExplorerItem` object. If so, we proceed to extract its mode property, which tells us the type of Explorer item it is. Typically, we add special processing here only if we have to build the child list dynamically as part of a database request. In this case, we have two nodes of this type: `"Products"` and `"Cities"`. We define all other child nodes statically as part of the `LoadRoot` method, with the `TreeView` automatically handling expansion. After we check for a child expansion, we proceed to transfer any child nodes over to the `ListView`, mimicking the functionality of the Microsoft Windows Explorer. If we are not performing a child expansion, we proceed to call the `LoadDetail` method that populates our `ListView`.

Our `LoadDetail` method is similar to many of our business layer methods in that we must dimension variable references for all our potential object collections that we load into the `ListView`. The code for the `LoadDetail` method appears in Listing 10.9.

Listing 10.9   **The *LoadDetail* Method on Our *NWExplorer* User Control that Manages the *ListView* on the Right Side of the Control**

```
Private Sub LoadDetail()
Dim i As Integer, iMode As Integer
Dim lId As Long
Dim oItem As ListItem
Dim NWExplorerItem As CNWExplorerItem
Dim ExplorerItem As IExplorerItem
Dim vCriteria As Variant
Dim vOrder As Variant

Dim AppCollection As IAppCollection
Dim AppObject As IAppObject
Dim CategoryItems As CCategoryItems
Dim CategoryItem As CCategoryItem
Dim ShipperItems As CShipperItems
Dim ShipperItem As CShipperItem
Dim ProductItem As CProductItem
Dim ProductItems As CProductItems
Dim EmployeeProxyItem As CEmployeeProxyItem
Dim EmployeeProxyItems As CEmployeeProxyItems
Dim CustomerProxyItem As CCustomerProxyItem
Dim CustomerProxyItems As CCustomerProxyItems
Dim SupplierProxyItem As CSupplierProxyItem
Dim SupplierProxyItems As CSupplierProxyItems
Dim OrderProxyItem As COrderProxyItem
Dim OrderProxyItems As COrderProxyItems
Dim CityItems As CCityItems
Dim CityItem As CCityItem

On Error GoTo ErrorTrap

    'load the detail items if any....
    If TypeOf CurrentNode.Tag Is IExplorerItem Then
        Set ExplorerItem = CurrentNode.Tag
        iMode = ExplorerItem.Mode
        CurrentListViewMode = iMode

        Select Case iMode
            Case EIT_CATEGORY
                Set CategoryItems = AppClient.LoadCollection(CT_CATEGORY, 0, 0)
                Set AppCollection = CategoryItems
                lvListView.Visible = False
                RaiseEvent ItemSelectable(False)
                CurrentListViewMode = iMode
                For i = 1 To AppCollection.Count
                  Set CategoryItem = AppCollection.Item(i)
                  With CategoryItem
                    Set oItem = lvListView.ListItems.Add(, , .Name, _
                                                IML32_ITEM, IML16_ITEM)

                    oItem.SubItems(1) = .Description
```

```
      End With
      Set oItem.Tag = CategoryItem
    Next i

  Case EIT_SHIPPER
    Set ShipperItems = AppClient.LoadCollection(CT_SHIPPER, 0, 0)
    Set AppCollection = ShipperItems
    lvListView.Visible = False
    RaiseEvent ItemSelectable(False)
    CurrentListViewMode = iMode
    For i = 1 To AppCollection.Count
      Set ShipperItem = AppCollection.Item(i)
      With ShipperItem
        Set oItem = lvListView.ListItems.Add(, , .CompanyName, _
                                         IML32_ITEM, IML16_ITEM)
        oItem.SubItems(1) = .Phone
      End With
      Set oItem.Tag = ShipperItem
    Next i

  Case EIT_EMPLOYEE
    Set EmployeeProxyItems = _
      AppClient.LoadCollection(CT_EMPLOYEE_PROXY, 0, 0)
    Set AppCollection = EmployeeProxyItems
    lvListView.Visible = False
    RaiseEvent ItemSelectable(False)
    CurrentListViewMode = iMode
    For i = 1 To AppCollection.Count
      Set EmployeeProxyItem = AppCollection.Item(i)
      With EmployeeProxyItem
        Set oItem = lvListView.ListItems.Add(, , .LastName & ", " & _
                                         .FirstName, _
                                         IML32_ITEM, IML16_ITEM)
      End With
      Set oItem.Tag = EmployeeProxyItem
    Next i

  Case EIT_CUSTOMER
    Set CustomerProxyItems = _
      AppClient.LoadCollection(CT_CUSTOMER_PROXY, 0, 0)
    Set AppCollection = CustomerProxyItems
    lvListView.Visible = False
    RaiseEvent ItemSelectable(False)
    CurrentListViewMode = iMode
    For i = 1 To AppCollection.Count
      Set CustomerProxyItem = AppCollection.Item(i)
      With CustomerProxyItem
        Set oItem = lvListView.ListItems.Add(, , .CompanyName, _
                                         IML32_ITEM, IML16_ITEM)
        oItem.SubItems(1) = .CustomerCode
```

continues

Listing 10.9 **Continued**

```
                    End With
                    Set oItem.Tag = CustomerProxyItem
                Next i

            Case EIT_SUPPLIER
              Set SupplierProxyItems = _
                AppClient.LoadCollection(CT_SUPPLIER_PROXY, 0, 0)
              Set AppCollection = SupplierProxyItems
              lvListView.Visible = False
              RaiseEvent ItemSelectable(False)
              CurrentListViewMode = iMode
              For i = 1 To AppCollection.Count
                Set SupplierProxyItem = AppCollection.Item(i)
                Set oItem = lvListView.ListItems.Add(, , _
                                   SupplierProxyItem.CompanyName, _
                                   IML32_ITEM, IML16_ITEM)
                Set oItem.Tag = SupplierProxyItem
              Next i

            Case EIT_COUNTRY_REGION_CITY
              Set AppObject = ExplorerItem.AppObject
              Set CityItems = AppClient.LoadCollection(CT_CITY, _
                                      AppObject.Id, AppObject.SubId)
              Set AppCollection = CityItems
              lvListView.Visible = False
              RaiseEvent ItemSelectable(False)
              CurrentListViewMode = iMode
              For i = 1 To AppCollection.Count
                Set CityItem = AppCollection.Item(i)
                Set oItem = lvListView.ListItems.Add(, , CityItem.Name, _
                                           IML32_ITEM, IML16_ITEM)
                Set oItem.Tag = CityItem
              Next i

            Case EIT_PRODUCT_CATEGORY
                CurrentListViewMode = EIT_PRODUCT
                Set ExplorerItem = CurrentNode.Tag
                Set CategoryItem = ExplorerItem.AppObject
                Set AppObject = CategoryItem
                vCriteria = Array(Array("CategoryId", "=", AppObject.Id))
                vOrder = Array("Name")
                Set ProductItems = AppClient.LoadQueryCollection(CT_PRODUCT, _
                                      vCriteria, vOrder)
                Set AppCollection = ProductItems
                lvListView.Visible = False
                RaiseEvent ItemSelectable(False)
                CurrentListViewMode = iMode
                For i = 1 To AppCollection.Count
                  Set ProductItem = AppCollection.Item(i)
                  With ProductItem
                    Set oItem = lvListView.ListItems.Add(, , .Name, _
```

```
                     IML32_ITEM, IML16_ITEM)
        oItem.SubItems(1) = .QuantityPerUnit
        oItem.SubItems(2) = .UnitPrice
        oItem.SubItems(3) = .UnitsInStock
        oItem.SubItems(4) = .UnitsOnOrder
        oItem.SubItems(5) = IIf(.IsDiscontinued, "Yes", "No")
      End With
      Set oItem.Tag = ProductItem
    Next

Case EIT_ORDER_ALL
  Set OrderProxyItems = AppClient.LoadCollection(CT_ORDER_PROXY, _
                                                  0, 0)
  Set AppCollection = OrderProxyItems
  lvListView.Visible = False
  RaiseEvent ItemSelectable(False)
  CurrentListViewMode = iMode
  For i = 1 To AppCollection.Count
    Set OrderProxyItem = AppCollection.Item(i)
    With OrderProxyItem
      Set oItem = lvListView.ListItems.Add(, , .CustomerName, _
                                    IML32_ITEM, IML16_ITEM)
      oItem.SubItems(1) = IIf(.OrderDate = vbEmpty, "", .OrderDate)
      oItem.SubItems(2) = IIf(.RequiredDate = vbEmpty, "", _
                            .RequiredDate)
      oItem.SubItems(3) = IIf(.ShippedDate = vbEmpty, "", _
                              .ShippedDate)
      oItem.SubItems(4) = .EmployeeLastName & "," & _
                         .EmployeeFirstName
    End With
    Set oItem.Tag = OrderProxyItem
  Next i

Case EIT_ORDER_OPEN
  vCriteria = Array(Array("ShippedDate", "is", "null"))
  vOrder = Array("RequiredDate", "CustomerName")
  Set OrderProxyItems = _
    AppClient.LoadQueryCollection(CT_ORDER_PROXY, _
                                  vCriteria, vOrder)
  Set AppCollection = OrderProxyItems
  lvListView.Visible = False
  RaiseEvent ItemSelectable(False)
  CurrentListViewMode = iMode
  For i = 1 To AppCollection.Count
    Set OrderProxyItem = AppCollection.Item(i)
    With OrderProxyItem
      Set oItem = lvListView.ListItems.Add(, , .CustomerName, _
                                    IML32_ITEM, IML16_ITEM)
      oItem.SubItems(1) = IIf(.OrderDate = vbEmpty, "", _
                            .OrderDate)
```

continues

Listing 10.9   **Continued**

```
                oItem.SubItems(2) = IIf(.RequiredDate = vbEmpty, "", _
                                    .RequiredDate)
                oItem.SubItems(3) = IIf(.ShippedDate = vbEmpty, "", _
                                    .ShippedDate)
                oItem.SubItems(4) = .EmployeeLastName & "," & _
                                    .EmployeeFirstName
            End With
            Set oItem.Tag = OrderProxyItem
          Next i
      End Select
    End If

ExitSub:
    lvListView.Visible = True
    Call SetObjectCount(lvListView.ListItems.Count)
    If lvListView.ListItems.Count > 0 Then
      Set lvListView.SelectedItem = lvListView.ListItems.Item(1)
      RaiseEvent ItemSelectable(True)
    End If
    Exit Sub

ErrorTrap:
    Call HandleError(Err.Number, Err.Source, Err.Description)
    Resume Next
End Sub
```

We start this method by extracting the ExplorerItem associated with the currently selected Node object in the TreeView. Based on the value of the Mode property of this ExplorerItem, we run through a Select Case statement to determine our course of action. As you might notice, most of the actions are simple calls to the LoadCollection method of the AppClient for a given class type. After we have loaded the necessary collection, we proceed to iterate through it, moving the information into the ListView. A convenient CurrentListViewMode property is responsible for setting up our ListView header columns, based on the type of collection we are loading. By placing all this ListView initialization code into a single property, we make it easier to maintain in the future.

We deviate a bit from this simple LoadCollection approach for our EIT_PRODUCT_CATEGORY and EIT_ORDER_OPEN cases in which we use a LoadQueryCollection to load the collection of products for a given category. We rely on the AppObject property of the ExplorerItem object to get the CategoryId for the query. We also use a LoadQueryCollection to help us load the detail for the open orders, where we check for a null ship date.

One of the other items you might have noticed is that we have defined new collection classes with the word Proxy in their names. We define these objects as scaled-down versions of their fully populated siblings. We must define this all the way back to the `NWServer` component, creating new class type constants and modifying the `GetClassDef` method to support these new classes. We also must define the necessary classes in `NWClient`. We take the extra development effort to define these lighter-weight classes so that we can minimize network traffic and latency during our browsing process. A user does not need to see every data element of every object to find what interests him.

Now that we have all the pieces in place, we must begin responding to user input. We start by attaching an event handler to our `ToolBar` control. To accomplish this, we must first define a set of constants that corresponds to the button indexes within the `ToolBar` control. For example:

```
Private Const TBR_NEW As Integer = 2
Private Const TBR_DELETE As Integer = 4
Private Const TBR_PROPERTIES As Integer = 5
Private Const TBR_UPONE As Integer = 7
Private Const TBR_LVLARGE As Integer = 9
Private Const TBR_LVSMALL As Integer = 10
Private Const TBR_LVLIST As Integer = 11
Private Const TBR_LVDETAILS As Integer = 12
Private Const TBR_HELP As Integer = 14
```

You should notice that these constants are not contiguous because of the separator buttons that are in use in the `ToolBar` control.

Next, we create a `DoToolEvent` function that is nothing more than a `Select Case` statement switched on the index value of the button the user clicks. We map the `ButtonClick` method of the `ToolBar` control to this `DoToolEvent` method (see Listing 10.10).

Listing 10.10 **Implementation of the *ButtonClick* Method of the *Toolbar* Control Used Within Our *NWExplorer* User Control**

```
Private Sub tbToolbar_ButtonClick(ByVal Button As MSComctlLib.Button)
    Call DoToolEvent(Button.Index)
End Sub

Private Sub DoToolEvent(iIndex As Integer)
On Error GoTo ErrorTrap
    Select Case iIndex
        Case TBR_NEW
          Call EventRaise(emInsert)

        Case TBR_DELETE
          Call DeleteItem

        Case TBR_PROPERTIES
```

continues

Listing 10.10 **Continued**

```
            Call EventRaise(emUpdate)

        Case TBR_UPONE
            CurrentNode = CurrentNode.Parent
            Set tvTreeView.SelectedItem = CurrentNode
            Call tvTreeView_NodeClick(CurrentNode)

        Case TBR_LVLARGE
            tbToolBar.Buttons.Item(TBR_LVLARGE).Value = tbrPressed
            lvListView.View = lvwIcon

        Case TBR_LVSMALL
            tbToolBar.Buttons.Item(TBR_LVSMALL).Value = tbrPressed
            lvListView.View = lvwSmallIcon

        Case TBR_LVLIST
            tbToolBar.Buttons.Item(TBR_LVLIST).Value = tbrPressed
            lvListView.View = lvwList

        Case TBR_LVDETAILS
            tbToolBar.Buttons.Item(TBR_LVDETAILS).Value = tbrPressed
            lvListView.View = lvwReport

        Case TBR_HELP
            MsgBox "Add 'Help' button code."
    End Select

ExitSub:
    If ErrorItems.Count > 0 Then
        ErrorItems.Show
    End If
    Exit Sub

ErrorTrap:
    Call HandleError(Err.Number, Err.Source, Err.Description)
    Resume Next
End Sub
```

You should notice that for our Add and Edit functionality we are calling a private method called EventRaise. We must use an event because we are within a user control, and this is the only mechanism to communicate outward. We must send this event out, along with critical information, to the host application whether it is a Visual Basic form or an IE5 HTML page. The host application is then responsible for taking the appropriate action. For all other button actions, we are relying on functionality within this user control. Our EventRaise code appears in Listing 10.11.

Listing 10.11   **The *EventRaise* Method on Our *NWExplorer* User Control Used to Relay *ActionRequest* Events Out to Our Container Control**

```
Private Sub EventRaise(eMode As EnumEditModes)
Dim ExplorerItem As IExplorerItem
Dim AppObject As IAppObject
Dim oListItem As ListItem
Dim ClassId As Integer, ActionClassId As Integer
Dim ClassName As String

If TypeOf CurrentNode.Tag Is IExplorerItem Then
  Set ExplorerItem = CurrentNode.Tag
  Set oListItem = lvListView.SelectedItem
  If TypeOf oListItem.Tag Is IAppObject Then
    Set AppObject = oListItem.Tag
    Call AppClient.GetClassInfo(AppObject.ClassId, ClassName, ActionClassId)
    With AppObject
      RaiseEvent ActionRequest(ExplorerItem.Mode, eMode, .Id, .SubId, _
                               Server, SecurityKey)
    End With
  End If
End If
End Sub
```

Upon entering the method, we attempt to extract an `AppObject` object from the `ExplorerItem` object that we receive via the `Tag` property of the currently selected `ListItem` object of the `ListView` control. If we are in delete mode for this method, we prompt the user with a confirmation message. We use a `CMessageBox` class in our `AppCommon` library, which we have defined specifically for this process. For other modes, we simply raise the `ActionRequest` event outward for handling. We cover the host application's response to this event in the section titled "The Tabbed Dialog," later in this chapter.

Within our host application, we have the following simple code within our `ActionRequest` event handler to manage our object addition and update logic (see Listing 10.12).

Listing 10.12   **The Implementation of the *ActionRequest* Event on Our *frmNorthWind* Container Form**

```
Private Sub NWExplorer_ActionRequest(EIT As Integer, _
                                     EditMode As EnumEditModes, _
                                     Id As Long, _
                                     SubId As Long, _
                                     Server As String, _
                                     SecurityKey As String)
```

continues

Listing 10.12   **Continued**

```
Select Case EIT
  Case EIT_ORDER, EIT_ORDER_ALL, EIT_ORDER_OPEN
    Load frmOrder
    With frmOrder
      If EditMode = emUpdate Then
          .Id = Id
          .SubId = SubId
      Else
          .Id = 0
          .SubId = 0
      End If
      .Mode = EditMode
      .Server = Server
      .SecurityKey = SecurityKey
      .Show vbModal
    End With
    Set frmOrder = Nothing
End Select
End Sub
```

Note that the frmOrder form contains our NWOrder control that we will be developing in the "The Tabbed Dialog" section.

The last remaining method of importance is SetStates. This method is responsible for enabling and disabling buttons on the ToolBar control, based on the settings of the ExplorerItem associated with the currently selected Node object in the TreeView control. We have also created a pop-up menu for which we must set state, using this method as well. We call this method from the NodeClick event of the TreeView control. The code for the SetStates method appears in Listing 10.13.

Listing 10.13   **The *SetStates* Method on Our *NWExplorer* User Control, Used to Set the States for the Toolbar Buttons and Pop-Up Menus**

```
Private Sub SetStates()
  Dim ExplorerItem As IExplorerItem
  If TypeOf CurrentNode.Tag Is IExplorerItem Then
    Set ExplorerItem = CurrentNode.Tag
    With ExplorerItem
        If SelectMode = EIT_ALL Then
          tbToolBar.Buttons.Item(TBR_NEW).Enabled = .CanAdd
          mnuObjectNew.Enabled = .CanAdd

          tbToolBar.Buttons.Item(TBR_DELETE).Enabled = .CanDelete
          mnuObjectDelete.Enabled = .CanDelete

          tbToolBar.Buttons.Item(TBR_PROPERTIES).Enabled = .CanUpdate
          mnuObjectEdit.Enabled = .CanUpdate
```

```
      Else
          tbToolBar.Buttons.Item(TBR_NEW).Enabled = False
          mnuObjectNew.Enabled = False
          tbToolBar.Buttons.Item(TBR_DELETE).Enabled = False
          mnuObjectDelete.Enabled = False
          tbToolBar.Buttons.Item(TBR_PROPERTIES).Enabled = False
      End If
          tbToolBar.Buttons.Item(TBR_UPONE).Enabled = .CanGoUp
  End With

 End If
End Sub
```

Now that we have the control basics down, we present NWExplorer running within the context of IE5 in Figure 10.3. Note that IE4 is also acceptable for ActiveX control hosting. It is also possible to host ActiveX controls within Netscape Navigator running on Windows 95/98/NT if you use a plug-in.

Figure 10.3   The Northwind Explorer control within IE5.

The HTML code required to embed the control and activate it appears in Listing 10.14. We will be spending much more time in later chapters demonstrating how to implement controls as part of Web pages. Note that the value for clsid might vary from that shown in Listing 10.14.

Listing 10.14   **The HTML for a Page that Hosts Our** *NWExplorer* **User Control**

```
<HTML>
<HEAD>
<META NAME="GENERATOR" Content="Microsoft Visual Studio 6.0">
<TITLE>Northwind Traders</TITLE>
<script LANGUAGE="VBScript">
<!—
Sub Page_Initialize
  On Error Resume Next
  Call NWExplorer.RegisterControl("server=PTINDALL2&securitykey=")
  NWExplorer.SelectMode = 999 ' EIT_ALL
  NWExplorer.InitControl
End Sub
—>
</script>
</HEAD>
<BODY ONLOAD="Page_Initialize"  rightmargin=0 topmargin=0
 leftMargin=0 bottomMargin=0>
<OBJECT classid="clsid:41AC6690-8E70-11D3-813B-00805FF99B76"
        id=NWExplorer style="LEFT: 0px; TOP: 0px"
        width=100% height=100%>
</OBJECT>
</BODY>
</HTML>
```

The HTML shown in Listing 10.14 was generated using Microsoft Visual InterDev 6.0. We demonstrate the use of this tool in Chapter 12, "Taking the Enterprise Application to the Net."

The Tabbed Dialog

Although the concept of a tabbed dialog is intrinsically simple, we must place some thought into the best layout of our elements on the various tabs. Remembering the statement about the user layer being an outgrowth of the business layer offers us some guidance here. Suppose we have an object hierarchy like the one shown in Figure 10.4. Here we have a root object containing several subobjects that are collections.

We want to handle this "bundle" of information using the root object CPortfolio; therefore, we might lay out our tabbed dialog as shown in Figure 10.5. This model should follow any well-designed business layer.

For a specific implementation example, we develop a tabbed dialog control for the COrder object and its contained COrderDetailItems collection. We will demonstrate not only the basics of user interface design but also the integration of user interface elements with our AppClient.

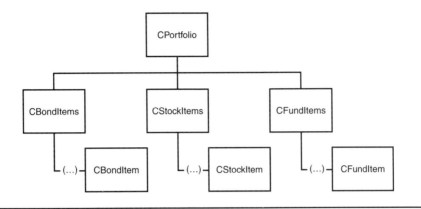

Figure 10.4   A sample object hierarchy.

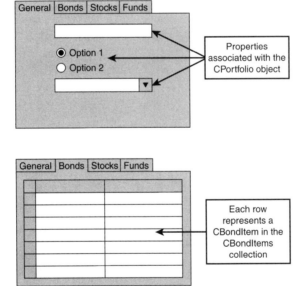

Figure 10.5   Our sample object hierarchy mapped to a tabbed dialog.

To start, we create a User Control project and name it NWOrder. We place a ToolBar control and a tabbed dialog with two tabs onto our layout space. We name the first tab General, as shown in Figure 10.6, and the other Detail, as shown in Figure 10.7.

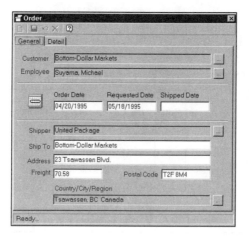

Figure 10.6   The `NWOrder` control's General tab.

Figure 10.7   The `NWOrder` control's Detail tab.

Our `Form_Activate` event in our host application for the `NWOrder` control is identical to the one we designed for our `NWExplorer`. Similarly, we implement `RegisterControl` and `InitControl` methods that connect to our `AppClient` component and initialize the control, respectively. Our initialization flow appears in Figure 10.8.

The implementation of our `InitControl` method is quite different in our `NWOrder` control than in the `NWExplorer` control. The code for the `NWOrder` implementation appears later in Listing 10.15.

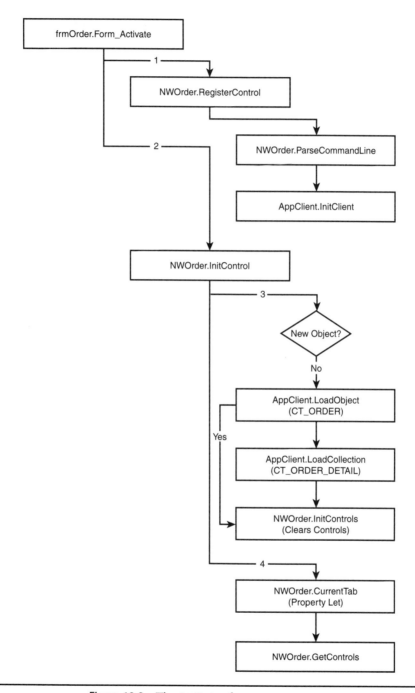

Figure 10.8   The frmOrder form startup process.

Listing 10.15 **The *InitControl* Method on Our *NWOrder* User Control**

```
Public Sub InitControl()
Dim i As Integer
Dim s As String
Dim AppObject As IAppObject
Dim AppCollection As IAppCollection

On Error GoTo ErrorTrap

    '1. initialize form properties....
    FormDirty = False
    For i = 0 To tabMain.Tabs - 1
        TabDirty(i) = False:    TabClick(i) = False
    Next

    Call SetStatusText("Initializing...")
    picGeneral.Visible = False
    Screen.MousePointer = vbHourglass

    '2. load this order object...
    If Mode = emUpdate Then
      Set Order = AppClient.LoadObject(CT_ORDER, Id, SubId)
      Set AppObject = Order
      Set OrderDetailItems = _
          AppClient.LoadCollection(CT_ORDER_DETAIL, Id, SubId)
      Set AppCollection = OrderDetailItems
    Else
      Set Order = New COrder
      Set AppObject = Order
      AppObject.Id = 0
      AppObject.SubId = SubId
      AppObject.IsDirty = True
      AppObject.IsLoaded = True
      Set OrderDetailItems = New COrderDetailItems
      Set AppCollection = OrderDetailItems
    End If

    If Mode = emUpdate Then
      s = ""
    Else
      s = "[New]"
    End If
    RaiseEvent SetParentCaption(s)

    '3. initialize all controls
    Call ClearControls(TAB_GENERAL)

    '4.  Set the current tab
    CurrentTab = TAB_GENERAL
```

```
        picGeneral.Visible = True
        Screen.MousePointer = vbDefault

    ExitSub:
        If ErrorItems.Count > 0 Then
            ErrorItems.Show
            RaiseEvent UnloadMe
        End If
        Call SetStatusText("Ready.")
        Exit Sub

    ErrorTrap:
        Call HandleError(Err.Number, Err.Source, Err.Description)
        Resume Next
    End Sub
```

To manage our tab states, we define two form-level property arrays known as
TabClick and TabDirty. We implement these two properties as arrays, with one
element for each tab. We also have a form-level property known as FormDirty. We initialize all these properties at the start of our InitControls method. We then proceed
to check for whether we are initializing in Update or Insert mode via our Mode property set by our host application. If the former, we load our global private Order and
OrderDetailItems using our AppClient. If the latter, we simply instantiate new objects
of these types. We then call our ClearControls method for the first tab, which clears
all controls on the tab. Finally, we set the CurrentTab property to the first tab.

The code for the CurrentTab property appears in Listing 10.16.

Listing 10.16   **The *CurrentTab* Property for Our *NWOrder* User Control**

```
Public Property Let CurrentTab(ByVal iTab As Integer)
    On Error GoTo ErrorTrap

    iCurrentTab = iTab
    bLoading = True
    If TabClick(iTab) Then GoTo ExitProperty

    Call SetStatusText("Initializing...")
    Screen.MousePointer = vbHourglass
    Select Case iTab

      Case TAB_GENERAL
        Call SetControlsFromObjects(TAB_GENERAL)

      Case TAB_DETAIL
        ' need to load listview here
        ' or else we get into a nasty loop
```

continues

Listing 10.16 **Continued**

```
        picDetailsTab.Visible = False
        Call LoadListView
        picDetailsTab.Visible = True
        Call SetControlsFromObjects(TAB_DETAIL)

    End Select
    TabClick(iTab) = True

ExitProperty:
    Call SetStatusText("Ready...")
    Screen.MousePointer = vbDefault

    iCurrentTab = iTab
    bLoading = False
    Call SetStates
    Exit Property

ErrorTrap:
     Call HandleError(Err.Number, Err.Source, Err.Description)
End Property
```

We first check to see whether the user has already clicked on this tab, by examining the TabClick property. If this returns True, we exit out of this property. If not, we proceed to load the controls. If we are on the TAB_GENERAL tab, we simply call the SetControlsFromObjects method. If we are on the TAB_DETAIL tab, we must first load the ListView control with the OrderDetailItems collection before we can call the SetControlsFromObjects method. The code for our SetControlsFromObjects method appears in Listing 10.17.

Listing 10.17 **The *SetControlsFromObject* Method on Our *NWOrder* User Control to Update the UI Based on Our *Order* Object**

```
Private Sub SetControlsFromObjects(iTab As Integer)
Dim b As Boolean
Dim sgDown As Single

  b = bLoading
  bLoading = True

  Select Case iTab
  Case TAB_GENERAL
    With Order
      lblCustomer.Caption = .CustomerName
      lblEmployee.Caption = .EmployeeLastName & ", " & .EmployeeFirstName
      txtOrderDate.Text = IIf(.OrderDate = "12:00:00 AM" Or _
                             .OrderDate = vbEmpty, "", _
```

```
                            Format(.OrderDate, "mm/dd/yyyy"))
        txtRequestedDate.Text = IIf(.RequiredDate = "12:00:00 AM" Or _
                                .RequiredDate = vbEmpty, "",_
                                Format(.RequiredDate, "mm/dd/yyyy"))
        lblShipper.Caption = .ShipperName
        txtShippedDate.Text = IIf(.ShippedDate = "12:00:00 AM" Or _
                                .ShippedDate = vbEmpty, "", _
                                Format(.ShippedDate, "mm/dd/yyyy"))
        txtShipToName.Text = .ShipToName
        txtShipToAddress.Text = .ShipToAddress
        txtFreight.Text = .FreightCost
        txtShipToPostal.Text = .ShipToPostalCode
        lblCRC.Caption = .ShipToCity & ", " & .ShipToRegion & "  " & _
                        .ShipToCountry
    End With
  Case TAB_DETAIL
    With SelectedOrderItem
      lblProduct.Caption = .Product
      lblSupplier.Caption = .Supplier
      lblUnitPrice.Caption = Format(.UnitPrice, "$ ###0.00")
      txtDiscount.Text = Format(.Discount, "##0.00")
      txtQuantity.Text = .Quantity
      lblStandardTotal.Caption = _
        Format(OrderDetailItems.OrderTotal(False), "$ #,##0.00")
      lblDiscountedTotal.Caption = _
        Format(OrderDetailItems.OrderTotal(True), "$ #,##0.00")
      If SelectedOrderItem.Product = "[New Product]" Then
        txtDiscount.Enabled = False
        txtQuantity.Enabled = False
      Else
        txtDiscount.Enabled = True
        txtQuantity.Enabled = True
      End If
    End With
  End Select
  bLoading = b
End Sub
```

Notice that our Detail tab contains a `ListView` control with a series of controls below it. The values in these secondary controls correspond to a row in the `ListView`, with each column mapping to one of the controls. We have chosen this approach for demonstration purposes only. In many cases, you might want to use an advanced grid control, which has embedded `ComboBox` and `CommandButton` capabilities.

After we have loaded our control with the necessary object information, we must begin reacting to user inputs. We use the `Validate` event on our `TextBox` controls to ensure that our application performs appropriate property validation. For example, our `txtFreight` `TextBox` control has the validation code shown in Listing 10.18.

Listing 10.18   **Implementation of the *Validate* Event on the *txtFreight TextBox*
Control to Implement Field-Level Validation**

```
Private Sub txtFreight_Validate(Cancel As Boolean)
  If IsNumeric(txtQuantity.Text) Then
    If CDbl(txtDiscount.Text) <= 0 Then
      Cancel = True
    End If
  Else
    Cancel = False
  End If
End Sub
```

We also use the KeyDown and KeyPress events to track whether a user changes a
value so that we can set our TabDirty and FormDirty properties. For an example, see
Listing 10.19.

Listing 10.19   **Implementation of the *KeyPress* and *KeyDown* Events on the
txtFreight TextBox Control to Track Dirty Status**

```
Private Sub txtFreight_KeyPress(KeyAscii As Integer)
  TabDirty(TAB_GENERAL) = True
End Sub

Private Sub txtFreight_KeyDown(KeyCode As Integer, Shift As Integer)
  If (KeyCode = vbKeyDelete Or KeyCode = vbKeySpace Or KeyCode = vbKeyBack) Then
    TabDirty(TAB_GENERAL) = True
  End If
End Sub
```

Notice that we have implemented many of our input fields as Label and CommandButton
controls. For these fields, we are relying on the SelectMode of our NWExplorer control to
help. Figure 10.9 shows the selection of the customer for the order.

After the user has made the necessary changes to the order and/or modified elements
in the OrderDetailItems collection, he or she can proceed to save the changes to the
database. For this, we reverse the process of loading the NWOrder control. The Save
method implements this process (see Listing 10.20).

Listing 10.20   **The *Save* Method on Our *NWOrder* User Control to Commit
Changes to the Database Through the Business Layer**

```
Private Function Save() As Boolean
Dim v
Dim i As Integer
Dim lRc As Long
Dim sMsg As String, sBase As String
Dim Errors As Variant
Dim AppObject As IAppObject
```

```
Dim AppCollection As IAppCollection

On Error GoTo ErrorTrap
    Screen.MousePointer = vbHourglass
    Call SetStatusText("Saving changes....")

    If TabDirty(TAB_GENERAL) Then
      If Not SetControlsToObjects(TAB_GENERAL) Then GoTo ExitFunction
      Set AppObject = Order
      If Not AppObject.IsValid(Errors) Then
        Call ErrorItems.MakeFromVariantArray(Errors, vbObjectError, _
                                             "NWOrder", "Save")

        ErrorItems.Show
        GoTo ExitFunction
      End If

        If Mode = emUpdate Then
          Call AppClient.UpdateObject(AppObject.ClassId, AppObject)
        Else
          Call SetStatusText("Inserting new object...")
          AppObject.ClassId = CT_ORDER
          Call AppClient.InsertObject(AppObject.ClassId, AppObject)
          If ErrorItems.Count > 0 Then
              ErrorItems.Show
          End If
          Mode = emUpdate
          Id = AppObject.Id
          SubId = AppObject.SubId
          Call InitControl
        End If
        TabDirty(TAB_GENERAL) = ErrorItems.Count > 0
    End If

    If TabDirty(TAB_DETAIL) Then
      Set AppCollection = OrderDetailItems

      If Not AppCollection.IsValid(Errors) Then
        Call ErrorItems.MakeFromVariantArray(Errors, vbObjectError, _
                                             "NWOrder", "Save")

        ErrorItems.Show
        GoTo ExitFunction
      End If

      For i = 1 To AppCollection.Count
        Set AppObject = AppCollection.Item(i)
        If AppObject.Id > 0 Then
          If AppObject.IsDirty Then
            Call _AppClient.UpdateObject(AppObject.ClassId, AppObject)
        Else
          AppObject.Id = 0
```

continues

Listing 10.20 **Continued**

```
        Call AppClient.InsertObject(AppObject.ClassId, AppObject)
      End If
    Next i
    Mode = emUpdate
    TabDirty(TAB_DETAIL) = ErrorItems.Count > 0
    Call InitControl
  End If

RaiseEvent ObjectSave
Call SetStates

ExitFunction:
  Save = ErrorItems.Count = 0
  Screen.MousePointer = vbDefault
  Call SetStatusText("Ready.")
  Exit Function

ErrorTrap:
  Call HandleError(Err.Number, Err.Source, Err.Description)
End Function
```

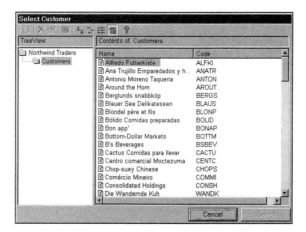

Figure 10.9 The Explorer control in selection mode for the customer class.

For a given tab, we call the SetControlsToObject method to move the control information into the appropriate properties. We then call the IsValid method on the AppObject or AppCollection objects to make sure that there are no issues across property values. An example could be that the ship date occurs before the order date. If validation succeeds, we call the necessary AppClient update or insert functionality for the AppObject or AppCollection objects, depending on which tab we are saving. We then clear the dirty flags and refresh the controls.

Summary

We have reached a milestone with the conclusion of this chapter because we have implemented the complete set of functionality necessary to build a three-tiered application. Figure 10.10 shows graphically what we have accomplished.

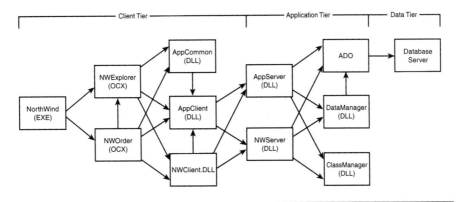

Figure 10.10   Our three-tiered application.

In the next chapter, we begin implementing our Internet/intranet functionality by developing a reporting component that uses ASP for simple reports or gets a little help from some MTS components for the more difficult reports.

11

A Distributed Reporting Engine

U P TO THIS POINT, FOCUS FOR THE FRAMEWORK has been on the input, or information generating, side of the application. When you look at our goal of moving the sample Northwind application into an n-tiered, distributed framework, you can see that the work is not complete because several reports I defined are now no longer available with this migration of functionality. This chapter shows how Active Server Pages (ASPs), coupled with the framework components running on Microsoft Transaction Server (MTS), can be used to replace most of the standard reporting functions in a manner that provides access to a much broader audience. For complex reports that cannot be handled within ASP directly, specialized reporting objects are built and deployed on MTS.

Design Theory

Many commercially available, third-party tools are available, which provide powerful report development capabilities. Tools like Microsoft Access are designed to support pure client/server environments, whereas tools like Seagate Crystal Reports and others have versions that can run as part of server process to serve up Web-based reports. With all other parts of our application framework executed in a distributed fashion, it is clearly desirable to continue with that design goal for reporting purposes. At a minimum, the logic to run reports should be implemented on a remote server machine so that report formats and logic can be changed in a single locale rather than on every client. Some developers (pre-intranet explosion) have cleverly achieved this type of functionality using a combination of Microsoft Access and Microsoft Message Queue (or using a home-grown version of a simple queue), setting up reporting servers that do nothing more than fulfill generation requests. After a report is run, it is emailed to the requestor as an attached document.

Although this type of report automation is impressive, in the intranet-enabled corporation of today, such extensive efforts are no longer needed because ASP can fulfill most of the same reporting requirements. Although some of the grouping and preprocessing routines that are normally processed by a report writer need to be handled programmatically in VBScript, they are not difficult to master. The use of ASP has another advantage in that its VBScript language supports COM, which allows reuse of our framework code.

Implementation

To build out our reporting functionality, we will be using Visual InterDev 6.0. If you have not ventured far beyond the Visual Basic environment, you will need to install the FrontPage 98 extensions on your Internet Information Server (IIS) development machine. You can perform this installation using the NT 4.0 Option Pack on the IIS machine. Be aware that running the NT 4.0 Option Pack on an NT Workstation will install Peer Web Services (PWS) instead of IIS. This is fine for our purposes because PWS and IIS are similar. When I refer to IIS from this point forward, it includes PWS installations.

Visual InterDev 6.0 tries to be many things, perhaps to the point of causing confusion. When we try to create a new project, in addition to a Visual InterDev project, we are given the choices of creating database projects, distribution units, utility projects, and Visual Studio Analyzer projects. A database project is simply a database development environment similar to Microsoft Access, with the added option to debug stored procedures within Microsoft SQL Server. A distribution unit can be one of several types. One option is a cabinet (CAB) file that is used by the Microsoft setup engine. A second option is a self-extracting setup that uses one or more CAB files to build a self-contained installer. The last option is simply a Zip file. It is difficult to discern the purpose of the last two options. Nonetheless, Visual InterDev's forte is in its capability to manage and edit Web projects. These Web projects will be the manifestation of our reporting engine in this chapter. We will continue with this same project in the next chapter as we create the entire Web site portal for our application.

Before proceeding with the details of building the reporting engine, it is important to understand that ASP represents a programming model that runs on an IIS server. ASP code never crosses over to the browser. Instead, it produces the HTML stream that is sent to the browser. Because of this, an ASP page that generates browser-neutral HTML can support both Netscape Navigator and Internet Explorer. This is no different from server-side Perl or C code that generates HTML to send back to the browser. No Perl or C code is ever passed back to the browser.

Creating the Web Project

After you have access to an IIS installation, you can create the Web project. The easiest way to do this is from within Visual InterDev. Start Visual InterDev and select File, New Project from the main menu. This brings up the New Project dialog as shown in Figure 11.1.

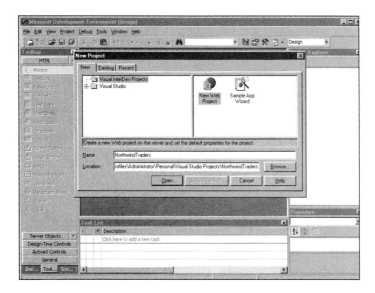

Figure 11.1   Creating a new Web application in Visual InterDev.

Enter NorthwindTraders for the project name, and then click the Open button. This launches the Web Project Wizard. On Step 1 of the wizard, choose or enter the name of the Web server that will host this application, and select Master mode to have the Web application automatically updated with changes as they are made. This mode should be switched to local after a Web application enters production. After you click the Next button, the wizard attempts to contact the server and to verify that it is configured appropriately.

On Step 2 of the wizard, select the Create a New Web Application option and accept the default application name. Click the Next button to arrive at Step 3 of the wizard. Ensure that <none> is selected so that no navigation bars are applied. Click the Next button one last time to arrive at Step 4. Once again, ensure that <none> is selected to make sure that no themes are applied either. Click the Finish button to tell Visual InterDev to create the project.

Upon completing this process, the Project Explorer shows the newly created process with several folders underneath it. The _private and _ScriptLibrary folders are used directly by Visual InterDev. The images folder can be used to place the images that are used by the Web site. A file titled global.asa also appears. This file is used globally to declare objects and to define application- and session-level events used by the Web application. It is discussed in further detail in Chapter 12, "Taking the Enterprise Application to the Net."

Making *NWServer* IIS Friendly

Because the NWServer component contains the functionality necessary to retrieve lists of objects, it makes sense to use it as the vehicle to deliver information to ASP for formatting into reports. In so doing, all information retrieval functionality, for both the data generator and data consumer sides of the application, is confined to a single code base. This bodes well for future maintenance of the application. Some applications instantiate ADO Command, Connection, and Recordset objects within an ASP page to retrieve data. This not only creates a second SQL code area within the application, meaning another potential maintenance point, but it also performs data access in one of the most inefficient manners possible. Remember that everything in ASP is scripted, whereas objects developed in Visual Basic can be compiled to native code for much higher performance. Also, remember that ASP pages are recompiled with every access (that is, not cached), meaning the re-instantiation of multiple objects. MTS-hosted objects are pooled and context-switched for higher performance and scalability. Additionally, IIS does not perform connection pooling unless a manual change to the registry is made, whereas MTS performs ODBC and OLE DB connection pooling automatically. The bottom line is that ASP should retrieve its data from the MTS objects that we have already put in place rather than re-creating data access functionality.

To make the functionality of NWServer available to IIS you must create specific wrapper functions because VBScript cannot deal with interface implementations as can Visual Basic. For example, the following code fragment does not work in VBScript:

```
Dim AppServer
Dim NWServer
Set NWServer = CreateObject("NWServer.CNWServer")
Set AppServer = NWServer
Call AppServer.InitServer
```

This code fails on the last line because VBScript considers AppServer to be of type CNWServer, but it does not have visibility to its IAppServer interface in which the InitServer method is defined.

To circumvent this issue, wrapper functions are built for each method that must be exposed to IIS. Listing 11.1 shows the code for each data access method on the IAppServer interface.

Listing 11.1   **Wrapper Methods on NWServer for IIS**

```
Public Sub IISQueryObjectListData(ByVal ClassId As Integer, _
                                  ByVal Criteria As Variant, _
                                  ByVal Sort As Variant, _
                                  ByVal Conjunction As Variant, _
                                  PropertyNames As Variant, _
                                  Data As Variant, _
                                  Errors As Variant)
  Call IAppServer_QueryObjectListData(ClassId, _
                                Criteria, _
                                Sort, _
                                Conjunction, _
                                PropertyNames, _
                                Data, _
                                Errors)
End Sub

Public Sub IISDeleteObject(ByVal ClassId As Integer, _
                           ByVal ObjectId As Long, _
                           ByVal ObjectSubId As Long, _
                           Errors As Variant)
  Call IAppServer_DeleteObject(ClassId, _
                            ObjectId, _
                            ObjectSubId, _
                            Errors)
End Sub

Public Sub IISDeleteObjectList(ByVal ClassId As Integer, _
                           ByVal ParentId As Long, _
                           ByVal ParentSubId As Long, _
                           Errors As Variant)
  Call IAppServer_DeleteObjectList(ClassId, _
                            ParentId, _
                            ParentSubId, _
                            Errors)
End Sub

Public Sub IISGetObjectData(ByVal ClassId As Integer, _
                            ByVal ObjectId As Long, _
                            ByVal ObjectSubId As Long, _
                            PropertyNames As Variant, _
                            Data As Variant, _
                            Errors As Variant)
  Call IAppServer_GetObjectData(ClassId, _
                                ObjectId, _
                                ObjectSubId, _
                                PropertyNames, _
                                Data, _
                                Errors)
End Sub
```

continues

Listing 11.1 **Continued**

```
Public Sub IISGetObjectListData(ByVal ClassId As Integer, _
                                ByVal ParentId As Long, _
                                ByVal ParentSubId As Long, _
                                PropertyNames As Variant, _
                                Data As Variant, _
                                Errors As Variant)
    Call IAppServer_GetObjectListData(ClassId, _
                                ParentId, _
                                ParentSubId, _
                                PropertyNames, _
                                Data, _
                                Errors)
End Sub

Public Function IISGetPropertyNames(ByVal ClassId As Integer) As Variant
    IISGetPropertyNames = IAppServer_GetPropertyNames(ClassId)
End Function

Public Sub IISInsertObjectData(ByVal ClassId As Integer, _
                                ByVal PropertyNames As Variant, _
                                ByVal Data As Variant, _
                                Errors As Variant, _
                                ObjectId As Long, _
                                ObjectSubId As Long)
    Call IAppServer_InsertObjectData(ClassId, _
                                PropertyNames, _
                                Data, _
                                Errors, _
                                ObjectId, _
                                ObjectSubId)
End Sub

Public Sub IISInsertObjectListData(ByVal ClassId As Integer, _
                                ByVal ParentId As Long, _
                                ByVal ParentSubId As Long, _
                                ByVal PropertyNames As Variant, _
                                ByVal Data As Variant, _
                                Errors As Variant)
    Call IAppServer_InsertObjectListData(ClassId, _
                                ParentId, _
                                ParentSubId, _
                                PropertyNames, _
                                Data, _
                                Errors)
End Sub

Public Sub IISUpdateObjectData(ByVal ClassId As Integer, _
                                ByVal PropertyNames As Variant, _
                                ByVal Data As Variant, _
                                Errors As Variant, _
```

```
                         ObjectId As Long, _
                         ObjectSubId As Long)
   Call IAppServer_UpdateObjectData(ClassId, _
                                PropertyNames, _
                                Data, _
                                Errors, _
                                ObjectId, _
                                ObjectSubId)
End Sub


Public Function IISInitServer() As Boolean
   IISInitServer = IAppServer_InitServer
End Function
```

As you can see from Listing 11.1, the implementation of these wrapper functions are trivial in nature.

An IIS Service-Layer Component

Before the report generators using ASP within IIS can be realized, a service-layer component needs to be built. There are two primary reasons for this. The first reason is to provide a mechanism to implement the functionality that is available in Visual Basic but not in VBScript. Specifically, the Visual Basic Format function—used to format dates, currency, and percentages—is not available in VBScript; therefore, a VBAFormat wrapper function is created. A CFunctions class is created to provide an anchor point for this and future wrapper functions. This class is defined within an ActiveX DLL component called AppIISCommon. The simple code for the CFunctions class is shown in Listing 11.2.

Listing 11.2   **A Wrapper Function Added to the *CFunctions* Class**

```
Public Function VBAFormat(StringToFormat As String, _
                          FormatPattern As String) As String
   VBAFormat = Format(StringToFormat, FormatPattern)
End Function
```

The second reason is to simplify the retrieval of information from the variant arrays that are returned from MTS. For this, a CDataArray class is also created within AppIISCommon. The CDataArray class has an Initialize method that accepts Data and PropertyNames arguments; both arguments are of the array data type. This method sets an internal private reference to the Data argument and proceeds to create a property index for the array using a Dictionary object. It does this by calling a private MakeDictionary method. The Dictionary object is defined in the Microsoft Scripting Runtime (scrrun.dll), which should be referenced by the AppIISCommon project. Several derived properties are also defined (MinRow and MaxRow) to simplify iteration through the data array. Finally, an Item method is implemented to extract from the array a particular property for a given row. The code for the CDataArray class is shown in Listing 11.3.

Listing 11.3   **The *CDataArray* Class**

```
Option Explicit
Private vData As Variant
Private dict As Dictionary

Public Sub Initialize(Data As Variant, PropertyNames As Variant)
  vData = Data
  MakeDictionary (PropertyNames)
End Sub

Private Sub MakeDictionary(PropertyNames As Variant)
  Dim i As Long
  Set dict = Nothing
  Set dict = New Dictionary
  If IsArray(PropertyNames) Then
    For i = LBound(PropertyNames) To UBound(PropertyNames)
      Call dict.Add(PropertyNames(i), i)
    Next i
  End If
End Sub

Public Function Item(PropertyName As Variant, Row As Variant) As Variant
  If dict.Exists(PropertyName) Then
    Item = vData(dict.Item(PropertyName), CLng(Row))
  Else
    Item = vbEmpty
  End If
End Function

Public Property Get MinRow() As Long
  MinRow = LBound(vData, 2)
End Property

Public Property Get MaxRow() As Long
  MaxRow = UBound(vData, 2)
End Property
```

A Simple Report with Grouping

With the NWServer component modified to handle calls from IIS and the development of the service-layer component AppIISCommon complete, the first report can be built. The first report to build is the Products by Category report from the original Northwind database. This report provides a simple grouping of products by category.

The original Microsoft Access report shows only the current product list. To demonstrate the flexibility of ASP as a reporting tool, the sample report will allow for the display of both current and discontinued products.

The first step of adding a new report is to make sure that the appropriate information set, in terms of a `ClassDef` instance, is defined within `NWServer`. If not, add the definition in the `GetClassDef` method, making sure that the appropriate view in the database has been defined as well. For this report, a new `ClassDef` is needed. As shown in Listing 11.4 using the code fragment from the `Select Case` statement in the `GetClassDef` method on `NWServer`. After this simple change is made, `NWServer` is recompiled and redeployed to MTS.

Listing 11.4   **Addition of the *ProductByCategory* Class to the *GetClassDef* Method**

```
Private Function IAppServer_GetClassDef(ByVal ClassId As Integer) As CClassDef
  Dim ClassDef As CClassDef

  If Not bInitialized Then IAppServer_InitServer
  If Not mIAppServer.ClassDefs.Exists(CStr(ClassId)) Then
    Select Case ClassId
      ' other cases as before

    Case CT_PRODUCT_BY_CATEGORY
      Set ClassDef = New CClassDef
      With ClassDef
        .DatabaseName = "NWIND"
        .ReadLocation = "View_Product_By_Category"
        .WriteLocation = ""
        .IdColumnName = ""
        .OrderByColumnName = "Category_Name, Product_Name"

        .AppendMapping "ProductId", "Product_Id", _
                       True, False, ctNumber, ""
        .AppendMapping "CategoryName", "Category_Name", _
                       True, False, ctString, ""
        .AppendMapping "ProductName", "Product_Name", _
                       True, False, ctString, ""
        .AppendMapping "UnitsInStock", "Units_In_Stock", _
                       True, False, ctNumber, ""
        .AppendMapping "IsDiscontinued", "Is_Discontinued", _
                       True, False, ctNumber, ""
      End With
      Call mIAppServer.ClassDefs.Add(ClassDef, CStr(CT_PRODUCT_BY_CATEGORY))
    End Select
  End If

  Set IAppServer_GetClassDef = mIAppServer.ClassDefs.Item(CStr(ClassId))
End Function
```

With this new `ClassDef` in place, attention returns to Visual InterDev to write the report in ASP and deploy it on a Web site. To create a new ASP page in the NorthwindTraders project, simply right-click the servername/NorthwindTraders node in the Project Explorer and select Add, Active Server Page from the pop-up menu. This launches the Add Item dialog with the ASP page type selected. In the Name field, enter `ProductReports.asp`, and then click the Open button to create the file. Repeat this process to create a `ProductReport.asp` file as well.

The `ProductReports.asp` file is used to gather some direction from the user before proceeding with the generation of the actual report in the `ProductReport.asp` file. This technique is used across all types of reports that require initial user input. For this set of reports, the only information needed from the user is which type of report to run: All Products, Current Products, or Discontinued Products. The script needed to implement a simple selector mechanism appears in Listing 11.5, whereas the resulting HTML page appears in Figure 11.2.

Listing 11.5   **ASP Script to Implement the Report Selector for Product Reporting**

```
<%@ Language=VBScript%>
<%Response.Expires=5%>
<HTML>
<HEAD>
<META NAME="GENERATOR" Content="Microsoft Visual Studio 6.0">
<TITLE>northwind traders</TITLE>
</HEAD>
<BODY>
<%
 Dim vReports(3)
 vReports(1)="Current Products"
 vReports(2)="All Products"
 vReports(3)="Discontinued Products"
%>
<H1>Product Reporting</H1>
<FORM action=ProductReport.asp>
<SELECT id=ReportType name=ReportType>
<%
   For i = 1 To UBound(vReports)
       If CInt(i) = 1 Then
%>
           <option selected value='<%=i%>'><%=vReports(i)%></option>
<%
       Else
%>
           <option value='<%=i%>'><%=vReports(i)%></option>
<%
       End If
   Next
%>
</SELECT>
```

```
<P>
<INPUT type="submit" value="Run Report">
</FORM>
</BODY>
</HTML>
```

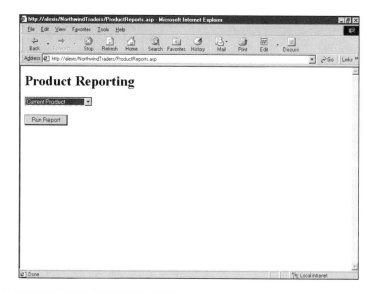

Figure 11.2   The Product Reporting mode selector.

There is nothing too exciting about the code in Listing 11.5 because it produces a simple HTML Form page. One item to note is that an array is being used for the report names rather than a hard-coded mechanism. This makes it easier to add new report types to a form by simply adding new elements to the array. The real excitement comes in the `ProductReport.asp` code because it is what interacts with MTS to produce the desired report. The code for this page appears Listing 11.6, with the resulting HTML page shown in Figure 11.3.

Listing 11.6   **ASP Script Code to Implement the Product Report**

```
<%@ Language=VBScript%>
<%Response.Expires=5%>
<HTML>
<HEAD>
<META NAME="GENERATOR" Content="Microsoft Visual Studio 6.0">
```

continues

Listing 11.6 **Continued**

```
<TITLE>northwind traders</TITLE>
</HEAD>
<BODY>
<%
  Dim Data, PropertyNames
  Dim DataArray
  Dim Errors, NWServer
  Dim ReportType, ReportTypeId
  Dim WhereClause, OrderClause
  Dim IsDiscontinued
  Const CT_PRODUCT_BY_CATEGORY = 201

  ReportTypeId = Request.QueryString("ReportType")
  Select Case ReportTypeId
    Case 1
      ReportType = "Current Products"
      WhereClause = Array(Array("IsDiscontinued","=","False"))
    Case 2
      ReportType = "All Products"
      WhereClause = ""
    Case 3
      ReportType = "Discontinued Products"
      WhereClause = Array(Array("IsDiscontinued","=","True"))
  End Select
  OrderClause = Array("CategoryName","ProductName")

  Set NWServer = Server.CreateObject("NWServer.CNWServer")

  If Not NWServer.IISInitServer Then
    Response.Write("Could not Initialize the MTS Server<br>")
  End If

  Call NWServer.IISQueryObjectListData(CT_PRODUCT_BY_CATEGORY, _
                                       WhereClause, _
                                       OrderClause, _
                                       "OR", _
                                       PropertyNames, _
                                       Data, _
                                       Errors)

  If IsArray(PropertyNames) and IsArray(Data) Then
    Set DataArray = Server.CreateObject("AppIISCommon.CDataArray")
    DataArray.Initialize Data, PropertyNames

  If IsArray(Data) Then
%><H1>Product By Category</H1>
<H2><%=ReportType%>
  <TABLE WIDTH="100%" CELLPADDING=2 CELLSPACING=0 border=0>
<%
      For i = DataArray.MinRow To DataArray.MaxRow
        vThisCategory = DataArray.Item("CategoryName",i)
```

```
            If (vThisCategory <> vLastCategory) Then
%>
    <TR><TD colspan=2> </TD></TR>
    <TR>
      <TD colspan=2>
        <B>Category:</B> 
        <%=vThisCategory%>
      </TD>
    </TR>
    <TR>
      <TH align=left>Product Name</TH>
      <TH align=left>Units In Stock</TH>
<%        If ReportTypeId = 2 Then %>
      <TH align=left>Discontinued</TH>
<%        End If %>
    </TR>
<%

          vLastCategory = vThisCategory
        End If
%>
      <TR>
        <TD>
          <%=DataArray.Item("ProductName",i)%>
        </TD>
        <TD>
          <%=DataArray.Item("UnitsInStock",i)%>
        </TD>
<%  If ReportTypeId = 2 Then
      If CBool(DataArray.Item("IsDiscontinued",i)) Then
        IsDiscontinued = "Yes"
      Else
        IsDiscontinued = "No"
      End If
      Response.Write("<TD>" & IsDiscontinued & "</TD>")
    End If %>
      </TR>
<%

    Next
    Else
%>
      <TR>
        <TD>No data found</TD>
      </TR>
<%
    End if
%>
    </TABLE>
<%
  End If
%>
</BODY>
</HTML>
```

Looking at Listing 11.6, the first item to pay attention to is the `Select Case` statement at the beginning of the script section. It is here that several variables are set based on the specific report type requested. This report type is retrieved from the `QueryString` collection on the `Request` object that ASP maintains automatically. Based on which report type is selected, different `WhereClause` arrays are created to pass to the `IISQueryObjectListData` method on the `NWServer` component. After `NWServer` is created using the `CreateObject` method on the `Server` object, the retrieval method is called. This passes control to MTS to perform the request. Remember that this is calling the exact same underlying code as that used by the Visual Basic client-side components developed in Chapters 9, "A Two-Part, Distributed Business Object," and 10, "Adding an ActiveX Control to the Framework."

After the request has been fulfilled, a `CDataArray` object is created and initialized with the resulting information. From this point, iterating through the array and formatting the report using a simple HTML table construct is easy. The `MinRow` and `MaxRow` properties help in this iteration process. Additionally, the script chooses whether to add the Discontinued column based on the report type because it only makes sense on the All Products version of the report. To handle grouping, a simple breaking mechanism that compares the current category with the last category is used. If the values are different, a category header is written to the HTML stream.

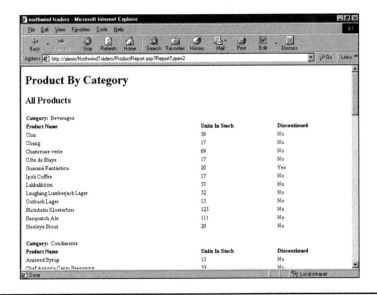

Figure 11.3   The product report rendered in Internet Explorer.

Amazingly, this is all that is needed to build a simple ASP-based report using the MTS infrastructure already created. One of the common statements about Web reporting is that it just looks ugly. Well, if you leave the formatting of these reports as it is in this example, then yes they do. Fortunately, HTML can be used to create appealing pages with only modest effort. As proof, look at the same two reports in Figure 11.4 and Figure 11.5 with some polish work added to them. The specific techniques that were used to make the reports look better are discussed in more detail in Chapter 12.

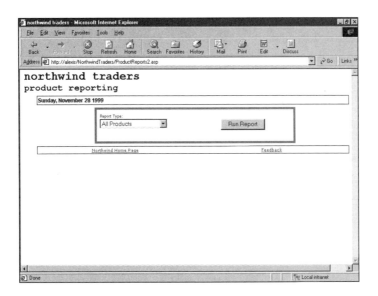

Figure 11.4   The product report mode selector with a makeover.

Our last little makeover to the product report also demonstrates one of the greatest advantages we have in using ASP as our reporting engine. We can change the look and feel, the structure, or the processing logic at any time in a development environment, and then push it to the production environment on the server. After it has been moved, the report is updated. There is no redistribution of anything to the client.

A Complex Report with Preprocessing

Some types of reports that are traditionally built in commercial report writers include not only single-level grouping functionality, as demonstrated in the previous section, but also multilevel grouping and preprocessing. ASP can easily accommodate these features as well. To demonstrate, the Employee Sales report from the original Northwind application will be transformed into ASP next. Again, to enable this report, several new views are created on the database and a new `ClassDef` is added to `NWServer`. The code fragment for this appears in Listing 11.7. Again, after this simple change is made, `NWServer` is recompiled and redeployed to MTS.

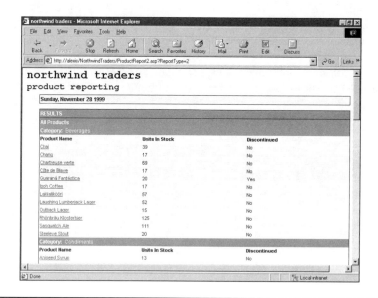

Figure 11.5 The product report with a makeover.

Listing 11.7 **Addition of the *EmployeeSales* Class to the *GetClassDef* Method**

```
Private Function IAppServer_GetClassDef(ByVal ClassId As Integer) As CClassDef
  Dim ClassDef As CClassDef

  If Not bInitialized Then IAppServer_InitServer
  If Not mIAppServer.ClassDefs.Exists(CStr(ClassId)) Then
    Select Case ClassId
      ' other cases as before

    Case CT_EMPLOYEE_SALES
      Set ClassDef = New CClassDef
      With ClassDef
        .DatabaseName = "NWIND"
        .ReadLocation = "View_Employee_Sales"
        .WriteLocation = ""
        .IdColumnName = ""
        .OrderByColumnName = "Country, Shipped_Date, Last_Name, First_Name"

        .AppendMapping "Country", "Country", _
                    True, False, ctString, ""
        .AppendMapping "LastName", "Last_Name", _
                    True, False, ctString, ""
        .AppendMapping "FirstName", "First_Name", _
                    True, False, ctString, ""
        .AppendMapping "ShippedDate", "Shipped_Date", _
                    True, False, ctDateTime, ""
```

```
            .AppendMapping "OrderId", "Order_Id", _
                           True, False, ctNumber, ""
            .AppendMapping "SalesAmount", "Sales_Amount", _
                           True, False, ctNumber, ""
        End With
        Call mIAppServer.ClassDefs.Add(ClassDef, CStr(CT_EMPLOYEE_SALES))
    End Select
  End If

  Set IAppServer_GetClassDef = mIAppServer.ClassDefs.Item(CStr(ClassId))
End Function
```

To continue the development of these reports, two new ASP files are added to the project: EmployeeSalesReports and EmployeeSalesReport. For this set of reports, the user criteria form is more complex than the previous example with the addition of start date and stop date selection mechanisms. The generation of the SELECT fields for these two dates is similar to the previous example. The code fragment in Listing 11.8 shows the initialization information necessary to generate the various form elements.

Listing 11.8 **The Initialization Information for the *EmployeeSalesReports* Form Elements**

```
<%
 Dim vStartMonth, vStartDay, vStartYear
 Dim vEndMonth, vEndDay, vEndYear, vEndDate

 Dim vMonths(12), vReports(2)

 vMonths(1) = "January"
 vMonths(2) = "February"
 vMonths(3) = "March"
 vMonths(4) = "April"
 vMonths(5) = "May"
 vMonths(6) = "June"
 vMonths(7) = "July"
 vMonths(8) = "August"
 vMonths(9) = "September"
 vMonths(10) = "October"
 vMonths(11) = "November"
 vMonths(12) = "December"

 vReports(1)="By Order ID"
 vReports(2)="By Sales Amount"

 vEndDate = Now + 120
 vStartMonth = Functions.VBAFormat(Now,"mm")
 vStartDay = Functions.VBAFormat(Now,"dd")
 vStartYear = Functions.VBAFormat(Now,"yyyy")
```

continues

Listing 11.8 **Continued**

```
vEndMonth = Functions.VBAFormat(CStr(vEndDate),"mm")
vEndDay = Functions.VBAFormat(CStr(vEndDate),"dd")
vEndYear = Functions.VBAFormat(CStr(vEndDate),"yyyy")
%>

<SELECT id=StartMonth name=StartMonth>
<%
For i = 1 To 12
  If CInt(i) = CInt(vStartMonth) Then
    Response.Write("<option selected value='" & i & "'>" & _
                    vMonths(i) & "</option>")
  Else
    Response.Write("<option value='" & i & "'>" & vMonths(i) & "</option>")
  End If
Next

%>
</SELECT>

<SELECT id=StartDay name=StartDay>
<%
For i = 1 To 31
  If CInt(i) = CInt(vStartday) Then
    Response.Write("<option selected>" & i & "</option>")
  Else
    Response.Write("<option>" & i & "</option>")
  End If
Next
%>
</SELECT>

<SELECT id=StartYear name=StartYear>
<%
For i = 1993 To 2010
  If CInt(i) = CInt(vStartYear) Then
    Response.Write("<option selected>" & i & "</option>")
  Else
    Response.Write("<option>" & i & "</option>")
  End If
Next
%>
</SELECT>
```

Note the use of the `VBAFormat` method of the `Functions` object to extract the month, day, and year components of the start and stop dates. This `Functions` object is declared in the `global.asa` file for the project, which has the effect of making the object reference available to all ASP pages within the application. By defining it in this manner, this often-used object does not need to be constantly re-created as users access the site. The following code fragment from the `global.asa` file makes this reference:

```
<OBJECT RUNAT=Server
        SCOPE=Application
        ID=Functions
        PROGID="AppIISCommon.CFunctions">
</OBJECT>
```

Additionally, the code to generate the `SELECT` form elements for the start date is shown. Notice the use of the `If CInt(i) = CInt(vStartDay)` construct. Because VBScript is based exclusively on the variant data type, these extra `CInt` functions are required to ensure that the comparison is made properly. In some cases, VBScript does not perform the appropriate comparison unless it is told to do so explicitly. It is a good idea to develop the habit of making comparisons this way so that you can avoid wasting hours by assuming the comparison would be made correctly when VBScript assumed something else.

The resulting code (this time with the makeover at the outset) appears in Figure 11.6.

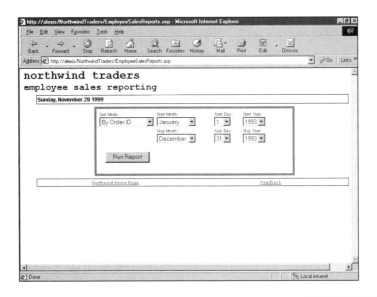

Figure 11.6   The employee sales report criteria selection screen.

The code in the `EmployeeSalesReport` that is called interacts with MTS in a manner similar to the `ProductReport` page. Again, a `Select Case` statement is used to set various report-specific variables that are used by the call to the `NWServer` object to retrieve the information in the appropriate sort order. The code fragment that performs this work is shown in Listing 11.9.

Listing 11.9   **The Initialization and Retrieval Code for the** *EmployeeSalesReport* **Page**

```
<%
  Dim Data, PropertyNames, Errors, NWServer
  Dim DataArray

  Const CT_EMPLOYEE_SALES = 200
  Dim diSalesByPerson, diSalesByCountry

  StartDate = Request.QueryString("StartMonth") & "/" & _
              Request.QueryString("StartDay") & "/" & _
              Request.QueryString("StartYear")
  StopDate = Request.QueryString("StopMonth") & "/" & _
              Request.QueryString("StopDay") & "/" & _
              Request.QueryString("StopYear")
  SortMode = Request.QueryString("SortMode")

  StartDateClause = Array("ShippedDate",">=",StartDate)
  StopDateClause = Array("ShippedDate","<=",StopDate)
  WhereClause = Array(StartDateClause,StopDateClause)

  Select Case SortMode
    Case 1
      OrderByClause = Array("Country","LastName", _
                            "FirstName","OrderId")
    Case 2
      OrderByClause = Array("Country","LastName", _
                            "FirstName","SalesAmount DESC")
  End Select

  Set NWServer = Server.CreateObject("NWServer.CNWServer")
  If Not NWServer.IISInitServer Then
    Response.Write("Could not Initialize the MTS Server<br>")
  End If

  Call NWServer.IISQueryObjectListData(CT_EMPLOYEE_SALES, _
                                       WhereClause, _
                                       OrderByClause, _
                                       "AND", _
                                       PropertyNames, Data, Errors)

  if IsArray(PropertyNames) and IsArray(Data) then
    Set DataArray = Server.CreateObject("AppIISCommon.CDataArray")
    DataArray.Initialize Data, PropertyNames
%>
```

For this report, the difference between the two report modes is simply the sort order, as indicated by the `Select Case` statement. Looking at the second case and the assignment of the `OrderByClause` variable, notice the keyword `DESC` that follows the `SalesAmount` property definition. This keyword is used by the `QueryObjectListData` method of `IAppServer` to sort in a descending order instead of the default ascending order. The remainder of the code fragment in Listing 11.9 is identical to that of Listing 11.6.

Because this report must calculate two aggregate fields based on the two grouping levels by Country and Employee, the DataArray object must be preprocessed before the report is actually written. To store these aggregates, Dictionary objects are used; the use of the Dictionary object is mandated because, unlike Visual Basic, VBScript does not have a Collection class. This Dictionary object is actually a more powerful version of a collection because it has a built-in method to check for key existence coupled with the capability to generate an array of key values. This preprocessing is shown in Listing 11.10. Once again, we monitor the values for the country and employee fields to determine when our groups break.

Listing 11.10   **Preprocessing of the *DataArray* Object**

```
<%
    Set diSalesByPerson = Server.CreateObject("Scripting.Dictionary")
    Set diSalesByCountry = Server.CreateObject("Scripting.Dictionary")
    For i = DataArray.MinRow To DataArray.MaxRow
      vThisPerson = DataArray.Item("LastName",i) & "|" & _
                    DataArray.Item("FirstName",i)
      If (vLastPerson <> vThisPerson) Then
        Call diSalesByPerson.Add(CStr(vLastPerson),vPersonTotal)
        vLastPerson = vThisPerson
        vPersonTotal = 0
      End If
      vThisCountry = DataArray.Item("Country",i)
      If (vLastCountry <> vThisCountry) Then
        Call diSalesByCountry.Add(CStr(vLastCountry),vCountryTotal)
        vCountryTotal = 0
        vLastCountry = vThisCountry
      End If
      vSales = DataArray.Item("SalesAmount",i)
      vPersonTotal = vPersonTotal + vSales
      vCountryTotal = vCountryTotal + vSales
    Next
    Call diSalesByPerson.Add(CStr(vLastPerson),vPersonTotal)
    Call diSalesByCountry.Add(CStr(vLastCountry),vCountryTotal)
%>
```

After the preprocessing is complete, a second pass through the DataArray object is made to format the report. The resulting report is shown in Figure 11.7.

This second report example demonstrates that multilevel reports with preprocessed data can easily be built in ASP. This section and the previous section also demonstrate the ease at which new ClassDef objects can be added to NWServer to enable these reports. Although this technique does involve a different development methodology from a traditional report writer, it broadens the audience of end users in a manner that these report writers cannot match. This technique also remains tightly integrated to the application framework we have put into place to this point, promoting our goal of maximum reuse.

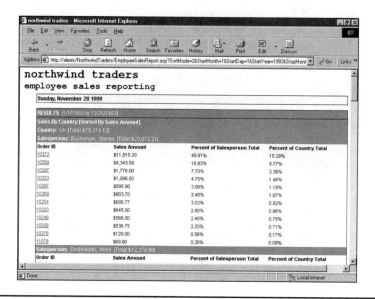

Figure 11.7   The employee sales reporting screen.

Complex Report Generation Through MTS

Although several techniques have been demonstrated that implement much of the basic functionality of standard report writers, there are still times when the formatting complexity of a report is more than ASP can efficiently handle. In these cases, a custom report generator can be built and deployed in MTS that writes the complex HTML stream back to ASP. As an example, several calendar-style reports are developed.

To begin development, a new ActiveX DLL named `AppReports` is created. This DLL is designed to be usable across various applications rather than just the one from our sample application. As such, it defines several core classes. For a basic calendar, a `CCalDay` class and its `CCalDays` collection class are defined. The `CCalDays` collection class has the intelligence necessary to build a basic calendar grid for a given month and year. It also has the capability to generate an HTML-formatted table for inclusion into an ASP page. The `CCalDay` class has a `TextRows` collection that enables the report developer to place HTML-formatted information snippets for a given day of the month. The details of the implementations of these two classes are not discussed, although their full source code accompanies this book.

The AppReports library also defines two other classes. One is an interface class called ICalendarReport, and the other is called CReportImplementation. These two classes are used to enable the addition of new reports to an application as administratively friendly a process as possible. The ICalendarReport interface is used simply to enable the implementation of multiple calendar-style reports that have as their only inputs the month and year of the calendar to generate. The CReportImplementation class is used to map report names to their implementation class for use by a Visual Basic CreateObject statement. Listing 11.11 shows the code for ICalendarReport, whereas Listing 11.12 shows CReportImplementation.

Listing 11.11   **The Code for the *ICalendarReport* Interface Class**

```
Option Explicit
Private mCalendarMonth As Integer
Private mCalendarYear As Integer

Public Sub DoReport(DataStream As Variant, _
                    ByVal CalendarMonth As Integer, _
                    ByVal CalendarYear As Integer)

End Sub

Public Property Let CalendarYear(ByVal vData As Integer)
    mCalendarYear = vData
End Property

Public Property Get CalendarYear() As Integer
    CalendarYear = mCalendarYear
End Property

Public Property Let CalendarMonth(ByVal vData As Integer)
    mCalendarMonth = vData
End Property

Public Property Get CalendarMonth() As Integer
    CalendarMonth = mCalendarMonth
End Property
```

Listing 11.12   **The Code for the *CReportImplementation* Class**

```
Option Explicit

Private mReportName As String
Private mLibraryName As String
```

continues

Listing 11.12   **Continued**

```
Public Property Let ReportName(Value As String)
  mReportName = Value
End Property

Public Property Get ReportName() As String
  ReportName = mReportName
End Property

Public Property Let LibraryName(Value As String)
  mLibraryName = Value
End Property

Public Property Get LibraryName() As String
  LibraryName = mLibraryName
End Property
```

With the core `AppReports` component complete, the component to build the reports can be built. The `NWReports` component is defined as an ActiveX DLL as well, and it is designed to run under MTS. First, a special class called `CNWCalendarReports` is created to do nothing more than to enumerate the calendar-style reports implemented by the `NWReports` component. The code for this `CNWCalendarReports` class is shown in Listing 11.13.

Listing 11.13   **The Code for the *CNWCalendarReports* Class**

```
Option Explicit
Private Index As Integer
Private mCol As Collection

Public Sub AppendType(ReportName As String, LibraryName As String)
  Dim ReportImplementation As New CReportImplementation
  With ReportImplementation
    .ReportName = ReportName
    .LibraryName = LibraryName
  End With
  mCol.Add ReportImplementation, ReportImplementation.ReportName

End Sub

Private Sub Class_Initialize()
  Set mCol = New Collection
  Call AppendType("Shipped Date", "NWReports.CShippedCalendar")
  Call AppendType("Requested Date", "NWReports.CRequestedCalendar")
End Sub
```

```
Public Property Get Item(Index As Variant) As CReportImplementation
  Set Item = mCol.Item(Index)
End Property

Public Property Get Count() As Long
   Count = mCol.Count
End Property

Public Property Get NewEnum() As IUnknown
   Set NewEnum = mCol.[_NewEnum]
End Property

Private Sub Class_Terminate()
   Set mCol = Nothing
End Sub
```

In the `Class_Initialize` event of `CNWCalendarReports`, the internal collection of `CReportImplementation` items is built. As new reports are defined, a new `CReportImplementation` instance is added to this class to tell the outside world of its existence. As you can see from the two library names in the `Class_Initialize` event (see Listing 11.13), there are two `ICalendarReport` interfaces implemented: one in the `CShippedCalendar` class and the other in the `CRequestedCalendar` class. Again, the implementation details of these two classes are not covered here, but the full source is available in the accompanying software.

One other class, `CNWReportServer`, is built within the `NWReports` component. This class is called into action by IIS to accomplish the generation of the complex HTML stream for the calendar reports through its `DoCalendarReport` method. Before this call, the user must select the desired report, which is provided to the user criteria page through a `CalendarReportNames` property on the `CNWReport` server. The code for the `CNWReportServer` class appears Listing 11.14.

Listing 11.14 **The Code to Implement the *CNWReportServer* Class**

```
Option Explicit
Public Property Get CalendarReportNames() As Variant
  Dim vRet As Variant
  Dim ReportImplementation As CReportImplementation
  Dim NWCalendarReports As New CNWCalendarReports
  Dim i As Integer

  vRet = Array(1)
  ReDim Preserve vRet(1 To NWCalendarReports.Count)

  For i = 1 To NWCalendarReports.Count
```

continues

Listing 11.14   **Continued**

```
      vRet(i) = NWCalendarReports.Item(i).ReportName
   Next i
   CalendarReportNames = vRet
End Property

Public Function DoCalendarReport(ByVal CalendarMonth As Variant, _
                                 ByVal CalendarYear As Variant, _
                                 ByVal ReportName As Variant) As Variant
   Dim vDataStream As Variant
   Dim NWCalendarReports As New CNWCalendarReports
   Dim CalendarReport As ICalendarReport
   Dim LibraryName As String
   On Error GoTo ErrorTrap

   LibraryName = NWCalendarReports.Item(ReportName).LibraryName
   Set CalendarReport = CreateObject(LibraryName)
   Call CalendarReport.DoReport(vDataStream, _
                                CInt(CalendarMonth), _
                                CInt(CalendarYear))

ExitFunction:
   DoCalendarReport = vDataStream
   Exit Function

ErrorTrap:
   '1. Send detailed message to EventLog
   Call WriteNTLogEvent("CNWReportServer:DoCalendarReport", _
                        Err.Number, _
                        Err.Description, _
                        Err.Source & " [" & Erl & "]")
   vDataStream = "<p>" & "CNWReportServer:DoCalendarReport" & _
                 Err.Number & " " & Err.Description & " " & _
                 Err.Source & " [" & Erl & "]" & "</p>"

   '2. Raise a more generic event to the client
   Err.Raise vbObjectError, "CNWReportServer:DoCalendarReport", _
             Err.Description & " [" & Erl & "]"
   GoTo ExitFunction
End Function
```

Turning to Visual InterDev, two new ASP files are added to the Northwind Traders project: CalendarReports and CalendarReport. To build the list of available reports for CalendarReports, the NWReportServer object on MTS is called as shown in Listing 11.15, to produce the page shown in Figure 11.8.

Listing 11.15   **Enumerating the Calendar Reports in ASP**

```
<%
  Dim HTMLStream, NWReportServer
  Dim i, vMonth, vYear, vReportNames

  Set NWReportServer = Server.CreateObject("NWReports.CNWReportServer")
  vReportNames = NWReportServer.CalendarReportNames

  vMonth = Functions.VBAFormat(Now,"mm")
  vYear = Functions.VBAFormat(Now,"yyyy")
%>
```

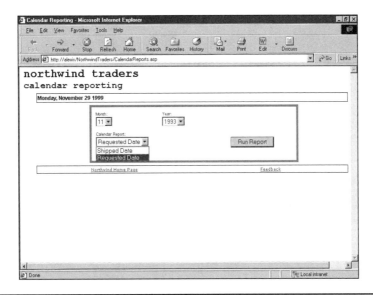

Figure 11.8   The list of available reports in the Calendar Reporting page.

In the Calendar Reporting page, the script is simple as well, as shown in Listing 11.16, producing the page shown in Figure 11.9.

Listing 11.16   **The ASP Code to Insert the HTML Fragment from Our Calendar Builder**

```
<%
  Set NWReportServer = Server.CreateObject("NWReports.CNWReportServer")
  vReportName = Request.QueryString.Item("ReportName")
  HTMLStream = NWReportServer.DoCalendarReport(vMonth, vYear, vReportName)
  Response.Write(HTMLStream)
%>
```

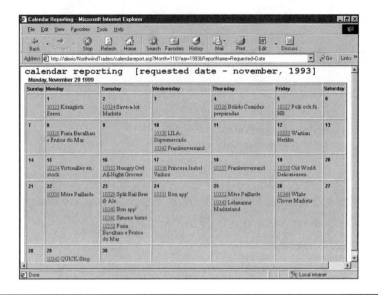

Figure 11.9   The Calendar Reporting page.

Summary

This chapter has provided examples of how to use ASP as a distributed reporting engine in place of traditional report writers. Several techniques have been demonstrated to generate both simple- and medium-complexity reports using just ASP coupled with the existing MTS business objects. Additionally, a technique to generate complex reports was demonstrated, which used ASP in conjunction with MTS-hosted reporting objects that subsequently tapped into the business objects.

In the next chapter, I discuss the development of an intranet portal site for the application. Some specific topics include how style sheets and server-side include files have been used to produce the nicely formatted pages shown in some of the examples seen in this chapter. Additionally, the portal concept is discussed as a means not only to provide reports to end users, but also to provide access to the underlying information sets managed by the system.

12

Taking the Enterprise Application to the Net

AN APPLICATION DEVELOPER WOULD BE REMISS to underestimate the capabilities that an intranet or Internet extension would add to their application in this modern Internet age. Simply noticing the current efforts of some traditional enterprise application vendors to enable their application for the Internet, or seeing the emergence of new companies with enterprise application products designed for the Internet from the outset, are indicators of others who have already gone through this thought process. Specific examples include the Enterprise Resource Planning (ERP) market, with such vendors as SAP and its mySAP.COM infrastructure; the Supply Chain Management (SCM) market, with such vendors as i2 Technologies and its TradeMatrix business portal; and the Customer Relationship Management (CRM) market, with such vendors as Pivotal and its eRelationship product or Vantive and its e-Customer suite.

With this trend in mind, this application framework has also been designed from the outset to easily support an Internet component. Part of this foresight is seen in the choice of tools and technologies that have driven the implementation to this point. The DNA underpinnings of this framework have played a dramatic role in this effort, as was evident during our first foray into Internet Information Server (IIS) in the previous chapter. In this chapter, much more attention is given to the development of the Internet portion of the framework, focusing specifically on both intranets and Internets.

Layout Standardization Techniques

Before getting into the details of intranets and Internets, some generic techniques are applicable to both domains. As should be clear by this point, two fundamental principles have driven design and implementation decisions to this point: flexibility and standardization. Development efforts in the IIS realm are no different. For maintenance efficiency, it is highly desirable to have the flexibility to make global application changes at singular locations. It is also desirable to have the implementation of similar functionality performed in standardized manners. The topics covered in this section are driven by these two requirements.

Style Sheets

A *style sheet* is a special HTML tag that enables a developer to control how textual content is rendered by the browser. Specifically, the developer can specify style classes that can be assigned to specific HTML tag types—for example, <TD>, <H1>, or <P> tags—or used globally by any tag type. The most often-used style properties include those for font, text color, background color, and text alignment. Style sheets enable one other type of formatting for the control of hyperlink rendering based on its various states.

As an aside, style sheets are gaining importance in their use beyond the simple HMTL format standardization discussed in this section. In the eXtensible Markup Language (XML) standard, style sheets are also used to automatically apply formatting to the data embodied in an XML block within an HTML page. The new eXtensible HTML (XHTML) standard also makes similar use of the style sheet mechanism for formatting. We discuss and use the XML standard in much more detail in the next chapter, although our primary purpose will be as a data transfer mechanism that does not need style. Nonetheless, it is important to understand the role that style sheets play today and where their use is headed in the near future.

Note

There are many more style properties than will be covered in this section, because complete coverage of them is beyond the scope of this book. Any good book on HTML should provide more than adequate information on this topic. The intent of this section is to introduce the concept of using style sheets to provide a flexible mechanism for driving Web site consistency.

Style sheets are placed into an HTML document using a <STYLE> block within the <HEAD> block of the HTML page, as shown in Listing 12.1.

Listing 12.1   **A Style Sheet Within an HTML Document**

```
<HTML>
<HEAD>
<TITLE>Some Title</TITLE>
<STYLE TYPE="text/css">
<!--
  A:active { color: mediumblue; }
  A:link {color: mediumblue;}
  A:visited {color: mediumblue;}
  A:hover {color: red;}
  TD.HeaderOne
  {
    BACKGROUND-COLOR: #009966;
    COLOR: #ffff99;
    FONT-FAMILY: Arial, Verdana, 'MS Sans Serif';
    FONT-SIZE: 10pt;
    FONT-WEIGHT: normal
  }
  TD.HeaderOne-B
  {
    BACKGROUND-COLOR: #009966;
    COLOR: #ffff99;
    FONT-FAMILY: Arial, Verdana, 'MS Sans Serif';
    FONT-SIZE: 10pt;
    FONT-WEIGHT: bold
  }
  TD.ResultDetailHeader-1
  {
    COLOR: black;
    FONT-FAMILY: Arial, Verdana, 'MS Sans Serif';
    FONT-SIZE: 8pt;
    FONT-WEIGHT: bold;
    TEXT-ALIGN: left
  }
  TD.ResultData {
    FONT-FAMILY: Arial, Verdana, 'MS Sans Serif';
    FONT-SIZE: 8pt;
    FONT-WEIGHT: normal;
    TEXT-ALIGN: left
  }
-->
</STYLE>
</HEAD>
<BODY>
</BODY>
</HTML>
```

In Listing 12.1, the information within the <SCRIPT> block is surrounded by the <!-- and --> comment tags to prevent older-vintage browsers that do not support style sheets from being unable to render the HTML page. In the <STYLE TYPE="text/css">

line, the css refers to the term Cascading Style Sheet, which is the name of the standard adopted by the World Wide Web Consortium (W3C) in 1996 to define style sheets for HTML. Internet Explorer (IE) 3.0 and Netscape Navigator 4.0 were the first browsers to adopt subsets of these standards, with later versions of each adopting more of the standard. The term *cascading* refers to the way style classes are merged if they are defined multiple times within an HTML document.

The formats associated with hyperlinks are formally known as pseudo-classes in the W3C standard because they are based on tag states instead of tag content. For the <A> tag given in the example, the four pseudo-classes include active, link, visited, and hover. The first three are formally defined by the W3C standard, whereas the last is a Microsoft extension for Internet Explorer. For each of these pseudo-classes, a color style property is defined using named color values. These color names are based on extensions to HTML 3.2, which initially defined only 16 colors. Netscape extended these names to several hundred to coincide with the colors available in the X-Windows system, with subsequent support by Microsoft Internet Explorer. Colors can also be provided as Red-Green-Blue (RGB) color triples using either the format #RRGGBB or the statement rgb(RRR,GGG,BBB). In the former case, the values are given in hexadecimal format, whereas in the latter case, the values are provided in decimal format. For example, the following are equivalent color property statements in HTML:

```
color: silver
color: #C0C0C0
color: rgb(192,192,192)
```

Looking at the example once again, the color properties for the active, link, and visited properties are set to mediumblue, whereas the color for the hover property is set to red. Having the common color scheme of the first three properties has the effect of preventing the browser from changing the color of the hyperlink after a user has clicked on the link. The effect of the last property is to have the link highlighted in red when the mouse pointer is directly over the hyperlink text. By placing this set of pseudo-class definitions in the style sheet, all the hyperlinks in the current HTML document follow these effects.

Looking next at the style properties for the various TD-based classes in Listing 12.1, we can see that font-, text-, and color-level definitions are given. Specifically, FONT-FAMILY, FONT-SIZE, and FONT-WEIGHT properties are defined for fonts. For text definitions, a TEXT-ALIGN property is defined. For color definitions, COLOR and BACKGROUND-COLOR properties are defined.

A comma-separated list of font names is provided for the FONT-FAMILY property. This tells the browser to search for installed fonts in the order given, using the first installed font found. If no installed fonts are found, a default font is used. Because the installed fonts can vary from user to user, it is a good idea to use common fonts, with the last one or two being fonts that are likely to be installed, such as Arial or Sans Serif. It is also a good idea to use Sans Serif fonts for online applications because studies have shown that they are the preference of most users.

There are several FONT-SIZE property definition options as in the color case discussed previously. For this property, size can be specified in absolute, relative, or named terms. For absolute definitions, either pt or % can be used. The pt definition, used in Listing 12.1, is the most common method that sets the size to an exact value. The % definition sets the size as a percentage of the size of the parent element. For relative sizes, a + or - precedes the value, as in +2pt, which would increase the font size by two points from the most recently used font size. In the named value case, keywords are mapped to absolute sizes that are defined by the browser. Valid keywords include xx-small, x-small, small, medium, large, x-large, and xx-large. For the purpose of style sheets, it is best to stick with using absolute, pt-based sizes, because this method offers the most control with the most predictability of how the final HTML page will be rendered by the browser.

In the example, the FONT-WEIGHT property is defined next. For this property, named values, such as bold and normal, can be used to indicate whether to use boldface. Alternatively, boldness values can be given in the form of numbers that are multiples of 100, between 100 (lightest) and 900 (boldest). The keyword bold corresponds to a value of 700, whereas the value 400 corresponds to the keyword normal.

The only text-based property defined in the example is TEXT-ALIGN. Values that can be assigned to this property include left, right, center, or justify. If this property is not defined, left is assumed. Other text properties that are available but not shown include TEXT-DECORATION for special effects, such as strikethrough and blinking; TEXT-INDENT to implement hanging and normal indents on the first line of a paragraph; and TEXT-TRANSFORM to modify letter capitalization.

Now that a style sheet is defined within the <HEAD> section of an HTML document, it is a simple matter to make references to the style classes from within the tags used throughout the remainder of the HTML document. As mentioned before, the style associated with hyperlinks is automatically enforced throughout the entire document after the definition is made. For the other classes, they must be explicitly used. As an example of style use, a fragment of HTML generated by the EmployeeSalesReport.asp page in the previous chapter appears in Listing 12.2.

Listing 12.2 **Using the Styles Defined in the Style Sheet**

```
<TABLE WIDTH="100%" CELLPADDING=2 CELLSPACING=0 border=0>
  <TR>
    <TD class="HeaderOne-B" width=150>Sales By Country</TD>
    <TD class="HeaderOne" colspan=3>
      [12/5/1993 to 4/3/1994]
      [Sorted By Order ID]
    </TD>
  </TR>
  <TR>
    <TD class="HeaderOne-B" width="150">Country:</TD>
```

continues

Listing 12.2   **Continued**

```
    <TD class="HeaderOne" colspan=3>UK [Total $52,840.06]</TD>
  </TR>
  <TR>
    <TD class="HeaderOne-B" width="150">Salesperson:</TD>
    <TD class="HeaderOne" colspan=3>
      Buchanan, Steven [Total $15,694.50]
    </TD>
  </TR>
  <TR>
    <TD class='ResultDetailHeader-1' width='10%'>Order ID</TD>
    <TD class='ResultDetailHeader-1' width='5%'>Sales Amount</TD>
    <TD class='ResultDetailHeader-1' width='10%'>
      Percent of Salesperson Total
    </TD>
    <TD class='ResultDetailHeader-1' width='5%'>Percent of Country Total</TD>
  </TR>
  <TR>
    <TD class='ResultData' width='10%'>
      <a href='OrderDetail.asp?orderid=10372'>10372</a>
    </TD>
    <TD class='ResultData' width='10%'>$11,515.20</TD>
    <TD class='ResultData' width='10%'>73.37%</TD>
    <TD class='ResultData' width='10%'>21.79%</TD>
  </TR>
  <TR>
    <TD class='ResultData' width='10%'>
      <a href='OrderDetail.asp?orderid=10378'>10378</a>
    </TD>
    <TD class='ResultData' width='10%'>$129.00</TD>
    <TD class='ResultData' width='10%'>0.82%</TD>
    <TD class='ResultData' width='10%'>0.24%</TD>
  </TR>
</TABLE>
```

As you can see in the various <TD> tags, a `class=` statement within the tag indicates the style to associate with the tag. You should also note that nothing special is done in the <A> tags to make them use the special pseudo-class effects defined in the style sheet.

You might be thinking to yourself that although this style sheet mechanism does offer flexibility, it still requires that each of the HTML documents making up a Web site has a style sheet in its <HEAD> section. For a Web site with hundreds or thousands of pages, it would be difficult to make style changes because each document, or more appropriately, each Active Server Page (ASP) generating these documents, would have to be modified to support the change. This would indicate that there is no real flexibility offered by the style sheet approach. This is a valid assessment, so the HTML specification allows for the linkage of style sheets into an HTML document. The mechanism for this is as follows:

```
<head>
<title>northwind traders</title>
<LINK REL=stylesheet TYPE="text/css" HREF="stylesheets/nw01.css">
</head>
```

With this approach, these same hundreds or thousands of documents can make this reference to a style sheet so that changes made to it are immediately reflected throughout the Web site.

Creating a style sheet is easy. Although it can be done directly in a text editor following the W3C specifications, Visual InterDev provides a simple editor for doing so. To add a style sheet to an existing project, simply right-click on the project node within Visual InterDev and select the Add option and then the Style Sheet option. The Add Item dialog appears with the Style Sheet option selected by default. Change the name of the style sheet to `nw01.css`, and click the Open button. This brings up the style sheet editor with a default `BODY` class created, as shown in Figure 12.1.

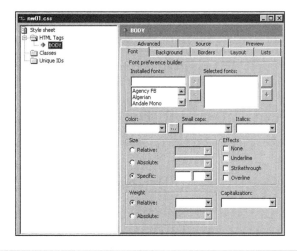

Figure 12.1   A new style sheet added to the Northwind Traders project.

To create a new class within a style sheet, right-click on the `Classes` folder within the style sheet editor, and then select Insert Class to bring up the Insert New Class dialog. To make a tag-specific class, select the Apply To Only the Following Tag checkbox and select the appropriate tag name from the list. Type the name of the new class in the Class Name field, and click OK. The new class is added under the `Classes` folder, and the properties page for your new class, in which you can set the various style properties, is brought up on the right side. Figure 12.2 shows the results of adding the `TD.ResultData` class after the font properties have been set on the Font tab.

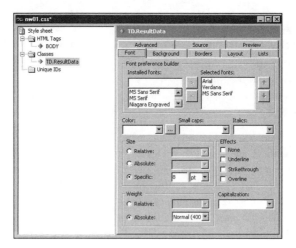

Figure 12.2   A new style class added to the Northwind Traders
project after the font properties were set.

Text properties are set on the Layout tab, whereas the background color is set on the Background tab. Clicking on the Source tab shows the HTML code for the style sheet with the currently selected style class in bold. Notice that this text is similar to the format of the original style sheet that was embedded in the <HEAD> section.

Server Side Includes

Although style sheets can control the look and feel of individual tags in an HTML document, they cannot provide an overall template for the document. For example, if you look at many commercial Web sites, you might notice that they have similar headers or footers across all their pages, or at least throughout various subsections of the site. One mechanism to accomplish this standardization, while following the flexibility mantra, is to use server side includes. These files are separate HMTL or ASP code snippets that are pulled into an ASP as a pre-processing step before the final generation of the HTML stream that is sent back to the client. An example of such a reference can be seen in the ASP script code from the `ProductReports2.asp` file given in the previous chapter. A fragment of this code is provided in Listing 12.3.

Listing 12.3   **Using Server Side Include Files**

```
<BODY TOPMARGIN=0 marginwidth=10 marginheight=0 LEFTMARGIN=10>
<!--#include file="ServerScripts\GetpageHeader.inc"-->
<%
 Dim vReports(3)
 vReports(1)="Current Products"
 vReports(2)="All Products"
```

```
   vReports(3)="Discontinued Products"
   FormWidth = 470
%>
<!--#include file="ServerScripts\GetFormHeader.inc"-->
  <FORM  action=ProductReport2.asp>
    <TABLE WIDTH="100%" CELLPADDING=2 CELLSPACING=0 border=0>
      <TR>
        <TD class="FormCaption" WIDTH=30%>Report Type:<BR>
          <SELECT id=ReportType name=ReportType>

<%
For i = 1 To ubound(vReports)  if cint(i) = 1 then
  Response.Write("<option selected value='" & i & "'>" & _
                    vReports(i) & "</option>")  else
    Response.Write("<option value='" & i & "'>" & _
                    vReports(i) & "</option>")      end if
next
%>
          </SELECT>
        </TD>
        <TD width=30% align="center">
          <BR><INPUT type="submit" value="Run Report">
        </TD>
      </TR>
    </TABLE>
  </FORM>
<!--#include file="ServerScripts\GetFormFooter.inc"-->
<!--#include file="ServerScripts\GetpageFooter.inc"-->
</BODY>
```

Four files are included in this simple script. The GetPageHeader.inc file is responsible for generating the standard header of the page, whereas its GetPageFooter.inc counterpart generates the standard footer. Similarly, GetFormHeader.inc and GetFormFooter.inc generate the table structures to give a consistent look and feel to all forms used throughout the Web site. Figure 12.3 indicates the specific areas that are generated by these include files.

Notice the .inc extension given to the server side include files to indicate that these are not fully functional ASP scripts but rather ASP fragments. Although this is good to identify them as included script files, it makes them more difficult to edit in Visual InterDev. Because Visual InterDev does not recognize these extensions, it opens them up in a standard text edit mode without the nice, yellow highlights at the beginning and end of script blocks, which have the <% and %> markers. Nor is it able to identify tags in black, keywords in red, values in blue, comments in gray, and so forth. Thus, if you give these files ASP extensions, Visual InterDev is able to interpret them and give you these visual clues. The choice is yours.

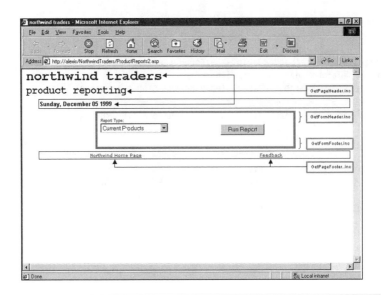

Figure 12.3   The areas of the user criteria screen contributed to by various server side include files.

Global Application Variables

One other area that can add a level of standardization and flexibility is the use of application variables. Under the IIS model, a Web application is defined based on all the files within a given directory, or any of its subdirectories, on or mapped by the IIS Web server. As briefly discussed in the last chapter, the global.asa file is used as a controlling mechanism for the entire Web application, and it must reside in the root directory of the Web application. After the Web site is first started (or restarted) using the Internet Service Manager, the first request for any page within the context of the Web application causes the Application_OnStart event to fire. If this happens, application variables can be defined using the following syntax:

```
Application(VariableName) = VariableValue
```

Any ASP page within the application can then retrieve these variables by using the reverse syntax as follows:

```
VariableValue = Application(VariableName)
```

This simple mechanism enables the application to store global variables for the entire application, much as constants are stored in traditional programming environments. Examples of usable information might be the name of specific page URLs, such as a NoAccessGranted.ASP file or a MailTo:-style URL to redirect mail to the site administrator. Examples appear in the following code fragment from the global.asa file:

```
Sub Application_OnStart
  Application("NoAccessURL") = "no_access.asp"
  Application("SiteAdministratorMailTo") = "mailto:ptindall@texas.net"
End Sub
```

Building the Internal Intranet Site

With some basic standardization techniques, we can now turn our attention to the development of an intranet site for our application. From surfing the Web and accessing commercial Web sites, you might have noticed that they typically have a home page that enables entry into the various navigation points of the system. In addition, there are typically links to frequently used, functional areas of the system (such as stock quotes or local weather forecasts) from this main page. Home pages designed in this format are often referred to as *portals* or *consoles*. We follow a similar design philosophy in designing the intranet site for our framework.

Our goal, for now, is to provide internal access to the various objects and reports of the application. In Chapter 13, "Interoperability," we will add a few new features to help us move information out of our application and into other applications using the portal as a launching point. Portal design can be accomplished in many ways. You can prove this to yourself by looking at commercial portal sites. For our purposes, we are going to stay somewhat basic, as shown in Figure 12.4. This page corresponds to a file `Home.asp` that we have created for our Northwind application.

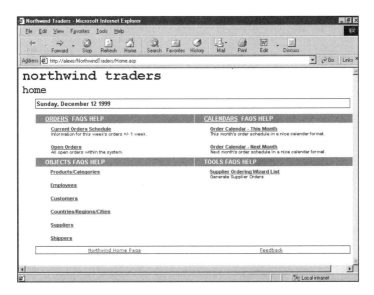

Figure 12.4   The intranet portal for the Northwind Traders application.

Looking at Figure 12.4, you should see four distinct areas. The first two have headers titled ORDERS and CALENDARS, whereas the other two have headers titled OBJECTS and TOOLS.

By clicking on the ORDERS hyperlink, we jump to an OrderReports.asp screen that enables us to run several queries against the orders stored in the database. These are similar to the All Orders and Open Orders nodes in the NWExplorer control that we developed in Chapter 10, "Adding an ActiveX Control to the Framework," although now they accept the entry of a date range. We develop the OrderReports.asp file using the EmployeeReports.asp file that we created in the last chapter as a template. To do this, we simply create the new ASP file in our project, copy everything in the EmployeeReports.asp file to the clipboard, and paste it into our new file. We then make a few minor modifications to the vReports section of the code, as shown in Listing 12.4. We also change a caption here and there, and change the target for the form to OrderReport.asp.

Listing 12.4   **Minor Modifications to the *EmployeeReports.ASP* Page to Create *OrderReports.ASP***

```
<%
...
Dim vMonths(12), vReports(2)
...
 vReports(1)="All Orders"
 vReports(2)="Open Orders"
...
%>
...
<FORM action=OrderReport.asp id=form1 name=form1>
  <TABLE WIDTH="100%" CELLPADDING=2 CELLSPACING=0 border=0>
    <TR>
      <TD BGCOLOR="#ffffee" WIDTH=30%>
        <FONT FACE="Arial,Helvetica,sans-serif" SIZE="-3" COLOR="#333333">
        Report Mode:<BR>
        <SELECT id=ReportMode name=ReportMode>
<%
  For i = 1 To UBound(vReports)
    If CInt(i) = 1 Then
      Response.Write("<option selected value='" & i & "'>" & _
        vReports(i) & "</option>")
    Else
      Response.Write("<option value='" & i & "'>" & vReports(i) & "</option>")
    End If
  Next
%>
        </SELECT>
```

```
        </FONT>
      </TD>
  ...
```

Listing 12.4 demonstrates how we've made the code for this user selection form as flexible as possible for future modification. By placing our report name information in an array at the top of the script and using the UBound function as we iterate through the array, we make it easy to modify this template if we need to create new criteria selectors. The screen generated by our OrderReports.asp file appears in Figure 12.5. Note that the default dates seen in the screen are set based on a base date of April 15, 1995. This is done to coincide with the dates in the Northwind database. In a real application, we would want our base date to be the current date. Leaving the defaults as is and clicking on the Run Report button produces the report shown in Figure 12.6.

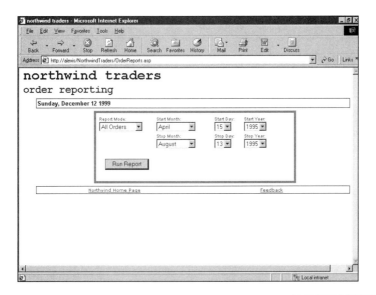

Figure 12.5   The OrderReports screen in Internet Explorer.

Note from Figure 12.6 that the columns in the ASP-generated screen are the same as those in the NWExplorer control. Looking at the code in Listing 12.5 should convince you that the techniques to retrieve the information in Visual Basic (VB) and ASP forms are strikingly similar. This is by design.

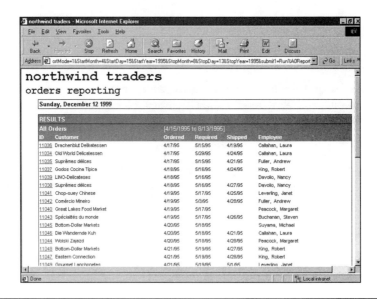

Figure 12.6   The `OrderReports` screen in Internet Explorer run using the default values.

Listing 12.5   **Comparison of VB to ASP Code**

```
' From VB
...
            Case EIT_ORDER_OPEN
               vCriteria = Array(Array("ShippedDate", "is", "null"), _
                                 Array("ShippedDate", "=", "12:00:00 AM"))
               vOrder = Array("RequiredDate", "CustomerName")
               Set OrderProxyItems = _
                  AppClient.LoadQueryCollection(CT_ORDER_PROXY, _
                                                vCriteria, _
                                                vOrder, _
                                                "OR")
               Set AppCollection = OrderProxyItems
...

' From ASP
<%
...
  Const CT_ORDER_PROXY = 104
...
  ReportMode = Request.QueryString("ReportMode")
  StartDateClause = Array("OrderDate",">=",StartDate)
  StopDateClause = Array("OrderDate","<=",StopDate)
  OrderByClause = Array("OrderDate","CustomerName")

  Select Case ReportMode
```

```
      Case 1 ' All Orders
        WhereClause = Array(StartDateClause,StopDateClause)
        ReportName = "All Orders"
        Conj = "AND"
      Case 2 ' Open Orders
        ' Note:  because this has a compound AND and OR in the WHERE statement,
        '        we have to grab all open orders here and then filter below
        WhereClause = Array(Array("ShippedDate", "is", "null"), _
                            Array("ShippedDate", "=", "12:00:00 AM"))
        ReportName = "Open Orders"
        Conj = "OR"
    End Select
...
    Call NWServer.IISQueryObjectListData(CT_ORDER_PROXY, _
                                    WhereClause, _
                                    OrderByClause, _
                                    Conj, _
                                    PropertyNames, Data, Errors)
...
%>
```

You might have noticed that the Order ID column, both in these reports and the ones from the previous chapter, have been hyperlinked to an `OrderDetail.asp` file. This file represents the first detail screen that we will create. All other object detail screens can be created in a similar manner. Because a `COrder` object has a collection of `COrderDetailItem` objects, we design our `OrderDetail.asp` screen to have a header section that contains the details for the order, followed by a section that lists the order line items. This screen appears in Figure 12.7.

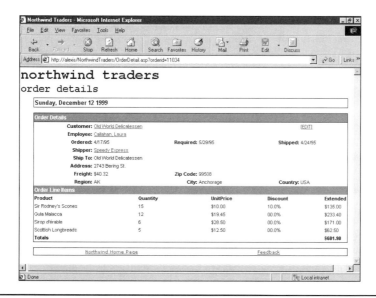

Figure 12.7   The `OrderDetail` screen in Internet Explorer.

There is nothing of a rocket-science nature in the `OrderDetail.asp` screen. We are first retrieving our `Order` object with a call to `NWServer.IISGetObjectData`, followed by a call to `NWServer.IISGetObjectListData` for the `OrderDetailItems` collection. The remainder of the script is used to build the table structure necessary to display the screen as shown. Notice that our Customer, Employee, and Shipper fields are hyper-linked to their respective detail pages as well. Such capability is the beauty of the World Wide Web (WWW).

What is new with this screen is the [EDIT] hyperlink in the upper-right corner. Clicking on this link takes us to the `OrderDetailControl.asp` page, which has our `NWOrderControl` embedded in it. This page appears in Figure 12.8, and the script code appears in Listing 12.6.

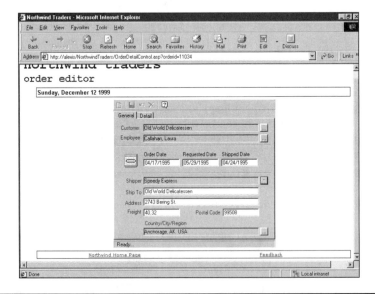

Figure 12.8   The `OrderDetailControl.asp` page with the `NWOrderControl` embedded in it.

We have chosen to use our `NWOrderControl` to implement the edit functionality instead of a series of ASP pages for several reasons. First, we have already built the functionality into this control, and it doesn't make sense to duplicate something that works so well. The second reason is that the architecture of the system requires the selection of items from lists. Although the selection process for the `Customer`, `Employee`, and `Shipper` fields could easily be implemented as `<SELECT>` elements within a form, the other fields are not. The hierarchical relationship of the `Country/City/Region` selection, more specifically, a tree, is not easily implemented in any form element available to us. This is similar to the product selection process in that we first must look under a category before selecting our product.

Listing 12.6 **Embedding the *NWOrderControl* in the *OrderDetailControl.asp* Page**

```
<html>
<head>
<meta NAME="GENERATOR" Content="Microsoft Visual Studio 6.0">
<title>Northwind Traders</title>
<LINK REL=stylesheet TYPE="text/css" HREF="stylesheets/nw01.css">
</head>
<%
  Id = CLng(Request.QueryString("orderid"))
%>
<script LANGUAGE="VBScript">
<!--
Sub Page_Initialize
  On Error Resume Next
  NWOrder.RegisterControl("server=alexis&id=<%=Id%>&subid=0&mode=2")
  NWOrder.InitControl
End Sub
-->
</script>
<body bgcolor="#FFFFCC"
      TOPMARGIN=0
      marginwidth=10
      marginheight=0
      LEFTMARGIN=10
      LANGUAGE="VBScript"
      ONLOAD="Page_Initialize">
<!--#include file="ServerScripts\GetpageHeader.asp"-->
<TABLE WIDTH="800" border=0 CELLSPACING="0" CELLPADDING="0" valign="TOP">
  <TR>
    <TD WIDTH="100%" align="CENTER" valign="TOP" BGCOLOR="#FFFFCC">
      <OBJECT classid="clsid:692CDDDA-A494-11D3-BF79-204C4F4F5020"
              id=NWOrder
              align="center">
      </OBJECT>
    </TD>
  </TR>
</TABLE>
<!--#include file="ServerScripts\GetpageFooter.asp"-->
</body>
</html>
```

We will demonstrate how an order can be created from the customer's perspective in the following section "Building the External Internet Site." It is here that we follow a pure HTML-based approach because we cannot run DCOM over the Internet, which is what is needed by the control.

Note

As an aside, Microsoft's recent proposal for the Simple Object Access Protocol (SOAP) promises to offer the capability to provide a rich control-based interface without having to run over a DCOM layer. This protocol uses standard HTTP (HyperText Transport Protocol) as its base, which is the same base protocol used by the World Wide Web for delivery of HTML pages. Using this communication protocol, XML data formatted requests are used to invoke methods on remote objects. Because this is a standard submitted to the Internet Engineering Task Force (IETF), it has the promise of being adopted as a true Internet standard. If this were the case, it would not matter what type of Web server we were running, such as IIS or Apache. Nor would it matter what type of application server we were running, such as MTS or WebLogic. Nor would it matter whether our rich controls were based on Win32 or Java. It will be interesting to watch the development of this standard.

Before completing this section, we still must cover a few more areas. The upper-right corner of our home page includes a hypertext link to the CalendarReports.asp page developed in the last chapter. You should notice from our home page that, under the ORDERS hyperlink, there are additional hyperlinks named Current Orders Schedule and Open Orders. These links jump directly into the OrderReport.asp page using default information based on the current date, bypassing OrderReports.asp's user criteria selection page. The reasoning for this is that these are the most frequently used reports; therefore, there is no need to go through the criteria selection page. Similar links can be found under the CALENDARS section of the page.

The final item to investigate in this section is the OBJECTS area of the portal. This text is not hyperlinked as the other items looked at so far. Instead, it provides a listing under it of all the objects available for viewing from the intranet. If we select the Products/Categories hypertext link, we jump to the Categories.asp page, which appears in Figure 12.9. Selecting any of the hyperlinks on this page jumps us to the ProductsByCategory.asp page, as shown in Figure 12.10.

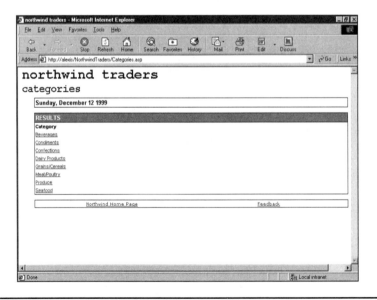

Figure 12.9   The Categories.asp page.

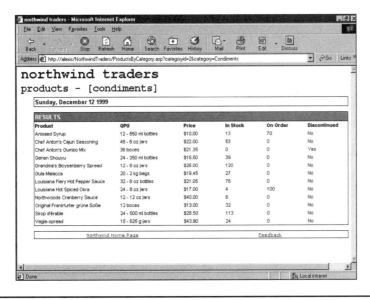

Figure 12.10   The `ProductsByCategories.asp` page.

The other objects listed under the **OBJECTS** caption on the home page can be implemented in a similar manner. We will postpone the discussion of the items under the **TOOLS** caption until the next chapter.

Building the External Internet Site

With our ability to generate an internal intranet site to accompany our application, we might begin to wonder how we can leverage the external access that an Internet can provide to enhance our system. Thinking from the perspective of a customer, we might want to create an order ourselves, or at least check on the status of an existing order. Enabling customers to create and access their own orders has the advantage of reducing the sales and support staffing for Northwind Traders, as well as the advantage of providing access in a 24×7 fashion. Other types of functionality can be placed on an Internet-based site as well, such as yearly or quarterly order histories and customer profile management. We focus on the online ordering process in this section.

To start, we must implement a customer logon process to ensure that only privileged users are granted access. We also use this login process to retrieve the **Id** and **CompanyName** properties for the customer and save them to session variables. The logon process assumes that a customer will use his or her customer code for the login name. We will add a column to the **Table_Customer** table to store the password, and we will modify the `View_Customer` view to also include this field. We will assign the password and provide a password change mechanism on the site. We also must make the appropriate change to our `GetClassDef` method on our `NWServer` class for `CT_CUSTOMER`.

If we have a corporate Web site, we should update it by placing a hyperlink to our customer login process. For our example here, we will simply create a `Home1.asp` page to serve as a surrogate for our corporate home page, with a hyperlink called `MY NORTHWIND` to enter into the customer-specific site. Figure 12.11 shows this entry page.

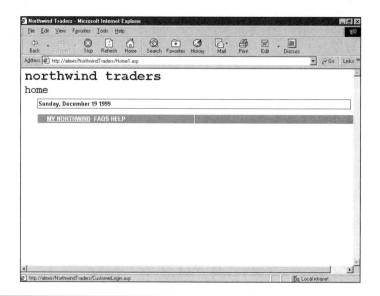

Figure 12.11   The mocked-up Internet corporate home page for Northwind.

Clicking on the `MY NORTHWIND` hyperlink takes us to the `CustomerLogin.asp` page, as shown in Figure 12.12.

The script code for `CustomerLogin.asp` uses standard `FORM` elements, although in this case we are using the `POST` method to prevent the password from being visible to a malicious user. We have designed this page to enable re-entry in case the login should fail in the `CustomerLogin2.asp` page that is called by the form. To enable re-entry, we simply check for two query string variables named `MSG` and `CustomerCode`. The `MSG` variable indicates the type of failure, whether it is from an invalid `CustomerCode` or an invalid `Password`. The `CustomerCode` variable is used in the case of an invalid `Password` so that the user does not have to re-enter it. If either variable is undefined or contains no data then nothing shows on the form. Listing 12.7 shows the code for the `CustomerLogin.asp` page.

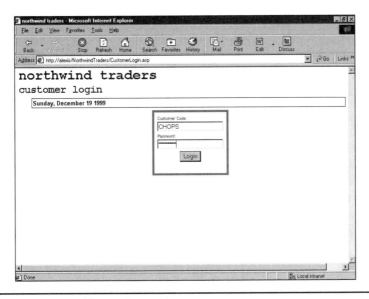

Figure 12.12   The CustomerLogin.asp page.

Listing 12.7   **The *CustomerLogin.asp* Page**

```
<%
  Msg = Request.QueryString("msg")
  CustomerCode = Request.QueryString("CustomerCode")
%>
<FORM  action="CustomerLogin2.asp" id=form1 name=form1 method=post>
  <TABLE WIDTH="100%" CELLPADDING=2 CELLSPACING=0 border=0 height=100%>
    <TR><TD class="ResultData"><%=Msg%></TD></TR>
    <TR>
      <TD class="FormCaption" width=100% height=100%>
        Customer Code:<BR>
        <INPUT type=text id="CustomerCode"
               name="CustomerCode" value=<%=CustomerCode%>>
      </TD>   </TR>    <TR>
      <TD class="FormCaption" width=100% height=100%>
        Password:<BR>
        <INPUT type=password id="pwd" name="pwd">
      </TD>
    </TR>
    <TR>       <TD class="FormCaption" width=100% height=100% align=center>
        <INPUT type="submit" value="Login" id=submit1 name=submit1>
      </TD>
    </TR>
  </TABLE>
</FORM>
```

Our `CustomerLogin2.asp` page produces no HTML; instead, it checks the validity of the `CustomerCode` and `Password` variables passed to it. Because we used the `POST` method to arrive here, we must retrieve the variables from the `Request.Form` collection rather than the `Request.QueryString` collection. After we have retrieved these values, we create an `NWServer` object, as in the other examples, and perform an `IISQueryObjectListData` on it to retrieve the customer object associated with the `CustomerCode`. If nothing is found, we redirect back to the `CustomerLogin.asp` page with a message indicating that the customer code was not found. If we do find the customer code but the password is incorrect, we also redirect back to the `CustomerLogin.asp` page, but this time with an invalid password message and the customer code. If the password is correct, we set several session variables and redirect to the `CustomerConsole.asp` page. Figure 12.13 shows a flowchart for this login process, and Listing 12.8 provides the code for the `CustomerLogin2.asp` page.

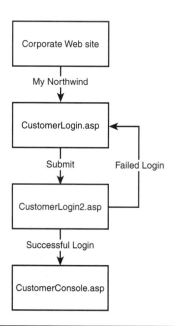

Figure 12.13 The customer login process.

Listing 12.8 **The Code for the *CustomerLogin2.asp* Page**

```
<%
   Dim Data, PropertyNames, Errors
   Dim DataArray
   Const CT_CUSTOMER = 4

   CustomerCode = Request.Form("CustomerCode")
```

```
  Pwd = Request.Form("pwd")

  Set NWServer = Server.CreateObject("NWServer.CNWServer")
  If Not NWServer.IISInitServer Then
    Response.Write("Could not Initialize the MTS Server<br>")
  End If
  WhereClause = Array(Array("CustomerCode","=",CustomerCode))
  OrderClause = Array("Id")
  Call NWServer.IISQueryObjectListData(CT_CUSTOMER,_
                                       WhereClause,_
                                       OrderClause,_
                                       "AND",_
                                       PropertyNames,_
                                       Data,_
                                       Errors)

  If IsArray(Data) Then
    Set DataArray = Server.CreateObject("AppIISCommon.CDataArray")
    DataArray.Initialize Data, PropertyNames
    If CStr(pwd) = CStr(DataArray.Item("Password",0)) Then
      Session("CustomerId") = DataArray.Item("Id",0)
      Session("CustomerName") = DataArray.Item("CompanyName",0)
      Response.Redirect("CustomerConsole.asp")
    Else
      Response.Redirect("CustomerLogin.asp?CustomerCode=" & _
                        CustomerCode & "&Msg=Password is Incorrect")
    End If
  Else
    Response.Redirect("CustomerLogin.asp?Msg=Customer Code Not Found")
  End If
%>
```

After the customer login is passed, we have defined two session variables: `CustomerId` and `CustomerName`. Session variables are similar to application variables in that they are shared across all the pages within the application. The difference is that session variables are destroyed after the user disconnects from the site, whereas application variables persist until the Web site is restarted from the IIS Management Console. Upon entering our `CustomerConsole.asp` page, we use the `CustomerName` session variable to add a little personalization to the site. The `CustomerConsole.asp` page appears in Figure 12.14.

Looking at the `CustomerConsole.asp` page, you should notice that its layout is similar to our intranet site. This is simply a matter of convenience on our part so that we do not have to create and maintain two sets of templates and styles. You might need to modify your Internet site over time, based on usability studies and so forth; so be prepared to make changes if necessary. For our example, we have chosen to place several pieces of functionality on the customer-specific site. The `Order Status` hyperlink is a straightforward implementation that is similar to the `OrderDetail.asp` page from the intranet section. Likewise, the `Order Listings` hyperlink is similar to the

`OrderReports.asp` and `OrderReport.asp` pages in the intranet section, except that here they must be filtered for a specific customer. You can create another set of ASP files to drive this process, or if you cleverly modify the existing reports, you can use them. The implementation of this set of pages is not provided here. You might also notice the `Change Profile` hyperlink available under the `Administrative` section. This link would lead to a series of ASP pages that enable the user to modify properties on the `Customer` object, such as address, contact person, telephone numbers, passwords, and so forth. Again, this implementation is not provided here. Many other types of functionality can be placed on this `CustomerConsole.asp` page. Fortunately, our architecture is robust enough to accept such future enhancements.

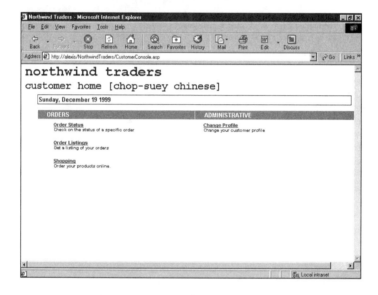

Figure 12.14   The `CustomerConsole.asp` page.

The remaining item to be discussed is the `Shopping` link. As you might guess, this link should enable the user to peruse the product catalog and create an order. To do this, we will implement a simple shopping and checkout process that enables the user to create an `Order` object and its associated `OrderDetailItems` collection.

Note

The solution presented for this process is simple in its design and implementation. It is meant to demonstrate the flexibility of our architecture to support creates, updates, and deletes from the intranet; it is not meant to represent a ready-to-deploy electronic commerce solution. Our architecture is merely the starting point for such applications.

If you have spent much time on commercial sites, you probably noticed that the process of shopping involves searching for a product and then adding it to a shopping cart. When you are finished shopping, you proceed to a checkout process. We follow a modified approach here. Figure 12.15 provides a flowchart of our order-creation process relative to the ASP pages that we will be creating.

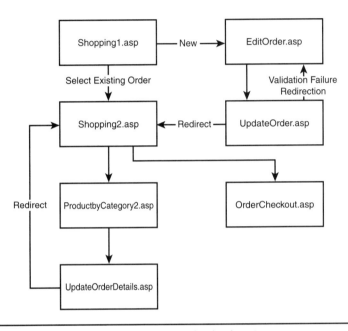

Figure 12.15   The flowchart for the shopping process.

Following the shopping link from the CustomerConsole.asp page takes us to the Shopping1.asp page, shown in Figure 12.16. This page retrieves the session variable for the CustomerId and performs a query using the IISQueryObjectListData method for the CT_ORDER class type. To enable this query, we must first add a field to the database to indicate whether an order is complete so that it can be submitted to the order fulfillment system—a topic that is discussed in detail in Chapter 13. This completion flag, along with the OrderDate, is set automatically during the checkout process that is discussed later in this section. Thus, we will add a simple Is_Complete field to the database table and view, along with the appropriate modification to the GetClassDef method on the NWServer class for CT_ORDER and CT_ORDER_PROXY. It is important to note how simple and unobtrusive this type of change is. Over time, as you are developing your application, you will find the need to make similar changes to support expanding business requirements. One of the underlying goals of this framework has been to enable such simple changes.

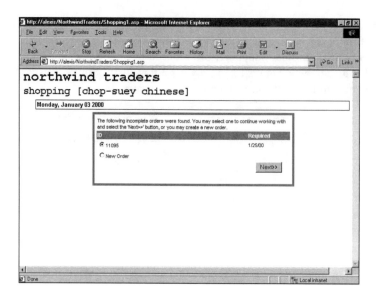

Figure 12.16   The Shopping1.asp page.

We are specifically looking for orders where the IsComplete flag is false. We build our page using standard HTML FORM methods, adding a New Order option at the end of the radio button list.

Clicking the New Order radio button and then clicking the Next button takes us to the EditOrder.asp page, as shown in Figure 12.17.

The EditOrder.asp page is built using similar techniques to the ones used to build the other pages developed to this point. We use our IISQueryObjectListData to help us build our Shipper and City combo boxes. Our choice to handle the City entry this way is for simplicity.

> **Note**
>
> In a real-world situation, a Web-based modal dialog would be required to enable the selection first of a Country, followed by a Region, and then a City. The change in the Country selection would trigger a reload of the page with the appropriate Region selection loaded. Similarly, a change in the Region selection would trigger a reload of the page with the appropriate City selection loaded. Implementing such a dialog requires the use of Dynamic HTML (DHTML) and client-side JavaScript, two topics that are outside the scope of this book.

After we have entered our information and made our selections, we click on the Next button. This submits the form to the UpdateOrder.asp page, which performs the validation. If the validation fails, the page is redirected back to the EditOrder.asp page with validation failure messages. The specific validation code appears in Listing 12.9.

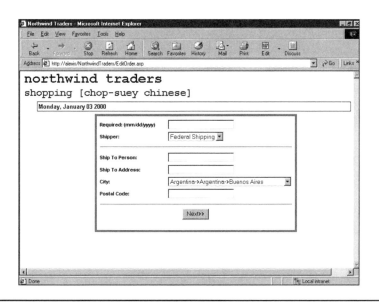

Figure 12.17   The `EditOrder.asp` page.

Listing 12.9   **The Validation Code in the *UpdateOrder.asp* Page**

```
CustomerId = Session("CustomerId")
OrderId = Session("OrderId")
ShipperId = Request.Form("ShipperId")
CityId = Request.Form("CityId")
ShipTo = Request.Form("ShipTo")
Address = Request.Form("ShipToAddress")
PostalCode = Request.Form("PostalCode")
ReqDate = Request.Form("ReqDate")

Msg = ""

If ReqDate = "" Then
  Msg = "- <i>Required Date</i> cannot be empty.<br>"
ElseIf Not IsDate(CStr(ReqDate)) Then
  Msg = "- </i>" & ReqDate & "</i> & is invalid.<br>"
End If
If ShipTo = "" Then
  Msg = Msg & "- <i>Ship To</i> cannot be empty.<br>"
End If
If Address = "" Then
  Msg = Msg & "- <i>Ship To Address</i> cannot be empty.<br>"
End if
If PostalCode = "" Then
```

continues

Listing 12.9 **Continued**

```
    Msg = Msg & "- <i>Postal Code</i> cannot be empty.<br>"
End If

If Msg <> "" Then
    Session("Msg") = Msg
    Response.Redirect("EditOrder.asp")
Else
    Session("Msg") = ""
End If
```

From Listing 12.9, you can see where we are pulling our form information from the Form collection of the Request object. We have chosen to use the POST method of form processing for several reasons. First, if we begin to place the information necessary to drive the pages on the URL as a query string, then unscrupulous users might be able to modify the orders of others simply by editing the URL. Using the POST methods keeps the information from users and eliminates a potential security hole. Although this method is still not foolproof, it is much more robust than using a query string approach.

If we fail validation, we place a message into a session variable and redirect back to EditOrder.asp. This page is designed to check this session variable and present the information at the top of the form. We have chosen to use a session variable to prevent the entry of free-form text as part of a query string. Figure 12.18 shows EditOrder.asp with a validation error message generated by UpdateOrder.asp.

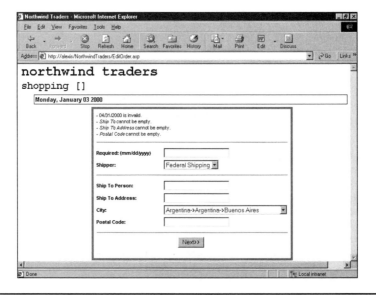

Figure 12.18 The EditOrder.asp page with validation errors.

If our update is successful, we insert a new order in the database and redirect to the
Shopping2.asp page, as shown in Figure 12.19.

Figure 12.19 The Shopping2.asp page after successful order creation.

To perform the insert, we use the IISInsertObjectData method. To build the variant
array needed by the method, we modify our CDataArray class in several ways. First, we
change our Item method to a property Let and Get. Second, we add a Data-property
Get statement to return the internal variant array. Third, we modify the Initialize
method to create an empty array if the Data variant passed in is not already dimensioned. These modifications appear in Listing 12.10.

Listing 12.10   **Modifications to the *CDataArray* Class**

```
Public Property Get Item(PropertyName As Variant, Row As Variant) As Variant
  If dict.Exists(PropertyName) Then
    Item = vData(dict.Item(PropertyName), CLng(Row))
  Else
    Item = vbEmpty
  End If
End Property

Public Property Let Item(PropertyName As Variant, _
                         Row As Variant, _
                         RHS As Variant)
```

continues

Listing 12.10 **Continued**

```
  If dict.Exists(PropertyName) Then
    vData(dict.Item(PropertyName), CLng(Row)) = RHS
  End If
End Property

Public Sub Initialize(Data As Variant, PropertyNames As Variant)
  Dim i As Integer

  Call MakeDictionary(PropertyNames)

  If Not IsArray(Data) Then
    Data = Array(1)
    ReDim Data(LBound(PropertyNames) To UBound(PropertyNames), 0)
  End If

  vData = Data
End Sub

Public Property Get Data() As Variant
  Data = vData
End Property
```

Our insertion logic within the UpdateOrder.asp page is straightforward and appears in Listing 12.11.

Listing 12.11 **Insertion of a *New Order* Object Within *UpdateOrder.asp***

```
Data = vbEmpty
PropertyNames = NWServer.IISGetPropertyNames(CT_ORDER)
Set DataO = Server.CreateObject("AppIISCommon.CDataArray")
DataO.Initialize Data, PropertyNames
DataO.Item("ShipperId",0) = ShipperId
DataO.Item("ShipToCityId",0) = CityId
DataO.Item("CustomerId",0) = CustomerId
DataO.Item("EmployeeId",0) = 10
DataO.Item("RequiredDate",0)= ReqDate
DataO.Item("ShipToName",0) = ShipTo
DataO.Item("ShipToAddress",0) = Address
DataO.Item("ShipToPostalCode",0) = PostalCode
DataO.Item("IsComplete",0) = False
Data = DataO.Data
Call NWServer.IISInsertObjectData(CInt(CT_ORDER), _
                                  PropertyNames, _
                                  Data, _
                                  Errors, _
                                  ObjectId, _
                                  ObjectSubId)
Session("OrderId") = ObjectId
```

On the `Shopping2.asp` page, we first present the user with a list of product categories. Selecting a category produces a list of products in that category. This list is presented in the `ProductsByCategory2.asp` page, as shown in Figure 12.20.

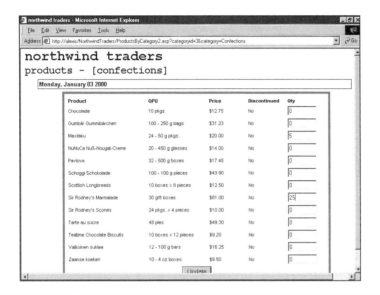

Figure 12.20 The `ProductsByCategory2.asp` page.

We present this list within the context of a `FORM`, with input fields to indicate the quantity of items desired for purchase. To support the creation of new `OrderDetailItem` objects, the user must change the quantity of a catalog item from zero to something other than zero. Changing a quantity from a non-zero value to zero causes a deletion to occur, whereas a change from one non-zero number to another non-zero number performs an update. After changes are made to the quantities, the `ProductByCategory2.asp` page is submitted to the `UpdateOrderDetails.asp` page that performs the various inserts, updates, and deletes. Upon completion, it redirects back to the `Shopping2.asp` page, showing the changes to the order detail items, as shown in Figure 12.21. The code to perform the inserts, updates, and deletes appears in Listing 12.12.

Listing 12.12 **The Code Driving the Inserts, Updates, and Deletes in** *UpdateOrderDetails.asp*

```
Dim Data, PropertyNames, Errors
Dim DataOD, ObjectId, ObjectSubId
Const CT_ORDER_DETAIL = 8

CustomerId = Session("CustomerId")
```

continues

Listing 12.12   **Continued**

```
OrderId = Session("OrderId")

MinRow = Request.Form("MinRow")
MaxRow = Request.Form("MaxRow")

Set NWServer = Server.CreateObject("NWServer.CNWServer")
If Not NWServer.IISInitServer Then
  Response.Write("Could not Initialize the MTS Server<br>")
End If

PropertyNames = NWServer.IISGetPropertyNames(CT_ORDER_DETAIL)

For i = MinRow To MaxRow
  vQty = Request.Form("_Qty_" & i)
  vOriginalQty = Request.Form("_OriginalQty_" & i)
  vProductId = Request.Form("_ProductId_" & i)
  vOrderDetailId = Request.Form("_OrderDetailId_" & i)

  If CInt(vQty) > 0 and CInt(vOriginalQty) = 0 Then
    ' Insert
    Data = vbEmpty
    Set DataOD = Server.CreateObject("AppIISCommon.CDataArray")
    DataOD.Initialize Data, PropertyNames

    DataOD.Item("OrderId",0) = OrderId
    DataOD.Item("ProductId",0) = vProductId
    DataOD.Item("Quantity",0)= vQty
    DataOD.Item("Discount",0) = 0

    Data = DataOD.Data

    Call NWServer.IISInsertObjectData(CInt(CT_ORDER_DETAIL), _
                          PropertyNames, _
                            Data, _
                            Errors, _
                            ObjectId, _
                            ObjectSubId)

  ElseIf CInt(vQty) = 0 and CInt(vOriginalQty) <> 0 Then
    ' Delete
    Call NWServer.IISDeleteObject(CInt(CT_ORDER_DETAIL), _
                          CLng(vOrderDetailId), 0, _
                          Errors)

  ElseIf CInt(vQty) <> 0 And CInt(vOriginalQty) <> 0 and _
        CInt(vQty) <> CInt(vOriginalQty) then
    ' Update
    Data = vbEmpty
    Set DataOD = Server.CreateObject("AppIISCommon.CDataArray")
    DataOD.Initialize Data, PropertyNames
```

```
        DataOD.Item("Id",0) = vOrderDetailId
        DataOD.Item("OrderId",0) = OrderId
        DataOD.Item("ProductId",0) = vProductId
        DataOD.Item("Quantity",0)= vQty
        DataOD.Item("Discount",0) = 0
        Data = DataOD.Data

        Call NWServer.IISUpdateObjectData(CInt(CT_ORDER_DETAIL), _
                                          PropertyNames, _
                                          Data, _
                                          Errors, _
                                          CLng(vOrderDetailId), _
                                          0)
    End If
Next

Response.Redirect("Shopping2.asp")
```

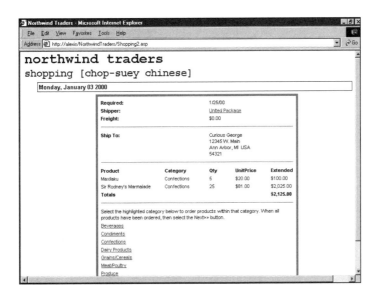

Figure 12.21   The products that have been added to the current order.

It is important to note that we have modified our `OrderDetailItem` object by adding a `Category` property. We have made this modification to support the usability of our `Shopping2.asp` page so that if we want to modify an existing `OrderDetailItem`, we know the category to which the product belongs. To make this update, we simply modify our `View_Order_Detail` view to add the column and make the changes to the `CT_ORDER_DETAIL` class in our `GetClassDef` method on `NWServer`. Again, it is important to note how simple and unobtrusive this type of change is.

After we have selected all our products, we click the Next button, which submits the page to the `OrderCheckout.asp` page. This page simply performs an update, setting the `IsComplete` flag and the `OrderDate` to the current date. Upon completion of this update, it redirects back to the `Shopping1.asp` page.

Summary

In this chapter, we explored mechanisms with which to extend our application to both the intranet and the Internet using functionality already built into our framework. We have also explored basic Web site standardization techniques using style sheets and server side include files. Finally, we looked at mechanisms to perform inserts, updates, and deletes from a Web site within the context of our framework.

In the next chapter, we will look at how our system interacts with others to integrate itself within the landscape of the enterprise. We will also look at techniques that involve both the movement of data between systems and the direct, real-time access of data in foreign systems.

13

Interoperability

T HE TOPIC OF INTEROPERABILITY is one that can fill an entire book by itself. Indeed, Enterprise Application Integration (EAI) books that are available in a variety of series deal with this topic in detail. Nonetheless, it is important in a book on enterprise application development to provide a basic level of coverage of this topic for completeness, because application interoperability is fundamental to the enterprise. Therefore, the ideas presented in this chapter are meant to discuss some of the theory as well as the implementation for the interoperability techniques related to our application framework.

Interoperability Defined

The term *interoperability* itself can mean several things. At one level, it can simply mean the movement of data from one application to another via simple file structures, with a person acting as an intermediary. On the other hand, it can mean the movement of data via a direct link between the two systems, without user involvement. This same sharing of data can also be accomplished without the physical movement of data from one system to another; it can be accomplished instead through the direct, real-time access of the data in the other system. At another level, interoperability can also require collaboration, which can include both sharing data and signaling other systems. In this mode, one application can pass a set of information to another system, asking it to perform some function. This second system might perform some additional work and send a signal to yet another system. At some point, the originator might receive notice of success or failure, possibly with some data that represents the end product of all the work.

For the sake of exposition in this chapter, let us suppose that Northwind Traders has an order-fulfillment system that is separate from its order-taking system—a somewhat plausible example of how such an operation might work. The order-taking system is the sample application that we have been working on up to this point. The order-fulfillment system is an in-house legacy system. It is necessary for our application to send the order information to the fulfillment system after an order has been created.

We assume that the initial sample mechanism to accomplish our goal of interoperability requires user intervention. We provide an example of this less-than-ideal solution because there are many instances in which this is the only option available. We follow this example with a more automated approach in which orders are "dropped" from our order-taking application into the fulfillment system at regular intervals (such as every two, four, or eight hours). We can assume, in this more automated approach, that orders can be changed up until the time they are dropped to the fulfillment system. In this automated approach, we have several options available for implementation; we will provide examples of each.

Interoperability Through Data Movement

The basis for any form of data movement is a stream. SQL Server uses what is known as a Table Data Stream (TDS) format when communicating with clients, Internet Information Server (IIS) uses an HTML stream when sending results back to a client, and so forth. In our example of moving the orders into the fulfillment system, our stream carrier becomes a simple file, although its format can take one of several forms.

Using Proprietary Formats in Data Transfer

Proprietary formats are typically brought about by the capabilities (or restrictions) of one of the two systems in question. For example, if the legacy-based fulfillment system has a defined file format for importing the orders, this is said to be a proprietary format that the order-taking system must support. Alternatively, we might choose to define a proprietary format within the order-taking system that the fulfillment system must import. Typically, the former solution is easier to implement because it is often more dangerous to make modifications to stable applications than to newer ones just going into production.

To implement an exporter that will support this movement of data, we need to create a new method on our IAppServer class called CreateExportStream. We will make our application-specific implementation in the NWServer class. This method is designed to be the only one called, regardless of the class type or the format needed, by passing in an `ExportClass` and an `ExportFormat` identifier. Our choice to create a single method to support all formats of all objects for all export activities is done for future flexibility, as the next section points out. Note that this implementation is yet another divergence from pure object orientation in that the `NWServer` surrogate object is hosting a method that would otherwise be implemented directly by the object in question.

To implement a specific export process, we must first define export class types. These differ from the normal class type definitions implemented so far. The reason for this is that we might have to combine or modify some of our existing class types to arrive at the export information needed by the foreign application, or we might need to export our existing class types in manners not specified in our original `ClassDef` definitions. If we must recombine existing class types to meet our export requirements, we first must create a new class type, for which there is no corresponding implementation in our `NWClient` component. Within the implementation of the `CreateExportStream` method, use a `Case` statement to select from among the various export class types, which then call an appropriate private method on `NWServer`, passing it the given export format identifier.

We start our implementation process by defining two new class type constants: `CT_ORDER_EXPORT` and `CT_ORDER_DETAIL_EXPORT`. We also define a new export format, `EF_ORDER_PROPRIETARY`. Listing 13.1 shows the implementation of the `CreateExportStream` method on `NWServer`.

Listing 13.1   **The *CreateExportStream* Method on *NWServer***

```
Private Function IAppServer_CreateExportStream(ClassId As Integer, _
                                    ExportType As Integer, _
                                    Stream As String, _
                                    Errors As Variant) As Variant

   Select Case ClassId
     Case CT_ORDER_EXPORT, CT_ORDER_DETAIL_EXPORT
        Call CreateOrderExportStream(ExportType, Stream, Errors)
   End Select
   ObjCtx.SetComplete
End Function
```

Before implementing our `CreateOrderExportStream` method, which we called in Listing 13.1, we must perform several development tasks. First, we must define a proprietary format to use for the example. Next, we must implement the appropriate `ClassDef` objects in our `GetClassDef` method.

Let us suppose that the proprietary format for our order information is such that both the order and the order detail information are included in the same data stream. Let us also assume that there is an order line followed by multiple detail lines, which might be followed by other order and detail lines. To accommodate this, the first character of a line is a line type indicator of either an O or a D, for order and detail, respectively. The remaining information on a given line depends on this type indicator, with each field being separated by the pipe (¦) character. We also assume that the fields in both line types are defined implicitly by the proprietary standard and cannot be changed without programmatic changes by both applications.

To implement the CT_ORDER_EXPORT class type, a new single-row, two-column table called Table_Last_Order_Export is created to track the last time an order drop was exported. It has an Id column to serve as the primary key to help us update the row, and a LastDate column that contains the date field in which we are interested. We create a new view called View_Order_Export that includes this table but does not explicitly join it to the other tables. This has the effect of returning the LastDate column for every row returned by the other join and where conditions for the query. We can then compare this date with our Order_Date column to only return the rows that have not been exported since the last export date. We also create a CT_LAST_ORDER_EXPORT class type to help us easily manage the value of this row in the database. We could have chosen to implement this last date tracking mechanism via a registry setting on the computer running the integration. Although this is plausible, it does not enable the data transfer to be run on more than one machine because it is difficult to keep these dates synchronized between the various machines. By placing this information in the database, we can run our data transfer on multiple machines, although not at the same time. The implementation of CT_ORDER_DETAIL_EXPORT follows the standard process that we use to add new class types. We make these additions to our GetClassDef function, as shown in Listing 13.2.

Listing 13.2 **Adding the New Class Types to *NWServer***

```
Private Function IAppServer_GetClassDef(ByVal ClassId As Integer) As CClassDef
    Dim ClassDef As CClassDef

    If Not bInitialized Then IAppServer_InitServer
    If Not mIAppServer.ClassDefs.Exists(CStr(ClassId)) Then

        Select Case ClassId
...

        Case CT_ORDER_EXPORT
            Set ClassDef = New CClassDef
            With ClassDef
                .DatabaseName = "NWIND"
                .ReadLocation = "View_Order_Export"
                .WriteLocation = ""
                .IdColumnName = "Id"
                .OrderByColumnName = "Order_Date, Id"

                .AppendMapping "OrderId", "Id", True, False, ctNumber, "ORDER_ID"
                .AppendMapping "CustomerCode", "Customer_Code", True, False, _
                            ctString, "CUSTOMER_CODE"
```

```
          .AppendMapping "CompanyName", "Company_Name", True, False, _
                         ctString, "COMPANY_NAME"
          .AppendMapping "OrderDate", "Order_Date", True, False, _
                         ctDateTime, "ORDER_DATE"
          .AppendMapping "RequiredDate", "Required_Date", True, False, _
                         ctDateTime, "REQUIRED_DATE"
          .AppendMapping "ShipperName", "Shipper_Name", True, False, _
                         ctString, "SHIPPER_NAME"
          .AppendMapping "FreightCost", "Freight_Cost", True, False, _
                         ctNumber, "FREIGHT_COST"
          .AppendMapping "ShipToName", "Ship_To_Name", True, False, _
                         ctString, "SHIP_TO_NAME"
          .AppendMapping "ShipToAddress", "Ship_To_Address", True, False, _
                         ctString, "SHIP_TO_ADDRESS"
          .AppendMapping "ShipToPostalCode", "Ship_To_Postal_Code", _
                         True, False, ctString, "SHIP_TO_POSTAL_CODE"
          .AppendMapping "ShipToCountry", "Ship_To_Country", True, False, _
                         ctString, "SHIP_TO_COUNTRY"
          .AppendMapping "ShipToCity", "Ship_To_City", True, False, _
                         ctString, "SHIP_TO_CITY"
          .AppendMapping "ShipToRegion", "Ship_To_Region", True, False, _
                         ctString, "SHIP_TO_REGION"
          .AppendMapping "LastExportDate", "Last_Export_Date", True, False, _
                         ctDateTime, ""
        End With
        Call mIAppServer.ClassDefs.Add(ClassDef, CStr(CT_ORDER_EXPORT))

    Case CT_ORDER_DETAIL_EXPORT
        Set ClassDef = New CClassDef
        With ClassDef
          .DatabaseName = "NWIND"
          .ReadLocation = "View_Order_Detail_Export"
          .WriteLocation = ""
          .IdColumnName = "Id"
          .ParentIdColumnName = "Order_Id"
          .OrderByColumnName = "Id"

          .AppendMapping "Id", "Id", True, False, ctNumber, "ID"
          .AppendMapping "OrderId", "Order_Id", True, True, _
                         ctNumber, "ORDER_ID"
          .AppendMapping "Product", "Product", True, False, _
                         ctString, "PRODUCT"
          .AppendMapping "Quantity", "Quantity", True, True, _
                         ctNumber, "QTY"
          .AppendMapping "QuantityPerUnit", "Quantity_Per_Unit", True, False, _
                         ctString, "QUANTITY_PER_UNIT"
        End With
        Call mIAppServer.ClassDefs.Add(ClassDef, CStr(CT_ORDER_DETAIL_EXPORT))

    Case CT_LAST_ORDER_EXPORT
        Set ClassDef = New CClassDef
        With ClassDef
          .DatabaseName = "NWIND"
```

continues

Listing 13.2   **Continued**

```
            .ReadLocation = "Table_Last_Order_Export"
            .WriteLocation = "Table_Last_Order_Export"
            .IdColumnName = "Id"
            .OrderByColumnName = "Id"

            .AppendMapping "Id", "Id", True, False, ctNumber, ""
            .AppendMapping "LastDate", "LastDate", True, True, ctDateTime, ""
        End With
        Call mIAppServer.ClassDefs.Add(ClassDef, CStr(CT_LAST_ORDER_EXPORT))
    End Select
  End If

  Set IAppServer_GetClassDef = mIAppServer.ClassDefs.Item(CStr(ClassId))

End Function
```

With our new `ClassDef` objects defined in `GetClassDef` and our new tables
and views created, we can turn our attention to the implementation of the
`CreateOrderExportStream` method, as shown in Listing 13.3. Although we currently
have only one format type defined, we implement a `Select Case` statement to switch
among the possible types. In this code, we simply obtain the list of current exportable
orders using our `GetObjectListData` method for the `CT_ORDER_EXPORT` class type.
Remember that this list is automatically controlled by the `View_Order_Export` view
that relies on the `LastDate` column in the `Table_Last_Order_Export` table. We iterate
through the returned orders, requesting the order detail information with a similar call
to `GetObjectListData`, this time using the `CT_ORDER_DETAIL_EXPORT` class type and the
ID of the current order. We then write out to our output string the "O" header
record, followed by the "D" detail records. We continue this for all orders.

Listing 13.3   **The Implementation of *CreateOrderExportStream***

```
Private Function CreateOrderExportStream(ExportType As Integer, _
                                        Stream As String, _
                                        Errors As Variant)
  Dim DataO As Variant, DataOD As Variant
  Dim PropertyNames As Variant
  Dim Criteria As Variant
  Dim cPIO As Collection, cPIOD As Collection
  Dim i As Integer, j As Integer
  Dim OrderId As Long
  Dim sOut As String

  On Error GoTo ErrorTrap

  Select Case ExportType
    Case EF_ORDER_PROPRIETARY

        ' get the collection of non-exported orders
        Call IAppServer_GetClassDef(CT_ORDER_EXPORT)
        Call IAppServer_GetClassDef(CT_ORDER_DETAIL_EXPORT)
```

```
          Call mIAppServer.GetObjectListData(CT_ORDER_EXPORT, 0, 0, _
                                      PropertyNames, DataO, Errors)
        If IsArray(DataO) Then
          Set cPIO = MakePropertyIndex(PropertyNames)
          For i = LBound(DataO, 2) To UBound(DataO, 2)
            ' get the order detail records
            OrderId = DataO(cPIO.Item("OrderId"), i)

            DataOD = vbEmpty
            Call mIAppServer.GetObjectListData(CT_ORDER_DETAIL_EXPORT, _
                                        OrderId, 0, PropertyNames, _
                                        DataOD, Errors)
            If IsArray(DataOD) Then
              Set cPIOD = MakePropertyIndex(PropertyNames)

              ' write out the order header
              Append sOut, "O¦"
              Append sOut, DataO(cPIO("OrderId"), i) & "¦"
              Append sOut, DataO(cPIO("CustomerCode"), i) & "¦"
              Append sOut, DataO(cPIO("CompanyName"), i) & "¦"
              Append sOut, DataO(cPIO("OrderDate"), i) & "¦"
              Append sOut, DataO(cPIO("RequiredDate"), i) & "¦"
              Append sOut, DataO(cPIO("ShipperName"), i) & "¦"
              Append sOut, DataO(cPIO("FreightCost"), i) & "¦"
              Append sOut, DataO(cPIO("ShipToName"), i) & "¦"
              Append sOut, DataO(cPIO("ShipToAddress"), i) & "¦"
              Append sOut, DataO(cPIO("ShipToPostalCode"), i) & "¦"
              Append sOut, DataO(cPIO("ShipToCountry"), i) & "¦"
              Append sOut, DataO(cPIO("ShipToCity"), i) & "¦"
              Append sOut, DataO(cPIO("ShipToRegion"), i) & vbCrLf

              ' write out the order details
              For j = LBound(DataOD, 2) To UBound(DataOD, 2)
                Append sOut, "D¦"
                Append sOut, DataOD(cPIOD("Product"), j) & "¦"
                Append sOut, DataOD(cPIOD("Quantity"), j) & "¦"
                Append sOut, DataOD(cPIOD("QuantityPerUnit"), j) & vbCrLf
              Next j
            End If
          Next i
        End If

      Stream = sOut
  End Select

  Exit Function
ErrorTrap:
    '1.  Details to EventLog
    Call WriteNTLogEvent("CNWServer:CreateOrderExportStream", Err.Number, _
                    Err.Description & " [" & Erl & "]", Err.Source)
    '2.  Generic to client - passed back on error stack
    Err.Raise Err.Number, "CNWServer:CreateOrderExportStream", _
            Err.Description & " [" & Erl & "]"
End Function
```

With this initial implementation of the `CreateOrderExportStream`, we are able to generate the proprietary format needed to move data from our application into the order-fulfillment application. Implementing a dialog within Visual Basic that runs this export process and saves the resulting stream to a file is a simple process. The simple code snippet to instantiate the process appears in Listing 13.4.

Listing 13.4 **Calling the Proprietary Export Process**

```
Dim NWServer As CNWServer
Dim AppServer As IAppServer
Dim Stream As String
Dim Errors As Variant

Set NWServer = CreateObject("NWServer.CNWServer", MTSMachineName)
Set AppServer = NWServer
AppServer.InitServer

Call AppServer.CreateExportStream(CT_ORDER_EXPORT, EF_ORDER_PROPRIETARY, _
                                  Stream, Errors)
```

After this output stream has been written to a file, it can be read into the fulfillment system using whatever process is in place that accepts this proprietary input. In some cases, it might be possible to implement a new custom loader in a language like Visual Basic or C++, assuming there is an application programming interface (API) to do so. Figure 13.1 shows a flowchart of how we have implemented this data movement process so far.

Standards-Based Formats

Although implementing a proprietary export format as shown in the previous example is somewhat trivial in nature, creating new formats becomes burdensome because the secondary systems are replaced over time. As these newer, secondary systems are created, our legacy data transfer processes are no longer needed. We might be remiss to take such functionality back out because of the time invested into developing it, even though we might never use it again. This is akin to all the clutter up in the attic or down in the basement that we find difficult to throw away. One solution is that our application writes out a generic, standards-based format that new systems coming online should support. We can either maintain our capability to write out proprietary formats alongside our generic format or just write out a single generic format and create secondary processes to convert the information into the appropriate target format. These secondary processes can be console applications written in your favorite language, such as Visual Basic or C++, or they can be simple Perl scripts.

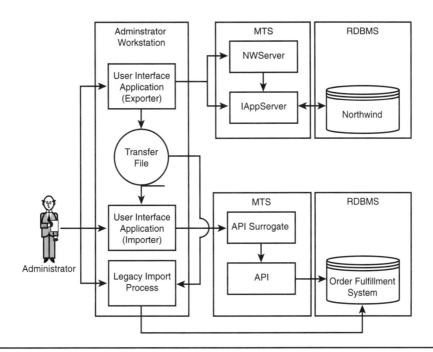

Figure 13.1 Manual data movement using a file-based process.

For our application, we have chosen to use the eXtensible Markup Language (XML) as the foundation for our standards-based format. Not only does this make it easier to implement the importation side of the data movement interface, it uses a technology that has gained widespread acceptance. XML parsers are available for most major platforms and operating systems, and most enterprise applications should offer some form of XML support in the near future. To implement this type of output stream, we must define a format identifier and implement the appropriate code under our `CreateOrderExportStream` method. We call this new constant `EF_ORDER_XML`. This code, as shown in Listing 13.5, leverages the XML-generation functionality that we have placed in `IAppServer`.

Listing 13.5 **The *CreateOrderExportStream* Method with Support for XML Format**

```
Private Function CreateOrderExportStream(ExportType As Integer, _
                                         Stream As String, _
                                         Errors As Variant)
    Dim DataO As Variant, DataOD As Variant
    Dim PropertyNames As Variant
    Dim Criteria As Variant
    Dim cPIO As Collection, cPIOD As Collection
    Dim i As Integer, j As Integer
```

continues

Listing 13.5 **Continued**

```
Dim OrderId As Long
Dim sOut As String

On Error GoTo ErrorTrap

Select Case ExportType
  Case EF_ORDER_PROPRIETARY
    ' same code as before
  Case EF_ORDER_XML
      Call IAppServer_GetClassDef(CT_ORDER_EXPORT)
      Call IAppServer_GetClassDef(CT_ORDER_DETAIL_EXPORT)

      ' write out the DTD
      Append sOut, "<?xml version='1.0' encoding='iso-8859-1' ?>" & vbCrLf
      Append sOut, "<!DOCTYPE ExportedOrderItems [" & vbCrLf
      Append sOut, "<!ELEMENT ExportedOrderItems (ExportedOrderItem*)>"_
                  & vbCrLf
      Append sOut, _
              "<!ELEMENT ExportedOrderItem (ORDER, ORDER_DETAIL_ITEMS*)>" _
              & vbCrLf

      sTemp = mIAppServer.CreateXMLCollectionClass(CT_ORDER_EXPORT)
      Append sOut, sTemp & vbCrLf

      vOrderProperties = Array("OrderId", "CustomerCode", _
                               "CompanyName", "OrderDate", _
                               "RequiredDate", "ShipperName", _
                               "FreightCost", "ShipToName", _
                               "ShipToAddress", "ShipToPostalCode", _
                               "ShipToCountry", "ShipToCity", _
                               "ShipToRegion")

      vOrderDetailProperties = Array("Product", "Quantity", _
                                     "QuantityPerUnit")

      sTemp = mIAppServer.CreateXMLClass(CT_ORDER_EXPORT, vOrderProperties)
      Append sOut, sTemp

      sTemp = mIAppServer.CreateXMLCollectionClass(CT_ORDER_DETAIL_EXPORT)
      Append sOut, sTemp

      sTemp = mIAppServer.CreateXMLClass(CT_ORDER_DETAIL_EXPORT, _
                                       vOrderDetailProperties)
      Append sOut, sTemp

      Append sOut, "]>" & vbCrLf

      ' write out the document data
      Append sOut, "<ExportedOrderItems>" & vbCrLf

      ' get the collection of non-exported orders
      Call mIAppServer.GetObjectListData(CT_ORDER_EXPORT, 0, 0, _
                                       PropertyNames, DataO, Errors)
```

```
        If IsArray(DataO) Then
          Set cPIO = MakePropertyIndex(PropertyNames)
          For i = LBound(DataO, 2) To UBound(DataO, 2)
            Append sOut, "<ExportedOrderItem>" & vbCrLf

            ' get the order detail records
            OrderId = DataO(cPIO.Item("OrderId"), i)
            sTemp = mIAppServer.CreateXMLObject(CT_ORDER_EXPORT, _
                                            vOrderProperties, DataO, i)
            Append sOut, sTemp

            DataOD = vbEmpty
            Call mIAppServer.GetObjectListData(CT_ORDER_DETAIL_EXPORT, _
                                          OrderId, 0, _
                                          PropertyNames, DataOD, _
                                          Errors)

            If IsArray(DataOD) Then
                sTemp = _
                  mIAppServer.CreateXMLCollection(CT_ORDER_DETAIL_EXPORT, _
                                              vOrderDetailProperties, _
                                              DataOD)
                Append sOut, sTemp
            End If
            Append sOut, "</ExportedOrderItem>" & vbCrLf
          Next i
        End If

      Append sOut, "</ExportedOrderItems>" & vbCrLf
      Stream = sOut
  End Select

  Exit Function
ErrorTrap:
    '1.  Details to EventLog
    Call WriteNTLogEvent("CNWServer:CreateOrderExportStream", Err.Number, _
                    Err.Description & " [" & Erl & "]", Err.Source)
    '2.  Generic to client - passed back on error stack
    Err.Raise Err.Number, "CNWServer:CreateOrderExportStream", _
            Err.Description & " [" & Erl & "]"
End Function
```

To build an XML document, we first must define a document type definition (DTD) section that describes the data contained in the remainder of the section. We must explicitly create the DTD ourselves because it is so tightly bound to our object model. If we had built an application to support an existing industry standard DTD—something that might become more common as XML use increases—then we would have adapted our object model to conform to the standard DTD at the outset or we would have to write some additional code to make sure that we can reproduce the standard DTD from our object model. Listing 13.6 shows the DTD for our export process.

Listing 13.6 **The DTD for Our XML-Formatted Order Export Process**

```
<?xml version='1.0' encoding='iso-8859-1' ?>
<!DOCTYPE ExportedOrderItems [
<!ELEMENT ExportedOrderItems (ExportedOrderItem*)>
<!ELEMENT ExportedOrderItem (ORDER, ORDER_DETAIL_ITEMS*)>
<!ELEMENT    ORDERS EMPTY>

<!ELEMENT    ORDER EMPTY>
<!ATTLIST    ORDER
        ORDER_ID CDATA #REQUIRED
        CUSTOMER_CODE CDATA #REQUIRED
        COMPANY_NAME CDATA #REQUIRED
        ORDER_DATE CDATA #REQUIRED
        REQUIRED_DATE CDATA #REQUIRED
        SHIPPER_NAME CDATA #REQUIRED
        FREIGHT_COST CDATA #REQUIRED
        SHIP_TO_NAME CDATA #REQUIRED
        SHIP_TO_ADDRESS CDATA #REQUIRED
        SHIP_TO_POSTAL_CODE CDATA #REQUIRED
        SHIP_TO_COUNTRY CDATA #REQUIRED
        SHIP_TO_CITY CDATA #REQUIRED
        SHIP_TO_REGION CDATA #REQUIRED
>
<!ELEMENT    ORDER_DETAIL_ITEMS (ORDER_DETAIL_ITEM*)>
<!ELEMENT    ORDER_DETAIL_ITEM EMPTY>
<!ATTLIST    ORDER_DETAIL_ITEM
        PRODUCT CDATA #REQUIRED
        QUANTITY CDATA #REQUIRED
        QUANTITY_PER_UNIT CDATA #REQUIRED
>
]>
```

You might notice that the keyword #REQUIRED is used for all the attribute default type settings. Other values could include #IMPLIED or #FIXED. If your DTD requires these settings, it is a simple matter to add this meta information to the Attributes collection for the required property in a ClassDef, while also modifying the appropriate DTD generation functions. The same applies to the CDATA keyword, which can be replaced with other attribute types, such as ENTITY, ENTITIES, ID, IDREF, IDREFS, NMTOKEN, NMTOKENS, NOTATION, and Enumerated. We have chosen the simplest CDATA and #REQUIRED methods as defaults because we are using XML as a simple data transfer medium, not as a mechanism to enforce business rules.

Looking back at the code in Listing 13.5, you should notice that in our XML version, we follow the same data retrieval logic that we used in our proprietary format case. The main difference is in how we write out the data. Notice the use of four methods on the IAppServer class that assist us in formatting the information into XML. They are CreateXMLCollectionClass, CreateXMLClass, CreateXMLCollection, and CreateXMLObject. The first two methods correspond to the creation of the DTD, whereas the second two methods correspond to the actual information being written out. To create our XML-formatted stream, we must first build the DTD. To accomplish this, we first write out some preamble information—including the first four lines of the DTD—to an XML output string to identify the contents as an XML document. We then call the `CreateXMLCollectionClass` method for `CT_ORDER_EXPORT` to write out the DTD information for the `ORDERS` collection, followed by a call to `CreateXMLClass` to write out the DTD information for the `ORDER` class. Notice that in our call to `CreateXMLClass`, we are passing a variant array call, `vOrderProperties`. This tells the `CreateXMLClass` method which properties of the class to write out as attributes in the `ATTLIST` section.

Notice that we have also followed the same approach in terms of object hierarchy in our XML as we have throughout the rest of our application base. Instead of defining the `ORDER_DETAIL_ITEMS` collection as a child object of the `ORDER` object, we have placed them side-by-side and wrapped them in an `EXPORTED_ORDER_ITEM` construct. The reason for this is that our metadata does not understand an object hierarchy, and thus it cannot generate a DTD to support one.

The `CreateXMLCollectionClass` method appears in Listing 13.7, and the `CreateXMLClass` method appears in Listing 13.8. Both are straightforward in their implementation. It is important to note that we are simply using the `Attributes` collections on both the `ClassDef` and `PropertyDef` objects.

Listing 13.7   **The** *CreateXMLCollection* **Method on** *IAppServer*

```
Public Function CreateXMLCollectionClass(ClassId As Integer) As String
   Dim sXMLOut As String
   Dim ClassDef As CClassDef

   Dim PropertyDef As CPropertyDef
   Dim AttributeItem As CAttributeItem
   Dim XMLCollectionClassName As String
   Dim XMLThingy As String
   Dim i As Integer

On Error GoTo ErrorTrap

   Set ClassDef = mClassDefs.Item(ClassId)

   ' 1. Output the ELEMENT section

   If ClassDef.Attributes.Exists("XMLCollectionClassName") Then
     XMLCollectionClassName = _
       ClassDef.Attributes.Item("XMLCollectionClassName").Value
   Else
     XMLCollectionClassName = ClassDef.ReadLocation ' assumes table name
   End If

   Call Append(sXMLOut, "<!ELEMENT" & vbTab & XMLCollectionClassName & " ")

   If ClassDef.Attributes.Exists("XMLCollectionClassChildren") Then
     XMLThingy = ClassDef.Attributes.Item("XMLCollectionClassChildren").Value
```

continues

Listing 13.7 **Continued**

```
  Else
    XMLThingy = "EMPTY"
  End If

  Call Append(sXMLOut, XMLThingy & ">" & vbCrLf)

ExitFunction:
  CreateXMLCollectionClass = sXMLOut
  Exit Function

ErrorTrap:
    '1.  Details to EventLog
    Call WriteNTLogEvent("IAppServer:CreateXMLCollectionClass", Err.Number, _
                        Err.Description, Err.Source)
    '2.  Generic to client - passed back on error stack
    Err.Raise Err.Number, "IAppServer:CreateXMLCollectionClass", _
                        Err.Description & " [" & Erl & "]"
End Function
```

Listing 13.8 **The *CreateXMLClass* Method on *IAppServer***

```
Public Function CreateXMLClass(ClassId As Integer, _
                                Properties As Variant) As String

  Dim sXMLOut As String
  Dim ClassDef As CClassDef

  Dim PropertyDef As CPropertyDef
  Dim AttributeItem As CAttributeItem
  Dim XMLClassName As String
  Dim XMLThingy As String
  Dim i As Integer

On Error GoTo ErrorTrap

  Set ClassDef = mClassDefs.Item(ClassId)

  ' 1. Output the ELEMENT section

  If ClassDef.Attributes.Exists("XMLClassName") Then
    XMLClassName = ClassDef.Attributes.Item("XMLClassName").Value
  Else
    XMLClassName = ClassDef.ReadLocation ' assumes table name
  End If

  Call Append(sXMLOut, "<!ELEMENT" & vbTab & XMLClassName & " ")

  If ClassDef.Attributes.Exists("XMLClassChildren") Then
    XMLThingy = ClassDef.Attributes.Item("XMLClassChildren").Value
```

```
      Else
        XMLThingy = "EMPTY"
      End If

    Call Append(sXMLOut, XMLThingy & ">" & vbCrLf)

    ' 2. Output the ATTLIST section

    XMLThingy = "<!ATTLIST " & vbTab & XMLClassName
    Call Append(sXMLOut, XMLThingy & vbCrLf)

    If Not IsArray(Properties) Then
      Properties = GetPropertyNames(ClassId)
    End If

    For i = LBound(Properties) To UBound(Properties)
      Set PropertyDef = ClassDef.PropertyDefs.Item(Properties(i))
      If PropertyDef.Attributes.Exists("XMLAttributeName") Then
          XMLThingy = PropertyDef.Attributes.Item("XMLAttributeName").Value
          If XMLThingy <> "" Then
            Call Append(sXMLOut, vbTab & vbTab & XMLThingy)
            Call Append(sXMLOut, " CDATA #REQUIRED" & vbCrLf)
          End If
      End If
    Next i

    Call Append(sXMLOut, ">" & vbCrLf)

ExitFunction:
  CreateXMLClass = sXMLOut
  Exit Function

ErrorTrap:
    '1.  Details to EventLog
    Call WriteNTLogEvent("IAppServer:CreateXMLClass", Err.Number, _
                         Err.Description, Err.Source)
    '2.  Generic to client - passed back on error stack
    Err.Raise Err.Number, "IAppServer:CreateXMLClass", _
                          Err.Description & " [" & Erl & "]"

End Function
```

The CreateXMLCollection and CreateXMLObject methods take our familiar data variant array that is retrieved from our various data retrieval methods. The code for CreateXMLObject appears in Listing 13.9, and Listing 13.10 shows the code for CreateXMLCollection.

Listing 13.9   **The *CreateXMLObject* Method on *IAppServer***

```
Public Function CreateXMLObject(ClassId As Integer, Properties As Variant, _
                                Data As Variant, Row As Integer) As String
    Dim sXMLOut As String
    Dim ClassDef As CClassDef

    Dim PropertyDef As CPropertyDef
    Dim PropertyNames As Variant
    Dim PropertyIndex As Collection

    Dim XMLClassName As String
    Dim XMLThingy As String
    Dim i As Integer

On Error GoTo ErrorTrap

    Set ClassDef = mClassDefs.Item(ClassId)
    PropertyNames = GetPropertyNames(ClassId)
    Set PropertyIndex = MakePropertyIndex(PropertyNames)

    If Not IsArray(Properties) Then
      Properties = PropertyNames
    End If

    If ClassDef.Attributes.Exists("XMLClassName") Then
       XMLClassName = ClassDef.Attributes.Item("XMLClassName").Value
    Else
      XMLClassName = ClassDef.ReadLocation ' assumes table name
    End If

    Append sXMLOut, "<" & XMLClassName & " "

    For i = LBound(Properties) To UBound(Properties)
      Set PropertyDef = ClassDef.PropertyDefs.Item(Properties(i))
      If PropertyDef.Attributes.Exists("XMLAttributeName") Then
        XMLThingy = PropertyDef.Attributes.Item("XMLAttributeName").Value
        If XMLThingy <> "" Then
          Append sXMLOut, XMLThingy & "=" & Chr(34) & _
                  Data(PropertyIndex(PropertyDef.Name), Row) & Chr(34) & " "
        End If
      End If
    Next i
    Append sXMLOut, "/>" & vbCrLf

ExitFunction:
  CreateXMLObject = sXMLOut
  Exit Function

ErrorTrap:
    '1. Details to EventLog
    Call WriteNTLogEvent("IAppServer:CreateXMLObject", Err.Number, _
                    Err.Description & " [" & Erl & "]", Err.Source)
```

```
      '2.  Generic to client - passed back on error stack
      Err.Raise Err.Number, "IAppServer:CreateXMLObject", & _
                          Err.Description & " [" & Erl & "]"
End Function
```

Listing 13.10   **The *CreateXMLCollection* Method**

```
Public Function CreateXMLCollection(ClassId As Integer, _
                                    Properties As Variant, _
                                    Data As Variant) As String

  Dim sXMLOut As String
  Dim ClassDef As CClassDef

  Dim PropertyDef As CPropertyDef
  Dim PropertyNames As Variant
  Dim PropertyIndex As Collection

  Dim XMLCollectionClassName As String
  Dim XMLThingy As String
  Dim i As Integer

On Error GoTo ErrorTrap

  Set ClassDef = mClassDefs.Item(ClassId)
  PropertyNames = GetPropertyNames(ClassId)
  Set PropertyIndex = MakePropertyIndex(PropertyNames)

  If Not IsArray(Properties) Then
    Properties = PropertyNames
  End If

  If ClassDef.Attributes.Exists("XMLCollectionClassName") Then
    XMLCollectionClassName = _
      ClassDef.Attributes.Item("XMLCollectionClassName").Value
  Else
    XMLCollectionClassName = ClassDef.ReadLocation ' assumes table name
  End If

  Append sXMLOut, "<" & XMLCollectionClassName & ">" & vbCrLf

  For i = LBound(Data, 2) To UBound(Data, 2)
      XMLThingy = CreateXMLObject(ClassId, Properties, Data, i)
      Append sXMLOut, XMLThingy
  Next i

 Append sXMLOut, "</" & XMLCollectionClassName & ">" & vbCrLf


ExitFunction:
```

continues

Listing 13.10   **Continued**

```
    CreateXMLCollection = sXMLOut
    Exit Function

ErrorTrap:
    '1.  Details to EventLog
    Call WriteNTLogEvent("IAppServer:CreateXMLCollection", Err.Number, _
                        Err.Description & " [" & Erl & "]", Err.Source)
    '2.  Generic to client - passed back on error stack
    Err.Raise Err.Number, "IAppServer:CreateXMLCollection", _
                        Err.Description & " [" & Erl & "]"
End Function
```

With our XML process now in place, we can modify the code snippet from Listing 13.4 to now generate an XML format of the same information, which appears in Listing 13.11.

Listing 13.11   **Calling the XML Export Process**

```
Dim NWServer As CNWServer
Dim AppServer As IAppServer
Dim Stream As String
Dim Errors As Variant

Set NWServer = CreateObject("NWServer.CNWServer", MTSMachineName)
Set AppServer = NWServer
AppServer.InitServer

Call AppServer.CreateExportStream(CT_ORDER_EXPORT, EF_ORDER_XML, _
                                Stream, Errors)
```

The rest of the standards-based process is the same process shown in Figure 13.1. The only difference is that now the format of the transfer file is XML versus a proprietary format. Figure 13.2 shows the XML Notepad (available from Microsoft) with a sample of our export file loaded.

File-Based Interoperability

With our capability to generate proprietary, or standardized, data streams, we now have the capability to transfer information from one system to another. In the simplest form, a simple file generation process that calls the `CreateExportStream` method can be implemented. We spoke of this same process in the previous section and diagrammed it in Figure 13.1. This process can be placed directly off the TOOLS section of the intranet Web site, or it can be placed in the Visual Basic client application. In either implementation, a user chooses to generate this information to a file. The user must then take this file to the order-fulfillment system and import it. This activity is typically performed at predetermined intervals, such as daily, every four hours, or whatever is needed. In many cases, this type of interoperability can be put into production quickly, while more automated solutions are developed.

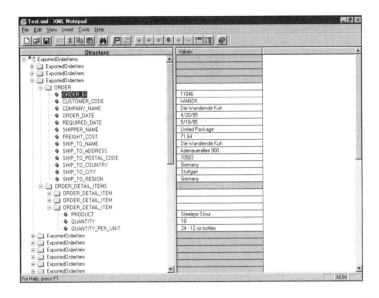

Figure 13.2   The XML Notepad showing a sample order export file.

In a more automated system, a task scheduler can trigger a process in the order-taking system that writes out the file to a shared directory and then calls the order-fulfillment system in which to read it. Task schedulers can come in various forms. The NT system has a built-in task-scheduling component through its AT command. The SQL Executive can be used as a triggering device, but this requires processing to occur on the same physical machine as the database server, which might not be desirable. Commercially available task schedulers can also be used, or a custom scheduler, which uses the Windows timer API and which is implemented as an NT service, can also be used. For our purposes, we use the native NT scheduler to call console applications written in Visual Basic.

If our order-fulfillment system has an API that enables us to automate our import process, we can automate this entire data transfer process. Figure 13.3 shows an overview of the architecture required to automate this process.

First, we create a shared file directory on our integration server machine to serve as a common data point. If we want an order drop to occur every four hours starting at 8:00 a.m. and a command file called DROPORDERS.CMD drives it, then we would enter the following AT commands on our integration server machine:

```
AT 8:00  /every:M,T,W,Th,F,S,Su DROPORDERS.CMD
AT 12:00 /every:M,T,W,Th,F,S,Su DROPORDERS.CMD
AT 16:00 /every:M,T,W,Th,F,S,Su DROPORDERS.CMD
AT 20:00 /every:M,T,W,Th,F,S,Su DROPORDERS.CMD
AT 0:00  /every:M,T,W,Th,F,S,Su DROPORDERS.CMD
AT 4:00  /every:M,T,W,Th,F,S,Su DROPORDERS.CMD
```

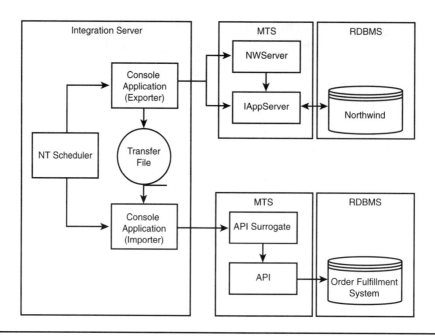

Figure 13.3   Automated data movement using a
task scheduler and an integration server.

First, the DROPORDERS.CMD file is designed to retrieve the file from the order-taking system via a console application. Assuming our Northwind MTS machine is named MOJO and our integration server is called CARTMAN, then our console application can be called as follows:

```
EXPORTORDERS.EXE MTS:MOJO PATH:\\CARTMAN\EXPORTS\ORDERS.XML
```

This console application would connect to the MTS machine named MOJO, calling the CreateExportStream method and saving the resulting information to a file called ORDERS.XML on the path \\CARTMAN\EXPORTS.

The next line in the DROPORDERS.CMD file would import the file into the fulfillment system. Assuming an MTS machine of ALEXIS, it might look something like the following statement:

```
IMPORTORDERS.EXE MTS:ALEXIS PATH:\\MOJO\EXPORTS\ORDERS.XML
```

This simple command file and the supporting console applications would be all that is necessary to automate the data transfer process. In a real-world case, the console applications would be designed to return errorlevel values back to the command processor.

For example, if the EXPORTORDERS.EXE were to fail, we would not want to run the IMPORTORDERS.EXE command. In fact, we would likely be interested in branching off to an alerting mechanism to inform support staff of the failed export.

There are still some issues with this process in that there is a "hole" in which a set of orders could be exported, but the import would fail and thus never have the chance of making it into the fulfillment system on the next export. The reason is that the LastExportDate field would have been adjusted in the CreateExportStream method, which assumes that the downstream import processes will succeed. To make this process as robust as possible, the CreateExportStream method should not update the LastExportDate field. Instead, a separate public method on NWServer named SetLastExportDate should be created. This method could be called by yet another console application upon successful completion of the IMPORTORDERS.EXE process. There is still an issue in that if the import fails midway into the process, no orders from the point of failure forward will be processed.

The most robust approach using the LastExportDate field would be to have the IMPORTORDERS.EXE process call the SetLastExportDate method after each successful import. Upon the first failure, the process aborts, writing an application event to the event log and sending an errorlevel back to the command processor. Again, this would signal support staff of the issue to be resolved. This process assumes that the orders are listed in date order.

Building a pseudo-console application in Visual Basic is not overly difficult. We use the term *pseudo-console* because Visual Basic cannot redirect stdin and stdout like most console applications can. Other than that, it can process command-line arguments and, with the help of a Windows API, can generate an errorlevel back to the command processor. It is advantageous for us to use Visual Basic to build the console applications for our application-integration efforts because we can use the COM and DCOM infrastructure functionality already built. It is also much simpler than using other alternatives, such as C++, Delphi, or even Perl. The only thing to consider is that using Visual Basic requires the installation of the Visual Basic runtime and our application framework components on the integration machine.

To create a console application in Visual Basic, we simply create a Standard EXE application. We remove the Form1.frm file, add a basic module called modConsole, and create a Main subroutine. This routine is called when the application starts up. We can gain access to the command-line parameters through the Command function and return an errorlevel via the ExitProcess function. This function simply provides us with the command-line argument as a string value. We must process it to determine the actual parameters based on whatever format we have defined. The code for EXPORTORDERS.EXE can be found in Listing 13.12. A similar application can be built for IMPORTORDERS.EXE.

Listing 13.12   **The Code for *EXPORTORDERS.EXE***

```
Option Explicit

Const CT_ORDER_EXPORT = 301
Const CT_ORDER_DETAIL_EXPORT = 302
Const EF_ORDER_PROPRIETARY = 1
Const EF_ORDER_XML = 2


Public Declare Sub ExitProcess Lib "kernel32" _
                    (ByVal uExitCode As Long)


Public Function ExportOrders(MTSServerName As String, _
                             FilePath As String) As Boolean
    Dim NWServer As CNWServer
    Dim AppServer As IAppServer
    Dim Stream As String
    Dim Errors As Variant
    Dim iFileNum As String

    On Error GoTo ErrorTrap

    Set NWServer = CreateObject("NWServer.CNWServer", _
                                MTSServerName)
    Set AppServer = NWServer
    AppServer.InitServer

    Call AppServer.CreateExportStream(CT_ORDER_EXPORT, _
                                      EF_ORDER_XML, _
                                      Stream, _
                                      Errors)

    iFileNum = FreeFile
    Open FilePath & "\OrderExport.XML" For Output As #iFileNum
    Print #iFileNum, Stream
    Close #iFileNum

    ExportOrders = True
    Exit Function

ErrorTrap:
    ExportOrders = False
End Function


Sub Main()
    Dim sCommand As String
    Dim sParms() As String
```

```
    Dim MTSServerName As String
    Dim FilePath As String

    Dim i As Integer

    sCommand = Command
    sParms = Split(sCommand, " ")

    For i = LBound(sParms) To UBound(sParms)
      Select Case UCase(sParms(i))
        Case "-S"
          MTSServerName = sParms(i + 1)

        Case "-P"
          FilePath = sParms(i + 1)
      End Select
    Next i

    If ExportOrders(MTSServerName, FilePath) Then
      ExitProcess (0)
    Else
      ExitProcess (1)
    End If
End Sub
```

Messaging-Based Interoperability

In our automated version in the previous example, we have had to go to great lengths to ensure that orders do not get lost during the process of moving the data between the taking and fulfillment systems. We did this by having the IMPORTORDERS.EXE console application perform the update to the LastExportDate field. Although this is a working solution, it is undesirable to have the IMPORTORDERS.EXE application, which is a part of our fulfillment system, performing updates to our order-taking system. Additionally, if the number of orders is large then this adds extra processing overhead onto the data transfer process. This section introduces the concept of a message queue to make this type of application integration cleaner. We then talk about using a much larger messaging system—electronic mail—to provide integration among systems that span corporate boundaries.

Using a Message Queue

A *message queue* is an enterprise component that has been around since the early mainframe days. The two larger message queue products include Microsoft Message Queue (MSMQ) and IBM's MQSeries. The former runs only on NT-based platforms, whereas the latter runs on NT and most others. There are commercial bridging products available that can move messages from one product to another, or you can build your own. For the purposes of our application, we use only MSMQ, although similar techniques should apply to other message queue products.

One of the benefits of using a message queue is the concept of guaranteed delivery. If one application places a message on the queue, it remains there until specifically removed by another application. In our order-information transfer example, the EXPORTORDERS.EXE console application could place the information into a message queue rather than to a shared file directory. In this case, the EXPORTORDERS.EXE would have the responsibility of setting the LastExportDate upon completion, because it is now guaranteed that the message it has created will remain in the queue until it is successfully processed. Figure 13.4 shows an architectural overview of this process.

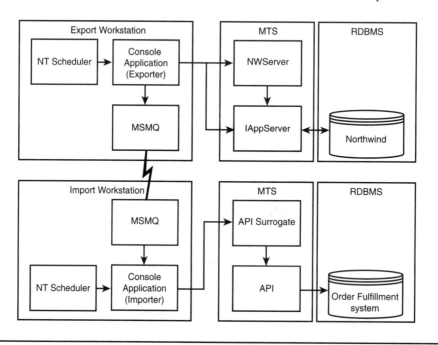

Figure 13.4   Automated data movement using a task scheduler, an integration server, and a message queue.

Modifying our EXPORTORDERS.EXE process to accommodate a message queue is straightforward. First, your development machine must have the MSMQ-independent client components installed. To do this, you must have access to an MSMQ site-controller installation. If your development machine is NT Server, you can simply install MSMQ on it. If you are running NT Workstation then you will need to use the NT Option Pak to install the MSMQ client. The reason for using an independent client is so that we can send messages over a potentially unreliable, or sometimes disconnected, network. In this mode, MSMQ writes to a local message store if the network is disconnected, and the message store sends the messages to the target queue after the connection is reestablished. The other option, the dependent client, does not have this local storage capability.

With these items in place, we can create a public queue using the MSMQ Explorer. To accomplish this, we right-click on the server name in the MSMQ Explorer and select New, and then Queue, as shown in Figure 13.5. This launches the Queue Name dialog seen in Figure 13.6. We then name this queue OrderTransfer and deselect the Transactional check box. Clicking on the OK button creates the queue.

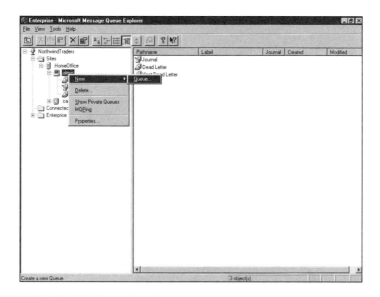

Figure 13.5   Creating a new queue in the MSMQ Explorer.

Figure 13.6   Naming the new queue in the MSMQ Explorer.

After the MSMQ-independent client is installed on our machine, we can reference it via the MSMQ object library. This ActiveX library is found in mqoa.dll. It appears as Microsoft Message Queue Library in the References dialog within Visual Basic. A C-level API provides access to all MSMQ functionality, whereas the ActiveX wrapper is suitable for many applications.

We modify our EXPORTORDERS.EXE code by first creating a public QSend function, as shown in Listing 13.13. The technique shown for opening a message queue and sending a message is taken directly from Microsoft documentation. It is important to note the statement that sets the Delivery property of the MSMQMessage object to MQMSG_DELIVERY_RECOVERABLE. The default mode of MSMQ is to store all local

messages in memory. In the case of a double fault, whereby the network is disconnected, if messages are sent and then the system is restarted before re-establishment of
the connection, the messages stored in memory will be lost. By setting this property as
described, the messages are written to local disk storage. Although this mode makes
these messages permanent, it does slow down overall message passing. Because we are
moving data between applications using MSMQ, we must be guaranteed of delivery,
so we set this property.

Listing 13.13   **The *QSend* Function**

```
Public Function QSend(QueueName As String, _
                      MsgTitle As String, _
                      MsgBody As String)
  Dim qry As MSMQQuery
  Dim qis As MSMQQueueInfos
  Dim qi As MSMQQueueInfo
  Dim q1 As MSMQQueue
  Dim msg As MSMQMessage

  Set qi = New MSMQQueueInfo
  qi.FormatName = QueueName

  Set q1 = qi.Open(MQ_SEND_ACCESS, MQ_DENY_NONE)
  Set msg = New MSMQMessage

  msg.Label = MsgTitle
  msg.Body = MsgBody
  msg.Delivery = MQMSG_DELIVERY_RECOVERABLE
  msg.Send q1
  q1.Close

End Function
```

We are not explicitly trapping for errors in this code because we are assuming our
calling process will want to handle it specifically.

We also modify our ExportOrders function to now send the XML-formatted stream
to the queue instead of the file used in the previous example, as shown in Listing
13.14.

Listing 13.14   **The Modified *ExportOrders* Function to Support MSMQ**

```
Public Function ExportOrders(MTSServerName As String, _
                             FilePath As String) As Boolean
  Dim NWServer As CNWServer
  Dim AppServer As IAppServer
  Dim Stream As String
  Dim Errors As Variant
  Dim iFileNum As String
```

```
    Dim QName As String

    On Error GoTo ErrorTrap

    Set NWServer = CreateObject("NWServer.CNWServer", _
                                MTSServerName)
    Set AppServer = NWServer
    AppServer.InitServer

    Call AppServer.CreateExportStream(CT_ORDER_EXPORT, _
                                      EF_ORDER_XML, _
                                      Stream, _
                                      Errors)


    QName = "Direct=TCP:128.128.128.126\OrderTransfer"
    Call QSend(QName, "ORDER_EXPORT", Stream)

    ExportOrders = True
    Exit Function

ErrorTrap:
    ExportOrders = False
End Function
```

Although we have hard-coded the queue name here for exposition, we would modify our calling convention into ExportOrders to implement a -q switch to provide the queue name. Notice the "Direct=..." format used for the queue name. This format tells MSMQ to delivery the message in a potentially disconnected status. If we do not use this format and the computer is disconnected when we send the message, an error is raised. After this method has completed successfully, the message is visible in the MSMQ Explorer under the OrderTransfer queue name, as shown in Figure 13.7.

On the import side, we implement a process that retrieves the messages for the queue. Although we won't provide the full implementation, we do show this retrieval process. The important item to understand is the difference between peeking and retrieving messages. *Peeking* enables you to pull a message from the queue without removing it from the queue. *Retrieving* a message removes it. Typically, we want to peek the message first, attempt to process it, and remove it from the queue if we are successful. Listing 13.15 shows the code for a queue processing procedure. We have implemented our reader function in a mode in which it loops through the entire queue, processes messages of interest, and then exits. An external task scheduler can fire off our console application periodically to scan the queue in this manner.

In an alternative processing technique, an MSMQEvent object is attached to an MSMQQueue object through its EnableNotification method. This MSMQEvent provides an event sink for an Arrived event, which fires every time a message arrives in the queue. This technique can be used to process messages as they arrive. There are many other ways in which to implement a queue reader process besides those provided. The specific implementation can vary between the tasks for which the message queue is being used.

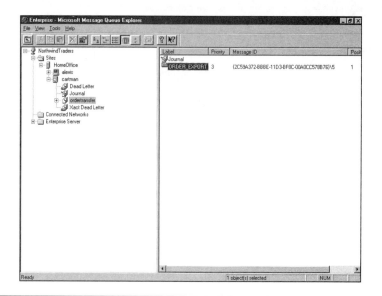

Figure 13.7   The newly delivered message in the queue.

Listing 13.15   **A Queue-Reading Function**

```
Public Sub Read_Queue()
  Dim qry As MSMQQuery
  Dim qis As MSMQQueueInfos
  Dim qi As MSMQQueueInfo
  Dim q1 As MSMQQueue
  Dim msg As MSMQMessage
  Dim bReceived As Boolean

  Set qi = New MSMQQueueInfo
  qi.PathName = "cartman\OrderTransfer"

  Set q1 = qi.Open(MQ_RECEIVE_ACCESS, MQ_DENY_NONE)

  Set msg = q1.PeekCurrent(ReceiveTimeout:=0)
  Do Until msg Is Nothing
    bReceived = False
    Select Case msg.Label
      Case "ORDER_EXPORT"
        If SomeProcess(msg.Body) Then
          ' remove the message
          Set msg = q1.ReceiveCurrent
```

```
              bReceived = True
          End If
      End Select

      If bReceived Then
        Set msg = q1.PeekCurrent(ReceiveTimeout:=0)
      Else
        Set msg = q1.PeekNext(ReceiveTimeout:=0)
      End If
    Loop
    q1.Close
  End Sub
```

Again, the queue-reading functionality is taken from Microsoft documentation. You should note that our queue name specifier is different for reading. Here we use the syntax `"cartman\OrderTransfer"` rather than the `"DIRECT=TCP:..."` from before. In addition, to open the queue for both receive and peek access, we must open it using the `MQ_RECEIVE_ACCESS` mode. As we loop through the queue, we first peek the method using the `PeekCurrent` message, and then we attempt to process it. If we are successful, we then remove it using the `ReceiveCurrent` method. This `PeekCurrent`, followed by a `ReceiveCurrent`, implicitly advances the underlying cursor used to iterate the queue but places it in an indeterminate state. If this has occurred, we must repeek the queue using the `PeekCurrent` method to restore it. This obscure fact can be found buried somewhere in the Microsoft Knowledge Base.

Using the Mail Subsystem

With the basic messaging system in place, there are still times when MSMQ cannot be used. For example, if the order-taking system is perhaps hosted at an Internet service provider (ISP) or an application service provider but the order fulfillment is running at the home office, it might be difficult to set up MSMQ if there is not a dedicated network in place connecting the two. Looking beyond our sample application, there might be times when data needs to move between applications in different companies. For example, a material requirements forecast for a manufacturing company might need to be sent to the material supplier. In these cases, we need something more than MSMQ alone.

One solution is to use the file-based approach, as we did before, with file transfer protocol (FTP) paths instead of local network paths. Another is to leverage the email system already in place and send the information over the Internet. It is easy to think of MSMQ in terms of an email metaphor. The `PathName` property of the `MSMQQueue` object becomes the `To` field, the `Label` property of the `MSMQMessage` object becomes the `Subject`, and the `Body` property becomes the text of the email.

We can use Messaging Application Programming Interface (MAPI), Collaborative Data Objects (CDO), or Collaborative Data Objects for NT Server (CDONTS) to assist us in our email generation and delivery on the export side. MAPI is a C-level API that is cumbersome to work with. CDO is an ActiveX DLL, but it requires Microsoft Exchange. CDONTS uses Simple Mail Transfer Protocol (SMTP), which bypasses Exchange. CDONTS is not available from Microsoft as a standalone install. Instead, it is installed on NT Server machines with IIS 4.0 and higher. The code for the mailing routing using CDONTS appears in Listing 13.16. Note that NT Server is required to implement and debug CDONTS.

Listing 13.16   **An Email Message Sender Using CDONTS**

```
Public Function MSend(ToAddress As String, _
                      FromAddress As String, _
                      Subject As String, _
                      Body As String)

    Dim oMail As NewMail
    Set oMail = CreateObject("CDONTS.NewMail")

    oMail.To = ToAddress
    oMail.From = FromAddress
    oMail.Subject = Subject
    oMail.Body = Body

    oMail.Send
    Set oMail = Nothing

End Function
```

By replacing our QSend function call in the ExportOrders function with MSend, we have bypassed MSMQ and gone directly to the Internet. On the receiving end, there must be a listener routine that checks an email inbox for the target address with the given subject line. The CDONTS library can be used to pull the message from the inbox. This is followed by an attempt to process the message, as was done in the PeekCurrent case in MSMQ. If successful, an acknowledge message can be sent back using the FromAddress in the original field; otherwise, an error message stream can be sent to the same address for diagnostic purposes. Because there isn't a mechanism to guarantee delivery, the export process must be able to store messages locally until a successful acknowledgement is received. Because only SMTP-based mail services are required for this process, it is not dependent on any one particular vendor of mail systems.

Cryptography

If we start sending data over the Internet as email message bodies, it might be important to encrypt the body to prevent unwanted eyes from deciphering its contents. Numerous cryptography solutions are available, including the CryptoAPI that comes with NT. Unfortunately, this is a C-level API that is both difficult to understand and proprietary to NT. To solve this problem, we can use a commercial product, or we can choose to build our own simple encryption/decryption mechanism, depending on the level of security required.

Without going into significant detail, the code in Listing 13.17 shows a basic encrypter and decrypter function using a single numeric key. For this process to work, both the sender and receiver must have an agreed-upon key value. These algorithms also ensure that the characters that make up the encrypted text remain within the ANSI character set (that is, character codes less than 128). It does this by converting three 8-bit bytes into four 6-bit bytes and vice versa.

Listing 13.17 **Basic Encryption and Decryption Algorithms**

```
Private Const C1 As Long = 52845
Private Const C2 As Long = 22719

Public Function Encrypt(ByVal S As String, Key As Long) As String
  Dim i As Integer, j As Integer
  Dim sRet As String, sRet2 As String, tKey As Long
  Dim a1 As Byte, b1 As Byte, b2 As Byte
  Dim n As Integer

  For i = 1 To Len(S)
    Key = Key And 32767
    tKey = Key
    For j = 1 To 8
      tKey = tKey / 2
    Next j
    sRet = sRet & Chr(Asc(Mid(S, i, 1)) Xor (tKey))
    Key = (Asc(Mid(sRet, i, 1)) + Key) * C1 + C2
  Next i

  'convert (3) 8 bit bytes into (4) 6 bit bytes
  n = Len(sRet)
  For i = 1 To n
    a1 = Asc(Mid(sRet, i, 1))
    b1 = ((a1 And &HF0) / (2 ^ 4)) Or &H40
    b2 = (a1 And &HF) Or &H40

    sRet2 = sRet2 & Chr(b1) & Chr(b2)
  Next i
  Encrypt = sRet2

End Function

Public Function Decrypt(ByVal S As String, Key As Long) As String
  Dim i As Integer, j As Integer
  Dim sRet As String, tKey As Long
```

continues

Listing 13.17 **Continued**

```
Dim sTemp As String
Dim b1 As Byte, b2 As Byte, a1 As Byte

sTemp = S
S = ""
For i = 1 To Len(sTemp) Step 2
  b1 = (Asc(Mid(sTemp, i, 1)) And Not (&H40)) * (2 ^ 4)
  b2 = Asc(Mid(sTemp, i + 1, 1)) And Not (&H40)
  a1 = b1 Or b2
  S = S & Chr(a1)
Next i

For i = 1 To Len(S)
  Key = Key And 32767
  tKey = Key
  For j = 1 To 8
    tKey = tKey / 2
  Next j

  sRet = sRet & Chr(Asc(Mid(S, i, 1)) Xor (tKey))
  Key = (Asc(Mid(S, i, 1)) + Key) * C1 + C2
Next i
Decrypt = sRet

End Function
```

Interoperability Through Data Sharing

To this point, we have looked at data transfer as a mechanism for application integration. Another form of integration can occur by simply accessing foreign data in real time. This can happen in several ways.

Direct Database Access

Direct data access is probably the easiest form of application integration. Using ADO or ODBC, we can connect our `DataManager` component to these other systems for data retrieval purposes. In many cases, we can create a `ClassDef` object to map these foreign tables and views into new classes within our system, although they might not follow our precise design guidelines, as covered in Chapter 8, "The DataManager Library." In some cases in which stored procedures are used for data retrieval, a read-only `ClassDef` can be implemented based on the columns returned. Data insert and updates, on the other hand, are much more difficult and might require direct access to the underlying system. The `Attributes` collection on a `ClassDef` object can be used to hold metadata associated with processing these types of situations.

With a `ClassManager` and `DataManager` created, we can bring the foreign data into our application, as well as provide information back to these same applications. In worse-case scenarios, we can bypass our `ClassManager` and `DataManager` altogether and place custom methods off our `NWServer` component. Figure 13.8 shows this form of integration and the various pathways between our application server components and the databases.

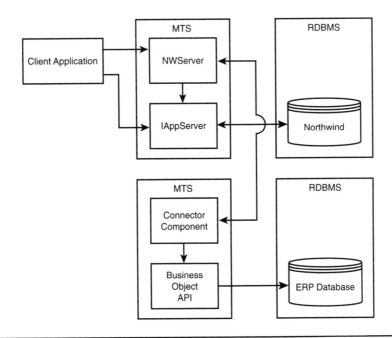

Figure 13.8   Application integration using direct database access.

Application Connectors

Many modern enterprise applications are beginning to offer integration objects to assist in hooking systems together. These integration objects are sometimes called connector components or object brokers. Depending on how they are designed, they can run as DCOM objects within MTS or as CORBA objects within an object request broker. Many application vendors are offering both forms.

With an application connector, we can make calls into it to retrieve the information we need or we can provide data inserts and updates. In many ways, our own framework is a form of an application connector into our system if used by other applications. In the case of a DCOM-based application connector, we can interact with it using variant arrays or XML-formatted data streams as in our own examples. Figure 13.9 shows this form of application in the context of an Enterprise Resource Planning (ERP) system.

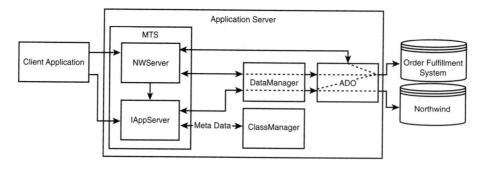

Figure 13.9   Application integration using connector components.

From Figure 13.9, you should note that we are performing our integration to the connector component through our NWServer class rather than IAppServer. The reason for this is that such integration is specific to the particular application being built using our framework, so it belongs with NWServer.

Summary

We have just gone through a whirlwind tour of application integration using our framework. We have covered data transfer techniques using proprietary and XML-based data formats as transfer mediums. We have covered the use of files, message queues, and emails as transfer conduits. We have also talked briefly of integration using direct connect techniques, either directly at the database level or through application connector components. Although this chapter has had a significant amount of content, it is by no means a definitive source. Other books go into much detail on the subject.

In the next chapter, we look at Windows 2000 and how it affects our framework components. We specifically look at compatibility issues with MTS, MSMQ, and IIS. We also address some of Windows 2000's new features that can enhance our application.

14

Windows 2000 and COM+ Considerations

IF VARIOUS SCHEDULES GO ACCORDING to plan, you should be reading this book in the months following the release of Windows 2000, the replacement for Windows NT. Within a few months, your company can begin making the long-anticipated migration to this latest Microsoft server platform and its COM+ model. At this point, you might be concerned that everything that has been demonstrated in this book is for naught with this new technology release, or you might be concerned that implementing an application based on the framework we have presented will have to be reworked after you do make the migration. Fear not; much of the functionality we have relied on to this point was released with the NT 4.0 Option Pack.

Component Services

To quote from the MSDN library at Microsoft's Web site at the time of this writing (with the appropriate disclaimer that it is preliminary and can change):

> "COM+ can be viewed as a merging of the Microsoft Transaction Server (MTS) and COM, along with the introduction of a host of new features. If you are currently using MTS, Windows 2000 makes the change to COM+ completely automatic.
>
> For the most part, your MTS packages are transformed to COM+ applications during the Windows 2000 setup procedure. Without doing anything beyond the typical setup, you can now take advantage of all the new COM+ features."

Migrating Existing MTS Components

The simplest way to move our existing MTS components from NT/MTS to COM+ is to export our components to a package file in MTS, and then import it into COM+. By following this approach, we preserve our GUID for our DCOM objects so that client-side applications do not have to be recompiled and redeployed. This technique will most likely be used in migration strategies, in which companies are moving existing MTS-based applications over to Windows 2000 Advanced Server.

The Transaction Server Explorer has been replaced with the Component Services snap-in for the Microsoft Management Console (MMC). Figure 14.1 shows how to navigate to the Component Services snap-in.

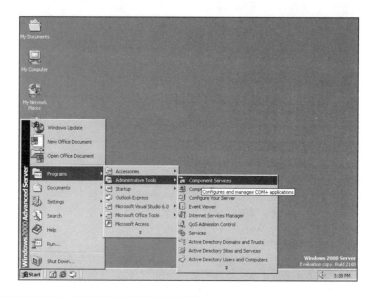

Figure 14.1   Navigating to the Component Services
snap-in in Windows 2000 Advanced Server.

Inside the Components Services snap-in, we see that it has a similar layout to the Transaction Server Explorer. The only differences in the look and feel of the new snap-in is that several of the old nodes in the tree view are gone and that the spinning balls have gone from green to gold. In addition, most of the wizards used to install new packages and components have been polished a bit, but they are fundamentally the same. To import our MTS-based package, we right-click on the COM+ Applications node and select New, followed by Application from the pop-up menu, as shown in Figure 14.2.

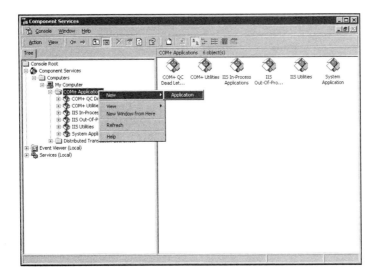

Figure 14.2   Launching the COM+ Application Install Wizard.

The first step of the wizard is simply informational. We click Next on the wizard to advance to the second step. From there we click on the Install Pre-Built Application(s) button, as shown in Figure 14.3.

Figure 14.3   Installing a prebuilt application.

This brings up a file selector dialog. We change the Files of Type combo box to MTS Package Files (*.PAK) and browse to our package file. We click on the Next button to take us to the Set Application Identity step. We leave the account set to Interactive User for now, but this should be changed later when the application is put into production. We click Next once again to take us to the Application Installation Options step. We click on the Specific Directory radio button and enter the name of the directory where our new components are to be installed. We select our directory and click on the Next button one final time to arrive at the last step. We click on the Finish button and find that our Northwind Traders application has been created, as shown in Figure 14.4. We also must remember to move our `ClassManager` and `DataManager` components over as well, although they can simply be registered using the REGSVR32 utility.

Figure 14.4   The Northwind Traders application added to COM+.

Installing MTS Components into Component Services

If we are developing a new application that has not yet been deployed, we might want to directly install our components into Component Services. To do this, we once again right-click on our COM+ Applications node, followed by the New and Application submenus in the pop-up menu. We click the Next button on the first step of the resulting wizard, followed by the Create an empty application button on step two. We enter `Northwind Traders` as the application name, and select the Server Application radio button. We click on the Next button, again leaving the account set to the Interactive User option. Then we click the Next button, followed by the Finish button to complete the process.

At this point, an empty package has been created. To add components, we right-click on the Components folder under the Northwind Traders folder, selecting New followed by Component from the resulting pop-up menus, as shown in Figure 14.5.

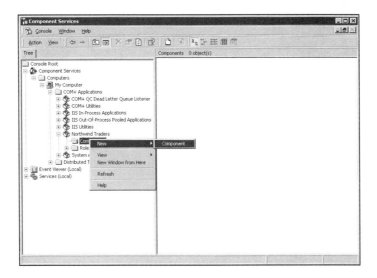

Figure 14.5 Adding components to an empty package in COM+.

The preceding steps launch the COM+ Component Install Wizard. Clicking the Next button on the informational screen takes us to the Import or Install a Component step. We click on the Install New Component(s) button to launch a file selection dialog. We browse to our DCOM components, select them, and click on the Open button. We click on the Next button, followed by the Finish button to complete the process. Our components are now added, as shown earlier in Figure 14.4.

By installing components in this manner, they have been assigned new GUID values and are not accessible to our client until we create new remote application installers. In Windows 2000 and COM+, these become known as *application proxies*. To create an application proxy, we right-click on the Northwind Traders folder, selecting the Export menu item from the pop-up, as shown in Figure 14.6.

The COM+ Application Export Wizard begins with the familiar informational first step. We click on the Next button to take us to the Application Export Information step. We select our output path for the export file, naming it `Northwind.msi`. We select the Application Proxy radio button in the Export As frame and click the Next button. A click on the Finish button completes the process. The result is the creation of an installer Cabinet file, otherwise known as a CAB file, and a Windows Installer Package file. These two files can be used on the client machine to create the remote registration entries required to access these components.

Note

If your client machine is not Windows 2000, you must download the Windows Installer from the Microsoft Web site. At the time of this writing, Windows 2000 was at RC3 level, and the Windows

Installer for NT 4.0 would not recognize the installation files generated by the COM+ export process. Until this issue is resolved, the easiest way to migrate existing applications to COM+ while keeping the clients at non-Windows 2000 levels is to perform the package import process from MTS-based components.

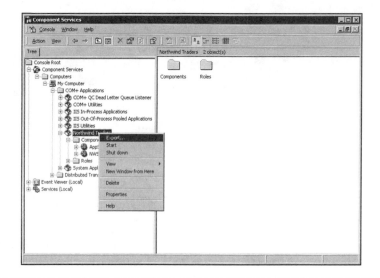

Figure 14.6   Exporting a package from COM+.

Message Queuing

Another major component of our model tied into the NT Option Pack is Microsoft Message Queue (MSMQ), which also has undergone some refinement. Although the client-side programming model is compatible with MSMQ 1.0, MSMQ has undergone several significant changes. One minor change is the name. Message Queue for COM+ is now called simply Message Queuing, although some references are made to it in the context of MSMQ 2.0. From a technical standpoint, MSMQ no longer needs to coexist with SQL Server because it now uses the Active Directory to store its topology information.

Note

When setting up MSMQ 2.0 on Windows 2000 that will be accessed by a NT 4.0-based client, it is important to set it up for Domain mode. To do this, you must choose the Message Queuing Will Access a Directory Service option when setting up the service.

Microsoft claims that there are no compatibility issues using an application written for an MSMQ 1.0 object model. Our framework components from Chapter 13,

"Interoperability," showed no issues, although we were using only a small subset of MSMQ functionality. Again, to quote from Microsoft's Web site:

> "MSMQ 2.0 has new versions of its COM components that are compatible with the MSMQ 1.0 components. The programmatic names of these components have remained the same, enabling you to use the same names you are familiar with (for example, MSMQQueue and MSMQMessage). However, the identifiers (GUIDs) of the objects have changed."

Microsoft further provides the information in Table 14.1 to help determine which version of the library to use if you are programming in a mixed NT 4.0 and Windows 2000 environment.

Table 14.1   **Microsoft's Matrix for Mixed NT 4.0 and Windows 2000 MSMQ Programming**

For...	Select...
Applications that will run on both Windows NT 4.0 and Windows 2000	Microsoft Message Queue 1.0 Object Library
Applications that will run only on Windows 2000	Microsoft Message Queue 2.0 Object Library

The MSMQ 1.0 Explorer has been replaced with a series of MMC snap-ins. To gain access to the queues themselves, we must go under the Computer Management snap-in, as shown in Figure 14.7.

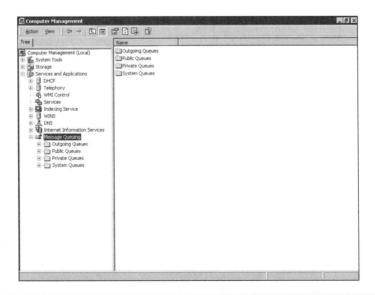

Figure 14.7   Accessing the Message Queues on a Message Queuing server.

New Features in COM+

Although our application framework ports over to COM+ and Windows 2000 relatively easily, several new features within COM+ can be used to enhance our framework. They are discussed in the following sections.

Component Load Balancing

One of the most anticipated features of COM+ has been Component Load Balancing. With this feature, you no longer have to marry your client or IIS server to a specific component server. In this environment, you can have a series of clients and COM+ servers operating in a parallel fashion, with a directory service dynamically determining the routing between the two. For example, if a request is made to instantiate a COM+ object on the Windows 2000 server, rather than "hard-coding" the server name into the application or the DCOM parameters on the client machine, the call is routed to one of several servers. With this architecture, the system can support both failover and scalability issues.

Unfortunately, based on customer feedback from the Windows 2000 beta releases, this feature was pulled out of Windows 2000. According to Microsoft at the time of the writing of this book, Component Load Balancing will be redeployed to the Microsoft AppCenter Server. However, the timing of this release was not given.

Queued Components

COM+ also releases a new feature known as queued components that runs atop MSMQ 2.0. With this new feature, components can be instantiated in an asynchronous fashion. For example, the client machine normally instantiates a COM+ object using an application proxy. In a queued component model, the queued component recorder acts as the application proxy, recording all method calls made on an object. These recorded calls are packaged into an MSMQ 2.0 message body and sent to the server where they are unpackaged and replayed.

Although the use of component queuing is unobtrusive (meaning that special programming at the component level does not need to occur to enable it), not all component uses and method calls lend themselves to queuing. Only parameters that are passed by value in a method call can be used. To gain access to return values, a response message must be issued.

Queued components are well suited to solve issues with availability, scalability, and concurrency, but these features come at the price of performance. Specifically, recording the method, packaging it into a message body, sending the message, unpacking the message, and replaying the method all add extra time to the process. If you are not concerned about the performance implications, this process is acceptable. If performance is an issue, you should investigate other mechanisms, such as writing your own messaging layer that bypasses the recording and playback steps.

In-Memory Databases

With COM+, Microsoft was to have released a feature known as the In-Memory Database (IMDB) to enable application servers to store critical information in a fast and easily accessible format. Unfortunately, based on Windows 2000 beta feedback, this feature was removed after Release Candidate 2 with no indication of when it might be added back. Microsoft recommends using the Shared Property Manager for local data caching. This feature, which we have not used in our framework, was originally released with the NT 4 Option Pack and has been carried forward with the COM+ release.

Summary

In this chapter, we covered the topics of moving our existing framework components into the COM+ environment offered by Windows 2000. We showed that our existing uses of MTS and MSMQ translate rather effortlessly (from a programmatic standpoint) into the new environment. We also talked about some of the new features available in COM+ that you might want to incorporate into the framework as you make the move into this environment.

In the next chapter, we wrap up the book by talking about a few items that did not fit elsewhere in the book. Specifically, we talk about making applications that are written using this framework scalable, as well as how programmatic security can be implemented across the application.

15

Concluding Remarks

WE HAVE MADE IT TO THE LAST CHAPTER of the book with several important stones unturned. It is our goal in this chapter to spend some time with these final topics so that we can say we are finished with the application framework. Specifically, we start by finishing the topic of error handling, followed by a discussion of programmatic security, and concluding with a discussion of scalability.

Error Handling

Up to this point, we have casually addressed the issue of error handling through our event-logging and error-raising mechanisms. In many of our method calls across the DCOM boundary, we included a parameter called `Errors`, meant to contain a variant array with which we have never specifically done much. We have even included some functions to add errors to this array and convert this array into a native `ErrorItems` collection in our `AppCommon` component. Although the only implementation example of these pieces has been to handle validation requirements, they can also be used to pass back general errors resulting from various business rules. Be sure to keep this in mind as you are building out your application using these framework components.

Security Mechanisms

When you are developing in a Windows NT environment using Microsoft infrastructure items, such as MTS, MSMQ, and SQL Server, you can resort to what is known as an integrated security mode. Although this enables you to control high-level access at the network level, it is often insufficient for the types of role-based security needed by enterprise applications. In addition, the management of this type of information must be relegated to a person with NT administration rights, which might be outside your realm of control or expertise. To understand this issue, we can implement a programmatic security model to give our application administrators the control necessary to ensure the appropriate individuals are able to do their needed tasks.

To implement this model, we follow a design pattern that enables us to classify users into one or more user groups. For each user group, we can assign a specific type of access to each implemented class within the system. Our approach is simple in concept but the implementation can be difficult to understand. For performance reasons, we implement our security as a hard-coded DLL for our specific application. We first define the various roles for our application, followed by our access modes, followed by the class types we want to secure. For example, Listing 15.1 shows these constants defined within a basic code module that is shared by both the security DLL and the client side.

Listing 15.1 **Shared Constants Necessary to Drive Our Security Model**

```
Option Explicit

' secured group type constants
Public Const SGT_CSR = 1            ' 2^(1-1) = 1
Public Const SGT_ACCOUNT_MGR = 2    ' 2^(2-1) = 2
Public Const SGT_MERCHANDISER = 3   ' 2^(3-1) = 4
Public Const SGT_TRAFFIC_MGR = 4    ' 2^(4-1) = 8

' access mode constants
Public Const AM_ADD = 1
Public Const AM_UPDATE = 2
Public Const AM_DELETE = 4

' secured class types
Public Const CT_CATEGORY As Integer = 1
Public Const CT_CITY As Integer = 2
Public Const CT_COUNTRY As Integer = 3
Public Const CT_CUSTOMER As Integer = 4
Public Const CT_EMPLOYEE As Integer = 5
Public Const CT_LIST_ITEM As Integer = 6
Public Const CT_ORDER As Integer = 7
Public Const CT_ORDER_DETAIL As Integer = 8
Public Const CT_PRODUCT As Integer = 9
Public Const CT_REGION As Integer = 10
Public Const CT_SHIPPER As Integer = 11
Public Const CT_SUPPLIER As Integer = 12
```

With these constants in place, we can implement an ActiveX DLL component named NWSecurity to implement the security. We define a class called CSecurityServer to host our security mechanism.

> **Note**
>
> Do not name your security component simply Security.DLL. This conflicts with a system DLL used by NT.

To implement our pattern, we use a simple matrix, aptly named mSecurityMatrix, defined as a two-dimensional array, with our first dimension representing the secured group type and the second representing the secured class type. The value of the array at a particular position is the access mode, which is the sum of the various constants. Because we have defined our constants as powers of the base 2, we can use bitwise comparisons to extract a particular access mode for a given combination of security group and class type. From the constants defined in Listing 15.1, assuming the value mSecurityMatrix(SGT_CSR, CT_CUSTOMER) is 3, we can establish whether a customer service representative can delete a customer object using the following statement:

```
If mSecurityMatrix(SGT_CSR, CT_CUSTOMER) And AM_DELETE = AM_DELETE Then ...
```

To initialize this matrix, we create a private method on our CSecurityServer class, called simply InitSecurityMatrix. We call this method from our Class_Initialize event. The code for our example appears in Listing 15.2.

Listing 15.2 **The *InitSecurityMatrix* Method and Its Supporting *SetSecurity* Method**

```
Private Sub InitSecurityMatrix()

  ' Customer Service Reps
  Call SetSecurity(SGT_CSR, CT_CUSTOMER, _
                   AM_ADD + AM_UPDATE + AM_DELETE)
  Call SetSecurity(SGT_CSR, CT_CITY, AM_ADD + AM_UPDATE)
  Call SetSecurity(SGT_CSR, CT_REGION, AM_ADD + AM_UPDATE)
  Call SetSecurity(SGT_CSR, CT_COUNTRY, AM_ADD + AM_UPDATE)

  ' Account Managers
  Call SetSecurity(SGT_ACCOUNT_MGR, CT_CUSTOMER, _
                   AM_ADD + AM_UPDATE + AM_DELETE)
  Call SetSecurity(SGT_ACCOUNT_MGR, CT_ORDER, _
                   AM_ADD + AM_UPDATE + AM_DELETE)
  Call SetSecurity(SGT_ACCOUNT_MGR, CT_ORDER_DETAIL, _
                   AM_ADD + AM_UPDATE + AM_DELETE)

  ' Merchandisers
  Call SetSecurity(SGT_MERCHANDISER, CT_CATEGORY, _
                   AM_ADD + AM_UPDATE + AM_DELETE)
  Call SetSecurity(SGT_MERCHANDISER, CT_PRODUCT, _
                   AM_ADD + AM_UPDATE + AM_DELETE)
```

continues

Listing 15.2   **Continued**

```
   Call SetSecurity(SGT_MERCHANDISER, CT_SUPPLIER, _
                    AM_ADD + AM_UPDATE + AM_DELETE)

   ' Traffic Managers
   Call SetSecurity(SGT_TRAFFIC_MGR, CT_SHIPPER, _
                    AM_ADD + AM_UPDATE + AM_DELETE)
End Sub
Private Sub SetSecurity(SecurityGroupType As Integer, _
                        SecuredClass As Integer, _
                        AccessMode As Integer)
   mSecurityMatrix(SecurityGroupType, SecuredClass) = AccessMode
End Sub
```

Now that we have our matrix, we must be able to assign a user to one or more security groups. To do this, we follow a bitwise pattern, as we previously used, and create a security key for each employee, storing this in the database and adding it to the CT_EMPLOYEE class type. Unfortunately, because the number of security groups we implement might exceed the acceptable range of a long integer, we must use a string to store this key value. To keep this string from becoming too large, we convert our bits to a hexadecimal string. Because Visual Basic does not have full binary and hexadecimal string-processing libraries, we must implement some of these features ourselves. Listing 15.3 shows a simple binary-to-hexadecimal converter.

Listing 15.3   **The *BinToHex* Function**

```
Public Function BinToHex(ByVal BinString As String) As String
   Dim i As Integer, j As Integer
   Dim nNibbles As Integer, szBinString As Integer
   Dim HexString As String, Nibble As String
   Dim byValue As Byte

   szBinString = Len(BinString)

   nNibbles = Int(IIf((szBinString / 4) = Int(szBinString), _
                   szBinString / 4, szBinString / 4 + 1))

   BinString = Right("0000" & BinString, nNibbles * 4)

   For i = 1 To nNibbles
     byValue = 0
     Nibble = Mid(BinString, (i - 1) * 4 + 1, 4)
     For j = 1 To Len(Nibble)
       byValue = byValue + 2 ^ (4 - j) * Val(Mid(Nibble, j, 1))
     Next j
     HexString = HexString & Hex(byValue)
   Next i
```

```
  BinToHex = HexString

End Function
```

Without going into significant detail, the `BinToHex` function takes a string in binary format, breaks it into 4-byte nibbles, and then coverts each nibble into a hexadecimal value.

With this `BinToHex` converter, we also create a function to convert a hexadecimal string into a byte array, with every two hexadecimal digits being converted to a byte within the array. Listing 15.4 shows this function.

Listing 15.4   **Converting a Hexadecimal String to an Array of Bytes**

```
Public Sub HexStringToByteArray(HexString As String, Bytes() As Byte)
  Dim nBytes As Integer
  Dim i As Integer, j As Integer

  If Len(HexString) / 2 <> Len(HexString) \ 2 Then
    HexString = "0" & HexString
  End If

  nBytes = Len(HexString) / 2
  ReDim Bytes(1 To nBytes)

  j = 1
  For i = nBytes To 1 Step -1
    Bytes(j) = Val("&H" & Mid(HexString, (i - 1) * 2 + 1, 2))
    j = j + 1
  Next i
End Sub
```

With these basic functions in place, we can implement two methods on our `CSecurityServer` class to enable us to convert our security key to an array of Boolean values, indicating group inclusion or exclusion. Listing 15.5 shows this process.

Listing 15.5   **Creating a Boolean Array from Our Security Key**

```
Private Sub MakeGroupMemembershipFromKey(SecurityKey As String, _
          GroupMembershipFlags() As Boolean)
  Dim Bytes() As Byte
  Dim i As Integer, j As Integer, iGroup As Integer

  ReDim GroupMembershipFlags(1 To MAX_SGT_GROUPS)

  Call HexStringToByteArray(SecurityKey, Bytes)
  For i = LBound(Bytes) To UBound(Bytes)
    For j = 0 To 7
```

continues

Listing 15.5   **Continued**

```
      iGroup = (8 * (i - 1) + j + 1)
      If iGroup > MAX_SGT_GROUPS Then Exit Sub
      If ((Bytes(i) And (2 ^ j)) = 2 ^ j) Then
        GroupMembershipFlags(iGroup) = True
      Else
        GroupMembershipFlags(iGroup) = False
      End If
    Next j
  Next i

End Sub
```

Assuming this MakeGroupMembershipFromKey method returned a Boolean array call Groups, we can now check whether a user's security key places them into a security group using a simple call like the following:

```
If Groups(SGT_ACCOUNT_MGRS) Then ...
```

We can now implement our final method on the CSecurityServer class, called simply AccessGranted, as shown in Listing 15.6.

Listing 15.6   **Our *AccessGranted* Method**

```
Public Function AccessGranted(SecurityKey As String, _
                              SecuredClass As Integer, _
                              AccessMode As Integer) As Boolean
    Dim IsGranted As Boolean
    Dim i As Integer

    Dim GroupMembershipFlags() As Boolean

    If SecurityKey = "" Then GoTo ExitFunction

    Call MakeGroupMemembershipFromKey(SecurityKey, GroupMembershipFlags)

    IsGranted = False
    For i = LBound(GroupMembershipFlags) To UBound(GroupMembershipFlags)
      ' check if user is a member of this group
      If GroupMembershipFlags(i) Then
        ' if so, see if this group has the appropriate access mode
        If ((mSecurityMatrix(i, SecuredClass) And AccessMode) = AccessMode) Then
          IsGranted = True
          GoTo ExitFunction
        End If
      End If
    Next i

ExitFunction:
```

```
        AccessGranted = IsGranted

    End Function
```

Our `AccessGranted` method takes, as parameters, the `SecurityKey` from the user profile, the secured class type, and the access mode to be tested. Using this information, the method converts the security key to a Boolean array using the `MakeGroupMembershipFromKey` method. It then iterates through this array, checking each group to see whether it grants the access mode desired. If so, the function exits with a `True` value. If no group is found with the desired access mode, the method exits with a `False` value. The implementation has been done in this fashion to accommodate overlapping security groups.

Because this security mechanism is implemented as an InProc ActiveX DLL, it is usable on all components of the system—IIS, MTS, or client. By simply making calls on the presentation layer, the application can enable the user interface to allow or disallow certain functionality, or to prevent entry into a particular area altogether.

Scalability Concerns

Although our framework design inherently maximizes scalability by minimizing object-state management on the MTS server, the DCOM/MTS model does not natively handle load balancing. To be sure, MTS has sophisticated pooling mechanisms so that a few physical object instances support many logical object instances. In addition, the multiprocessor, multithreaded capability of NT Server can further expand the workload afforded by a single server to increase performance. Nonetheless, MTS reaches a saturation point as the number of users rise. In these cases, mechanisms must be in place to balance MTS server loads relative to database server loads. If IIS is part of the picture, it must be load balanced as well.

The Single Server per Site/Organization Model

In this model, each site or organization maintains its own instance of the MTS server, database, and IIS servers. This is the easiest manner in which to address scalability concerns because the application needs no additional components to support it. The client applications direct their DCOM calls to the appropriate MTS server, based on client-side registry settings. An installer program or configuration utility running on the client can create these settings. Here, we assume that the single server instance is sufficient to handle the user load for the site.

If each site maintains its own database server as well, a replication mechanism must be in place to keep global information synchronized across all database server instances. SQL Server has integrated replication support to accomplish just this activity. Figure 15.1 shows the single server set per site model.

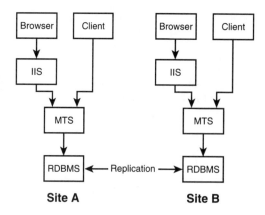

Figure 15.1 The single server set per site model.

One drawback to this approach is that it has no failover mechanism. If the server instance goes offline, it is not easy to redirect the client applications to a different server because the mappings are stored in the client registries.

The Multiple Servers per Site/Organization Model

In some cases, a single server set instance cannot handle the load generated by a site or organization. We can further segregate the client applications to access different server instances, as in the previous case. This model appears in Figure 15.2. Although this is a simplistic solution, it does not guarantee that each server instance is loaded appropriately. Some servers might be over-used, whereas others are under-used. Load balancing must occur by modifying client registries. Worse still, if you achieve a good balance, there is no guarantee that it can be maintained, because new users are added and others are removed. There is also the same failover problem that plagues the first model.

To circumvent this, we need a server broker. In this model, the client application might first connect to a DCOM object on a single brokerage server thats only function is to reply with a target server for the application to use. The method that this broker object uses to determine load can be simplistic or complicated. One method is that the brokerage server randomly determines a target server name from a list of available servers in the pool. Other techniques include a round robin approach where the brokerage server iterates through the list of servers, giving out the next server name in the list with each request. Although these are probably the two simplest mechanisms, there is still no guarantee for proper server balancing.

Another method is to employ load-balancing software such as the Microsoft Windows NT Load Balancing Service (WLBS). In this method, the brokerage server periodically pings each available server to determine its relative load. The server with the lowest load is the next one handed out. Unfortunately, determining relative server load is a complex issue because of the same multiprocessor, multithreaded concerns previously mentioned. MTS pooling further confounds the problem. Because such load-balancing software typically requires the development of NT services, it is not something easily accomplished using VB. In this case, prebuilt, load-balancing software might be the only solution. Otherwise, a programming language, such as Visual C++, and a developer with NT service skills are required.

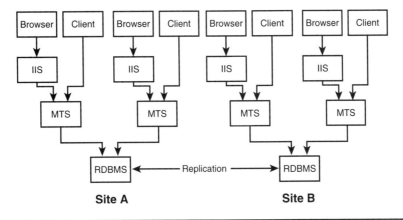

Figure 15.2   The multiple server sets per site model.

As mentioned in the previous chapter, the Windows 2000 Advanced Data Center will be releasing a form of COM object load balancing. This will be a software-oriented solution that models the CORBA and Enterprise Java models.

Server Clustering

Another solution to the load balancing and failover issue is to use a server cluster. In this mode, you would employ special software (and sometimes hardware) to make multiple servers act like one large virtual server. The application software itself does not have to be cognizant that it is operating on a cluster, because the clustering mechanisms are bound tightly in the NT Server operating system. Microsoft supplies a cluster software solution through its Microsoft Cluster Server (MSCS) software, which allows a clustering of two nodes. The Windows 2000 Data Center version of MSCS will allow four nodes. Several other clustering solutions are available from other vendors as well; one is HolonTech's HyperECS product, which is a hardware- and software-based solution. IBM has added extensions to MSCS for its line of Netfinity servers to allow for clustering for up to 14 servers.

Typically, the database portion of the system operates in a cluster fashion, while other parts of the system operate in an IP load balanced fashion. The reason for this is that the database is the place where concurrency of information is maintained, which requires more than simple load balancing. Microsoft SQL Server can be clustered in a two-node fashion on top of MSCS in a fairly straightforward fashion. Other database vendors, such as Oracle and IBM, provide clustering capabilities using their own technology.

Hardware-based load balancers are available as well from vendors such as Cisco, F5 Networks, and QuickArrow. These solutions provide load balancing at the IP address level. This means that anything that can operate purely on an IP address can be load balanced. The advantage of a hardware solution is their outright speed at performing the load-balancing act, versus the software-oriented solutions mentioned in the previous chapter. The downside is that hardware solutions can become rather expensive. You will have to balance price and performance in your application.

Figure 15.3 shows the final, fully scaled and failover-protected solution. Note that this model works well because we are not maintaining state on our MTS servers.

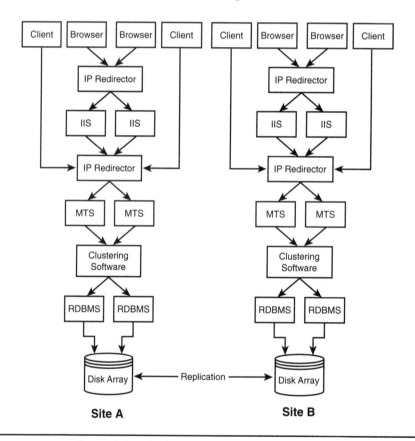

Figure 15.3 The fully scaleable and failed over model.

Summary

This chapter covered two topics: programmatic security and the issues associated with scalability and failover. With the conclusion of this chapter comes the conclusion of this book. Although it has been a long journey, it is my hope that, for some, the topics covered in this book were helpful in a total sense. For the rest, I hope that it provided insight and useful information, at least in a piecemeal fashion, that can be incorporated into your enterprise-level projects going on within the corporate development landscape.

Index

K

L

N

O

P

Q

R

S

que®
Professional

Dedicated to creating and delivering solid technical content to
professional developers, designers, and software engineers in the areas of networking,
enterprise application integration, middleware, e-commerce, and component development.

OTHER BOOKS IN THE QUE PROFESSIONAL SERIES

Written by a senior software architect at Candle Corporation. This book focuses on how to build real-world applications with Microsoft's Message Queue Server and IBM's MQSeries. In-depth coverage of the architecture, design, and implementation of message queuing applications.

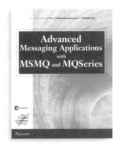

ADVANCED MESSAGING APPLICATIONS WITH MSMQ AND MQSERIES
ISBN: 0-7897-2023-x
December 1999

A leading expert in Enterprise Application Integration provides the IT professional with practical information and guidance on how to successfully design and implement an EAI solution. Readers will receive insight into decomposing business processes, analyzing integration patterns, deriving the architecture, and understanding how to apply the relevant technologies to solve the problem.

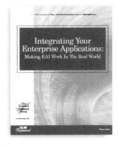

INTEGRATING YOUR ENTERPRISE APPLICATIONS: MAKING EAI WORK IN THE REAL WORLD
ISBN: 0-7897-2421-9
August 2000

A member of the ASP Industry Consortium provides in-depth coverage of the emerging Application Service Provider technology. These vendors are making Enterprise Application Integration and the promise of e-commerce available to smaller businesses without vast IT resources. Readers will explore the core concepts and building blocks of e-business, leading to a comprehensive understanding of the opportunities of the future.

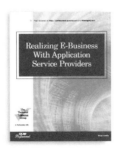

REALIZING E-BUSINESS WITH APPLICATION SERVICE PROVIDERS
ISBN: 0-7897-2408-1
August 2000